A Practical Approach to Legal Advice & Drafting

Susan Blake LLB, MA, Barrister

Senior Lecturer in Law, Inns of Court School of Law

First published in Great Britain 1985 by Financial Training Publications Limited, Avenue House, 131 Holland Park Avenue, London W11 4UT

ISBN: 0 906322 49 9

Typeset by Kerrypress Ltd, Luton
Printed by Livesey Ltd, Shrewsbury

Contents

List of examples

Preface

I wrote this book with two main objectives, both of which have grown out of a period of practice at the Bar and the experience of several years teaching a course for those who intend to become barristers. Both objectives are very important for those who wish to become practising lawyers, and neither is fully covered by any existing book.

The first objective is to give guidelines to the young lawyer on the practical way to deal with a client and go through the various stages of preparing a case for court. There is a great transition to be made from the law student to the practising barrister or solicitor giving advice to a real client with a real problem. Some make the transition easily, but some find it difficult, or fail to realise how important it is to move from concentrating solely on the details of academic law to take a wider, more realistic and more imaginative approach to the entire situation in a real case. Inevitably some things can only be learned with experience in pupillage or in articles, but increasingly the emphasis in professional legal training has turned to the practical approach which will prepare the lawyer for helping the client. Of course, this practical approach cannot ultimately be taught by a book, but I have tried to give a basic framework with ideas for the young lawyer to build on.

My second objective is to give some guidance on the principles of drafting documents for court. Although cases will now rarely turn on technical points of drafting in the way that they once did, concise and clear pleadings are still an important part of bringing a case to court in the right way. There are some precedent books, but it can be very difficult for the young lawyer to learn how to draft, as there are no books that really deal with drafting comprehensively. There are reasons for this — there are some technical rules for drafting in the Rules of Court which must be followed, but many drafting points are a matter of practice and are not easy to identify and explain. In drafting, many things are a matter of personal style rather than right or wrong, and what the young lawyer needs is a sense of what to include and how to express it, rather than trying to tie himself down too much to precedents and detailed rules. What I have tried to do is to include the rules for drafting that must be followed, and to indicate the wider principles from which the young lawyer can build on.

In dealing with a client, preparing a case, or drafting, each lawyer will inevitably develop his own approach and style, which will build up as he does pupillage or articles and as he begins to do his own cases. All I have tried to do here is to give a foundation of principles and ideas to build from. Because lawyers will do things in different ways I have tried to distinguish those points where there are rules that must be followed, and those points where I suggest a way of doing things, but where other lawyers might well have other suggestions and ideas that would be useful.

I would like to thank my colleagues at the Inns of Court School of Law, whose discussions on many points of law and drafting have often proved stimulating and useful, and also friends in practice who have made suggestions to me. The staff at Financial Training Publications have also been efficient and encouraging in the preparation of this book, and have made constructive comments.

The law is stated as on 1 April 1985, and the precedents should be read as having been written on that date.

Susan Blake
Ealing, London W5

1 *The lawyer as a professional adviser*

It takes time to learn to deal with the practical problems and the realities of being a practising lawyer. The law student may study in detail various areas of law, but he or she will then have to undergo a transformation to deal with real people with real problems. The purpose of this book is to give the young lawyer guidelines on how this transformation comes about, and the new skills that he will have to learn to become a good practising lawyer. Some things can only be learned with experience—which is why the lawyer has to do articles or pupillage as part of his training—but I hope to be able to outline the main areas that are important in preparing a case as a professional lawyer.

The places where the young lawyer needs to develop his technique are as follows:

(a) He must learn how to advise a client properly. This involves being able to talk to the client, whether he is a rich property developer or an unemployed teenager, to understand the practical side of his situation and his case, and to tell him what can be done in the case and how.

(b) He must learn how to prepare a case in an efficient and practical way. This involves not only preparing legal arguments, but also making full use of every procedural step to the client's advantage and ensuring that all the necessary evidence is obtained and presented in the best possible way, so that the client both wins the case and gets all the remedies he seeks from it. Good advocacy begins with proper preparation, and the lawyer can only hope to convince a judge of his case if he has it clear in his own mind.

(c) He must learn how to draft pleadings and other documents for court. Clear and concise drafting clarifies the issues in the case which helps the lawyer to present it in court and helps the judge to understand it. It is a good draft that really does show that a lawyer has understood and prepared a case properly.

In the first chapter of the book I will deal with how to advise a client and prepare a case for court, following the stages of a civil case that goes to the High Court with the client going first to a solicitor who then briefs a barrister, as this is the best model. In later chapters I will deal with the differences arising in cases in a county court and in criminal cases. I will mention appropriate points of procedure and evidence where they are important in dealing with the case in a practical way and in developing a good technique, because these are the things that the lawyer really needs to know in bringing a case, but I will not go into detail, as there are a number of books dealing with them.

I will then go on to deal with drafting, looking at formal and informal rules and matters of style, and giving outlines of the forms of the most important types of drafting for court actions. Although drafting is an important skill for the practising lawyer, there are surprisingly few books on the subject, except for major reference works that need to be used with care. What I hope to do is to cover the principles of drafting, including the relevant Rules of Court and case law, to give the young lawyer an idea of what he is trying to achieve and how. There is a strong element of style in drafting, and lawyers will often disagree as to how a particular point should be dealt with in a draft, but once the young lawyer is aware of the basic rules he will hopefully be able to use those rules to develop his own style properly, and to use reference books on drafting properly.

In the second part of the book I will go on to look at advising and drafting in particular types of case, showing how general principles should be applied and how to deal with special issues and problems that may arise. To do this I have chosen basic areas of law with which most young lawyers will be familiar, that is contract, tort, crime, trust law and family law. Although lawyers going into practice may well deal with other areas of law, the skills that they need can usually be developed from these areas, unless they are going into specialist practices.

There are some general points that will come up time and again. 'Practice' and 'practical' are just two different grammatical forms of the same word, but it is surprising how difficult young lawyers who intend to go into practice find it to be practical. The purpose of the lawyer in practice is to advise someone with a problem on the best way of solving it, and he should never lose sight of that. Right through every case the lawyer is there to gather all the information that he can from the client, and any other relevant source and organise it to see what legal possibilities there are in it. From this he gives advice and drafts documents for the court. But at the end of the day the lawyer is there to get what he can for the client, so it is the remedies available, and the procedure and evidence for getting them that matter. Also the lawyer should never lose sight of the fact that the case is the client's, and that the client must therefore be kept informed of everything that is happening, and have each step in the case explained to him as far as possible.

This means that the lawyer going into practice has to modify his approach to law and develop new techniques. When studying law at University or College, the student learns detailed law, reads judgments in detail, and discusses complex points where the law is not clear. This will still be important in some cases in practice, especially if he goes into a specialist area of law, or as he becomes more senior in his profession, but for most cases early in practice the emphasis changes completely. Most clients will not care greatly what a particular judge said in a case in the House of Lords some years ago; what they will care about is whether they have a cause of action, what chance of success it has, and exactly what remedies they may be able to get at the end of the day, so this is what the lawyer advising a real client needs to concentrate on.

This means that the lawyer who goes into practice does not need to carry round a great deal of detailed law in his head—he can look that up and make notes on it when he does have to argue a particular point in court—but he does need a thorough and up-to-date knowledge of the general principles of law in every area of law that he practices in. When reading a brief or advising a client he must be able to identify all the main points of law involved quickly so that he can give outline advice without delay, and also so that he is aware of all the points on which he will have to do further research in the case. It is only possible to research efficiently if you have been able to identify all the legal arguments accurately.

The areas of law that the practising lawyer does need to know in some detail are procedure and evidence, as these are things that he may not have time to look up if he needs them. It may be necessary to know on the spur of the moment how to deal with a procedural point that has arisen, or whether it is possible to object to the admissibility of a piece of evidence that has been produced by the other side. A case that is good in law can be let down if proper use is not made of all procedural steps, or if there is not sufficient evidence to prove it.

The main thing is that the young lawyer going into practice must open his mind to the realities of the job that he is doing and the needs of his clients. While he needs to be able to use academic law, he should not cling to it too much. The professional courses for both solicitors and barristers now place great emphasis on this need for a practical approach, and it is of course necessary to do articles or pupillage before the lawyer is able to take cases of his own. It is important to make full use of the experience of this training to learn as much as possible about preparing and presenting a case, and this is a matter not only of learning all the basic skills, but also of looking at the different skills and approaches that different practising lawyers have. In that the law is a profession, it is a matter not only of rules, but also of technique, style and personal skills in preparing and presenting a case, and this must be learned as much as anything else.

The young lawyer will go on learning matters of professional skill from the more experienced members of his profession for many years in getting their advice and watching what they do, and he should bear two things in mind. Firstly, he should distinguish between when a lawyer does something in one way because it must be done in that way, because of a statute or rule of court, and when he does it purely because it is his way of doing things. This distinction is important especially in presenting a case in court and in drafting legal documents. Sometimes a particular thing has to go into a draft, and sometimes a lawyer only puts it in as a matter of his own style. In the latter case the young lawyer can of course decide whether it is something that he wishes to follow or not. Secondly, the young lawyer should take full use of his opportunities to learn from older members of the profession because it is such an important way of learning—though obviously not to the point where he makes a nuisance of himself! There is inevitably some problem in getting articles or pupillage that will give a good range of good quality work, but it is worth making all possible efforts to do this. A good firm of solicitors or set of Chambers will try to arrange for the articled clerk or pupil to get experience of different types of work within their practice, but the young lawyer must also make an effort himself to read papers in a case rather than just sitting in court and listening, to make himself useful by taking notes of a conference or of a speech or evidence in court, or by tactfully asking questions or volunteering an opinion where appropriate. The articled clerk will normally be given work to do on a case at quite an early stage, and a pupil may be asked to research a point or do some work on a brief, but he should make sure that he not only does what he is asked, but also learns as much as he can from the case as to what legal steps should be taken and what documents will be needed. There is a lot for the young lawyer going into practice to learn and he should take every opportunity that he can.

The preparation of a case

There are many types of lawyers in practice, and many ways in which they may be involved in a case. The model used here, that of a client going to a solicitor, who then briefs a barrister to advise on and prepare a civil case to be brought in the High Court, will need to be adapted where necessary, where for example the solicitor has advocacy skills and chooses to conduct the case himself in a court where he has the right of audience. The model will also need to be modified where for example the lawyer is employed, rather than working as a solicitor or barrister in his own right, or where he works for a Law Centre, and there are different rules on the role he may take in advising a client.

There will obviously also be differences in preparing a case depending on the type of practice that the lawyer has. The heavy commercial case will need a different approach from the smaller domestic one, and the smaller country practice will be very different from the large city practice. The young barrister in a criminal set of Chambers will have a working life rather different to that of the Chancery barrister, with much more emphasis on court appearances rather than paper work. All these different circumstances will require a slightly different relationship with the client and a slightly different development of skills. The good lawyer will need the sensitivity to modify his technique to his type of practice.

The first stage in a case will normally be the client going to a solicitor for initial advice. It is vital for the proper development of the case that this first interview be handled well, and there is a chapter on how the solicitor should handle this meeting to get all the information he needs from the client and to get the case on a strong footing. Normally the client cannot go directly to a barrister, but there are limited exceptions, such as the dock brief. A barrister may give informal advice to a friend, but if he goes on to act for the friend in court or in proceeding with the case in any other way, he will have to be briefed by a solicitor in the normal way. A barrister may represent himself in court, but if there is no solicitor he should appear unrobed as an individual and not as a barrister. Another anomalous case concerns the special rules for the barrister in the Law Centre, who may interview clients, take statements, write letters and the like without being briefed but, if he is paid a salary by the Law Centre, he will have limited rights of audience and will not be able to work from Chambers at the same time. The last exception is where the barrister is employed by the Civil Service or a company, where again he will be able to give legal advice and draft documents for his employer, but will have limited rights of audience and will be unable to practice from Chambers while he is salaried.

The solicitor may well be able to deal with the case himself, by giving advice or drafting a letter or document, but if there are any problems, he may well consider briefing a barrister. Careful thought should be given to the reasons why the barrister is to be briefed and what he will be asked to deal with, and the instructions in the brief should be drawn up carefully, and the right documents attached. There are chapters on the drawing up of a brief, the reading of the brief, and the way that counsel should approach drafting his opinion on the brief. These are all areas where the practising lawyer must develop skills to see the problem in a practical way, to think through all the legal and practical possibilities, and really do the best that he can for his client.

It is vitally important for the barrister and the solicitor to build up a good working relationship to see that the case is properly conducted and that everything is done as it should be. There are few rules on how the barrister and solicitor should work together, and this makes it all the more important that they should personally make an effort to see that things function as they should. The brief is not a contract, so there is no legally enforceable agreement. Once the barrister has been briefed, he is in charge of the case and the solicitor cannot give him directions on how to act, though equally the barrister should remember that the solicitor is in closest contact with the client, and that everything relayed from the client must be properly taken into account.

A problem that has arisen from the fact that the brief is not a contract which does sometimes complicate the relationship between barristers and solicitors is that a barrister cannot sue for brief fees, *Wells* v *Wells* [1914] P 157. There are many good reasons why a barrister should not actually be subject to a contract of employment with the solicitor, but difficulties over money should not be allowed to cause any deterioration in their professional relationship. Various legal aid fees are now paid direct to the barrister rather than being paid through the solicitor, and negotiations between the Bar Council and the Law Society have led to terms being agreed whereby the barrister should normally be paid within three months of the fee note's being sent to the solicitor, or of the solicitor's being paid by the client, and in any event within three months of the case ending. The solicitor should take all reasonable steps to get payment from the client, and if there is any difficulty the Bar Council may take the matter up with the firm of solicitors or the Law Society.

The essential thing is for the barrister and solicitor in the case to establish a strong and clear working relationship as soon as possible, and not allow anything to complicate it unnecessarily. The solicitor must give clear instructions and full information to the barrister, and the barrister must in his turn give clear instructions as to how the case should proceed and what steps he would like the solicitor to take. Each must give the other the respect due to a legally trained professional, but must also be prepared to bring up tactfully anything that may have been overlooked. If the lawyers do not work efficiently together on the case, the person who will suffer is the client.

The best working relationship will of course build up where the solicitor regularly briefs the same barrister, but there are many possibilities that the lawyer may have to adapt to. Sometimes the experienced solicitor will be briefing a young barrister, sometimes a newly qualified solicitor will be briefing a leading silk, and both lawyers may have to make some allowances to work properly together. This may include personal matters as well as working efficiently, not least because the barrister will hope to get more work from the solicitor! It may well help both lawyers as well as the client if there is a friendly atmosphere, and it is for example quite proper for the barrister and solicitor to lunch together while a case progresses, but both sides must take care that the social side of the relationship does not exceed the correct limits. There must never be any suggestion that the barrister is improperly seeking work, and he should not normally give the solicitor presents, or accept any from him, or attend social functions held by the Law Society. If a barrister and solicitor are friends they should keep this separate from their professional work.

Once the brief has been sent to the barrister and he has sent his opinion back to the solicitor, the next stage will be for them to work together to prepare the case. This may well involve the barrister having a conference with the solicitor and the client, and will certainly involve a proper and full use of any appropriate procedural steps. The legal points in the case must be researched thoroughly, and all the necessary evidence must be collected. The barrister should tell the solicitor what he should collect for the trial, and the solicitor may need to get further advice from the barrister. There are chapters dealing with the most important points in preparing a case for court.

If it is decided to take the case to court, the necessary legal documents will have to be drafted. Because there are relatively few books available to help the young lawyer, one of the main aims of this book is to deal with the main principles of drafting rules and practice, dealing particularly with the main documents needed for a High Court action from the writ onwards, and also with originating summonses and affidavits.

Representing the client

This is one of the main things that the young lawyer has to learn to do. He is no longer concerned with academic points but with real people. From the time that he first sees the client to the end of the case, the solicitor or barrister is not judging the client, but is trying to find out all he can about his case, and is trying to achieve as much as he can for him. Comments on how to do this will be made right through the book, but there are a few general points.

The main point is for the barrister and the solicitor to communicate fully with the client at all stages in order to get all the information about the case from him (with points against him as well as points in his favour) and to keep him informed as to what is going on. This matters not only at his first meeting with the solicitor and when he sees the barrister in conference, but also when evidence is being collected, when the case is being prepared for court, and at every stage when there is some new development.

The importance of communication is not just a matter of questions and answers. It is also a question of having a quick and imaginative mind that can readily take new concepts into account and see things from different angles. The best way for a lawyer to ask a client or a witness the right questions is by being able to visualise the situation in his own mind, to try to find out what really happened and what things the client or witness may have forgotten to say. In addition, the lawyer needs to be able to communicate by using words well and accurately, whether on paper or in speech, and this is especially true of the barrister who is being paid to use words on behalf of someone who is not able to put his case himself. This does not mean talking a lot—it is quite possible to talk for hours without saying anything of real importance—but it does mean having ability and confidence to use words when necessary.

The other main element of proper communication between a lawyer and his client is the ability to get on with people. Especially in a general practice the lawyer may be representing the Managing Director of a company one day and an unemployed youth the next, and he should be able to talk equally to both. This does not mean that the lawyer has to like his client—inevitably there will be times when he will not, and professional standards require that the lawyer should not become too friendly with his client—but he does need an ability to talk to people of different kinds, and to show sufficient interest, tolerance and sensitivity for the client to be able to feel that he is being understood and properly represented. In a matrimonial or criminal practice in particular it may take a great deal of strength and energy to communicate well.

Advising a client is not only a matter of telling him what the law is and whether he has a case, it is also a matter of looking at the law from his point of view to see what arguments can be developed for him. The objectives of the client and whether they can be achieved are more important than clever legal argument. There is no point in advising the client in a contract case that he can sue for damages if what he really wants to do is end the contract, and in negotiating a settlement on divorce there is no point in getting a home for the wife if she will not have enough money to keep herself and pay the mortgage.

There are some circumstances where the lawyer must take particular care to represent his client properly. The most important of these are negotiating the settlement of an action and representing a client on legal aid. The vast majority of actions do settle out of court, and this will be dealt with in the chapter on preparing a case for court, but as a general rule, whenever any possibility arises of settling an action at any stage, the lawyer must ensure that he is properly representing the interests of his client to get as good a settlement as he reasonably can which covers all the points that the client is concerned with. Once a compromise is reached, the client will only be able to take further legal action in very limited circumstances, so nothing must be left uncertain or left out. The difficulties of agreements which do not cover everything have been seen in cases concerning consent orders on divorce.

As for the costs of the action, the lawyer is clearly not representing his client properly if he allows the costs of an action to build up unnecessarily, or if he does not keep the client informed of the costs of the action, especially where the action does not have a good chance of success. This is even more important where the client is on legal aid, where the lawyer has a duty not only to his client but also to the legal aid fund to see that money is not wasted. The lawyer should of course help the client to apply for legal aid if he needs it, and should ensure that legal aid is extended if necessary to cover later stages in the case, such as an appeal, *R & T Thew Ltd* v *Reeves* [1982] QB 1283, but he should not advise that legal aid should be granted if the case is not strong enough to justify it. If the lawyer fails in his duties to the legal aid fund, he may not be able to claim his costs.

There have been several cases where judges have commented on the duties of lawyers representing clients on legal aid. In *Kelly* v *London Transport Executive* [1982] 2 All ER 842 the court made it clear that a lawyer should only press an action for a legally aided client if he feels that the action is so well-founded that a client paying his own costs would be advised to sue, and the fact that one side has legal aid should not be used to force the other side into a compromise. In the case the plaintiff, an alcoholic, banged his head at work, got legal aid, and was advised to sue his employers, but the case snowballed to include leading counsel and 19 medical reports, and progressed very slowly. An offer of £4,000 by the defendant was rejected, but the plaintiff finally recovered only £75, at great expense to the legal aid fund. Further comments were made by the judge in the case of *Davy-Chiesman* v *Davy-Chiesman* (1983) *The Times*, 21 November, where counsel sought to argue that a husband should get a lump sum on divorce although he had been made bankrupt and the money would therefore have gone to his trustee in bankruptcy. The husband had legal aid, and the judge made it clear that the application for a lump sum should not have been pursued at the expense of the fund and that if a solicitor is aware of anything affecting the possible success of the case he should report it to the legal aid authorities, because otherwise the fund might not pay his costs, and indeed he might have to pay costs personally if there was any serious misconduct or dereliction of duty. The solicitor could normally rely on the advice of counsel, but he should also use his own discretion.

In the interests of the client, the lawyer representing him must keep him informed of whether he may have to pay a contribution to his costs, or whether there may be a legal aid charge on any property recovered or preserved by the client. The client must not be forced into a bad settlement, but the lawyer should not allow a case to be argued to the point where a legal aid charge will substantially remove any benefit the client gets from the action. This has been made especially clear in family law cases; in *Hanlon* v *The Law Society* [1981] AC 124 both spouses were legally aided, and although the matrimonial home worth £10,000 net was transferred to the wife the total costs of the case were £8,025, so that the home was subject to a charge leaving little for the wife. The House of Lords held that the charge could be postponed until the home was sold or transferred to another property, but although this was of practical help to her, the real value of the home was still ultimately lost.

Professional standards for the lawyer

The professional standards that a lawyer should abide by when giving advice to a client are primarily maintained by the professional bodies, the Bar Council and the Law Society. Both have disciplinary proceedings that can be used if a lawyer does fall short of proper standards, and he may, if appropriate, be disbarred or struck off. The young lawyer will learn the professional approach to many situations from the older members of his profession, and if in doubt what to do in any circumstance he should ask. Some rules are also specifically set out, and for example a barrister should read the Code of Conduct for the Bar of England and Wales published by the Senate and the book on Conduct and Etiquette at the Bar written by Sir William Boulton.

There are a variety of professional standards which vary between mere politeness (for example, telling another barrister when you take over a case in which he has already advised) and vital duties where a failure to keep up to standard may be a ground of appeal for the other side (for example where the prosecution fails to tell the defence that it knows of witnesses that may help the defence). Some professional standards relate to dealings with the client and others are duties to the court in conducting a case, for example once a client has told his lawyer something the lawyer cannot mislead the court by saying something to the contrary, and in an extreme example, if the client in a criminal case has told his lawyer that he is guilty, the lawyer cannot defend him on a plea of not guilty. Sometimes there is also a positive duty to reveal information to the court if it may have a direct bearing on the case and the reliability of a witness, see *Meek* v *Fleming* [1961] 2 QB 366.

Professional standards can be enforced other than by the professional bodies, for example the conduct of a lawyer may occasionally be taken into account when a costs order is made. As regards the solicitor, if he conducts a case in such a way that costs are incurred improperly or without reasonable cause, or if there is any undue delay or other misconduct in bringing the case, he may be ordered to pay costs personally. Certain costs may be disallowed, or otherwise he may be ordered to repay money to the client, though he must be heard by the court before such an order is made, see RSC Order 62, rule 8 and *Currie & Co* v *The Law Society* [1977] QB 990. As for the barrister, if his conduct in the case merits it, the judge may make remarks on what costs should be allowed to be taken into account by the taxing master, *R* v *McFadden* (1978) *The Times*, 10 December.

If the standard of work of a lawyer falls so far short of good professional standards that his client loses a case that he should have won, it may be possible for the client to sue the lawyer. The action will normally be for negligence, in that the lawyer has not satisfied the duty of care owed to the client, though the lawyer will only be liable if he has quite clearly not taken a step that he ought to have taken, or has given patently wrong advice. The mere fact that advice given by the lawyer was not ultimately successful cannot found an action, *Buckland* v *Farmar & Moody* [1978] 3 All ER 929, or no lawyer would risk giving advice if the law was not clear.

The mere fact that an action has failed does not mean that the client might sue the lawyer forthwith. If the action is not yet out of time a new writ may be issued or an existing writ extended, *Chappell* v *Cooper* [1980] 2 All ER 463. If the action is out of time then the possibility of an action in negligence can be examined and an action brought against the solicitor, but only if there is a real chance of an action against him succeeding, and not merely because the client is upset at losing the case.

A barrister in a case can only be sued for negligence in limited circumstances, and cannot be sued for the way that he conducts a case in court, or any preparatory work connected with court work, which would seem to include the pleadings, *Rondel* v *Worsley* [1969] 1 AC 191. One reason for this immunity is that the barrister has a duty to accept any case brought to him in an area in which he normally practises (the taxi rank principle), and it would be unfair if he could be sued for losing a case that he had no option but to take. It is also in the public interest in the proper conduct of cases that a barrister should be free to act fearlessly and independently in a case as he sees fit without the threat of being sued hanging over him. It is not a problem that there is no contract between the solicitor and client and the barrister as there could still be a duty of care in tort, and the barrister's immunity is a matter of public policy.

In the case of *Rondel* v *Worsley* the plaintiff was charged in 1959 with causing actual bodily harm by cutting someone's hand and biting their ear. He was defended on a dock brief by the defendant barrister, his case being that he admitted the injury caused, but said that he was justified in inflicting it. He was convicted, and in 1965 sued the barrister for negligence in losing the case, drawing up the statement of claim himself. The House of Lords held that a barrister could not be sued in negligence for his conduct and management of a case in court or preliminary work for it, though he was not immune from action for work not directly connected with a court case. This decision was upheld in *Saif Ali* v *Sydney Mitchell & Co* [1980] AC 198 where the plaintiff was injured by a car whose driver admitted driving without due care and attention. However, the barrister advised suing the driver's husband, who owned the car, and when eventually the plaintiff changed his solicitors he was advised to sue his former solicitors for conducting the case badly. The solicitors joined the barrister as a third party as they were acting on his advice, but it was held that he was immune from action not only for trial work but also for pre-trial work that was intimately connected with the court case, though there were dicta that an opinion which stopped the case from coming to court in the way it should might be the basis for a negligence action.

Thus the limits of a barrister's potential liability are far from clear. Because of the possibility of being sued, solicitors have taken out insurance against claims for many years, and in 1982 the Bar Council agreed rules for practising barristers to be insured on approved terms for at least £250,000, though commercial sets will be insured for much greater claims than this. Policies must cover everyone in Chambers, though of course each barrister will only be liable for his own work.

Working with other lawyers

An important part of conducting any case is working with other lawyers. Some points on this have already been made, and others will arise at various stages in this book. There are many ways in which relationships with other lawyers are important in learning the profession of the lawyer, and in the progress of individual cases.

As has already been mentioned, the young lawyer will learn many professional techniques from older members of his profession by observing and asking questions as to the right way to do things. This process does not stop with articles or pupillage. Discussions with other lawyers can always be useful to find out about areas of law or procedure that one is not familiar with, to keep up to date by asking about the experiences of others, or to test arguments before going into court. In any firm of solicitors or set of Chambers discussions about cases will be frequent and useful for all members.

However, cases must be discussed in a professional way. The name of a client who has come for advice in confidence should not be given, but a phrase like 'I have a client who . . .', 'I'm for a wife who . . .' or even 'I'm the sister claiming the will is a forgery and . . .' should be used. Only the details needed to discuss the legal or procedural difficulty should be given, and not personal matters that the client would regard as private, however strong the temptation is where the case is newsworthy or has salacious facts. It goes without saying that the details of a case should never be discussed with a person who is not involved in the case and is not a lawyer, though there is an accepted practice that a lawyer writing an autobiography can give some details of the major cases that he was involved in.

The confidential relationship that a client should enjoy with his lawyer has a legal basis in the doctrine of privilege. So that a client can talk freely to the lawyer any communication made in a conference or interview or a document prepared for the lawyer to give his advice does not have to be disclosed and cannot be used in evidence. However, the privilege is that of the client rather than of the lawyer, and the privilege may be waived if the client does wish evidence to go in, as in *George Doland Ltd* v *Blackburn, Robson & Co* [1972] 1 WLR 1338 where the plaintiff called his solicitor to give evidence of a telephone conversation. The actual advice given by a lawyer to his client will rarely be admitted in evidence except in exceptional cases, as in *Marriman* v *Vibart* [1963] 1 QB 528 where policemen overheard a barrister in a criminal case advising his client to escape. There may be some difficulty about when privilege in a case begins, for example where no decision has been taken to begin proceedings, *Alfred Crompton Amusement Machines Ltd* v *Customs & Excise Commissioners* [1974] AC 405. If for example an employer prepares an accident report for his own records and potential legal action is not a dominant reason for preparing it, it will not be privileged, *Waugh* v *British Railways Board* [1980] AC 521.

The importance of working well with other lawyers in the case has already been touched on—it is vital for the solicitor and barrister in a case to establish a good way of working together so that nothing is overlooked. This must be extended where there are other lawyers, for example where a provincial solicitor brings in a London Solicitor or his agent in a case he must communicate well with him rather than just sending off the file. In an important case more than one barrister may be briefed, either a silk with a junior or more than one junior, and both barristers must be clear about the division of work between them. If there is a silk, he will be primarily responsible for presenting the case in court, with the junior preparing the documents for court and researching points, but the junior may well be asked to deal with part of the case in court, and this should be clearly agreed.

In addition to building a good working relationship with the lawyers on the same side, it can also be important to work properly with the lawyers on the other side. There can be difficulties with any extreme. There is no need to be aggressive or unreasonable with the lawyers on the other side purely because they are the other side—it can often be the role of the lawyers to help defuse the situation and negotiate a settlement rather than build up hostility. On the other hand the lawyers on both sides should not be too friendly and accommodating or the clients may not be properly represented. This is especially important for barristers, who may well know each other because they are members of a relatively small profession. While this may mean that they can work easily together, they should be wary of showing friendship in front of the client, who may feel some resentment if he loses a case but then sees his barrister go off chatting happily with the barrister for the other side. His feeling will almost certainly be unjustified, but the barrister must take care to tell the client everything about negotiations with the other side, and must take care of the impression he gives the client.

It is important to establish the relationship with the other side in a case as soon as possible. Sometimes the different versions of facts or the antagonism of the parties will mean that the relationship with the other side will be rather formal, just following the procedural stages, but sometimes there may be the chance of some kind of compromise or settlement to be explored. It may be possible to avoid legal action at all, or at a later stage reach a formal agreement or consent order, and exploring such possibilities is one of the most practical roles of the lawyer. However, only real chances of agreement should be pursued, and negotiations should never be allowed to drag on, building up piles of correspondence with little chance of achieving anything. This will only create more work to prepare the case for court.

In particular, care should be taken with 'without prejudice' letters. One sometimes gets the impression that lawyers put this on the top of every letter as a matter of course! It should only be used where the letter is a genuine attempt to deal with the case without prejudice to the position of the party writing it at trial, either suggesting a settlement or trying to speed the conduct of the action, for example by making an admission. The use of the phrase should not encourage the writing of many letters with no real purpose. If a letter is expressed to be 'without prejudice' it will generally not be admissible at the trial, but it may be let in as evidence of a binding agreement, *Tomlin* v *Standard Telephones and Cables Ltd* [1969] 1 WLR 1378, if further evidence has been obtained as a result of the letter, *Rabin* v *Mendoza & Co.* [1954] 1 WLR 271, or if the party who wrote the letter has reserved the right to put it in when costs are considered, to show that the other side prolonged the case unnecessarily, *Cutts* v *Head* [1984] 1 All ER 597.

Finally, there is the relationship between the lawyers on both sides and the judge. A clearly and precisely presented case is inevitably going to impress a judge most, and this requires a lot more than just legal research. The arguments and evidence in each case must be prepared with a view to conveying them clearly to the judge. If a map or a photograph will help the judge to understand the case more easily it should be obtained, and the points in the case should be argued in the way that it is easy to follow, which will begin with good drafting and pleading. Sometimes the lawyer will know something of the judge he is to appear before, but in any event he should try to tailor the way he puts a case for the type of court in which he will appear, whether it be magistrates', county court, High Court or the Court of Appeal.

There are many other points to bear in mind when presenting a case to a judge. The mannerisms of an advocate can make quite an impression on a judge watching (as anyone who has been marshalling and sat with a judge will appreciate) and a good lawyer will need to be sensitive as to when he is irritating rather than impressing a judge, and when it is worth pushing an argument strongly in the hope of winning a judge over, or when this will merely make the judge more strongly opposed. However, the way to actually present a case in court and the skills of advocacy are beyond the scope of this book.

The public image of the lawyer

In general, the public image of lawyers in Britain is good, and the legal system is held in great respect, but there is some criticism of lawyers. People who have been involved in litigation will tell you that their case took a very long time to come to court, that it was very expensive, that their lawyer did not keep them informed of how the case was progressing, that he did not seem to grasp all the things that the client told him, or that some things were left unresolved by the case. Many of these criticisms can be at least partially answered—it does take a long time for a case to go through all the necessary stages and be properly prepared, and a good legal system will never be cheap. A good lawyer is busy and may not have time to explain every little point to a client, and many clients who have little knowledge of the law may not fully understand what they are told anyway.

However, the good professional lawyer will have some concern for the image that his profession presents to the public. Both barristers and solicitors have tended to be inward looking, and they should never lose sight of the fact that they are essentially in a service industry that is there for the good of the clients and the public. There has been an increased awareness of the need to serve the public well in recent years, not least because of the need to consider various matters for the Royal Commission on Legal Services (Cmnd 7648, 1979), and many modifications have been made and considered in the need to brief a junior counsel with a silk, the solicitors' conveyancing monopoly and so on.

However, some members of the public may still be slow to consult a lawyer even if they need one, because they are not confident of getting an efficient and reasonably priced service. The growth of do-it-yourself divorce, conveyancing and will writing is not really in anyone's interests if it means that things are not done properly. The best answer must be for every lawyer who goes into practice to ensure that he does deal with every case in a professional and efficient way, giving full, practical advice to the client, preparing the case thoroughly, and considering every real as well as every legal aspect of it. Clear thought and understanding should show at every stage of the case, especially in the drafting of pleadings and other documents.

2 *The first interview with the client*

The first time that the lawyer sees the client will be important for both. The lawyer must ensure that he discovers all the information he needs to give advice on the case, and the client should leave feeling confident that his problem is being dealt with, and should understand as far as possible what the first steps in the case will be.

The first interview between the lawyer and the client will normally take place when the client makes an appointment to go to the solicitor's office, as he cannot go direct to a barrister. He may see a barrister in conference later, and this is dealt with in a later chapter. The client may have been to the solicitor for advice before, or he may have found him through personal recommendation or the pages of a telephone book. The solicitor will need to take this into account in meeting the client, who may be nervous or very unsure whether he has come to the right person for the job. The client may also be unsure whether he has a legal problem at all or what sort of legal problem he has.

The lawyer will get a wide variety of clients, and the good solicitor will adapt his approach and manner for each as soon as he can in the first meeting. A business man may already know the solicitor well, may know some law himself, and may want detailed advice on a particular transaction. An angry man who has bought a defective car, or an unhappy man who does not want his wife to divorce him may never have been to a lawyer before and may find it difficult to discuss his problem coherently. To some extent the elements of the meeting with each of these will be the same, but the lawyer will have to adapt to represent all of them equally well.

As well as different types of clients, different types of case will need a slightly different approach and emphasis—interviewing a man who has been injured at work will require different things from interviewing a person who wants to buy a house. In this chapter I will try to give broad indications of the most important things in the first interview with the client, but they will have to be adapted to the individual case.

The relationship with the client

Many lawyers, even the most efficient, do not pay sufficient attention to building a good relationship with the client. It is not that he needs to be too friendly—any lawyer will like some clients and not others and this should be irrelevant to the conduct of the case. What is necessary is to build a relationship which does have real confidence and communication from both sides. The client will not feel that he is getting a good service if he feels that the lawyer does not listen to all he says or clearly understand his views and the objectives. Equally, the lawyer will not be able to conduct a case as well as he could if he does not manage to encourage the client to tell him everything he knows that might possibly be relevant. This is something the young lawyer may have to work at, but if he does not get his client to tell him something, the other side may surprise him by telling him at trial.

Lawyers sometimes tend to be like some doctors, in that they begin to see clients or patients as objects, or just something to be studied and argued about, rather than as real people with real problems that they may be very worried about. A consultant doing his round in a hospital may go up to a bed and discuss the patient as though he were not there, hardly speaking to the patient at all except to make a superficial comment. Some lawyers also see cases rather than people, and they must always remember that they are only there to advise and help the clients.

Lawyers will inevitably relate to their clients in different ways, but their essential objectives should be:

(a) To show a reasonable degree of sympathy for the client. This does not mean emotional support, but giving the client the feeling that the lawyer is on his side. The lawyer is there to develop the arguments for the client as far as possible, and to try to achieve what he wants, and the client should never get the feeling that his own lawyer is judging him, or is doing more for the other side than for him.

(b) To give the client confidence to discuss his case fully and not to intimidate him.

(c) To try to appreciate the realities of the situation that the client is in. This may require thought and imagination, to try to establish the full facts of the case and what can best be done about it. Especially in a case where facts may be in dispute or evidence may be difficult to gather, the lawyer will need to develop skills to put a case together.

(d) To keep the client fully informed of how the case is progressing. This applies to all aspects of the case, from giving a rough explanation of the procedural steps involved to letting the client know the current size of the bill for costs.

To put it in a nutshell, the client is paying (or the taxpayer's legal aid is paying for him), so he must come first in everything. The lawyer has no right to impose his own solutions on the client, or to be paternalistic. It is the client's case not the lawyer's, and it is especially important to remember this when negotiating a settlement, or the client may be left in a very difficult position. For example in *Waugh* v *M.B. Clifford & Sons* [1982] Ch 374 the solicitors negotiated a settlement for a claim arising from defects in houses without the client's consent. It was held that the clients were still bound by it as the solicitors had actual or ostensible authority to act on behalf of the clients, and full agreement had been reached. However it may be possible for the agreement to be set aside if the lawyer did not have authority and the agreement has not been perfected or put into effect. In *Marsden* v *Marsden* [1972] Fam 280 the wife's counsel agreed maintenance, gave up the wife's share in the home and released her charge on it without any instructions to do so. It was held that the order agreed could be set aside as counsel should not go beyond his instructions, and the order had not at the time been perfected.

The client must come first even if the lawyer does not agree with his views. If a landlord asks him to draw up leases to reduce tenants' rights to a minimum the lawyer should comply even if he does not think that this is a good thing to do. The lawyer must forget his personal views, and the most he can do is to suggest that the client might do better to go to another lawyer if he does feel so strongly that he feels he cannot represent the client properly. However the lawyer has no duty to do anything improper or unlawful for the client, and can certainly tell the client that in the eyes of the law he is asking too much, if for example he is representing a wife who is making unreasonable financial demands on her husband.

Although the lawyer should put the client first he does need to keep a balance. He must also use skills in communication and imagination to find out what the case against his client may be. Just as he has a duty to develop every argument in the client's favour he equally has a duty to give the client a realistic view as to whether his case will succeed. Although the lawyer should not take decisions for the client he can give him very strong advice, and he has no duty to accept his directions on the conduct of the case. For example the lawyer should not make unpleasant allegations against a witness purely because the client asks him to, but only if he feels it will be useful in winning the case.

Having said that the lawyer will be in charge of the actual conduct of the case it is not entirely clear how far he can go. Balancing the need to win the case with the instructions given by the client may not be easy. The barrister is solely in charge of the case in court, and it is for him to decide what witnesses to call and what questions to ask, whatever the client would like him to do, though he should try to follow the client's wishes unless he has good reason to do otherwise. In more than one of the 'Rumpole' stories by John Mortimer the barrister wins the case by calling a witness or asking a question directly contrary to his client's wishes, but winning by doing it. It is a difficult professional question whether he really should do this!

Finally, the lawyer must of course adapt all these points of general technique to the case in hand and according to the type of work he does. It is clearly much more important to be able to put people at their ease and talk sympathetically in a matrimonial case than when dealing with a building contract. To some extent this is just a question of degree, but there is also an element of temperament, and a lawyer should avoid going into an area of law where he cannot deal easily with his clients or he will not work well.

It is also necessary to adapt to the seriousness of the case. This is not just an objective test of the value of property in dispute, but also an awareness of how important the case is to the client. A neighbour cutting down a hedge can be more important to one person than a £100,000 contract is to another, and the lawyer should take that into account. He should let the client let off steam by telling him all about the problem, he should do what he can to help the client who is worried about something, but should give him an objective view of whether the cost and effort of suing will really help him.

Preliminary issues

There are a few matters to be considered even before the solicitor sees the client. Firstly there is the question of why and how the client first contacts the solicitor's office to make an appointment. A person may go to a solicitor because he is his family solicitor, because he has advised him before on business matters, or because a friend has recommended him. But it is also quite possible that the client had no idea which solicitor to go to and has just found one in the Yellow Pages, seen the solicitor's nameplate outside, or been referred by a person or a body such as a Citizens' Advice Bureau. This may cause a difficulty in that the client has not necessarily been able to choose a solicitor who is used to dealing with his type of case. Many firms of solicitors can cope with this as they have partners specialising in different areas, but many members of the public do find this a real problem. The rules that restricted advertising by solicitors were relaxed in October 1984, though there are still limitations on the types of advertisements that may be used. Hopefully this will help potential clients.

The client may decide to go to a solicitor for all sorts of reasons; he may just need advice on a matter that is not very urgent, such as the making of a will, or he may have a more urgent problem such as being summonsed for a criminal offence. The case may clearly involve a complicated study of documents, or it may not really be a legal problem at all but just something that the client does not know how to deal with.

All this should be taken into account when the client first contacts the lawyer's office for an appointment. Of course he will probably not speak to the solicitor himself at this point, but the solicitor should give clear directions to his secretary or receptionist on how to deal with a new client. It is useful if the client who wants to make an appointment is asked:

(a) What type of case is involved, so that an appointment can be made with the right partner, and the solicitor can at least be ready for the type of case.

(b) Whether the case is urgent, so that an appointment can be made soon if necessary.

(c) To bring any appropriate documents with him, and perhaps also a written summary of the main dates and facts that he might otherwise forget. This will save his having to come back for a second appointment when he has found the documents.

Conducting the first interview

The first thing to do is give the client the right impression when he arrives, and this has two main elements—the client should feel that he has come to an efficient office, but also should feel comfortable enough to be able to discuss his case freely. This will of course not be possible if the first interview has to take place elsewhere, for example in a court where the solicitor is taking part in the duty solicitor scheme, but in his own office the solicitor will be able to create the atmosphere.

Having met the client and put him at his ease, the solicitor will want to establish immediately what problem the client has and what sort of case he is concerned with. Sometimes this can be quickly established, if the client wants to make a will or has a summons to appear in court on a charge, but sometimes it will not be so easy to establish exactly what the problem is, and the client may have to explain a lot of factual background before the solicitor can identify what he can help with. The solicitor may have to develop his line of questioning carefully to get to the heart of the matter, and sometimes the client may not have a legal problem at all, and may have to be told to go elsewhere to get advice.

Having established what the problem is, the solicitor will be able to develop the interview by asking questions to establish all the facts that he needs to know. He should keep a note of the main things that are said, or should arrange for a note to be taken by someone else who is present, or by recording the interview. He should take care to establish all dates and main events in the case and identify all documents and people that may be relevant. He should also establish what it is that is bothering the client and what he hopes to achieve. Once he decides that a particular type of legal action may be taken he should run through all the necessary elements for that, so as not to have to call the client back for a further interview if this is avoidable. However, even once a possible cause of action has been decided on, the solicitor should keep an open mind, to change his view if necessary as further facts emerge.

Even though he will normally take control of the interview and direct what is said by his lines of questioning, the solicitor should ensure that the client does have the chance to say all that he wants to. While he should not be allowed to ramble on for too long a time on matters that are not relevant, the client must be given sufficient opportunity to speak for himself in case he does bring up matters that should be investigated, or which give a different complexion to the case. The client may well feel more confidence in the lawyer if he is allowed to say all he wants to, even if it is not legally relevant. The client should also be specifically asked whether he knows of any particular problems or points which could be argued against him. This needs to be done tactfully, but the solicitor can only give full advice if he has the full facts.

Once he has all the information that is available, the solicitor will need to make decisions on how the case should proceed in the future, and tell the client what should be done. By the time he leaves the office, the client should have clear in his mind what his position is and what will happen next, including such legal detail as he is capable of understanding. He should know as far as possible what type of case he has, what remedies he may get, and how long it will take. He should also know whether he has to do anything else, such as collect further information, whether the next step will be taken by a solicitor, or whether the opinion of a barrister will be sought, in which case the process of briefing a barrister should be explained to him.

In practical terms, he should also be made aware of what any possible action might cost. If there is a possibility that the client might be entitled to legal aid, the appropriate tactful inquiries should be made as to his means, and the solicitor can help him apply as soon as possible. If the client is not likely to get legal aid, it is in the interests of both the solicitor and the client that the possible costs should be made clear so as to try to avoid any difficulty about payment. If the case is likely to be quite expensive and take some time the solicitor may well ask for some payment to be made in advance. Any other point that may directly affect the client in the conduct of the case should also be made clear to him, for example the possibility that if a case goes to trial he will have to make discovery of documents, which he may not know, and which may not be welcome to him, *Rockwell Machine Tool Co Ltd* v *E.P. Barrus (Concessionaires) Ltd* [1968] 1 WLR 693.

The progress of the case

As has been said, by the end of the first interview the solicitor should have made some decisions on the future conduct of the case, and should have explained those decisions to the client. If the solicitor feels that he can give no further help, he should explain why, and if possible he should try to help the client to find somewhere else to go for advice. If the case will not need any court action but just requires the giving of advice and possibly drawing up a document such as a will, a conveyance or a lease then the solicitor can proceed to deal with the matter and contact the client again when the work is done, or if he needs further contact with the client for some other reason.

The solicitor may need further information before he can decide how to proceed, whether it be the names of witnesses, documents or reports, in which case he should decide exactly what he needs and how it should be obtained. If the client can get further information it should be made completely clear to him what to get, otherwise the solicitor himself must decide where the information is to come from and set about getting it. Once the further information has been obtained, the solicitor can decide how to proceed from there, and see the client again if necessary.

If the case needs to go to court, but can go to a court where the solicitor has a right of audience, then the solicitor can prepare the case for the hearing, drafting the necessary documents, collecting evidence, preparing his arguments and so on. In such a case the points made in the following chapters will be relevant to how the case will proceed.

If it is clear that the case is complicated, or that it will have to be heard in a court where the solicitor does not have a right of audience a barrister will need to be briefed. What this involves should be fully explained to the client, and a further appointment with the client will need to be made to discuss counsel's opinion when it arrives. The following chapter deals with the preparation of the brief. If the case is going to go to counsel it is preferable that the solicitor takes no further steps, or there may be difficulties if what he does conflicts with the way the barrister feels the case should be conducted, though he may need to take steps, for example by issuing a writ if a limitation period has nearly expired. If it becomes clear at a later stage that the case is more serious than was thought, a barrister may have to be briefed then.

In any event, the solicitor should keep an eye on the progress of the case to ensure that it does go through the necessary steps properly—both strategy and timetable should be kept under review. For this purpose it is useful to keep a sheet of paper in the front of the client's file to record the main stages in the case and important dates. This can be used to ensure that nothing is forgotten and that there is no undue delay in the case. If a barrister does take a long time to give an opinion on a brief he should be contacted to check on progress, and if the solicitors open negotiations with the other side in the case they should ensure that these do not drag on if they are not really achieving anything.

There are two particular things to watch in the progress of the case, especially if it does go on for some time. The first is to ensure that the limitation period for the action does not expire without a writ's being issued, which can happen if there is difficulty getting information or negotiations proceed without reaching any agreement. These periods are now governed by the Limitation Act 1980, and I have included a brief table of its main provisions for convenience. It may be possible to issue a writ after the expiry of the limitation period, but the court will look at the whole conduct of the case and any possible prejudice to the parties and will be slow to give leave. It is also worth remembering that it is difficult to add a new party to an action after the limitation period has expired, so even if the action is begun in time it may be a good idea to check that the right person has been sued if there is a possible choice of defendants, see *Liff* v *Peasley* [1980] 1 All ER 623 and *Lipton's Cash Registers and Business Equipment* v *Hugin Kassaregister AB and Hugin Cash Registers* [1982] 1 All ER 595.

The other thing is to watch the bill for costs, especially if a number of applications to court are made or a lot of evidence has to be collected. It should become clearer what chance of success the case has, and even if negotiations are proceeding, the relative size of the bill for costs should be taken into account. In *Singer* v *Sharegin* (1983) *The Times*, 28 June there was an application for a lump sum of £6,000 in a matrimonial case which was met by an offer of £3,000 which was rejected. The court ordered a lump sum of £4,500, but the legal costs were £5,000, and the judge made it clear that lawyers do have a duty to keep the client aware of the costs, and to bear in mind what effects costs may have on any judgment finally given. The solicitor will have difficulty as well as the client if costs reach a level that the client cannot afford to pay, and in any event costs should normally be kept in reasonable proportion to what can be achieved in the case.

TABLE OF MAIN LIMITATION PERIODS

Limitation periods are now governed by the Limitation Act 1980, and the references to sections are to that Act.

Type of action		*Limitation period*
Contract	Action on a contract or for an account	6 years, running from date of breach, s 5
	Contract under seal	12 years
Tort	Most tort actions	6 years, running from date tort committed, or if damage must be proved, from date of damage, s 2
	Personal injury actions	3 years, running from date tort committed, or date plaintiff knew he had a cause of action, s 11
	Fatal accident actions	3 years, s 12
	In personal injury and fatal accident cases the court has a discretion to override the 3 year limitation period if it would be equitable in the circumstances, s 33. This will depend on the length of and reasons for delay, whether evidence is likely to be less cogent due to the delay, the conduct of the defendant, whether the plaintiff acted promptly and the steps he took to get advice.	
Trust	Breach of trust actions	6 years, s 21
	Fraudulent breach of trust, or action to recover trust property from trustee	No limitation period
Land	Recovery of land or claim by mortgagee	12 years, running from date right to sue or recover land arose
	Rent or mortgage action	6 years

3 *The brief to counsel*

The brief is the written set of instructions, together with any relevant documents and statements, that the solicitor sends to the barrister when he is asking him to advise in a case, to advise on a particular point, or to conduct the case in court. The documents are collected together with the instructions and a backsheet with the name of the case and the name and address of the barrister and the solicitor is either folded round them or placed on top, and the papers are all tied together with pink tape. The brief is important as, with very few exceptions, the barrister can only act in a case if he has a brief, and should only act on the documents and instructions contained in it.

Not only must the barrister have a brief in the case, but he must have a separate brief for each piece of work he does. For example, a barrister may well be sent an initial brief to give general advice in an opinion, a later brief in the case to give specific advice on the quantification of damages or evidence, a brief to conduct the case at trial and, if necessary, a brief to advise on appeal. It is not possible for a barrister to act under any general brief or agreement to give advice to a particular solicitor or client whenever necessary—he must have a separate brief for each case as and when it arises, though he may have a retainer to act for a client provided he does have separate briefs for each case.

Each barrister in a case must have a separate brief, whatever his degree of involvement. If there is a silk and a junior counsel then each must have their own brief, and if there is more than one junior counsel each must act under his own brief. However, if a barrister is representing more than one client in a case he will normally have only one brief (if there is any conflict of interest or substantial difference in their cases then each should have a separate barrister). If one barrister does 'devilling' work on a brief sent to another he will not have a brief of his own, but will just do work on the brief and return it to the barrister to whom it was sent.

The 'taxi rank' principle as to the acceptance of briefs by a barrister was mentioned earlier. The idea is that there should be equal access to justice and that therefore the barrister, like the taxi driver, should accept any customer who reasonably requires his services, and should not pick and choose only those people he likes and whose cases he thinks are strong. A barrister should normally accept any brief in the courts in which he normally practises that concerns any type of work he normally does, and for which he is offered a fair fee. There are only limited circumstances in which a barrister can properly refuse to accept a brief, and these are dealt with later.

The brief is not a formal contract or agreement between the solicitor and the barrister—the solicitor in no way employs the barrister—but the contents of the brief are the basis of the work done by the barrister, who should only act on those contents and within the instructions he is given. The backsheet itself can be used for many purposes, such as the marking of the fee for the work to be done on the brief, the marking of an indorsement by the barrister when the case is over to show that he has completed the work in the brief, the recording in writing of any special instructions given by the client to the barrister, or the recording in writing of an agreement on the case made by the parties.

Because the brief is the whole basis of the work done by the barrister, it must be prepared carefully by the solicitor. It is not just a question of collecting together all the papers in the case and sending them off to the barrister asking him to advise. The brief should only include relevant documents, and all the relevant documents, and it should have clear instructions as to what the barrister is being asked to deal with. If the brief is properly prepared, the barrister should be able to deal with it quickly and reasonably easily, but if it is not well prepared the barrister will inevitably have to spend a lot longer dealing with it to sort out the contents and to write his opinion.

The decision to brief a barrister

There are many reasons why a solicitor may decide to brief a barrister. Amongst the most common are the following:

(a) The case may involve a difficult point of law needing special advice or research.
(b) The case may need to be brought in a court where the solicitor has no right of audience.
(c) The case may be outside the normal work done by the solicitor.
(d) There may be a need for an opinion on a particular point.

The solicitor should try to make the decision whether he will need to brief a barrister in the case as soon as he can. If he takes steps in the case before sending it to a barrister, this may make it more difficult for the barrister to deal with the case as he thinks right. Once the decision to brief a barrister has been made, the brief should be sent off as soon as all the necessary documents and information are available, but not before, unless there is real urgency. If the brief is sent off without the right documents there will still be a delay while the barrister asks for them before he writes his opinion. If there is real urgency, the solicitor may telephone the barrister for advice, and send the brief on later.

As to choosing the right barrister to brief, this may be a difficulty. An established firm of solicitors will regularly brief the same barristers, which is advantageous to all in building up a working relationship, but the solicitor may get a case outside his normal areas of work, his usual barrister may not be available and the small firm of solicitors may not be able to build up a regular relationship with a particular barrister. The solicitor may then have a problem, due to the strict limits on advertising by barristers. These do prevent any improper touting for work, but can make it difficult for the solicitor to find out information he does need to know. The basic sources of information are the Bar List, which gives the name and address of all barristers and the types of work that they do, other solicitors and barristers who may be able to make comments on someone appropriate, or the clerk of a set of Chambers, who is in a good position to be able to recommend a barrister from his experience.

The young barrister also has a difficulty in getting briefs sent to him. He cannot get briefs until he builds up a good reputation, and he can only build up a reputation if he gets briefs to do. To some extent the problem is inevitable, as there is a limited amount of work and a lot of people wanting to come to the Bar. A good set of Chambers will normally have some small matters for pupils to deal with once they have finished their first six months pupillage, but the pupil will himself have to make a real effort to impress solicitors and his clerk to get more work and build up the kind of practice that he wants. The young barrister must reasonably expect a struggle and competition, but in recent years the Bar has gone some way to deal with the more unfair aspects of competition with better organised pupillage schemes, and recognition that it is difficult for black barristers to get places. It has also been said that 'squatters' who have finished their pupillage should be given a clear indication of their position as soon as possible, and not be kept in Chambers unsure of their future.

Preparing the brief

Once the decision has been taken to brief a barrister, the solicitor should collect together the relevant documents and prepare the brief. Generally the brief should not be sent off until all the documents can be included, but sometimes it may be sent and the extra document sent on when it is available. Sometimes no documents will be needed beyond the instructions of the solicitor setting out what has happened, though then the instructions must be full and written with care.

The documents needed in a brief will vary with every case, but as a general guide, the following types of information may be included:

(a) Any existing legal documents in the case, such as a summons or writ. What has actually been pleaded will be crucial in the case.

(b) Any other document which is central to the case, such as a contract, deed or will. A solicitor will sometimes just write out the relevant clauses of the document in his instructions, but although this may be sufficient, it is better to send the whole document so that the barrister can see if there are any other relevant clauses for the arguments he develops.

(c) There may be a statement from the client, especially where there is an important issue of fact, such as how an accident occurred. Again the solicitor may summarise what the client says in his instructions, rather than including a separate statement, but he must ensure that such a summary is accurate and complete. The statement or summary should cover all the matters the barrister will need to know about, and the solicitor must see that he covers everything when he meets the client for this purpose.

(d) Any relevant map or plan should be included, for example in a road traffic accident or a boundary dispute. Alternatively, if the case involves something technical, such as the working of a machine, the solicitor should try to send sufficient information and diagrams for the barrister to be able to understand as far as possible what has happened.

(e) Any statement from any other witness that is available, for example a statement from a witness to the accident or someone who is aware of the background.

(f) Any existing correspondence with the other side which may be helpful. It is not helpful to send all the correspondence that there is, which will just waste the barrister's time, but only those things which may affect the advice given. Essentially the solicitor should use his common sense. He will already have taken some preliminary view of what sort of case he is dealing with, and he should make sure that he sends all the things the barrister will need to deal with a case of that kind. But the other general rule is not to send too much; if there are piles of documents or correspondence, the solicitor should try if possible to do some preliminary preparation (perhaps done by an articled clerk) so that the barrister only gets what is relevant and does not have to spend hours going through papers before he can begin to deal with the brief. It is only if all the papers really could be relevant that they should all be sent.

With the brief the solicitor has to send his instructions, which will normally be on the reverse side of the backsheet, or on a separate sheet which can be seen as soon as the brief is opened. In a very simple case it is sufficient to give very brief instructions along the lines of 'Counsel is requested to advise our client Mrs. X in this case', but normally the instructions will need to be more detailed. Essentially the instructions should firstly summarise the main points in the case so that the barrister can immediately see what it is about and how complicated it is, and secondly they should summarise exactly what the barrister is being asked to do so that there is no misunderstanding.

There are no binding rules for the writing of instructions, and in practice they vary a lot in length, in what they cover and in style. If the barrister and solicitor have worked together before they may be fairly chatty and informal, or sometimes they read like a formally drafted document. The solicitor will develop his own style for himself, but I suggest that as a general guideline the following things should be included. If many of the details are in documents contained in the brief the documents need only be referred to, but if there are few or no other documents in the brief the instructions must give all details.

(a) The instructions should begin with a brief summary of the case, that is the main facts together with any provisional decision that the solicitor has made as to the type of case, such as that it is one of negligence, misrepresentation, etc. If any particular line of legal argument has occurred to the solicitor then he may mention that as a possibility, but generally decisions should be left to the barrister.

(b) It is useful for the solicitor to list the contents of the brief beginning with 'Counsel has herewith . . .'. This has two uses—it encourages the solicitor to think of what documents should be there, and it is a useful guide for the barrister when he comes to read the brief as to what documents he has.

(c) The solicitor should specifically mention in the instructions any special points about the case to make sure they are brought to the barrister's attention.

For example he should say clearly if the limitation date is near or there is some other need for special urgency.

(d) It should be made completely clear what the barrister is asked to do. ‘Counsel is asked to advise’ will do for a simple case, but it will often be necessary to say more, and to say exactly what advice is sought. For example it may be about liability, damages, who should be sued, what evidence is needed, etc. Also counsel should be specifically asked to deal with any special points that the solicitor or the client feel are important, for example whether an injunction should be sought, or anything the client particularly wants to achieve.

The main thing is for the instructions to be clear. They go from one lawyer to another, but they should sum up succinctly what is in issue. It is quite open for the solicitor to make suggestions of any points that occur to him, and he should say exactly what he would like the barrister to do.

Uses of the backsheet

The backsheet will be folded round the rest of the brief or placed on top of it, and it will have written on it the basic details of the case. The elements that will appear are:

(a) The name of the case. If the case has not yet begun this will just be a simple ‘In the matter of Mrs Jones’ or ‘Re Mr Smith’, that is the name of the client. If the case has begun the full title should be given, the court the case is in, the number of the case, and the names of the parties set out as they would be on the top of a writ.

(b) The instructions to counsel. This is put between two solid black lines about half the way down the backsheet. The instructions should specify basically what counsel is being asked to do, for example ‘Instructions to counsel to advise’, ‘Instructions to counsel for the defence’, ‘Instructions to counsel to settle a Notice of Appeal’ as appropriate.

(c) The name of the barrister briefed and the address of his Chambers.

(d) The name and address of instructing solicitors.

There are no formal rules for the drawing up of a backsheet, it just provides basic information, but in practice it is used for many purposes. It is the document which counsel is acting under in the case. He has to be instructed by solicitors to be able to appear, and the backsheet provides these instructions. Once the case is finished, or the piece of work requested in the instructions done the barrister will endorse the brief to this effect and return it to the solicitor. The brief is endorsed by making the mark ℓ, through the title and writing the date when the work was completed with counsel’s signature.

The backsheet is also used to mark the brief fee. In a legal aid case the barrister will be paid the sum allowed on taxation so no fee should be marked (though the words ‘Legal Aid’ may appear on the backsheet) but in any other case the fee must be agreed and written on the brief before the barrister goes into court. There must be a separate fee for each brief, not a fixed fee for several briefs. If a barrister often does work for the same client or solicitors he must still have a separate fee for each brief. A fee must be marked, though it is possible for the barrister to waive all or part of the fee if he wishes to. A contingent fee under which payment depends on whether the case is won or lost and how much is recovered is not allowed by English law.

The fee for the brief will normally be agreed by the barrister's clerk and the solicitor, though the former may well consult the barrister, and the latter consult the client. The fee will of course depend on the complexity of the brief, the amount of work involved and the experience of the barrister, and it will usually be necessary for the barrister or his clerk to glance through the brief to decide on this. An experienced clerk will know the type of fee that should be asked for different types of work, and for the different barristers in his Chambers.

The fee agreed covers all the work to be done under the brief, that is reading it and drafting any documents necessary as a result of instructions. The fee may only be altered by specific agreement between the clerk and the solicitors, for example if the brief turns out to need much more work than was expected. If the brief is for the barrister to conduct the case at trial and the case may go on for some time it is normal for there to be not only a brief fee but also daily 'refreshers', that is the sum to be paid for each day of the hearing (see RSC Order 62). There must of course be a separate fee for every barrister instructed in the case, but each fee is agreed separately, and there is no longer a rule that a junior should necessarily be paid two-thirds of the fee paid to his leader, it will depend on the amount of work done by each. The fee agreed will normally be payable even if the case settles, or if the brief is returned in certain circumstances, *Taylor* v *McKenzie* (1984) *The Times*, 10 July.

Sometimes the fee agreed for a brief may seem very high, but various recent surveys have shown that the average barrister's income is often no more than he would earn in any other profession, and in the early years will be much less. It is only the leading silks at the top of the profession that do have a very high level of income. There are also many things that the fee has to cover; the barrister will be paid only the fee and it must therefore take into account all expenses, his travelling costs and Chambers expenses from the clerk to the paperclips. National Insurance contributions and payments for his own pension. Finally, since the barrister cannot sue for his fees he must take into account the fact that it may be some time before he is paid (with no interest on the fee) and that some fees will inevitably prove to be irrecoverable.

The backsheet may be used to record in writing a decision or agreement in the case which needs to be formally recorded. For example the client may insist on acting against the advice of the barrister, by accepting an offer of damages that is too low or pleading guilty when he is told he should not. To ensure that he cannot later be criticised or sued for allowing this to happen the barrister may write on the back of the brief that he has advised the client on his rights and the client has taken this course of his own free will, and get the client to sign it. Alternatively, the parties may agree to settle a case before going into court, and the barristers may record the terms of the agreement by indorsing it on their briefs and each signing it. This may be useful when they wish to agree detailed terms or give undertakings that the court could not itself order.

The barrister and the brief

When a brief is sent to a barrister he should have a preliminary look at it as soon as possible. He should see if there is any particular urgency in the case needing quick action or any legal difficulty needing long research and also how much work is involved for his clerk to agree a fee. Also the preliminary review may show that something is missing from the brief which he will need to give full advice, in which case he should contact the solicitor to send it.

If there is any need for quick action, for example because the limitation period is running out or because an injunction or some other order should be sought quickly, then the barrister should work on the brief as soon as he can, perhaps leaving other work which is not so urgent. If there is no particular urgency the brief will have to wait its turn, but it should only be left for a reasonable amount of time. If the brief involves a study of many documents or research on a complex point of law then a delay of a few months may be justified, but not if there is no particular complication. If the barrister does have so much work that there may be a long delay he should tell the solicitor. A barrister will inevitably have an uneven flow of work, but he should still try to be known for his efficiency rather than for keeping briefs too long.

The barrister should refuse to accept a brief if the case involves any business interest of his own that might affect his impartiality, or if he is aware that a close friend or relative of his is concerned in the case.

Sometimes the barrister should explain his position to the solicitor and ask if he really wishes him to accept the case, for example, if the brief is in an area of law that the barrister does not normally practise in and he does not feel he can do the case as well as a barrister who specialised in that area might. It may also happen if the barrister would feel some difficulty or embarrassment in accepting the brief, for example, if he had previously acted for the other side in a different case, or if he has any personal interest in the case at all. The barrister should also consult the solicitor if he feels for some reason that he cannot properly represent the client, if for example the brief is to represent a body whose views he strongly disagrees with. The barrister cannot refuse to take a case because of his personal views, but he can suggest to the solicitor that it might be better for the client to use some other barrister.

Once a barrister has accepted a brief he is bound as a matter of professional duty to do the work requested in the brief. However there are limited circumstances in which he may return the brief. If the barrister gives strong advice to the client on the way that the case should be conducted which the client refuses to accept, then the barrister can tell the client that in those circumstances he does not feel that he can go on representing him, though this should only be done as a last resort in an extreme case. In a criminal case, if the client admits his guilt to the barrister then the barrister cannot go on defending him on a plea of not guilty but must return the brief (though he should first question the client to see that the client really is guilty of all the legal elements of the offence charged).

Sometimes a barrister will have to return a brief because he finds that when the case comes to court he is already doing another case. This means that the brief may be sent back at a very late stage, and this should obviously be avoided whenever possible because the brief will be sent to a new barrister who will have relatively little time to acquaint himself with the details of the case. Clients will be very concerned if their barrister is replaced at the last moment, especially if he has already met them in conference or at a previous hearing.

To some extent the late return of briefs is inevitable. The Listing Officers have to make the best use they can of the courts' time and cannot always say when a particular case will come on. Some cases listed to go on for some days will settle, some that are expected to take only a couple of days may go on much longer. The Bar has considered the problem, and has made it clear that a barrister has a duty to do all that he can to avoid having to return a brief at a late stage—as soon as it becomes clear that he may have to he should explain the situation to the solicitor, and his clerk should make all efforts to find a suitable replacement barrister. If the replacement comes from the same Chambers it should be possible for him to discuss the case with the person who has had to return the brief. A brief to defend someone on a serious criminal charge must take precedence over a civil matter, and it should never be necessary to return a brief in a fixed date trial. A barrister should especially try to avoid returning a brief in a case where he has already met and advised the client in conference, and should of course never return a brief for social reasons.

If a barrister is briefed in a case where another barrister was previously asked to advise he should as a matter of etiquette telephone the former barrister to tell him.

Reading the brief

The whole conduct of a case stems from the first reading of the brief and the impressions that are formed then, so it is important to read it carefully and properly. If the brief has been properly prepared by the solicitor it should be easy to read, but if he has just sent off the papers without consideration the brief may need a lot of preparatory work by the barrister. As was said earlier, the barrister should have a quick look at the instructions in the brief as soon as he receives it, then later he will have to read it fully.

The first step will of course be to read the instructions themselves. If the instructions have been written well they should immediately tell the barrister what type of case he is concerned with, what the basic facts are, and what documents he should have. It should also be clear what stage the case has reached if the action has already begun, and exactly what the barrister is asked to do. If any essential information is not in the instructions then the barrister should try to establish it as soon as he can in reading the rest of the brief.

The next step will be to sort out the other papers in the brief. They should not be read haphazardly in whatever order they happen to be in, but should be sorted and read in a sensible order to avoid confusion. If the solicitor has given a list of documents on the instructions it should be relatively easy to decide on the best order for reading them—indeed the very good solicitor will have listed them in the order in which they should be read.

If there are any formal pleadings in the case these should be read first because, if they have been properly drafted, they will give a clear idea of the case. The next stage is to read any statement by the client, which will often be in the form of a summary by the solicitor of what the client says, and will give the barrister the view of the client that he is asked to represent. After this any other crucial document should be read, for example any contract, will or trust instrument. The next thing is to read any statements or reports by experts or witnesses, to find more detail of what has happened, and finally anything else that has been put in the brief, such as correspondence between the solicitors.

Obviously this is a general line of approach and will have to be modified for different types of case. The main thing is always to read the most important documents first so as not to be bogged down in irrelevant detail. If there is any map, plan or diagram it should be put where it can be seen while the brief is read. All through the reading the barrister should remember that he may not have all the documents he needs, or that some of the documents that have been sent may not be directly relevant.

It is important to try to approach reading the brief in the right way, because the impressions formed on first reading may well affect the whole conduct of the case. Therefore the barrister should avoid if possible first reading the brief while travelling, or when something is distracting his attention. It is vital not to miss a point or misread a point that may alter the advice given, and to keep an open mind as to what sort of action if any should be begun. It is also important to question everything that there is in the brief to see if there are any facts missing, gaps in the story or problems. At this stage the barrister will probably not have anything like the whole story, and it is important to bear in mind what is not in the brief as well as what is.

It is useful to have pen and paper available while reading the brief. On one sheet of paper notes should be made of all the important dates, all the people involved and all the main facts and figures. After reading the brief this information should be sorted into a logical order and a neat copy made that can be kept. The extra work involved in making this note of the main facts is well worth it—it helps to clarify the bare bones of the case, and can be referred to on many occasions:

(a) When writing an opinion it is useful to have a summary of the facts rather than continually searching through the whole brief.

(b) When advising in conference the barrister can leave the summary of facts on the desk in front of him and refer to it quickly while he talks to give the solicitor and client the feeling that he really does have the case at his fingertips.

(c) If the case comes back to the barrister for further advice he can use the summary of facts rather than having to re-read the whole brief in detail.

(d) When preparing the case for court the summary of facts will again reduce the amount of work to be done on the brief, and the summary can often be used as the basis of a speech opening the case to the court.

On another sheet of paper the barrister can note as he reads all the points on which he needs more information and a list of documents, witnesses or reports that should be sought. He can then ask the solicitor to provide these by telephone, in conference or in his opinion.

If the brief is a large one with lots of documents it will need extra work, which the barrister's pupil may well be asked to help with. If there are a large number of letters, reports or other documents they should be read separately. It is usually best to read the documents in chronological order, the earliest first, and as they are read to take notes of any relevant facts or points with a clear reference to which document the fact is in. Again a neat copy of these notes should be made and kept as it will be very useful later for easy reference, and will save having to read all the documents again. The notes will also be useful when preparing a bundle of the relevant documents for court.

The main objective while reading the brief is to decide what course of action should be taken in the case. As soon as the barrister has taken a preliminary decision he should bear in mind all the legal elements that he will need to prove for the case to succeed. While he reads he should see whether he does have all those elements and whether he can get the evidence necessary to prove each one. All the elements of the case must of course come from what he is told, and the barrister must beware of assuming anything—if he is not told something he should make a note about it and ask.

Action after reading the brief

Once the barrister has finished reading the brief he must make a decision as to what should be the next step in the case. The main possibilities are as follows:

(a) The case may need some immediate action such as the seeking of an injunction or an Anton Piller order. If there is real urgency, the barrister should telephone the solicitor and arrange with him for the appropriate application to be made with the appropriate documents as soon as possible. A full opinion on the case can be written later. If there is less urgency then the barrister should write his opinion as soon as he can and send it back to the solicitor, advising quick action.

(b) If there is no need for immediate action and the barrister has in his brief all the information he needs then he can proceed to write his opinion. He will of course need to research the relevant points of law first. The writing of an opinion is dealt with in the next chapter.

(c) If the barrister does need extra information before he can proceed then he should contact the solicitor to get it as soon as possible. If he has made a list of what he needs while reading the brief then he can easily ask for everything he needs. Once he has the extra information he can proceed to write his opinion.

(d) It may be that the barrister will feel that he needs to see the client before he can give full advice. It may be important for him to hear what the client personally has to say, for example in a divorce case or a personal accident case, or it may be that the case is especially important for the client and the barrister wants to discuss with him all the details and what the client hopes to achieve. In this case he should arrange a conference with the solicitor and client, and then write his opinion afterwards. Advising in conference is dealt with later.

(e) The barrister may feel that leading counsel should be brought into the case. This may happen if the law in the case is especially complex, or if the case involves something of great value or great importance, or if it may need particular skill in court with speeches and cross-examination, or if it is going on appeal and may need extra strength to conduct it. He must consult the solicitor and the client, because the client may well have to pay greater costs (*re Solicitors* [1982] 1 WLR 745), or if he is on legal aid the costs of bringing in the leader will not be allowed if the leader is not really necessary (*Gorfin* v *Odhams Press Ltd* [1958] 1 WLR 314). If a leader is to be brought in this should be done as soon as possible so that he can give advice on how the case should be conducted, though in fact the junior counsel may still do much of the work on the brief as regards research and preparing documents.

Other types of brief

The above comments apply primarily to a preliminary brief to counsel to advise, though many points will also apply to other briefs too. A brief may be sent to counsel at many stages in the case, to advise on evidence, to conduct the case at trial, or to advise on whether to appeal, as appropriate. Each type of brief requires a slightly different approach, and I will deal with some of the points to be taken into account. Briefs in criminal cases and appeal cases will be dealt with in a later chapter.

(a) A brief for the defence in a civil case. The points about reading the brief and noting the main points are dealt with above. In addition the barrister should in particular consider the reaction of the defendant to every point in the case against him. If necessary he should see the client in conference to decide what is admitted, what is denied, and what is challenged. In particular he should look for the elements of every possible specific or general defence, any way in which he may challenge the measure of damages or other remedy that the other side is claiming and whether any other party should be added to the action. The barrister acting for the defence needs much more imagination than the barrister acting for the plaintiff as he has to try to think of all the possible weaknesses in the case against him, which can be more difficult than building up a case.

The barrister for the defence should also always inquire whether his client has any claim to bring against the plaintiff, whether as a set-off or counterclaim, even if this is not specifically in his instructions, and he should also examine the plaintiff's pleadings to see if they should be challenged in any way.

(b) A brief to advise on quantum. It may well be difficult or impossible for the barrister to advise on the exact measure of damages when the case first comes to counsel, although he should be as specific in his advice as he can be. Especially in a personal injury case counsel may well be briefed again later to give advice on the measure of damages when details of injury and loss are available.

(c) A brief to advise on evidence. This will often be sent when it is clear that the case will go for trial. At the trial it will be essential to give evidence of every element of the case, so the barrister should give advice on exactly what the elements of the case are and precisely how he will prove each point.

(d) A brief to make a specific application to court. If it becomes apparent that a particular interlocutory application will need to be made the solicitor may instruct the barrister to make it.

There are two other types of brief that deserve special mention. Firstly there is the dock brief, which has fallen into disuse with the growth of legal aid. A prisoner at a Crown Court has the right to be represented by counsel for a nominal fee. He may choose any barrister in the court, who should only refuse if he already has a conflicting commitment to another case. The barrister may well only have a limited time to consult the client and prepare to conduct his defence. Secondly and more important is the noting brief or the watching brief. Someone who is not actually a party to a court case may still have an interest in what is said and the outcome, and they may brief a barrister to sit in court to take a note of the legal arguments and evidence, or to watch that nothing is said or decided which may affect the client's interests. Since the client is not a party to the action the barrister will not take a part in the proceedings but just note their implications. This type of brief would usually be given to a young barrister.

Devilling a brief

Sometimes someone other than the barrister named on the backsheet will work on a brief. If one barrister has to return a brief because of pressure of work and it is sent to another then the second barrister will take over the case completely, doing the work and being paid for it. However two barristers will sometimes arrange between them that one will do work on a brief for another, and this is referred to as devilling. The original barrister who was briefed remains responsible for the case and will be paid for it with the second barrister merely doing the work that he has been asked to do and being paid for it as agreed between the two.

Devilling is normally done by a young barrister for an older one, often in the same Chambers. It is quite common in Queen's Bench actions but rare in Chancery. A leading counsel would not ask someone to devil for him as he would normally have a junior to help him with the case. The devil may be asked to do a variety of different types of work, whatever is agreed by him and the barrister briefed. Normally devilling would involve research into a difficult legal point, or helping to sort out the documents in a long and complicated brief, but the one devilling the brief should not normally be left to do pleadings or an opinion in the case. He should at most do a draft for the barrister originally briefed to consider (though in practice little may be changed, it is only that the barrister originally briefed is still responsible for the case). The barrister devilling the case should not appear to conduct the case in court unless the solicitor has been consulted and has agreed to send a separate brief for the devilling barrister for the court appearance. Work on a murder brief should not normally be left for a devil to do but should be done by the barrister briefed.

The amount the devilling barrister should be paid is for the two barristers to agree between them, but the devilling barrister should be paid at least half the fee if he appears at a hearing, and should otherwise be paid according to the complexity of the work done, the time spent on it and his own experience. It is possible for devilling work to be done on a legally aided brief as well as a privately paid one.

If a pupil does work for his pupil master he is not entitled to be paid as this is regarded as part of his training. This is so even if his pupil master accepts any draft pleadings or opinions he does without a change. In fact some pupil masters will make some payment where work is done that they do use, or will at least show some mark of appreciation by taking the pupil out to dinner!

4 *The opinion*

Once he has been sent an initial brief in a case a barrister will normally have to send back a written opinion setting out his advice to the solicitor and the client. Once he has read the brief properly the barrister should have a basic idea what his advice is, though he may need to get extra documents or information, talk to the solicitor and client in conference, or research legal points in detail before he writes the opinion.

It is important to appreciate exactly where the opinion fits into the legal process. The opinion is not a formal legal document, it is just the written legal advice that the barrister gives on the brief sent to him. There are therefore no formal requirements about what it should contain or how it should be written, and each barrister will develop his own style, though in practice there are certain things that a good opinion should contain and they do need to be expressed in a way that is suitable and clear. However, there are a few cases where the opinion is needed for a specific purpose, such as assessing whether a case is strong enough for legal aid to be granted, or where a court is asked to give approval on the behalf of children and in these cases the appropriate matters must be covered.

When he has done all the appropriate preparation the barrister will write out his opinion (or speak it into a dictaphone), it will then be typed up by the secretary in Chambers and sent back to the solicitor with the brief. The solicitor will then call the client into his office and explain the points made in the opinion to the client. If the client is a local authority or a company running a business, they may well want to have a copy of the opinion so that they can consider it in detail, but in any event the solicitor should explain to the client everything that is in the opinion and give the client the chance to read it if the client is capable of understanding it.

This is what will happen where an opinion is asked for at the start of a civil case, but if a further brief is sent to the barrister later in the case for further advice, he will again send back his views in writing. Normally where further advice is sought on for example the quantification of damages or the evidence that will be needed then the written document sent back is normally called an 'Advice' rather than an opinion (and this term is also used in a criminal case) but many of the general points about how to write an opinion will still apply.

Most barristers will develop their own style for writing opinions, and some are very idiosyncratic—some write long opinions and some very short ones, some are very formal and academic and some are peppered with wit and exclamation marks—but some general points should be taken into account in developing a good style for writing opinions. Clarity and comprehensibility are indispensable.

Also the barrister must always remember what the purpose of the opinion is and who it is going to.

The purpose of the opinion will usually be to tell the client whether he has a legal case or not, and if he has what he can expect to get out of it. These are the matters to concentrate on—the opinion should not be an academic thesis. The second purpose of the opinion is to give directions on how the case should be conducted, and to that end it should be practical and deal with any appropriate procedural or evidential points.

The person to whom the opinion is going is a solicitor, so there is no need for an opinion to explain basic legal concepts; on the other hand specialist legal points that the solicitor is not likely to come across in his practice should be explained fully. It is also important to take care in phrasing the comments made to instructing solicitors and be tactful when necessary. If it is possible that the solicitors themselves drew up a document which is causing problems this should be taken into account when commenting on it—it has amazed me in teaching intending barristers how often they write opinions effectively telling instructing solicitors to sue themselves. If the solicitor has or has not done something important this should be pointed out clearly, but the way that the barrister writes should be directed primarily to building up a good working relationship with the solicitor.

It is equally important to remember that the opinion may well be read by or to the client, and that it is being paid for by him, or on his behalf. This can to some extent be taken into account in the style, which a business client may appreciate in more detail than the layman, but more than that the opinion really should try to deal with the problems the client has from the client's point of view. The barrister is not the client's judge but his adviser, and he should try to make his opinion as helpful as is possible in the circumstances.

Finally, the barrister should bear in mind that the opinion he writes may be useful to himself in the future. The opinion clarifies his initial view of the facts and law of the case, and will be the basis on which the case proceeds. A well thought-out and clearly presented opinion will not only help the solicitor to proceed with the case in the best way, but may well be useful to the barrister himself if the case comes back to him for further advice or to prepare for trial, and he can reread his own opinion to refresh his mind quickly.

Preparing to write the opinion

It is much easier to write a good opinion if proper preparation is done before a word is written. Usually the brief should be properly read (and reread to insure that the barrister has not misunderstood anything), notes of the important points made, any extra documents and information sought from the solicitor, and any necessary legal research done, but there are some exceptions. It may be necessary to give an initial view on the case before full information is available, especially if reports are needed to give a full assessment of damages. In this sort of case the barrister will have to write his opinion giving his views on the case as far as he can, but making it completely clear what extra information is needed, and the case can then be sent back to him for a further opinion on the area that was in doubt later. An alternative possibility is that some action will have to be taken quickly before there is time to write a full opinion, for example an injunction may need to be sought as a matter of urgency, and the barrister should then contact the solicitor to tell him this, and proceed with the application for the injunction, writing a full opinion later.

As for researching the law, the barrister should have been able to form a view of what types of action may be available and the elements that he will need to show to succeed in each as he read the brief. The practising lawyer will not need to carry a great deal of detailed law in his head, but he will need to have a good working knowledge of the main principles of law in the areas in which he practises, so that he does know exactly what to look up when the time comes. Research on a case will normally involve checking particular points of difficulty in a good, up-to-date practitioner's textbook, and reading all the appropriate statutory sections, regulations and cases. In doing this research it is useful to keep a note of references to cases and important points in books so that they can be easily found again, and so that they can be referred to in the opinion if necessary. Even if the lawyer has done a similar type of case before, he will need to do the necessary research to ensure that his knowledge is not out of date, and that there have been no new statutes or cases. Publications like *New Law Journal*, *The Law Society Gazette* and *Current Law* can be very helpful for this. The lawyer should of course not only research points in his favour but also points against him to realistically assess the chances of success.

A particular thing that may need research in a case is the amount a client may be awarded for damages for personal injury. A specialist with a number of years experience may be able to put a figure on an injury, but the general practitioner or the young lawyer will usually have to look up awards in other cases to estimate a figure. The best sources of cases on damages for personal injuries are *Kemp and Kemp* and *Current Law*, which both give cases of injuries suffered and awards made. It is best to try to find at least three or four cases with injuries similar to those of the client, noting carefully in what ways they are better or worse, and taking some sort of average. If the cases are more than a few months old the award must of course be increased slightly to take inflation into account, and it is better not to go back more than a few years as the practice of the court changes.

Style of writing

There are some things that a good opinion must include, but many things are a matter of style. The young barrister will be heavily influenced, quite rightly, by the style of older barristers, but he must keep a critical eye open to pick up those things which will help him write a good, clear, practical opinion, rather than just copying someone else's style without question. While it is useful for the young barrister to read opinions written by others, he should do this only to get ideas of approach, and not trying to find something to follow exactly in his own opinions.

The first point is what the opinion should cover, the essential point being that it is not an academic article but advice given to a real person with a real problem. It must give clear advice as concisely as possible which covers all the vital points, but only the vital points, and which tries to reach definite conclusions.

Next, the opinion should approach the problem in a suitable way. The barrister is giving advice, he is not the judge. It is not for the barrister to decide whether the client should succeed, only to advise if he has a reasonable prospect of doing so. Some barristers write an opinion in a categorial way as if they were giving orders, seeming almost to lose sight of the fact that the case is the client's. Certainly the barrister is in charge of the way that the case is conducted once he has been instructed, but only within the instructions that the solicitor and client give—he can advise in strong terms what decision he thinks should be taken, but he cannot actually take the decisions himself. Thus the point of the opinion is to develop the strengths and weaknesses of the client's case to suggest whether he might succeed and what he might recover, not to tell him.

One further point—the barrister is advising one side in the case. If he has a misrepresentation case the point of the opinion is not to set out the detailed law on misrepresentation, but to develop the arguments in favour of and against the client's case. It is not for the barrister to say 'I have decided that this client has no case', it is for him to put forward the ways in which the case could be most favourably put for the person he is representing, developing whatever arguments he can to achieve what the client wants within existing legal principles. Certainly he can conclude that he does not think that the best arguments that can be put forward in the client's favour will convince a judge, but that is as far as he can go.

It is important to present the opinion properly. Normally the document will be headed OPINION and typed (on A4 or foolscap paper), and it will have at the end the address of the barrister's Chambers, the date and the barrister's signature. For the sake of clarity and easy reference it is a good idea to divide the opinion up into different sections with sub-headings and numbered paragraphs. This will help the barrister to present his arguments clearly and makes it possible for the solicitor to grasp the elements of the opinion quickly. Many barristers have a habit of putting a brief summary of their advice at the beginning of the opinion, then going on to elaborate each point in more detail later. In addition or alternatively there can be a summary of all the main points and conclusions at the end of the opinion.

As for the type of language used to express an opinion, the more clear and concise it is the better. There is no magic in long words—as far as possible everything should be expressed so that the client as well as the solicitor can understand it easily. It should go without saying that an advocate needs to develop a skill of dealing with words that avoids the vague and the tautological to communicate immediately and readily with whoever he is addressing. The opinion is not paid for according to length, so while it should cover everything, it should not be too long. On the other hand, the barrister is advising as a professional lawyer and should certainly give full and detailed advice on everything he is asked about. He should ensure that he does cover everything that the solicitor or the client may be concerned about.

As to the terms to use, it is normal to refer to the solicitors as 'instructing solicitors' or 'those instructing me', and the brief itself is often called 'my instructions'. The person that the barrister is representing is referred to as 'the client' or 'our client' or perhaps by name as 'Mr X' or 'Mrs X', and when referring to the case against the client it is normal to say 'the other side', or again to use the name 'Mr Y' or 'Mrs Y'. Once the action has begun it is acceptable to refer to the parties in the opinion as 'the plaintiff' and 'the defendant' as appropriate (or 'the petitioner' and 'the respondent' etc).

As a matter of style, the barrister should avoid too much use of 'I' and 'In my opinion'; it is assumed that the opinion is the personal professional view of the barrister, and it is not suitable for him to keep projecting himself into what he advises. Equally he should make a clear distinction between what is clear undisputed law and what is his own view of how the case should be argued—it is important not to mislead the solicitor and client by confusing the two. He should not include his own purely personal views in the advice he gives.

References to legal authorities should be made where relevant to show the basis on which the barrister has developed his arguments. The solicitor can then look up the reference if he wishes, and the barrister will have them if the case comes back to him. A reference to a relevant provision of a statute or regulation should always be as specific as possible, and even the actual wording may be set out in the opinion if the provision is not a common one that can easily be looked up, or if the actual wording is very important in the argument in the case.

Textbooks and other academic works are of course not normally accepted as authorities in court, but again for the sake of the barrister and the solicitor it may be useful to include a reference to a particular passage in a textbook where it is important to an argument in a case, and it can then easily be found again. However, such references should be limited, as the barrister is essentially developing his own arguments on the facts of the case.

There is a wide variation in the practice of different barristers when it comes to quoting cases, some quoting many cases at length and others quoting very few. Perhaps the best rule to begin with is that a case should be quoted if it really is directly relevant to an argument in the case, if it is the authority for a particular proposition (such as that a particular thing is recoverable in damages), if the facts of it are particularly close to the facts that the lawyer is advising on or if the case is a recent one showing the current approach of the courts. If a case is referred to in the opinion, the full name of the case should be given (and may be underlined) and a full reference for finding it if possible. It is not necessary to set out the facts of the case unless they have some special relevance or similarity to the case the barrister is advising on, in which case the main facts or the relevant facts should be summarised briefly. Actual dicta from the judgments may be quoted if they help an argument that is being advanced, set out as a quotation.

In deciding whether to quote cases, the barrister should remember that in recent years the courts have discouraged the excessive quotation of cases in trials, especially in appeal cases. For example, Lord Diplock has said:

> The citation of a plethora of illustrative authorities, apart from being time and cost consuming, presents the danger of so blinding the court with case law that it has difficulty in seeing the wood of legal principle from the trees of paraphrase (*Lambert* v *Lewis* [1981] 1 All ER 1185).

Similarly, Lord Roskill said:

> I hope I shall not be thought discourteous or unappreciative of the industry involved in the preparation of counsel's arguments if I say that today massive citation of authority in cases where the relevant legal principles have been clearly and authoritatively determined is of little or no assistance and should

be discouraged (*Pioneer Shipping Ltd.* v *B.T.P. Tioxide Ltd.* [1981] 2 All ER 1030).

In summary, the style of an opinion is a personal matter for the barrister to evolve himself, not something governed by rules. However, to best serve its purpose it should be clear and concise in the way it is set out, in the wording used, in what is covered and in the references to authorities. It should be written for a particular person with a particular problem, and should be directed to help him rather than judge him. Sometimes a lengthy and rambling opinion is justified by the complexity of the case, but it is not something to aim for.

What to include in the opinion

I have given a suggested basic outline for an opinion in a civil case, this is obviously not a rigid format but just a brief guide to what may be covered and a logical order for dealing with points. Sometimes one area will not need to be dealt with at all, and the importance of each area will depend on the individual case. In any event the barrister should try to ensure a clear lay-out for his advice, and sub-headings and numbered paragraphs may well be useful to this end.

By the time the barrister has studied the brief and done any necessary research, he should have a fairly clear idea of the advice he wants to give, but it may still be helpful for him to make short outline notes before he begins to write, to clarify in his own mind all the points he needs to cover, and a suitable order for dealing with things. If an opinion does not deal with things in a suitable order it may be difficult to follow, and especially if it rambles round to come back to something dealt with earlier it may give a bad impression, especially if it seems to contradict itself.

To deal with each of the stages in the suggested outline in more detail:

(a) Introduction. It is generally useful to begin with a brief summary of the facts. This is not vital, but putting the opinion in context with a nutshell guide to the case is valuable to the person reading the opinion. The solicitor in a busy office, or the barrister doing further work on the case some time later may well not remember it well, and an introduction to the facts will help them to recall what the opinion is about. Also, if the barrister sets out the facts on which his opinion is based he should be able to avoid any later allegation that his advice failed to take account of something in the brief.

The summary should not be done in any great detail. There is no need to copy out sections of the instructions or of documents in the brief, as they will go back to instructing solicitors with the opinion. All that is needed in most cases is a few sentences summarising the facts, and perhaps a brief note of the documents enclosed, for example:

> I am asked to advise in a case involving a breach of a contract of employment. The client, Mr A was employed by B Ltd for a fixed term of five years, but has been dismissed after two years without good reason. Instructing solicitors have supplied me with a copy of the contract of employment and the letter dismissing Mr A.

> Instructing solicitors have asked me to advise in a case involving a running down accident. It appears that in January 1985 the client Mr C was knocked down by a car driven by Mr D while he was crossing a zebra crossing. He suffered a broken arm and some head injuries, the full effects of which are not yet clear.

It is only if the case is quite complicated that it is useful to do more. Then it is useful to outline all the facts in the first few paragraphs.

(b) Summary of advice. This is useful to the solicitor, as he can tell immediately the brief is sent back to him with the opinion what counsel's view is, without having to read through pages of legal argument to try to discover what advice is given. It will also help the solicitor to put the barrister's opinion across to the client clearly. The summary of advice may also be useful to the barrister as it does ensure that he has his objectives clear before he begins to write his opinion.

(c) Cause of action. The first thing the client wants to know is whether he can sue or not. To advise him, the barrister should examine in appropriate detail every possible cause of action that the client may have, not just the most obvious one. Even if the barrister is going to recommend a particular cause of action, it is valuable to mention any alternatives to see if they may be any use, and to show the instructing solicitor that every possibility has been considered. Even in a fairly straightforward case there may be a variety of causes of action, such as negligence/occupier's liability/breach of statutory duty or fraud/misrepresentation/breach of contract, and it is important to consider which will be best on the facts and the evidence available.

For each likely cause of action the barrister should check:

(i) Whether all the necessary legal elements are present in the facts.
(ii) Whether he will be able to prove all the elements at trial.

This must be done in a carefully objective way; the barrister should not read anything into the brief which is not there or assume something or he may well find himself in difficulty later. In the opinion he should ask the solicitors to check anything that he does not know. It is useful to note each element that he needs, for example in a misrepresentation case, was the representation false, did it lead to the contract, if so was it innocent, negligent or fraudulent, and what loss did the misrepresentation lead to?

It may not be easy to find the appropriate cause of action. If it was a fairly straightforward case the solicitor would probably have dealt with it himself, so the barrister must expect that in many of the cases he gets there will be no easy legal answer. One thing which young barristers do sometimes find difficult to adapt to is the overlap between various areas of law. At university they study land law, contract and tort as entirely separate subjects, but in practice they will sometimes overlap. It may be difficult to decide whether it is better to frame a particular case in negligence or breach of contract, but the barrister must develop the ability to deal with them all and make a decision.

As was said earlier, it is the job of the barrister to develop every possible argument that he can in his client's favour; he is there to help him, not to judge him. A young barrister may find this difficult as he is used to learning what the law is, and he does tend to want to decide the case himself, but once he begins his training as a legal adviser he should break away from this. Obviously he must not be falsely optimistic and give the client the impression that he will win the case if the barrister really thinks he will not. There are some cases that cannot be won on any view, and the client should be told this, but the barrister should develop every argument that he reasonably and realistically can before he advises on the strength of the case.

Having said that the barrister should develop legal arguments where he can, he should beware of a complicated and clever legal argument that is academically interesting if it has no real chance of success. In many cases there are no very complicated legal points, it is basically a question of getting all the evidence together, clarifying the main points and discussing damages, but if there is a complicated legal point the barrister should weigh up whether it is worth arguing in that it will take a lot of research and preparation, may well take some time in court and, although it may put names in the law reports, if the client loses he will have to pay for it all. If there is a lot at stake the argument may be worth it, but the client must be warned of its chances of success.

Similarly the barrister should ensure that there is a genuine cause of action. He should try to avoid bringing an action before the court that he feels is frivolous and vexatious unless he feels that there is good reason or the client insists. Also he should consider whether there is any reason that the case could not come before the court at all even if there is apparently a cause of action. For example it may be a term of the contract that there should be arbitration, or there may be some other body having jurisdiction. For example in *Patel* v *University of Bradford Senate* [1979] 2 All ER 582 a student failed his first year examination twice and sought a declaration that the refusal to readmit him to the university was unreasonable and unlawful. It was held that the Board of Visitors at the university had jurisdiction over such a matter so that the case could not be considered by the court at all.

Once the barrister has considered all the possible causes of action he should go on to advise which should actually be pursued and what their chances of success are if possible. It is quite possible to use every cause of action open to the client and it may well be possible to put all or most of them in the same action if they arise from the same facts. But there are reasons for not using every possibility, for example, there is little point in preparing a second cause of action when it is quite clear that the first will succeed as it may waste time and, even more important, costs. Generally the best choice of action will be the one or two with which there are fewest legal problems, and which will be easiest to prove. However there is a question of tactics here, and there may be some reason for adding a cause of action that one may not finally wish to pursue as such to show how badly you feel the defendant has behaved, or to get discovery. If there is any real doubt it is probably better in most circumstances to put the cause of action in and then cease to pursue it at the earliest point possible, rather than to try to add it later.

Lastly, the barrister must not only advise what sort of actions may be brought, but against whom. There may well be a choice, and the opinion should mention all the possible causes of action against each possible defendant. For example if someone is injured by something in a building it may well be possible to sue the person using the thing which inflicted the injury, the person who made the thing which inflicted the injury and the occupier of the building. There are also the possibilities of vicarious liability, agency, and other types of indirect involvement such as inducing breach of contract. The barrister needs to consider whether there is a cause of action against each person who is connected with what has happened. He will then go on to advise which people should actually be sued, which will usually be the person against whom there is the strongest legal case which is easiest to prove. If damages are sought there is also the question of which possible defendant will be able to pay them. If there is any choice, the barrister should also advise which court to sue in. This is dealt with in the chapter on drafting writs and the chapter on county courts.

(d) Defences. It is a part of advising the client to try to anticipate what the case against him may be and how strong it is. Whatever loss or harm your client has suffered there may be little point in suing if the potential defendant has a complete defence. This needs some imagination, as it is not just a question of reading your instructions, but also of trying to put yourself in the position of the defendant to decide what he may say. The best way for the young barrister to begin to do this is to pretend that he is acting for the other side to see what he would argue in their favour. The practitioner will soon get used to the types of defences that are often raised in particular types of cases.

One should try to contemplate every possible line of defence. There may be a defence on the law, a defence on the facts, a complete defence so that the action should not be brought at all, or a partial defence which will only reduce damages. The barrister will also have to try to assess the possible strength of each line of defence, and decide whether it does mean that the action should not be brought, or that the action should still be brought but less will be recovered. This may involve a careful questioning of the client to try to assess the strength of his story.

(e) Remedies. After the client has been told that he can sue, the other main thing that he will want to know is what he can really hope to get out of the action at the end of the day. Therefore the remedies available must be a major element in the opinion, and if the other side has admitted or is likely to admit liability, the entire opinion may need to centre on remedies and the measure of damages. Therefore if there is any cause of action that might succeed, the barrister must go on to deal with the remedies that will give rise to. Every remedy that may be available should be considered to see what will best achieve what the client wants. Sometimes the lawyer will only look at the most obvious remedy, which will usually be damages, but he should give some thought to whether there is any alternative. Interlocutory remedies may be appropriate as well as final remedies, and these are considered in the chapter on preparing the case for court. Particular remedies in particular types of cases are considered in the second part of the book.

In many cases the most important remedy will be damages, and the lawyer will need to advise specifically and in detail on what may be recovered, if possible saying what sort of figure the client can hope to get. If figures are given in the instructions, the opinion should deal with these as far as possible. If further figures or facts will be needed to make an assessment, the barrister should make it clear to the solicitor exactly what he will need to know and, if the case is very complicated, whether the help of an accountant may be needed. If necessary a separate later opinion can give further advice on the measure of damages.

The first stage will be to comment on the basis on which damages will be assessed, that is the relevant principles of foreseeability and remoteness and what type of thing will be recoverable. If there may be more than one way of assessing damages, for example if it may be possible to sue in tort or contract on the same facts, the relative merits of each possiblity should be examined.

The second stage is to look in detail at special damage, that is those things which have been lost for which a figure can already be given, so that they should be pleaded, for example existing loss of earnings, and expenses of repairing or replacing things which have been lost.

The next stage is to go on to look at general damage, that is wider categories of loss that cannot yet be quantified, such as loss of future earnings and damages for pain and injury. Here the lawyer will need to develop his arguments for how such loss should be quantified, as he will have to argue this in court rather than just leave it to the judge, do any research as to what should be paid for the injuries suffered, and try to give a figure, or at least a very general estimate of what the client should get.

The next stage will be to see if there is anything that needs to be deducted from the damages, for example if statutory benefits have been received. A major possibility to investigate is whether the other side may allege contributory negligence and, if they do, exactly what proportion of the damages is likely to be lost. The other main possibility is that the plaintiff may be in a position to mitigate his loss, and he should be advised on this as he may not realise that he has a duty to mitigate.

The next stage is to see whether there is anything else that might affect the final figures awarded, for example any question of taxation or a legal aid charge, which may reduce what the plaintiff actually gets in his pocket. The relevance of tax may necessitate quite complex calculations where damages are awarded for breach of a contract of employment, *Shove* v *Downs Surgical Ltd* [1984] 1 All ER 7, and it may also have some impact in other cases, like *Tate & Lyle Food and Distribution* v *Greater London Council* [1981] 3 All ER 716, where the defendant caused the river to silt up and the plaintiff claimed £550,000 because he had to dredge it to use it, but it was held that the £240,000 that he had saved in tax should be taken into account. Finally, the lawyer should consider whether interest may be awarded on all or any part of the damages so as to alter the figure payable. Having reached a final figure he might also consider whether the defendant will be able to pay it, as there is little point in suing a man of straw, and it may be worth seeking a Mareva injunction if assets are likely to disappear overseas.

(f) Other points. There are a variety of other things to be considered when writing an opinion, though they may be dealt with at a suitable point rather than at the end. Any point on which the solicitor particularly asks for advice should of course be covered. Evidence must be kept in mind right through, as the most ingenious legal argument is worth little if you cannot prove your case. For the law student evidence is a separate subject, but for the practitioner it is an inherent part of every case he does. In deciding whether the client has a case the lawyer must consider not only all the elements of a possible cause of action, but also whether he has evidence on each point which is admissible. If further evidence will be needed on any point the barrister should make this clear in his opinion so that the solicitor can get it, whether it be documents, witnesses, expert evidence, reports or anything else. If the case does go to trial the barrister may be asked to supply a more detailed advice on evidence at a later stage.

There may also be procedural points that should be raised. This is again something that is a separate subject for a student but an inherent part of a case for a practitioner. If there is a procedural point that may help the client, then it should be mentioned in the opinion. Usually the solicitor will be responsible for initiating the procedural steps, but if a barrister is briefed he should mention any appropriate points. This is an area where both the barrister and the solicitor should consider what can best be done in the client's interests and both work to help him.

Finally the good barrister should also give any practical advice he can which may help the client. This goes back to the point that an opinion is not an academic legal treatise but is advice to a person with a real problem, and the barrister should try to imagine all sides of the problem to appreciate it fully and to suggest what it is best to do. This is something that may be more important for the solicitor with the client in front of him rather than for the barrister writing an opinion, but it is something for both to bear in mind. The client will be much more impressed with a lawyer who does really seem to understand his difficulties.

(g) Conclusions. This may not be necessary if the barrister has summarised his advice at the start of the opinion, but he should at some point list clearly the main points in his opinion. This list of conclusions might well contain the following elements:

(i) What cause or causes of action may be open to the client.

(ii) The main defences or difficulties that may prevent success.

(iii) Clear and specific directions to the solicitor as to what extra information and evidence may be needed, and as to any particular steps that should be taken in the conduct of the case.

(iv) As specific an indication as possible of what the client may hope to get if he wins.

(v) Some indication of the chances of success of the case. This can usually be done in adjectives such as likely, unlikely, doubtful, highly unlikely, or in some other way such as 'something like a 60% chance of success'. But whatever evaluation a barrister gives he should make it clear that the final decision is that of the client; the barrister can advise that a case is unlikely to succeed but he cannot decide not to sue.

(vi) If the barrister does advise that some type of drafted document is needed he should normally draft the document to return to the solicitor with the opinion, e.g. a Statement of Claim, an Originating Summons, a deed, a lease or an agreement.

Other types of opinion

The above outline applies primarily to an initial opinion in a civil case, and it will need to be adapted as appropriate for different types of case. For example an opinion in a trust or land law case might well require much more detailed legal argument, an opinion in a tort claim for injuries would normally concentrate on finding and proving the facts of the case and the measure of damages. Giving advice in a criminal case is dealt with separately later.

After the initial opinion the brief may well come back to the barrister for further advice on a particular point. The instructions should make it clear exactly what counsel is being asked to deal with, and the above general principles should be applied as appropriate. For example there should still be a brief introduction as to the point in the case that has been reached, a clear summary of conclusions, a detailed examination of the points in the client's favour and against him, and a mention of any appropriate procedural or evidential points, depending on the stage the case has reached.

Advice on damages

One particular point on which a barrister may get a further brief is the quantification of damages. While the initial opinion will deal with potential liability it may well be difficult at that stage to give more than a very vague figure for damages, because further details of accounts or loss suffered are needed, or because the full extent or long-term effect of the client's injuries are not clear at that stage. If the solicitor does send a further brief to counsel for advice on damages he must enclose all the facts and figures that are in any way relevant to damages, such as detailed accounts, medical reports, any benefits received that may be deducted and so on. In writing his opinion the barrister should deal in detail with all the sums that may be recovered and all the things that may be deducted to mitigate damage. The figure that the barrister suggests may well be used as a basis for settling the action before it comes to trial, so it should be correct. It may be necessary to call in an accountant to advise if the case involves company or personal accounts, or a difficult calculation because for example tax is relevant. The solicitor should see the accountant, and if necessary he can be taken for a conference with the barrister.

Advice on evidence

In anything but a straightforward case the barrister may also be briefed to supply an advice on evidence. This will normally be sought after discovery and before the case comes to trial. There is little point in seeking an advice on evidence before all the potential evidence is available, but it should not be left too late in case it is necessary to make further enquiries on any point. The purpose of the advice on evidence is to concentrate the minds of the lawyers on the things they will have to deal with at the trial—the issues in the case and the way each will be proved.

A good way of setting out the advice (possibly useful for reference at the trial itself) is to list separately each issue in the cause of action that will have to be proved, on whom the burden of proof rests, and what witness or document will be used to prove the point. The list should cover not only the elements of one's own case, but also points that the other side may raise in defence that will have to be countered, as it may well be too late to get further evidence once the hearing has begun. If any further evidence will be needed, the solicitor should be told specifically what to get.

While writing an advice on evidence, it is also useful for the barrister to consider the state of the pleading in the case, to see if any amendments should be made, or any facts admitted. He may also consider the actual presentation of the evidence at court, such as whether there should be agreed bundles of documents and what they should contain, whether any maps, diagrams or other evidence will be needed, and the presentation of any expert or medical evidence.

EXAMPLE 1 SUGGESTED BASIC OUTLINE FOR AN OPINION IN A CIVIL CASE

OPINION

1. Introduction
The facts of the case are summarised briefly and the main issues to be dealt with identified.

2. Summary of advice
The main elements of the advice the barrister gives may be summarised so that they may be easily and quickly understood.

3. Cause of action
In numbered paragraphs each possible cause of action in the case is set out and analysed. It is important to decide whether all the necessary legal elements are present, and whether there are any legal, factual or evidential difficulties with any necessary element. If there is more than one possible cause of action the barrister should advise which one or more it would be best to follow. All the possible arguments in the client's favour should be examined.

4. Defences
In numbered paragraphs, each possible defence to the client's claim should be examined. This should include any raised by instructions, and any other that the barrister feels may arise, and should include partial and full defences to the client's claim. Again the barrister should weigh up as far as possible the legal and evidential value of any defence, and whether it may succeed.

5. Remedies
All the possible remedies that may be available to the client if he succeeds should be dealt with. If damages are sought, the barrister should try to give as close an idea as possible of the amount that may be awarded.

6. Other points
These are things which should be dealt with in the course of the opinion, or at the end.

(a) Anything which instructing solicitors have specifically asked the barrister to advise on.

(b) Evidence, that is what evidence there already is and also what more will be needed. The solicitor should be given clear instructions on the evidence he should seek.

(c) Procedural points. The barrister should bear in mind and mention any procedural step that may be valuable, e.g. an interlocutory injunction or summary judgment.

7. Conclusions
Especially if he has not summarised his advice at the start of the opinion, the barrister should set out his conclusions clearly.

Address of barrister's Chambers Signed by barrister.

Dated

5 *Advising in conference*

It may be necessary to hold a conference at various stages during a case. This will vary according to the type of case and the stage that it has reached, and one can only make general remarks about when a conference should be held and what should be covered.

Essentially a conference is a meeting between the barrister and the solicitor at which the client is often present, and which an expert witness may attend. The conference should be sought by the solicitor rather than the barrister, though a barrister may well suggest that a conference would be useful. The main purpose of a conference is usually to allow the barrister to explain his advice to the solicitor and client, to get further information from them, or to discuss the future progress of the action.

A conference will normally take place at the barrister's Chambers, though it may be elsewhere, for example there may well be a meeting outside court before the case begins to discuss necessary aspects of the case. Care should be taken as to where the conference does take place—it should not normally be at the solicitor's office unless there are special circumstances, for example where the case is to be heard at a town some way from the barrister's Chambers, or age or infirmity make it difficult for the solicitor or client to come to the barrister's Chambers. A conference should never be held at the barrister's home.

There are limits as to who should be present at a conference. The solicitor should always be there if possible, and it is improper for a barrister to see the client alone unless there is no alternative, for example where the case is due to be called in court and no representative from instructing solicitors has arrived. Although the barrister can see the client in conference, he should not normally talk to the witnesses before the case comes to court—the witnesses will be seen by the solicitor and copies of what they say supplied to the barrister as part of his brief. The exception is that the barrister can see expert or professional witnesses, as he may need to talk to them to understand what they have to say.

There are other forms of conference. If two barristers have been briefed in a case they may hold a joint conference. If a silk has been briefed in the case then the meeting will normally be held with the silk and junior barrister in the silk's room, and is called a consultation. The barristers, solicitors and clients on both sides in a case may hold a joint conference in an attempt to settle the case, and this will normally be held in the room of the senior barrister.

It is very important to use the conference to establish a good working relationship, and to get the confidence of the client. Although a barrister will hold conferences frequently, a client will normally go to a barrister rarely, possibly only once in his life. The case and the conference on it will usually be a great event in the life of the client, and the barrister should always remember this, however tired he is, and however much work he has to do. The barrister must communicate with the solicitor and client as fully as possible, show that he understands the case, and give the feeling that he is doing the best he can for the client. While this will generally mean that the barrister has to be in charge of what is happening, he must make sure that he gives the solicitor and client chance to say anything that they wish and to ask questions. In the well-run conference all present should feel involved, and should leave feeling that they understand the situation fully, that they know what the next stage in the case will be and that the case is proceeding as well as possible.

Preparation for a conference

Firstly it must be decided when a conference needs to be held. It will basically be for the solicitor to arrange, but he may well do so at the suggestion of the barrister or the client. The barrister must be briefed by the solicitor for the conference, and this may be done as part of a general brief to advise in conference and in a written opinion, or by a separate brief to advise in conference. A conference may be called in the following circumstances:

(a) A conference may be arranged as soon as the barrister has the initial brief in the case if it is necessary for the barrister to meet the client to fully understand the case. This will be the case if the case depends on disputed facts rather than documents. If the case may turn on what the client says and his version of events then the barrister may well need to see the client to get details from him, and to see how he may appear as a witness in court.

(b) If the case turns largely on written documents or points of law then there may well be no need to have a conference until after the barrister has written his opinion. Once the solicitor and client have read the opinion there may be a conference to decide how to proceed with the case.

(c) The client may particularly wish to have a conference with the barrister in any event if the case is particularly important to him, if it is personally important or if it involves a large amount of property or money, and he may wish to arrange this at an early stage.

(d) Once proceedings have begun it may be necessary to have a conference or further conference to decide how the case should proceed.

(e) A conference may be called to discuss terms if there is any chance of settling the case.

(f) If the case does go to trial it may well be necessary to have a conference shortly before the trial to review the arguments and evidence and strategy and to ensure that everything is ready.

Whenever a conference is arranged, it is essential that everyone attending should be properly prepared so that they can get full benefit from it and time will not be wasted. Occasionally a conference has to be arranged at short notice so that this is not possible, but generally everyone should give prior thought to what they want to say and ask. The solicitor should ensure that he has sent the barrister all the relevant documents, or that he gets them to take with him. He should also ask if there is anything that the client wishes to cover at the conference, and tell him of anything that he should bring with him. It may be useful for the solicitor to make notes of anything that should be covered at the conference, so that he can remind the barrister if anything is left out. If there are any major matters they should be put in the instructions in the barrister's brief if possible, so that he can prepare to deal with them.

If the client has not been to a conference before, the solicitor should explain to him as far as possible the purpose of the conference and how it will be conducted. Although the client will often spend most of the conference listening to what the lawyers say, he should be prepared so that he is not too overawed to take part in discussions where appropriate and to raise points he is concerned about.

As for the barrister, he should form some plan as to what he wants to cover in the conference, as it will essentially be for him to run it. Sometimes he may be delayed in court or with some other case just before the conference so that he does not have time to reread the papers, but he should be able to find them to do preparation in advance unless the brief was sent to him late. The solicitor and client may well have come some distance to see him, and the conference may be of major importance to the client, so the barrister should be ready for them.

The amount of preparation that the barrister can do will depend on the stage that the case has reached. If the barrister needs to have the conference to get further information from the client before he can write his opinion then there is only a limited amount that he can do in advance, familiarising himself with the undisputed facts and deciding what lines of questioning he wants to follow with the client. If the barrister has the relevant documents and information before the conference then he should have done enough work and research to be able to give detailed advice, so that the conference can centre on what to do next. In any event, the most useful preparation that the barrister can do is to make a note of the main dates and facts in the case which he can refer to in the conference (with which he can impress the solicitor and client with his grasp of the case even if he hasn't had time to reread the papers). Also he can make a brief note of the points that he does wish to raise in the conference, so that he has clear objectives in mind and does not waste time rambling and waffling. This note of points may relate to any of the points that should be covered in the conference, which are listed below.

What to cover in the conference

The following points are a brief guide to what the barrister may consider covering in the course of a conference. Depending on the type of case and the stage that it has reached, some things will not need to be covered and others will need to be emphasised. The order in which things are covered may also need to be modified as appropriate.

(a) The conference should be started properly, with everyone present being introduced so that everyone knows who is present and what their involvement in the case is. If the barrister has a pupil, the pupil should also be introduced and it should be ascertained that there are no objections to the pupil's being present.

(b) The barrister will start the conference. He will normally do this by briefly summarising the facts in the case and the stage that the case has reached, establishing and clarifying any points that are in doubt. If the client's version of events is particularly important to the case then the barrister may ask the client to tell the story in his words so that the barrister can spot the strengths and weaknesses in what he says.

(c) If there are any further facts or other points of information that the barrister needs to know he should ask about them. It will be useful for him to note in advance what he wants to ask about.

(d) The barrister will normally go on to advise on the relevant law, hopefully in a way which the client as well as the solicitor can follow, but without being too simplistic. If the wording of a statute or case is especially relevant, it may be useful to have a copy on hand for the solicitor and client to see. The advice should cover not only the legal aspects of the case, but its chance of success, and especially the remedies that may be available.

(e) It will be useful to examine the strength of any legal or factual arguments that the other side may raise. The barrister can deal with possible legal arguments, and then ask the client if he knows of any points that the other side may raise (it is better to hear of them from the client than from the other side).

(f) The barrister and solicitor may wish to review any procedural, evidential or practical points that may arise in the case and decide how to approach them.

(g) Before the conference ends, all the main points should be summarised and pulled together so that everyone there is fully aware of what case there is and what may reasonably be expected from it, what decisions have been taken or need to be taken, and what should be done next by the solicitor, the barrister and the client.

Although some outline decisions on the conduct of the conference need to be taken in advance for the sake of efficiency it is best if the plan is not too strict and too rigidly followed, but that the meeting is fluid enough to discuss any points that arise, so long as all the important things are covered at some point. The barrister should not let any preconceived views that he has got from the papers take over, and should not give the impression that he has taken important decisions—he is there to advise the client.

Conducting the conference

It is important to get the right atmosphere in conducting a conference, to inspire confidence, to ensure that everyone does say all that they want to and to ensure that everything is covered. It will normally be for the barrister to establish the atmosphere in setting the tone and controlling the order and the depth in which things are covered. It will be his role to draw from the client, or the witness, the information that he needs, and to communicate his views on the case clearly. The role of the solicitor will tend to be to introduce the people present, and to tactfully bring up any points which he feels the barrister has left out or which he knows that the client wishes to raise for discussion.

The atmosphere will need to be friendly but efficient, with the barrister seeking to maintain an understanding and unflustered control. The need to be able to communicate easily and encourage communication is essential for the lawyer, but it is not always easy. The barrister may find that he has little sympathy with the client, but he must not let this show or get in the way of his conduct of the case. Also it may not be easy to get the respect and trust of the client, for example where a young barrister has been briefed to advise an experienced and older business client. Sometimes the client will be very unhappy or very angry about what has happened, and the lawyer must learn to deal with this in a sympathetic way. Sometimes it will be necessary to give the client advice that he does not want to hear, that he cannot sue, or will not be able to recover the things he wants.

It does take real skill to handle different types of client well, and this is something that can only be learned with practice. Some will need a lot of encouragement to talk, whereas others will need a lot of control to make them realistic. A conference with a woman whose child has been taken away by her former husband will usually be of a totally different character to a conference with a businessman concerned with a breach of contract. A balance must be kept between letting the client talk, but not letting him waste time with too much that is irrelevant. As has been said, in many cases it may be useful to ask the client to tell his version of what has happened in his own words, in case this suggests anything new to the barrister, and it is also generally useful to ask the client if he knows of any weaknesses in his case, and to put the weaknesses that there are to the client.

In addition to encouraging or controlling the client, the barrister may have to weigh him up and to make decisions about the strength of his case and how good a witness he will be. One thing to be wary of is the client who has been so upset or worried by something that he has gone over and over it in his own mind to the extent that his own mind has modified or embroidered the real facts of the case. If the barrister feels that this may have happened he should try to challenge the client gently to establish the real facts—if he does not the other side certainly will in court. Another type of client to take particular care with is the one who is so bitter or angry that he has twisted facts in his own mind to blacken the person he feels is responsible for what has happened. It is usually a good idea to let the client let this bitterness out, but to try to pull him back to a more reasonable and objective state of mind, without losing his confidence, so that he will not be further disappointed by the outcome of the case.

In weighing up the client as a witness, this is something that is essential where the case turns on disputed fact, and may well turn on the client's word against someone else's. This can be dealt with by asking the client to say exactly what happened, and then gently cross-examining him to explore weaknesses in what he says, and any points that could be followed up. The barrister may have to be especially imaginative to try to see in his own mind what happened so that he can question the client fully.

As well as dealing with the client himself, the barrister may have to see a specialist witness in conference. This may be necessary for him to understand all the relevant details of the case—in a general common law practice you have to find out all about growing wheat one week and all about pre-stressed concrete the next like an intellectual chameleon. Sometimes this can be done by reading about the subject—the client may be able to suggest suitable reading material (a small medical dictionary is a useful investment for a personal injury or criminal practice). There are also some areas where most barristers will need a working knowledge of a fairly specialist area, such as accounts, which they are likely to have to deal with in a variety of cases, so that they should know enough to be able to hold a reasonably intelligent conversation with an accountant.

If reading or general knowledge are insufficient then an expert witness may be needed, and the barrister may need to see him in conference to understand what he says. The client or the solicitor may know of someone suitable to ask as an expert witness, someone else in Chambers may be able to suggest someone, or there may be an appropriate professional organisation to contact. Normally a solicitor can tell the expert witness what point he is asked to deal with and get a statement from him which can be sent to the barrister in his brief. If further investigation is necessary a conference can be arranged, which may differ from a conference with the client in that it is for the lawyers to make clear exactly what points they are concerned with, and to ask questions so that they understand enough to put the case in court.

When dealing with an area that needs expert knowledge, the lawyer should remember that the judge will wish to have things explained to him, and it is important to devise a way of doing this as quickly and simply as possible. If plans, diagrams, models or photographs may help the presentation of the case to the judge and aid understanding, they should be obtained.

While the conference goes on, at least one person should be responsible for taking a note of what is said and decided. If necessary this should be decided before the conference starts. The barrister and solicitor may each wish to take their own notes, or they may agree that one of them should take a note to be included with the papers in the case. If the barrister has a pupil or the solicitor brings an articled clerk with him, they will normally be responsible for taking the note. In a consultation with a silk, the junior barrister in the case will normally take the note.

After the conference

The conference should end with a summary of what has been said and decided, and everyone should be clear as to what they have to do in the future conduct of the case. If the barrister has written an opinion and advised fully, the brief may be returned to the solicitor for him to proceed with the case. Otherwise the barrister will retain the brief to write an opinion or draft a document or pleading as appropriate, or to do any necessary legal research, and it should be completely clear what the solicitor and client are expecting from him.

The solicitor may well leave with a list of things to do, as regards the procedural steps in the case, or as regards the seeking of further information or evidence, and it should be clear to him what he is expected to get. If the barrister has finished all his work on the brief, it may well be that there is an understanding that the barrister will be sent a further brief at a later stage in the case, to advise further on a particular point or to conduct the case at trial.

It may also be that the client is left to collect further information, or to take decisions as to what he wants to do. It should be completely clear to him what he is to get, or what options are open to him with what possible consequences.

6 *Preparing the case for court*

Once it has been decided that there is a good basis for bringing an action, it will need to be conducted, and hopefully won, with good use of the rules for procedure and evidence. There are a variety of expert books on these areas, and here I will only summarise some of the main practical and tactical points. There is sometimes a tendency to see procedure and evidence as boring necessities, and to have a superficial or cavalier approach to them, but they are the things with which a case can be won or lost, and the practising lawyer really does need to know them to achieve things for his clients. It is imaginative use of existing procedures that lead to the extremely practical developments of the Anton Piller order and the Mareva injunction.

Thorough preparation of a case can be a real strength for a young lawyer. Older clients and business clients may find it difficult to have faith in someone who is only recently qualified, but if the lawyer is clearly in control of the case and seems to know what he is doing without getting flustered, his confidence will communicate itself to both client and judge. Therefore at every stage of the case the lawyer should be considering what procedural steps may be of use to his client, and what further information or evidence will be needed for the case, making full use of compulsory steps and thinking about optional steps. Generally it will be for the solicitor to deal with the procedural steps and collect the evidence, subject to any directions given by the barrister, but both should be actively on the look out for things that should be done.

The stages of a High Court action

I have included an outline of the main stages in a High Court action begun by writ, the basic type of action dealt with in this book. Originating summons and county court actions are dealt with in other chapters, though they have points in common. It can be seen from the outline that a case could come on for hearing in less than three months if all the time limits were strictly adhered to (or quicker if both sides took less than the time allowed for each step). However, in practice, most High Court actions will take many months to come on, as a substantial time may be spent collecting information before a writ is issued, it will take longer than the strict time limits to draft documents, collect evidence and possibly try to negotiate a settlement, and once each side has prepared its case it will still take some time to come on for hearing.

STAGES IN A HIGH COURT ACTION

(a) Writ issued. This is normally done by the solicitor taking it to the appropriate court office. It should be done within the limitation period for the action.

(b) Writ served. This should be done by the appropriate method within 12 months of issue, though the writ may be renewed or a new writ issued if the limitation period is not over.

(c) Acknowledgement of service. This should be done by the defendant within 14 days of the service of the writ, or there may be judgment in default of appearance.

(d) Statement of Claim. This must be served within 14 days of the notice of intention to defend, unless the full statement of claim was indorsed on the writ, RSC Order 18, rule 1.

(e) Summary judgment. Once this stage in the action has been reached, the plaintiff may apply for summary judgment, RSC Order 14.

(f) Defence. This should be served within 14 days of the expiry of the time for acknowledgement of service, of the service of the statement of claim, or of leave to defend being given if an Order 14 judgment is sought, whichever is the later.

(g) Reply and/or defence to counterclaim. If the plaintiff wishes to serve such a pleading, it should be served within 14 days of the defence. If it is not, pleadings will be deemed to be closed 14 days from the service of the defence.

(h) Further pleadings. These can only be served with the leave of the court, and will rarely be necessary if previous pleadings were drafted properly or can be amended.

a Rejoinder, served by the defendant.
a Surrejoinder, served by the plaintiff.
a Rebutter, served by the defendant.
a Surrebutter, served by the plaintiff.

(i) Close of pleadings. This is deemed to be 14 days from the service of the defence, or from the service of the reply or further pleading if there is one, RSC Order 18 rule 20.

(j) Discovery. A list of the documents for discovery should be sent within 14 days of the close of pleadings, together with a notice of the time and place where inspection can take place within the following 7 days.

(k) Summons for Directions. The plaintiff should take this out within one month of the close of pleadings, returnable within not less than 14 days, and an appointment will be made.

(l) Setting down for trial. An order for this will be made when the Summons for Directions is heard.

These stages quite justifiably take time, and delay may also be necessary in a personal injury case where it takes time to estimate the likely long term effects, or a contract case where it takes time to establish the damage done. There is thus of necessity a lot of flexibility in the time limits for bringing an action, and the time for filing or serving any document can be extended with the written consent of the parties (or informally) or by the court on such terms as are just, RSC Order 3 rule 5. The timetable may also be altered or abridged in some way, for example by summary judgment, or an order for trial without pleadings, RSC Order 18 rule 21. Both sides should consider applying for orders to alter the normal timetable, or to get the other side to observe it if they are being unnecessarily slow. Although some delay is inevitable, it should not be longer than necessary, especially if it may be detrimental to the client at all.

The first possibility is to apply for judgment in default of appearance, if the defendant fails to enter an appearance within the specified time, though some cases will need leave, RSC Order 13. Final or interlocutory judgment may be given for the plaintiff, though it may be set aside or varied on the application of the defendant. Application for summary judgment under Order 14 can be made where there is a full statement of claim if the plaintiff believes that there is no real defence to the action, and the summons applying for it must be supported by an affidavit setting out fully the grounds for the application (the defendant does not have to prepare an affidavit, but he may to put his side of things). The lawyers must consider not only the affidavit, but also the variety of orders the court can make, such as giving conditional or unconditional leave to defend, and the orders as to costs to decide exactly what they should argue for. There are some cases where an Order 14 judgment is not available, and one alternative is summary judgment under RSC Order 86, where there is an action begun in the Chancery Division by writ claiming specific performance, rescission, or the forfeiture or return of a deposit.

If the action does proceed but goes slowly, the next possibility is dismissal for want of prosecution, under the inherent powers of the court or the rules of court. The case will only be dismissed where there is an intentional delay which is inordinate and inexcusable and which leads to a substantial risk that a fair trial will not be possible, *Biss* v *Lambeth, Southwark and Lewisham Health Authority* [1978] 2 All ER 125. The court may well impose a timetable for steps to be taken, and only dismiss the action if that is not complied with, *Pryer* v *Smith* [1977] 1 All ER 218. An action will rarely be dismissed within the limitation period because the plaintiff could just issue a new writ, *Birkett* v *James* [1977] 2 All ER 801, but it may be done, *Thorpe* v *Alexander Fork Lift Trucks Ltd* [1975] 1 WLR 1459. If the action is dismissed, it may be possible for the party to sue his solicitor for negligence.

The last main possibility is that the action may be withdrawn. The plaintiff may withdraw all or any part of his claim up to 14 days after the service of the defence, RSC Order 21, rule 2 (which he may choose to do if there is a complete defence to his case, or he has found a fatal flaw in it). The defendant can withdraw his defence at any time, or his counterclaim within 14 days of getting a defence to it. After this either party can only withdraw with the leave of the court, which may be subject to terms, and in particular terms as to paying costs, RSC Order 21, rule 3. Normally one will only wish to withdraw from a case if something unforeseen comes up, but an unusual case was *Castanho* v *Brown & Root (UK)* [1981] 1 All ER 143, where the plaintiff was a Portuguese sailor injured on a Panamanian ship in an English port, who sued here and got an interim payment, but was then persuaded to bring his action in the United States to get higher damages. It was held that he could not be prevented from withdrawing his action here.

In all these possibilities for altering the timetable for an action there is an element of tactical advantage. In many cases each party allows the other to fail to comply with strict time limits and the case plods on. It must be said that there is little point in applying for summary judgment or dismissal for want of prosecution if there is little chance of success and one will merely end up paying the costs. But on the other hand, if the other side really is being slow, something should be done, and an application to court may be made even if it will fail to show the other side that you mean business (and perhaps to prod them into making a settlement), and because even if the application does fail it will be in the papers for the case to show how the other side has behaved.

Interlocutory applications

Once the action has begun there are a variety of applications that may be made before it comes to trial, some as part of the action and some purely optional, and the good lawyer will make full use of the opportunities open to him to help in the preparation of the case, and to aid the practical situation of the client. Some types of application are well known, such as the interlocutory injunction, some only apply in particular circumstances, like security for costs, and some are appropriate to particular types of action, such as interim payments, but the lawyer should acquaint himself with all the possibilities. Different applications are made in different ways, and here I can only make some general points on interlocutory applications and deal with a few particular types of application, from which the lawyer can build depending on the type of practice he goes into.

Where an action is begun in the Queen's Bench Division, an interlocutory application is likely to be made by summons (see Example 1) to a judge in chambers or to the Master to whom the action has been assigned for the hearing of applications and summonses. Because of problems arising from applications being made at a late stage or without the proper paperwork there is guidance in Practice Directions and particularly in the *Practice Note* [1983] 1 All ER 1119, providing that not only should proper notice be given, but that where the hearing is likely to last more than 30 minutes it should be given a set date, and affidavits should always be filed at least 24 hours in advance, with appropriate pleadings and exhibits.

If the action is begun in the Chancery Division, an application may be made by notice of motion (see Example 2) to be heard in open court on a motion day. For many years there were specific motion days, but now every weekday is a motion day, and there is guidance on applying for a notice of motion to be heard, *Practice Direction* [1980] 2 All ER 750.

Most kinds of interlocutory application will need to be supported by an affidavit setting out and verifying the relevant background facts. This is dealt with in more detail in the chapter on affidavits. The lawyer should also try to prepare a draft of the order that he would like the judge to make, to clarify exactly what he wants and covering matters such as undertakings as to damages, or to issue the writ if it has not yet been issued. If the application is ex parte there may be an undertaking to notify the defendant, and a clause allowing the defendant to apply to set aside the order, and so on, depending on the type of order sought, *Practice Note* [1983] 1 All ER 1119. The judge will not necessarily make the order in the terms drafted, but it will form a basis for argument.

EXAMPLE 1 SUMMONS SEEKING AN INTERLOCUTORY ORDER IN THE QUEEN'S BENCH DIVISION (here an injunction)

IN THE HIGH COURT OF JUSTICE 1985.B.No.1234

QUEEN'S BENCH DIVISION

BETWEEN A. B. *Plaintiff*

and

C. D. *Defendant*

Let all the parties concerned attend the Judge in Chambers, Room , Royal Courts of Justice, Strand, London on the day of 1985 at o'clock on the hearing of an application on the part of the Plaintiff for an order that the Defendant be restrained from (state exactly the wording of the injunction that you wish the judge to grant) until the trial or until further order, and that the costs of the said application be (state the order as to costs that you would like the judge to make).

Dated the day of Signed

EXAMPLE 2 NOTICE OF MOTION SEEKING AN INTERLOCUTORY ORDER IN THE CHANCERY DIVISION (here an injunction)

IN THE HIGH COURT OF JUSTICE Ch.1985.B.No.1234

CHANCERY DIVISION

BETWEEN A. B. *Plaintiff*

and

C. D. *Defendant*

TAKE NOTICE that the Honourable Court will be moved before Mr Justice on the day of 1985 at o'clock or so soon thereafter as Counsel can be heard, by Counsel for the Plaintiff for an order that:

(1) The Defendant be restrained from (state exactly the wording of the injunction that you wish the judge to grant) until judgment in this action or until further order; and that
(2) The costs of this application be (state the order for costs that you would like the judge to make).

Dated the day of Signed

An application for an interlocutory order should be made on proper notice with both parties attending, but the application may be ex parte if there is a real risk that the defendant will dispose of or destroy an asset or otherwise prejudice the position of the applicant if he has notice. The application can be heard quickly, though normally the application, the affidavit and a draft of the order sought should be lodged with the judge's clerk the day before the hearing. However, if the case is urgent an application can be made at 10.00 a.m. or 2.00 p.m. before the judge hears his other cases if his clerk is warned and the appropriate papers handed to him. In an extreme emergency a judge can interrupt a case to hear an application, or an affidavit can be granted over the telephone, if for example there is a fear that a child will be snatched. Although the possibility is there if necessary, applications should only be made ex parte if there really is good reason. There is too great a tendency to rush straight off to court with a badly prepared application without real justification. Even if an ex parte order is made, it will normally only last a few days until there can be a full hearing with both parties present, and if the ex parte application fails the party will just end up paying the costs, so there must be a good reason for applying.

There is an element of tactics as well as the practical in most interlocutory applications. When he begins practice a lawyer may well feel overwhelmed and confused by the possibilities but if he does always try to think of the types of application open to him he will soon appreciate what can be achieved. The hearing of an interlocutory application will often be short, but that is no reason for underestimating what it can do, or for failing to prepare properly for it.

Interlocutory injunctions

This is probably the most important and most frequently used type of interlocutory relief. It can be a very positive and possibly a decisive step in many types of case, where it is desirable to stop the other side doing something, disposing of something or destroying something. By the Supreme Court Act 1981, s. 37 the High Court has power to grant an interlocutory injunction where it is just and convenient, and on such terms and conditions as are just. This gives the court a very wide discretion for a party to make use of. Much of the procedure for seeking the interlocutory injunction comes from RSC Order 29, which allows an application before or after the trial of an action, which can be inter partes or ex parte but which must be supported by an affidavit. An application can be made even before a writ or other originating process is issued, but only if the case is urgent and an undertaking to issue the writ is given.

In preparing his arguments as to why an interlocutory injunction should be granted, which may have to be done quickly, the lawyer will of course have to consider the tests developed in the case of *American Cyanamid Co* v *Ethicon* [1975] AC 396 and the cases following it:

(a) Is there a serious issue to be tried? The applicant has got to show a prima facie case for the injunction, even if he might not succeed at trial.

(b) Is the balance of convenience in favour of granting the injunction? This may involve detailed factual arguments as to whether the defendant will suffer more if the injunction is granted than the applicant will if it is not.

(c) Will damages be an adequate remedy? This is not a question of whether the applicant can claim damages, but whether they could really compensate him—if he will lose something that cannot be measured in money or that will be difficult to assess they could not.

(d) If all other factors are equal, the court will tend to preserve the status quo, but this may mean granting the injunction to prevent it being altered.

It seems that the *American Cyanamid* test may not be used where the application is for an injunction to enforce a restrictive covenant in a contract, and the injunction should normally be granted, unless there is real doubt as to whether the clause is valid, or it is clear that the injunction would be unreasonable, *Fellowes & Son* v *Fisher* [1976] QB 122, where the defendant would have lost his job if the injunction had been granted.

A practical point that often arises when an interlocutory injunction is sought is whether there should be an undertaking as to damages. If it is possible that the granting of the injunction may cause some loss to the defendant, the plaintiff may have to give an undertaking to reimburse him for that loss. This is something for the lawyers for the defendant to consider, as well as preparing their arguments why there should be no injunction. Another thing the defendant may choose to do is to give an undertaking to the plaintiff so that an injunction does not have to be granted, the undertaking being given to the judge or in negotiations outside court, though it must be recorded in an enforceable form, either in a consent order from the judge, or by being indorsed on counsel's brief. If no cause of action has arisen, there cannot be an application for an interlocutory injunction, but a *quia timet* injunction can be sought if the applicant can show a well-founded fear that he will suffer severe damage, the standard of proof being high. In *Redland Bricks* v *Morris* [1970] AC 652, excavations by the defendant led to a landslip and the plaintiff sought an injunction to prevent further excavation and to have his land shored up, but this was refused by the House of Lords because the proposed terms were too wide and the cost of complying would be high.

Mareva injunctions

This type of injunction has been developed over the last few years from the general power of the court to grant injunctions, and is now based on the Supreme Court Act 1981, s. 37, the purpose being to prevent a party to an action removing assets from the jurisdiction or otherwise dealing with them so as to prejudice the outcome of the action and prevent any judgments being enforced. It is obviously something to consider where a party has foreign connections and there is any reason to mistrust him, whether or not he is domiciled, resident or present in the jurisdiction, see *Prince Abdul Rahman bin Turki al Sudairy* v *Abu-Taha* [1980] 3 All ER 409.

As always, the applicant will have to prepare good arguments as to why he should get the order, rather than just turning up in court and asking. The principles for granting the injunction come primarily from the original case of *Mareva Compania Naviera SA* v *International Bulk Carriers SA* [1980] 1 All ER 213 and *Z Ltd* v *A–Z and AA–LL* [1982] 1 All ER 556:

(a) The applicant must give full and frank disclosure of the facts of his position.

(b) The applicant must give particulars of his claim against the defendant, showing a strong prima facie case and that he is likely to recover a substantial sum in damages.

(c) The applicant should give his grounds for belief that the defendant has assets within the jurisdiction, identifying them as far as possible.

(d) The applicant must give his grounds for believing the defendant will remove his assets from the jurisdiction so that they will not be available to satisfy a judgment.

As with an injunction, the plaintiff may well be expected to give an undertaking as to damages, to indemnify the defendant for any loss he suffers by the injunction's being granted and all the necessary information must be set down in a supporting affidavit. The form of order made will normally freeze specified assets until a specified time, usually when judgment is satisfied.

The order will bind not only the defendant, but also any third party at whom it is directed and who has knowledge of it, which in many cases will mean the bank at which the defendant has an account (the courts have acknowledged that it is often banks that administer the operation of Mareva injunctions). The interests of people who are not parties but who will be affected by any order will be taken into account, as in *Galaxia Maritima SA* v *Mineralimportexport* [1982] 1 All ER 796, where the making of an order would have severely disrupted the christmas arrangements made by the crew of a ship, so no order was made.

Although a Mareva order can be very helpful to a plaintiff, he may have to put some effort into investigating what assets the defendant has so as to have sufficient information to get an order. An order may be used to get documents connected with the running of the bank account if appropriate, but otherwise the order cannot put the plaintiff in a better position that he would have been in—he cannot use it to get priority over any other creditor, or to force the defendant into a settlement, *Iraqi Ministry of Defence* v *Arcepey Shipping Co SA* [1981] QB 65. The terms of the order must only be sufficient to cover a possible judgment, and not otherwise tie up the defendant's assets so that he does not have enough to live off, *PCW (Underwriting Agencies)* v *Dixon* [1983] 2 All ER 697.

Anton Piller orders

This type of order has again been developed from existing procedures over the last few years. Under RSC Order 29, rule 2 the court has the power to order the detention, custody or preservation of any property which is the subject matter of a case, and may authorise someone to enter property to carry out the order. This basic power has been widened in the cases to orders that allow the plaintiff to enter the defendant's premises to seize any specified property that is relevant as evidence as well as the subject of the action. In the case of *Anton Piller KG* v *Manufacturing Processes* [1976] Ch 55 the plaintiff was afraid that the defendant would improperly supply information to a rival, and might destroy relevant evidence if he was aware of the action. It was held that in such a case there could be an order for the plaintiff to enter the defendant's premises to inspect and copy documents on an application made ex parte at an early stage in the case (though after the issue of the writ).

As always, particularly as the application is ex parte, the plaintiff's lawyers must be sure of their facts, and prepare a strong and clear case. The principles for the grant of an order come from *CBS United Kingdom* v *Lambert* [1983] Ch 37:

(a) The applicant must show a prima facie case on the facts, and that the actual or potential damage to him is serious.

(b) The applicant must show a clear case that the defendant has incriminating evidence, or other assets derived from his wrongdoing.

(c) The applicant must show there is a real danger that the defendant will destroy or dispose of the evidence or assets unless an order is made.

Again the plaintiff may have to give an undertaking to reimburse the defendant for any loss he suffers if the order is made. The defendant will be in a difficult position, as of necessity he will know nothing of the order until it is enforced. A solicitor should attend when the order is carried out to ensure that it is done properly and no force may be used. If the defendant prevents the order's being carried out he will be in contempt of court. The court will wish to ensure that the wording of the order is very specific to avoid difficulty, *EMI Ltd* v *Pandit* [1975] 1 All ER 418.

The order has especially been used in cases of breach of copyright or the 'pirating' of music or video films, though it has a much wider potential. In *Universal City Studios Inc* v *Mukhtar & Sons* [1976] 2 All ER 330 the plaintiff had the copyright for merchandise connected with the 'Jaws' film, but the defendant produced unlicensed 'Jaws' T-shirts. The order granted required the defendants to hand over all the T-shirts they had, including some that did not belong to them, though the rights of the other owners were protected. The order may also be used to protect evidence that may be destroyed, *Yousif* v *Salama* [1980] 3 All ER 405, but cannot be used to get evidence that the plaintiff is not otherwise entitled to have, for example because it is privileged, *Rank Film Distributors* v *Video Information Centre* [1981] 2 All ER 76. Nor can the Anton Piller order be used by the plaintiff as a 'fishing trip' to see what he can find—his application and the order made must be specific.

Other types of application

Just to give a few other examples of applications that could be made, the plaintiff's legal advisers may consider applying for an interim payment under the Supreme Court Act 1981, s.32 and RSC Order 29, rule 10, primarily where there is a case for personal injuries. The defendant must have admitted liability, or the plaintiff must have judgment for damages to be assessed, or the court must be satisfied that the plaintiff will get substantial damages, and in addition it must be shown that the defendant is insured, or is a public authority, or has adequate means to make a payment. An action for personal injuries may take a long time to come to trial, and his lawyers should keep aware of the client's situation, and make an application for an interim payment if he is in any financial difficulty, or may need money to pay for treatment.

The lawyers for the defendant may advise him on making a payment into court under RSC Order 22, and should if appropriate reconsider the possibility as extra evidence comes to light. It is clear that if there is no real defence to the action, a payment in should be considered in the hope of encouraging the plaintiff to accept less than he might otherwise get, and to save costs. In any action for damages or debt the defendant can make a payment in at any time after he has entered an appearance, and there is an art to deciding whether a payment in should be made, when it should be made, and how much should be paid in. One needs to weigh up whether the plaintiff will win (payment in should not be made where there is a real chance that the plaintiff will lose), and exactly what amount in damages he can hope to get, then decide how much less than that one can pay in that the plaintiff might still accept. The lawyer will usually need to have quite a lot of information about the case to make these judgments, and may for example not be able to make a payment in until after discovery. With experience the lawyer will learn when and what to offer, and the lawyer for the plaintiff will know when and what to accept. A settlement of the action may be negotiated as an alternative to a payment in.

Costs

On these different types of interlocutory applications separate orders can normally be made for costs, even though costs at trial will normally follow the event, and this is something the lawyer should always consider. Clearly an application should not be made unless it has a reasonable chance of success as the party making it will only have to pay the costs (unless there is some tactical point to make), but as. well as preparing the affidavit and arguments for the application, the lawyer should also think of what order for costs to ask for, as the court has a wide discretion. The basic possibilities are:

(a) Costs reserved (who pays will be decided at trial).

(b) Costs in the cause (the party who loses at trial will pay).

(c) Plaintiff's or defendant's costs in the cause (if the party specified wins at trial he will get the costs of the application too).

(d) Plaintiff's or defendant's costs in any event (the party specified will get the costs of the application whatever happens at trial).

(e) Plaintiff's or defendant's costs (the party specified should be paid the costs of the application immediately).

(f) Costs of the day (e.g. if one party gets an adjournment they should pay the costs of the day that the other side has incurred in turning up).

(g) Costs thrown away (e.g. if a party gets a default judgment set aside they may be ordered to pay the costs thrown away by the other side in getting it).

The defendant's lawyers may consider seeking security for costs where the plaintiff has little real chance of success and may not be able to pay costs ordered against him if he loses, but under RSC Order 23 security for costs can only be ordered in limited circumstances where the court thinks it is just, and in practice the lawyer may only be able to point out to the other side strongly the weakness of their case in the hope of getting them to withdraw it or reach a quick settlement.

The main point about costs while preparing a case for court—that both sides should take care to keep the costs bill as low as is reasonably possible, and keep the client informed of the position—has been made, but cannot be stressed too much.

Collecting and preparing the evidence

Evidence is central and vital in the preparation of any case. The solicitor and barrister will both need to collect information when the client first comes to them for advice, to see if he has a case. If an action is brought, they may well need further evidence to assess exactly the extent of injury or the amount of damages to claim, and when the case comes to trial evidence may be crucial, to the extent that just before trial the barrister may be asked to provide an advice on evidence to ensure that all is in order. Some cases will turn on a complicated legal point, but many more will turn on whether the plaintiff can actually prove what he alleges as his cause of action and as the injury and loss he has suffered. The lawyer can make a speech, but he cannot give evidence—he must find something to prove every part of his case.

This is not something the young lawyer finds easy. He usually first encounters evidence as a complicated academic subject, and it is not until he gets into practice that he begins to see the practical importance of it (it is when you hear a real witness say 'Well, he told me that . . .' that you understand what the rule against hearsay is about—the witness did not see what happened, he was just told something). Thus many lawyers do come to practice without a good working knowledge of the rules of evidence, and they must make an effort to develop their skill. It is largely inevitable that the rules of evidence should be complex as they have to balance the interests of the parties in the action, be adaptable to many different sorts of action and cover many types of things that are potentially evidence, but there is no excuse for the lawyer not to learn and use the rules of evidence to the best possible advantage.

The main points are to find evidence on every issue in the case, that is every single element in the cause of action and the claim for loss or damage, to know whether the evidence he has is admissible or not, to know whether there are any procedural formalities before the evidence will be admitted, and to keep the mind open to all the possible types of evidence. Not only documents and witnesses may be used, but also plans and photographs. These may not only help to prove the case, but they may also improve the presentation of the case in court, holding the attention of the judge or jury and helping them to grasp a point much more quickly than words can, however eloquent the lawyer is.

In addition to proving one's own case, it is of course important to be aware of what evidence the other side has or may have, to decide whether one could challenge it, or collect evidence to contradict it.

The types of evidence available

Here is a brief check-list of some of the main types of evidence that may be available:

(a) Documents. Original documents on which a cause of action is based will usually not only be admissible but also be essential to the case, such as a contract, will, deed or lease. The original should be produced if available, or if not a properly authenticated copy.

(b) Witnesses. Everything that cannot be proved by an essential written document should be proved by a witness giving oral evidence in open court, especially in an action begun by writ (RSC Order 38, rule 1). It may not always be easy to find a witness, but every effort should be made, for example by trying to find people who live or work in the area and may know something; local papers may help. The witness will normally only be able to give evidence of things of which they have direct personal knowledge, everything else being excluded by the rule against hearsay. The barrister should not see witnesses other than the client and experts before the case, but the lawyers in a case must try to weigh up how good the witnesses they have are likely to be in court, and if necessary to choose the best. Very early in practice the lawyer will get used to the witness who does not come up to proof, sounds unreliable, or keeps going off at tangents, and he must be ready for it. To ensure that witnesses attend court, witness orders may be needed (RSC Order 38, rules 14–19).

(c) Other documents. There may be a variety of documentary evidence that may be relevant to the action, such as records, reports and letters. If such documents are sufficiently relevant they will normally be admissible, though this may depend on the correct procedural approach, such as giving notice (see the Civil Evidence Acts 1968 and 1972 and RSC Order 38). There are special requirements for expert evidence and medical reports that will be mentioned later, and for specific types of documents, as in the Bankers Books Evidence Act 1879.

(d) Affidavits. Sworn written evidence in the form of affidavits will be admissible, and often essential, for many interlocutory applications, and for actions begun by originating summons. In writ actions the oral evidence of witnesses is preferred and affidavits can only go in with the consent of the parties, or in other limited circumstances, which are dealt with in the chapter on affidavits (see RSC Order 38, rule 9).

(e) Maps, plans etc. These should be properly prepared by an appropriate person (see RSC Order 38, rule 5) and unless there are special reasons, they can only be used at trial if the other parties to the action have had chance to inspect and agree them. This may be dealt with at the summons for directions.

(f) Photographs and films. Photographs of places, machines etc. may be very useful, but again they can normally only be used at trial if the other parties have had an opportunity to inspect and agree them. The photographs need not be taken by the parties. In *Senior* v *Holdsworth ex p Independent Television News* [1976] QB 23 the plaintiff sued a policeman for an assault at a pop-concert, and he was granted an order that ITN should produce film that they took of the event, but only that part of it that was relevant.

Having gathered information and evidence for his own case the lawyer will need to ensure that it and the evidence produced by the other side is admissible.

The first thing to check is that any procedural points have been complied with—has proper notice been given under the Civil Evidence Acts? Was inspection allowed if necessary? Is it a case where affidavits are admissible?

The next thing to check is the source of the evidence and how it was obtained, for example, involuntary confessions will not be admissible in a criminal case. In *ITC Film Distributors* v *Video Exchange* [1982] 2 All ER 246 the defendant picked up documents accidently left by the plaintiff after a hearing and an injunction was granted for the return of the documents to the plaintiff and to prevent their use. Generally, however, the court will accept evidence from any source where it is not contrary to justice or public policy, if it is relevant. The court will also require to know the source of the evidence, as in the well-publicised case of *British Steel Corporation* v *Granada Television* [1981] 1 All ER 417, where the television company made a programme about a steel strike using material from secret B.S.C. files and the majority of the House of Lords held that the identity of the source of the information should be revealed.

The last main rule is to look at generally admissible evidence to see if part of it may be inadmissible, because it is prejudicial or hearsay. This must be done while reading documents before the trial and at the trial itself. It does take practice to learn to spot hearsay, but if one remembers that the essential point is that a witness cannot give evidence of something of which he does not have direct knowledge it becomes relatively easy. Small pieces of hearsay that do no harm to the case are not worth objecting to, but the lawyer should always be on his guard to object to things which should not be permitted and which may prejudice his client.

Expert evidence and medical reports

The parties may wish to call expert evidence of various kinds, to deal with how a machine works, a trade practice, a building technique and so on. Experts may be needed at an early stage to decide if there is a case at all, or at a later stage to advise on a particular point. It is quite open to any party to consult experts where they feel they may be useful, subject to whether the cost justifies it, and once they have an expert report they can decide whether or not they wish to use it. It is clearly important to get someone with appropriate qualifications and experience to convince the court, and the client, a lawyer, or a professional or trade organisation may be able to suggest someone.

Once an expert has been found, he should be told objectively the facts of the case, and what aspects of it he is being asked to advise on. No pressure must be put on him to draw conclusions favourable to the client—if the report is not favourable it does not have to be used, see dicta in *Whitehouse* v *Jordan* [1981] 1 WLR 246. If anything is left out of the report or is not clear the lawyer should clarify it to avoid any difficulty in court, and the barrister can see the expert in conference. It is useful to ask the expert if there are any alternative conclusions possible or any questions or doubts in his mind to see what might come up at trial, when the expert may well be vigorously cross-examined.

There are some limits on the use of expert evidence at trial in the Civil Evidence Act 1972, s.2 and RSC Order 38, rules 35–44. The number of experts allowed may be limited, and the substance of the expert evidence to be used will normally have to be revealed before the trial, *Ollett* v *Bristol Aerojet Ltd* [1979] 3 All ER 544, though the court does have a discretion where the report is based on disputed facts, or where disclosure would be expensive or impractical, *Kirkup* v *British Railways Engineering* [1983] 3 All ER 147.

The rules for expert medical reports are broadly similar, though slightly different. Again the case must be put objectively to the doctor and he must be left to draw his own conclusions. The number of medical witnesses may be limited, and the substance of the reports must normally be disclosed before the trial if they are to be used, though not in a personal injury action, when the defendant is also entitled to have the plaintiff medically examined by a doctor nominated by him, as he may well wish to dispute whether the claimed injuries are genuine. The plaintiff cannot refuse this merely because he is elderly or nervous, but the court can attach conditions, *Hall* v *Avon Area Health Authority* [1980] 1 All ER 516. However the plaintiff can refuse to undergo a long series of tests or tests that are painful, *Prescott* v *Bulldog Tools* [1981] 3 All ER 869. The plaintiff has no right to see the report, unless the defendant does decide to use it at trial, *Megarity* v *DJ Ryan & Sons* [1980] 2 All ER 832.

Discovery of evidence

The general discovery of documentary evidence is an obligatory stage in many types of civil action, and an optional stage in others, but many litigants are not aware of this. In most actions begun by writ, RSC Order 24 provides that discovery should take place after the close of pleadings, with each party providing the other with a list of relevant documents which he has or has had in his possession. They must also give notice of when these documents will be available for inspection. This may be unwelcome to a client, and the lawyer must make it clear to him at an early stage that he will have to be open about what he has, *Rockwell Machine Tool Co. Ltd.* v *EP Barnes (Concessionaires)* [1968] 1 WLR 693. Discovery can be a very useful process in preparing a case, but it is two-sided.

There may be some difficulty in deciding what to include in the list for discovery, but essentially everything relevant must go in, even if the party is going to object to producing it or claim privilege. The existence of the documents must be revealed, but the party can then argue the privilege against self-incrimination, or any other kind of privilege or reason why the document should not be revealed. When a party gets a list of documents he should of course check it thoroughly to see if there is anything interesting there, or whether anything has obviously been omitted. The court has wide powers to order that a new list of documents be drawn up or a specific document be produced. It can also limit or dispense with discovery, or order it in a case where it is not compulsory, taking into account all the circumstances of the case and public interest, as in *Church of Scientology of California* v *D.H.S.S.* [1979] 3 All ER 97 where the defendant had criticised the practices of the plaintiff in medical matters, but it was held the defendant did not have to disclose specific complaints made to them. If a document is very relevant there will have to be very good reasons to prevent its disclosure, see *Waugh* v *British Railways Board* [1980] AC 521 and *Campbell* v *Tameside Metropolitan Borough Council* [1982] QB 1065.

Since discovery is intended solely to help the parties in the preparation of their case there are strict limits on the ways in which documents obtained can be used.

In the case of *Distillers Co (Biochemicals)* v *Times Newspapers* [1975] 1 QB 613, where documents on thalidomide were disclosed on discovery and came into the possession of *The Times*, an injunction was granted to stop the paper using the documents as they were only disclosed for the action. In *Home Office* v *Harman* [1983] AC 280, a prisoner sued the Home Office for being kept in solitary confinement and on discovery documents passed to his solicitor, Harriet Harman. She argued that since these documents were read in open court she did no wrong in showing them to a journalist, but it was held that since she had given an undertaking that the documents would only be used in the case she was in contempt.

There are also some special types of discovery that may be useful. A potential plaintiff may need to see a document even before he begins an action to see if he has a case at all, and this may be possible under the Supreme Court Act 1981, ss.33–35 and RSC Order 24, rule 7A. In a case of personal injury or death, the High Court can order pre-action discovery by a person who is likely to be a party against another person who is likely to be a party. The order may allow for the disclosure, inspection or preservation of documents or other property likely to be relevant to an issue in possible proceedings, or for the taking of samples of property and the carrying out of experiments. In *Shaw* v *Vauxhall Motors* [1974] 1 WLR 1035 the plaintiff was injured at work while driving a fork lift truck and was allowed discovery of its maintenance records before he began his action.

Pre-action discovery may be ordered in other cases under the general power of the court to order discovery to fairly dispose of a case (see RSC Order 24), but only where it is really necessary. In *R.H.M. Foods* v *Bovril* [1982] 1 All ER 673 the plaintiff complained that the defendants were marketing their product of Gravymate to make it look like Bisto, the plaintiff's product. They sought pre-action discovery of the defendant's directions to their advertising agency, but this was refused on the grounds that they were only trying to substantiate a suspicion.

It is not generally possible to get discovery against someone who is not a party to an action, though orders may be made for them to appear as witnesses and bring documents with them where appropriate. However, orders may be made under the Supreme Court Act 1981, s.34 and RSC Order 24, rule 7A where someone does appear to have relevant documents in their possession, custody or power. The court also has a general inherent power to order discovery, as in *Norwich Pharmacal Co.* v *Customs & Excise Commissioners* [1974] AC 133, where the plaintiff believed there were illicit imports of patent medicines, and the defendants were directed to give discovery of information in their possession on the basis that there was a duty of disclosure where a person innocently became involved in the tort of another.

The summons for directions

The summons for directions is intended to deal with any outstanding matters to prepare the case for trial, to review the state of the case and see that both sides are ready. Thus it should encourage both sides to see that they have left nothing undone, and because of the wide variety of matters that must and can be dealt with, both sides should prepare for the hearing of the summons and decide in advance what they hope to achieve, rather than just seeing it as something they must go through.

The summons for directions should be taken out by the plaintiff after the close of pleadings (RSC Order 25). It is a set form dealing with specific issues, and the party taking it out should cross out those things which he does not in fact want the court to deal with. In the Chancery Division the set form is not necessarily used, and there may just be agreement as to the mode of trial and the setting down of the action. The summons will be heard by a Master in Chambers.

Decisions will be made on the trial itself, that is as to the place and mode of trial, and whether the case should be consolidated with another or transferred to another court. Any arguments on any of these points must be prepared. Most trials in the High Court will be by judge alone, but there may be a trial by judge and jury, or in special circumstances by some other mode such as an official referee (see the Supreme Court Act 1981, s.69 and RSC Order 33). Jury trial is available in cases of fraud, defamation and similar cases, though generally not where prolonged examination of documents will be needed. Jury trial is more expensive, and will only be ordered where there is good reason, *John L. Williams* v *Beesley* [1973] 1 WLR 1295.

There will also be consideration whether the pleadings of both parties are in order, and orders can be made for amendment or further and better particulars if necessary. Although the pleadings may initially have been drafted properly, points may have arisen making amendment desirable, and both parties should consider whether they do wish to go to trial on their existing pleadings. Amendment is still possible at trial, but only if the other side will not be prejudiced and costs are paid.

On the hearing of the summons for directions, orders can also be made as to the evidence for trial. It can be agreed what maps, models and photographs and so on will be used, or how a particular point will be proved. The use of medical and expert reports can be considered, and orders made as to whether the contents of reports should be revealed or the number of expert or medical witnesses limited. A party can admit a point to save costs, and any further orders that are needed as to discovery and inspection can be made. Normally a time limit will be set within which the plaintiff should set the action down for trial. The case will have to be set down in the correct List depending on what type of case it is, such as the Jury List, the Non-Jury List, the Short Cause List, the Commercial List and so on, *Practice Direction* [1981] 3 All ER 61. The parties will be warned as the case moves to the top of the List, which will of course depend on the number and length of the cases above it, though it is possible to apply for a fixed date for a trial. The parties should try to give a realistic estimate of how long the trial will last, and revise it if necessary to help the listing system work efficiently (see RSC Order 34 and *Practice Direction* [1981] 2 All ER 775).

Settling actions

The vast majority of actions that are begun will not proceed to trial. The parties may well try to seek a settlement to save costs, time and worry, and many writs are issued in the hope of persuading the other side to negotiate rather than with a real desire to take the case to court. The plaintiff may wish to settle because of possible weaknesses in the law or evidence in his case, and the defendant may try to settle to get the plaintiff to accept less than he might get if he goes to court. The parties need to communicate regularly anyway because of the procedural steps that they need to fulfil, and they may well try to reach a compromise solution in the course of correspondence. There is inevitably some risk in going to trial—a witness may prove weaker than one thought, the other side may come up with surprise evidence, or it may be more difficult to convince the judge of a line of argument than one had hoped, and these risks can be avoided with a good settlement.

When advising the client, the lawyer will be trying to advise him exactly what he can hope to get from the action, and once the remedies sought are decided on and the lawyer has been able to give a rough estimate of damages taking all relevant factors into account, the client will know the best that he can achieve and can negotiate from that point. The lawyer can advise in detail on the basis of a proper settlement if he thinks this appropriate and should take into account any risks or weaknesses that he can foresee in the case. The solicitor may negotiate through 'without prejudice' letters, and the barrister can advise on the basis for a settlement in his opinion.

A settlement can be reached at any stage in the case from before the case is begun to negotiations outside court before the case is called on (or even during the case itself if the judge is prepared to make a consent order agreed by the parties rather than letting the case continue). Whatever stage the case has reached, the lawyer should not reach a settlement until he really does feel sure that he knows what the client's case is worth, which may mean waiting for medical reports or accident reports. Also the lawyers must negotiate a settlement within the instructions from the client, and must consult the client before accepting any terms. The client may have particular problems or views, and the lawyer should not accept a settlement merely because he thinks it is reasonable (though he can certainly try to persuade the client to accept a settlement if he feels the client has unreasonable expectations). A lawyer has ostensible authority to reach an agreement on his client's behalf, but should specifically consult the client first, *Waugh* v *H.B. Clifford & Sons* [1982] 1 All ER 1095.

Although it may take some time to negotiate the details of a settlement, this must never prejudice the case in any way. If there is no settlement within a reasonable time the party should press on with the case, not least because this may encourage the other side to settle. The possible dangers of delay can be seen in *Easy* v *Universal Anchorage Co* [1974] 1 WLR 899 where a man was injured at work but his solicitors did not serve a writ because negotiations were continuing. However, the client refused the offer made and it was then too late to serve the writ, and the court refused to renew it.

In reaching a settlement, the lawyers for both sides must of course ensure that it covers everything and that the wording is absolutely correct, not least because there are a variety of ways of settling an action, and the rules for enforcing different types of settlements and consent orders are not entirely clear. Since so many actions are settled it would be helpful if the law were more specific and clear. As it is, the essential points are to draft the settlement clearly so as to leave nothing open to doubt, and to try to take into account not only all the client's existing requirements, but everything foreseeable in the future, because once the settlement is reached it can normally only be challenged on specific legal grounds such as fraud, misrepresentation or operative mistake. If anything is left out it may be impossible to do anything about it, unless it is possible to start a new action or reapply to court in the action that was settled.

A settlement may need the approval of the court to be effective if a party is an infant or a patient (see RSC Order 80, rule 10), or if a party is representing others (see RSC Order 15 rule 13).

The settlement of the action must be formally recorded in some way that is enforceable. There are various ways of doing this, of which the following are examples:

(a) Agreement before action. Before the action is begun the parties can settle the issues between them by contract, either both making concessions, or one giving up the right to sue in return for something. The contract should be written, and can be enforced by the usual contractual remedies, for example by specific performance, or an action can possibly still be begun within the limitation period unless the plaintiff is estopped.

(b) Proceedings may be stayed or adjourned on terms. Once the action has started, any settlement should include some provision that the case should proceed no further, and might take into account existing costs. If the action is stayed, it may be possible to re-open the proceedings if there is any difficulty, and the agreement reached may be enforced either as a contract, or by enforcing any terms given by the judge in ordering a stay of proceedings, as appropriate.

(c) Endorsement on briefs. Especially if an agreement is reached outside court, the terms may be written on the backsheet of the briefs and signed. This will be a form of contract, and will need to be enforced as such with a fresh action, unless the terms relate only to an interlocutory matter and the main action continues. In *Green* v *Rozen* [1955] 1 WLR 741 the terms were indorsed on counsel's brief with the words 'By consent all proceedings stayed on terms indorsed on briefs. Liberty to apply', but despite this it was held that the plaintiff would still have to begin a new action to enforce payment of the money agreed.

(d) Consent orders. The judge in the action may agree to make an order in the terms agreed by the parties rather than passing his own judgment. The parties should themselves draw up the order that they would like the judge to make, taking all possible care, but the judge is not bound to make an order in the terms they suggest if he does not think it right. The order made will be enforceable as a judgment, but is also a contract between the parties, and it seems that once the parties have agreed the terms of a consent order, neither can withdraw, *Chanel* v *F.W. Woolworth* [1981] 1 All ER 745. A consent order can only order those things which the court has power to order, but it can also include undertakings by a party to do something, which can therefore make it quite flexible to achieve what the parties want. The words 'Liberty to apply' tend to be used rather indiscriminately in consent and other orders, but they should in fact only be used where specific difficulties are foreseen—the words will not allow the party to return to the judge when what he should do is take action to enforce the order, *Practice Direction* [1980] 1 All ER 1008.

Preparing a case for hearing

If the case does not settle, the lawyers will have to prepare for trial. It will be primarily for the solicitor to ensure that the case goes smoothly through the necessary procedural steps to come to trial, and to this end it may be useful to keep a sheet of paper in the front of the file on the case, noting the main stages to go through and the dates by which things should be done. The solicitor should also keep a note of the things that he has to do, such as collecting items of evidence. If the case is slowed down by the need to wait for reports, or because negotiations are proceeding the solicitor should ensure there is no unnecessary delay, and he should keep the client informed of what is happening. As the time for the hearing of the case approaches the solicitor will need to prepare a brief for counsel with all the appropriate documents. He may also need to prepare documents for the court—if there are a lot of documents in the case it is normal to have a bundle agreed with the other side of the most important documents, bound together in order with page numbers for the easy use of the lawyers and the judge.

The case may be returned to the barrister with a brief to make an interlocutory application, to advise on a settlement or on evidence. If the case comes to trial, the brief should be sent well in advance for him to work on it. The list of main facts and dates made when first reading the brief can be a useful starting point to remind him of the case, and the barrister should update and improve it if necessary so that it can form the basis for his opening speech at the hearing, and for easy reference as the hearing proceeds.

When preparing his initial opinion on the case the barrister will have checked the relevant statutes and cases and if he has kept a list of references he should be able to find them again quickly. The exact wording of every relevant section and regulation will need to be checked, and it may be useful to have a photocopy of them to work with. Cases will need to be re-read, and the page numbers of relevant dicta noted. It is necessary to work on cases against you as well as for you to find ways of distinguishing them, not least because it is a good technique of advocacy to bring up a case and explain why it should not be followed before the other side has a chance to mention it. It will of course be necessary to provide a full list of authorities for the court.

Most barristers, especially early in practice, will also find it useful to prepare notes of their main lines of argument in the case. It is not a good idea to prepare speeches in detail as something that is just read out will inevitably be less effective, but outline notes that can be easily referred to will mean that one does not need to waffle or leave anything out. In addition it can be useful to make brief notes of the lines of questioning to be followed with each of one's own witnesses and in cross-examination (though to some extent the latter can only be done as the witness is heard in court). The notes can include those points the barrister wishes to emphasise and those he wants to challenge.

Such notes will help the barrister to develop a clear and concise presentation of his case when it comes to court. The actual presentation of a case and techniques of advocacy are beyond the scope of this book, but the case that has been properly prepared will be the basis for success.

7 *Basic principles of drafting and pleading*

This chapter will deal with the basic principles for drafting legal documents, especially pleadings for court. Examples of particular types of pleading are given in the second part of the book. People tend to regard legal documents with suspicion and mystification; the general public tend to regard them as incomprehensible, and lawyers themselves may find it difficult to master the principles of drafting, and take years to develop a good style and feel confident. There is a tendency to treat legal phrases as magic formulae, and some feeling that a conveyance or a statement of claim should sound grand to impress people in the way that a judge in robes does.

There is something to be said for the view that a legal document should be special—if someone is summoned to court they should feel it is something more than an ordinary letter. But on the other hand, they should be able to understand the document that they have received, whether it is a pleading of the court or some other document drafted by a lawyer. Good drafting is not necessarily long words and lots of sub-clauses, but the essential facts of a case set out in a clear and concise way, and using the right words in good English. A good draft should usually feel simple and right, but that is not easy to achieve and the lawyer may take some time to learn a good style. However, it is important that he should, as a good technique in drafting legal documents is the basis of a clearly presented case, and the first step to winning in court.

There are strong historical reasons for the involved legal documents that still sometimes appear today. The concept of legal pleadings began in the reign of Henry II, when each party gave a brief oral statement of their case which was written onto parchment rolls (hence the title of Master of the Rolls). The original idea was simple and logical—that it was necessary to define clearly and simply what the case was about—but it soon became hedged about with a number of strict rules and formalities which had to be observed. The correct formula of words had to be used for each case and the right form of action had to be chosen or the plaintiff would fail, whatever the facts and justice of the case. Common law and equity actions had to be brought separately, and a defendant could only record one defence, even if a variety of defences might be open to him on the facts.

Increasingly complex rules for pleading lasted well into the last century, and reached a climax for the early Victorian lawyer. It was necessary to plead positively every part of the case and to exclude all possible exceptions so that lengthy pleadings with many sub-clauses were inevitable, even though much of what they said was not strictly relevant to the case. Equally the defendant had to deal with every possible argument in the case and every possible defence. Anything not in the pleadings could not be argued in court, however relevant it was, so pleading was not only complex but vital, and cases could easily be won or lost on it. The lawyer needed to be not so much an expert at arguing a case in court but an expert at drafting, and the technical rules of pleading predominated over the need for justice in a case.

Fundamental reform came with the Common Law Procedure Acts 1852–60 and the Judicature Act 1873, which form the basis for the modern system of pleading. The rules had become so complicated that pleading tended to obscure rather than clarify the case, and these old rules were removed so that it was no longer necessary to plead on a wide number of matters that were not directly relevant to the case itself, but only to plead on the central facts and arguments in the case. Also it is now very much easier to amend a pleading, so that a defect in pleading will rarely be fatal to a case because it can usually be remedied.

Although the basic theory is now that the pleadings should summarise the facts and issues in a case as briefly and clearly as possible, there are still some drawbacks in the present system. Firstly, the old Victorian approach with a heavy style, cumbersome and old-fashioned words and complex grammar has died hard, being passed on from one generation of lawyers to another as they learn drafting techniques, and there are still far too many documents and pleadings that are much less comprehensible than they should be for no very good reason. Secondly, the fact that it is now relatively easy to amend a pleading has meant that some pleaders have become rather lax. They do not bother to make a pleading as accurate as it should be because they feel that they can always sort it out later at relatively little cost in time and money.

It goes without saying that the good pleader should avoid both of these tendencies, and should do so from the first moment that he begins to learn how to plead, as bad habits will be very difficult to lose once they have been picked up. It is vital to find a clear and concise style right from the start that gives the essence of the case and uses good, reasonably simple English. Also the good lawyer should only need to amend a pleading if new facts or arguments emerge, and not merely to correct mistakes.

There tends to be a feeling that now that the complicated rules of drafting are gone there is no real need for a lawyer to take great care with his drafting, but there are many reasons why it is still important to develop a skill here. Firstly, a good draft is part of preparing a case properly. If the lawyer has thought out all the issues clearly and developed his arguments sufficiently, a good draft should come automatically; it is only if he has not yet got the case straight in his own mind that the draft will be woolly and vague. Secondly, the pleadings in a case are the first thing that a judge will read. He may well read them before he comes into court, and in any event they will be the first things brought to his attention. Therefore a good, strong, clear pleading is the best way to get the attention of the judge to the central issues of the case. This can matter in little things as well as in big ones. Many judges will be prepared to ignore small mistakes because they are not important, but some will be irritated by them, or see them as being the sign of an inefficient lawyer. Lastly, there are still some cases where mistakes in drafting can be vital, even though the old rules are gone. For example, in the well-known case of *Leaf* v *International Galleries* [1950] 2 KB 86 the plaintiff bought a painting for £85 having been told that it was a Constable, and when he found out that it was not he sued claiming rescission. The judge held that the remedy of rescission was not available due to lapse of time before the claim, and the plaintiff could not get damages because they were not claimed in the pleading. A further example is *Esso Petroleum Co.* v *Southport Corporation* [1956] AC 218, where a ship was stranded and a beach polluted by it. The case went to the House of Lords, and it was held there had been no negligence but the accident was due to a defect in the ship. As unseaworthiness had not been pleaded the defendant did not have to deal with it and the plaintiff failed.

Even if bad or insufficient pleading does not lose a case, it may deprive a party of a remedy. This is especially so when pleading a claim for damages, where each head of damage claimed and the basic facts on which each claim is based should be pleaded, especially for a head of damage that is not obvious. To give one example, in *Perestrello E Companhia Limitada* v *United Paint Co* [1969] 1 WLR 570 there was an action for breach of contract which the plaintiff won, but the pleading claimed only some wasted expenditure and not general loss of profit, and it was held they could only recover what was pleaded.

Many judges still stress the importance of good pleadings in cases, as in the remarks made by Lord Edmund Davies in *Farrell* v *Secretary of State for Defence* [1980] 1 All ER 166 where he said:

> It has become fashionable in these days to attach decreasing importance to pleadings, and it is beyond doubt that there have been times where insistence on complete compliance with their technicalities puts justice at risk, and indeed may on occasion have lead to its being defeated. But pleadings continue to play an essential part in civil actions.

Types of drafting and pleading

There is a wide variety of different types of drafting and pleading that a lawyer may need to deal with. The basic types are:

(a) Essential court pleadings, such as the statement of claim and the defence.
(b) Other types of pleadings and applications for court, such as the originating summons or the petition.
(c) Drafting in criminal cases.
(d) Drafting affidavits for various procedural or evidential purposes.
(e) Drafting documents which are not part of court proceedings, such as wills and deeds.

Some general points will apply to all these categories, but the rules for each are different in various respects. This book deals primarily with the rules for the first two categories, where there are most technical rules for pleading and drafting, concentrating on High Court actions. Later chapters deal with the slightly different rules for county court and criminal actions and there is also a chapter on drafting affidavits, which can have an important role in a case. The points come from court rules and case law and what points really are matters of personal style are distinguished. Minor types of drafting will not be covered specifically, many of them being relatively straightforward or relatively uncommon. More minor drafts will usually be a matter of applying general drafting principles, and can be found in a reference work or learned in practice quite easily. Also, specialist drafting skills will not be covered, as these will often be a matter of applying general drafting principles in a particular area of law, with some special rules to be learned by the lawyer going into that type of work.

The drafting of documents which are not for use in court proceedings, such as deeds, wills, contracts and conveyances, is beyond the scope of this book, though to some extent similar principles will apply to them.

Choosing the appropriate type of draft

In many cases it will be fairly obvious what type of draft is needed at any point in an action, but there can be some difficulty about the type of pleading or other document needed to commence an action, especially in the High Court. The rules for commencing a civil action in the High Court are contained primarily in RSC Order 5, which provides that, subject to any provision of an Act or of the rules of court, proceedings can be begun by writ, originating summons, originating motion or petition (see RSC Order 5, rule 1). Sometimes a specific one of these must be used, but if there is a choice it is for the plaintiff to decide which to use.

The basic rules for making the choice are as follows:

A writ must be used in the following cases, unless there is any provision in an Act or rule to the contrary:

(a) In proceedings in which a claim is made by the plaintiff for any relief or remedy for any tort, other than trespass to land.

(b) In proceedings in which a claim made by the plaintiff is based on an allegation of fraud.

(c) In proceedings in which a claim is made by the plaintiff for damages for breach of a duty (whether the duty exists by virtue of a contract or of a provision made by or under an Act or independently of any contract or any such provision), where the damages claimed consist of or include damages in respect of death of any person, or in respect of personal injuries to any person, or in respect of damage to any property.

(d) In proceedings in which a claim is made by the plaintiff in respect of the infringement of a patent.

A writ should also be used for a probate action (see RSC Order 76, rule 2).

These provisions are reasonably straightforward as to the cases when a writ must be used. In practice any similar type of case should also be begun by writ, and usually not only tort actions but also many contract actions will be begun by writ. The writ will also be appropriate in other types of actions where there is any substantial dispute of fact between the parties, or where witnesses are likely to be needed for examination in court. This is because the procedure following a writ is designed to deal with these things, whereas the simplified procedure following an originating summons which is based largely on documents is not.

An originating summons must be used to begin an action where any application is made under any Act, unless the Act or rules of court expressly require or authorise some other means of beginning the action, or the proceedings are already pending (see RSC Order 5, rule 3). This will apply where the basis of the court's power to deal with the action comes from a statute, not where the statute merely happens to be relevant to the action.

An originating summons may be used in various other cases. It is appropriate to use an originating summons if the sole or principal question at issue is, or is likely to be, one of the construction of an Act or of any instrument made under an Act, or of any deed, will, contract or other document, or some other question of law, or in which there is unlikely to be any substantial dispute of fact (see RSC Order 5, rule 4(2)).

There are other cases in which an originating summons should normally be used, such as where there are proceedings for possession of land (RSC Order 113), an application under the Inheritance (Provision for Family and Dependants) Act 1975, and many types of proceedings in connection with a company (RSC Order 102).

A motion is to be used if the rules of court or any act require or authorise it (see RSC Order 5, rule 5). This will generally be for specialist or procedural matters. A motion would be used for a variety of applications under the Companies Acts (RSC Order 8). It would also be used to apply for a committal for contempt (RSC Order 52, rule 1), to apply for judicial review (RSC Order 53, rule 1), and also in connection with various other types of appeals by way of case stated (RSC Order 56, rule 8), from some tribunals (RSC Order 94, rule 9) and from an arbitration (RSC Order 73, rule 2).

A petition is to be used if the rules of court or any Act require or authorise it (RSC Order 5, rule 5). The most well-known use is of course to apply for a divorce, but it is also used to seek an order winding up a company, or to seek an order of bankruptcy.

In many cases there will be no choice between these four, as one of them must be used in the case in question. If there is a choice the answer may still be fairly obvious because a particular type of draft is normally used in practice, or a particular type of draft is clearly right on the facts. Occasionally there will be a real choice and the plaintiff can then decide which type of action he would prefer. In any event if a wrong choice is made it cannot prove fatal to the action, as a court cannot now wholly set aside proceedings, a writ or an originating summons on the ground that the proceedings are required by the rules of court to be begun by some other type of originating process. What may well happen is that the case will proceed as if it had been begun by the correct type of originating process, though there may be some penalty to the plaintiff in costs, and delay.

As a general guide for making a choice the first point is that if the case is like one in which a particular form should be used, then that one will probably be appropriate. Secondly, if there is any substantial dispute of fact or witnesses are likely to be needed in court then a writ will normally be more appropriate. The motion and the petition are used in particular circumstances, so the choice will generally be between a writ and an originating summons. Lastly there may well be strategic points involved if there is a real choice, for example the originating summons action does not have the wide possibilities for discovery, interrogatories etc. that the writ action does.

The writ will normally be appropriate for almost all tort actions and most contract actions, and it will also be appropriate for trust actions where there is a dispute over what someone has done, for example where a trustee is sued for breach of trust. The originating summons is appropriate where the plaintiff wishes the court to interpret the meaning of a document, or possibly of a series of actions, and will usually be used to decide the meaning of a will or trust document.

Principles of pleading

It is important to remember always that the basic purpose of pleading is to summarise a case and define the issues in it. This is to help the parties in the preparation of their case, and to help the judge to see immediately what the case is about. Good pleading helps the party drafting the pleading to clarify their own case, helps the party receiving the pleading to know what case they have to meet, and should help to keep costs down. Good pleading will also make a good impression on a judge, and one can only agree with Megarry V.C. in the case of *Re Brickman's Settlement* [1982] 1 All ER 336 in saying 'brevity, clarity and simplicity are the hallmarks of the skilled pleader'.

Many general principles will apply to most types of drafting. A preliminary decision will always have to be what should go into the draft, and this is something a young lawyer often finds difficult to distinguish. A legal opinion or conference must cover everything that has any relevance to the client's case, but the pleading must only contain the basic elements of the case that is being brought to court. Where it is quite clear at an early stage what the case will be, and that only a fairly straightforward draft will be needed then it can be done straight away, but normally it is advisable for the lawyer to do any necessary background work and write his opinion before he begins to draft. Only then will his views be clear in his own mind so that he can refine the case into the form needed for a draft.

An opinion should deal with every possible cause of action open to the client, but it should reach a conclusion as to which is the best cause of action to follow, and this is all that should go into the draft. It is important that everything that is in the draft should come from the opinion, and if necessary be explained by it. The two will go back to the solicitor and client together, and should make sense together. If there is anything unusual in the draft, it should be explained in the opinion; if anything has been left out of the draft this should be explained in the opinion or in a note at the end of the draft, although these explanations should not be long.

In an opinion a barrister may well make assumptions, or theorise on a possible fact to develop his arguments and see what further information may be needed, but a draft must only be based on known facts from instructions. This is the only proper way to draft, not least because it is dangerous to put something on record in a draft that has not been checked as there is a danger that a different version of things may come out at trial. Problems can usually be checked by telephoning the solicitor. The alternative is leaving a gap in the draft for the solicitor to fill in, but there can be a risk in this if the solicitor misunderstands what he should do and fills in the gap wrongly. As the barrister signs the pleading he is responsible for it, so he should be wary of leaving blanks unless their purpose is clear.

There is one special rule in the case of fraud. As a matter of professional conduct, an allegation of fraud should never be made in a civil case lightly, because it is a quasi-criminal allegation. Firstly the lawyer should be sure in his own mind that he does have sufficient evidence to justify the making of an allegation of fraud, that is a prima facie case. Secondly, the barrister must consult the solicitor and the client and should only make an allegation of fraud if they agree (there may be a penalty in costs if the allegation is made and does not succeed). The lawyer can certainly advise the client on the possibility of fraud and seek evidence, but the allegation should not actually be made in the pleading without these steps being taken.

As to deciding which cause or causes of action to plead, it is generally possible to have any number of causes of action in the same pleading, with some sensible limits. Obviously criminal and civil allegations cannot be made in the same pleading but will have to initiate separate actions. Otherwise any causes of action which can be put in the same pleading, e.g. every type of case that can be begun by writ can be put in the same pleading. Thus it is quite possible to have claims in tort, contract and trust in the same pleading, either cumulatively or in the alternative.

However there is a reasonable limitation in that the cases pleaded can only be joined in the same action if the plaintiff claims and the defendant is alleged to be liable in the same capacity in all of them, or if the plaintiff claims and the defendant is alleged to be liable as executor or administrator of an estate in one and in a personal capacity with respect to the estate in the other. Alternatively the causes of action can be joined with the leave of the court, which can be obtained by an ex parte application supported by an affidavit made before the writ of originating application is issued (see RSC Order 15, rule 1).

Provisions of the Rules of Court

There are relatively few Rules of Court relating to the details of pleading, but those rules that there are form the basic regulations of pleading, and the young lawyer should make himself familiar with them. However, only a fundamental failure to comply with the rules can be fatal to a case, as one of the underlying principles in the modern system of pleading is that more minor defects should be dealt with by amendment, or if necessary by setting aside the pleading. This comes from RSC Order 2, rule 1, which provides that if at any stage in the proceedings something is done or left undone so that there is a failure to comply with the rules, that failure will be treated as an irregularity and shall not nullify the proceedings, any step in them, or any document. If there is a failure to comply with the rules then the court can set aside all or part of the proceedings or any step in them or any document on such terms as to costs or otherwise as the court thinks just, or the court may allow amendments or make an order dealing with the proceedings generally as it thinks fit.

If a party does wish to complain of a failure of the other side to comply with the rules they should apply within a reasonable time of the defect and before the next step has been taken in the proceedings.

Then there are more specific rules:

Order 18, rule 6. The form of a pleading.

(a) Every pleading in an action must bear on its face:

(i) The year in which the writ in the action was issued and the letter and number of the action,

(ii) The title of the action,

(iii) The division of the High Court to which the action is assigned and the name of the judge (if any) to whom it is assigned,

(iv) The description of the pleading, and

(v) The date on which it was served.

(b) Every pleading must, if necessary, be divided into paragraphs numbered consecutively, each allegation being so far as convenient contained in a separate paragraph.

(c) Dates, sums and other numbers must be expressed in a pleading in figures and not in words.

(d) Every pleading of a party must be indorsed:

(i) Where the party sues or defends in person, with his name and address;

(ii) In any other case, with the name or firm and business address of the solicitor by whom it was served and also (if the solicitor is the agent of another) the name or firm and business address of his principal.

(e) Every pleading of a party must be signed by counsel, if settled by him, and, if not, by the party's solicitor or by the party, if he sues or defends in person. Paragraphs (a) and (d) are formalities, and will be dealt with later. Paragraphs (b) and (c) are matters of style and will be dealt with in more detail later in this chapter. As for signing a pleading, this must be done by the person who settles it, as specified, and the person signing is responsible for everything in the pleading. An originating summons should not be signed as it is not technically a pleading, but in practice the person who did settle it should acknowledge it as his work, which is normally done by the barrister informally signing the end of the draft, in a place different from the formal signature, or the backsheet.

Order 18, rule 7. This sets out generally what should be pleaded.

(a) Subject to the provisions of this rule, and rules 7A, 10, 11 and 12, every pleading must contain, and contain only, a statement in summary form of the material facts on which the party pleading relies for his claim or defence, as the case may be, but not the evidence by which those facts are to be proved, and the statement must be as brief as the nature of the case permits.

(b) Without prejudice to the previous paragraph, the effect of any document or the purport of any conversation referred to in the pleading must, if material, be briefly stated, and the precise words of the document or conversation shall not be stated, except in so far as those words are themselves material.

(c) A party need not plead any fact if it is presumed by law to be true or the burden of disproving it lies on the other party, unless the other party has specifically denied it in his pleading.

(d) A statement that a thing has been done or that an event has occurred, being a thing or event the doing or occurrence of which, as the case may be, constitutes a condition precedent necessary for the case of a party is to be implied in his pleading.

The basic wording of the first paragraph should be learned by heart by every young lawyer before he does his first draft. The rules listed as exceptions deal with pleading convictions, the rule preventing departure from a previous pleading, the rule that points of law may be pleaded, and the rule listing the cases in which particulars should be pleaded. All the paragraphs in this rule will be elaborated on later.

Order 18, rule 9. This allows no time limit on what may be pleaded.

Subject to rules 7(1), 10 and 15(2), a party may in any pleading plead any matter which has arisen at any time, whether before or since the issue of the writ.

Obviously the cause of action itself must have arisen before the initial pleading can be issued. This rule merely allows facts happening at any time to be included, which is particularly useful for later pleadings. The exceptions are the rule that only material facts should be pleaded, the rule preventing departure from a previous pleading and the rule that a statement of claim cannot depart from the allegations in the writ.

Order 18, rule 10. The rule against departure.

(a) A party shall not in any pleading make an allegation of fact, or raise any new ground or claim, inconsistent with a previous pleading of his.

(b) The first paragraph shall not be taken as prejudicing the right of a party to amend, or apply for leave to amend, his previous pleading so as to plead the allegations or claims in the alternative.

This is a simple rule which makes sense. If a party can contradict himself he will confuse the case. If you do for some good reason wish to plead more than one possibility (having weighed up whether it will strengthen or weaken your case to do so), then you must do it clearly in the alternative.

Order 18, rule 11. Law may be pleaded.

A party may by his pleading raise any point of law.

Note the 'may'. As a general rule you do not need to put legal principles into a draft, as the judge is presumed to know the law. The legal basis of a case is argued by the lawyer in court, and not in the pleading which is there to summarise the facts. The point is that you may plead law when there is some special reason to do so, as where for example there is a statutory defence or exception to be dealt with, or there is a particularly unusual point of law.

Order 18, rule 12. This deals with what particulars need to be pleaded.

(a) Subject to the following paragraph, every pleading must contain the necessary particulars of any claim, defence or other matter pleaded including, without prejudice to the generality of the foregoing words:

(i) Particulars of any misrepresentation, fraud, breach of trust, wilful default or undue influence on which the party pleading relies; and

(ii) Where a party pleading alleges any condition of the mind of any person, whether any disorder or disability of mind or any malice, fraudulent intention or other condition of mind except knowledge, particulars of the facts on which the party relies.

(b) Where it is necessary to give particulars of debt, expenses or damages and those particulars exceed three folios, they must be set out in a separate document referred to in the pleading and the pleading must state whether the document has already been served and, if so, when, or is to be served with the pleading.

Note that this is subject to the principal that the draft should be limited to the material facts, so that detailed particulars should not normally be given, but only if there is good reason (as a matter of policy it is normally better not to plead particulars unless you have to as it gives away part of your case, and you are tied to the pleadings in court). The rule itself lists the areas in which particulars must be given, but in practice particulars are normally given of any general allegation such as negligence, or the damages that have been suffered. If an allegation is general the other side must be given sufficient particulars to know the case that they have to meet.

These are the general rules of pleading. There are also some more special rules for things that should be pleaded in particular types of cases which come from the Rules of Court and from statutes, and these will be dealt with later.

General principles of drafting

These principles have their origin in the rules of court, but they are also principles of practice which although they are not specifically enforceable have grown up over the years. The young lawyer learning a style of drafting only has to comply with the rules of court, but in practice he will usually be strongly influenced by the more experienced lawyers he works with. This is a good method of learning drafting, but the system does have faults, in that lawyers will pass on their weaknesses as well as their strengths. The young lawyer should be wary of this and try to avoid picking up bad habits. If he is told to do something in a certain way he should ask himself if there is a reasonably good reason for doing this, and if there is all well and good. If there is not he should try to find a chance to ask an older lawyer why it is done that way. If there is no good answer it may just be that way that one lawyer after another has done it without one of them bothering to ask why, and it may not be a good way of doing things! The young lawyer should not of course make a nuisance of himself asking questions, nor always expect a detailed reason for each drafting point as there are so few rules and so many styles, but he should have an open mind and ask questions.

The most fundamental principles come from the Rules of Court already outlined.

(a) *Only material facts should be pleaded.*

This comes straight from RSC Order 18, rule 7, that a pleading should be a statement in summary form of the material facts. The whole point of any pleading, especially a statement of claim, is to set out the story as clearly and concisely as possible. A good exercise for a young lawyer starting to learn to draft is to take a postcard and write on that in brief numbered sentences what happend, for example:

1. The plaintiff bought a car from the defendant.
2. It broke down one week later.
3. It cost £600 to have it repaired.

This is the skeleton of a pleading, and even the most complicated case can be dealt with in this way, there are just more sentences and more details to be added.

This approach needs to be modified slightly for later pleadings, but the basic idea is still the same. For example, when drafting a defence, many of the facts have already been pleaded by the plaintiff so that the defendant needs only to fill in the gaps or modify the facts to give his own version, but this will be dealt with later.

The sentences telling the story should be just the main elements. They do not normally need to include things which are only vaguely relevant or which are just a matter of surrounding circumstances, nor do they normally need to include something that the other side may argue—you are telling your own story.

The main difficulty when learning how to plead is to decide what is and what is not a material fact. The test is whether the fact is directly connected with and essential to the case to be argued in court and which must be proved. A simple test for this is to write down the type of case it is and the elements that you need to prove for that type of case, for example:

Misrepresentation

(i) The defendant made a misrepresentation to the plaintiff.
(ii) As a result, the plaintiff made a contract with the defendant.
(iii) The misrepresentation turned out to be untrue.
(iv) As a result the plaintiff suffered damage.

Negligence

(i) There was a duty of care between the plaintiff and the defendant.
(ii) While the duty of care was operative the plaintiff was injured.
(iii) This injury was caused by the negligence of the defendant.
(iv) As a result of the negligence the plaintiff suffered loss and damage.

(b) *All the material facts should be pleaded*

Principle (a) gives the basic skeleton of what should be pleaded, but it is only in the simplest cases that this kind of skeleton will be sufficient pleading, and appropriate further details should be added. One of the most important skills of pleading is deciding which details are necessary and which are not. A basic guide is that the point of a pleading is to set out the essential case of the party for the other side, and to clarify the issues between the parties. An obvious sort of detail that will be needed for this purpose is clear identification of dates, places and exact people involved, as far as they are known and as far as they are relevant to the action.

More generally, details will be needed where they are specifically relevant to a factual or legal issue in a particular case. This does not mean that something should go in because it has a vague link with the case—this kind of sloppiness is one of the main signs of bad pleading—but means that a decision must be made whether a point really is specifically and directly a part of the case so that it should be pleaded, or is just general background information that should not. As examples, it would be necessary to plead that one person was the agent of another, or that a person had authority for a particular action, or that someone was acting in the course of their employment, or that someone had fulfilled a condition giving rise to a right.

Deciding what are material facts that need to be pleaded is not only an important part of good pleading, it can also be a vital part of the tactics in the case that the good lawyer will use. An argument for putting things in is that if you do not plead something you will not be able to give evidence on it at trial, unless the judge gives leave, as you will take the other side by surprise, and they may not have time to prepare to rebut the point. In an extreme case this may result in losing the case, or not getting all the remedies you hope for. Equally, if something is not pleaded, it cannot be raised on appeal.

However, it is equally important not to plead more than one has to. Although the other side need to know your basic case, you do not want to give away more than you have to before trial or you will just give them the chance to prepare their case more thoroughly. In addition, once a point has been put in the pleading, the party will be tied to it at trial, so it is better not to put too much detail in so as to leave freedom to adapt arguments depending on how things go at trial.

There is therefore a fine and important balance between what facts are material and must be pleaded and what can and should be left out. Sometimes the answer as to whether something should go in or not is clear, sometimes not, and different lawyers would have a different approach. This is where style and technique in drafting and in bringing cases comes in. It is not necessarily a matter of right and wrong but of good and better.

One area where extra detail may be needed is where a general allegation needs to have particulars given. This applies where the plaintiff makes an allegation and the immediate reaction of the defendant will be to ask 'How?' or 'Why?' or 'How much?', which is most likely to arise where there is an allegation of negligence or of damage suffered, or of knowledge of a particular fact. If particulars are needed they can just be pleaded as part of a paragraph, but the common practice is to give a sub-heading of 'Particulars', or 'Particulars of Negligence' or 'Particulars of Damage' and list the details under that, which is usually the clearest way.

Again it is a matter of technique to decide when particulars should be given. They will be needed for negligence, damage, and an allegation that a person was in a particular state of mind, but beyond that the decision may be tactical, and one can only say that particulars should be given where the other side will certainly apply for further and better particulars if a pleading or draft is sent out as it is. In *Selangor United Rubber Estates* v *Cradock* [1965] 1 Ch 896 it was said that if there was an allegation of a breach of a duty arising from a confidential or trust relationship, particulars of that relationship should be given. In *Cannock Chase District Council* v *Kelly* [1978] 1 All ER 152 there was an allegation that the Council had acted in bad faith, and it was held that particulars of the breach of faith or abuse of power should be given. As a further example, in *Fox* v *H. Wood (Harrow)* [1963] 2 QB 601 the plaintiff was injured at work in putting his foot through the floorboards, but his employers denied liability. It was held that where it was alleged that a party ought to have known something, particulars of the circumstances from which that knowledge was said to have arisen should be given.

(c) *Plead facts not law*

The point of the pleading of each party is to set out the facts and allegations from his point of view, not to set out the law and the parties' legal arguments. The court is presumed to know the law, and the other side can have lawyers to explain the law. Therefore no pleading will normally need to contain any legal argument or to draw any legal conclusions. At trial it will always be possible for a party to raise any legal arguments that he likes from his pleading, *Re Vandervells Trusts (No 2)* [1974] Ch 269. In *Drane* v *Evangelou* [1978] 2 All ER 437 the plaintiff's pleading contained all the facts necessary to establish a case of trespass and it was held that he could therefore succeed in trespass even though that was not what he had actually sued for. The lawyer will of course explain the legal arguments to the client in his opinion or in conference, and research them for the trial, but legal principle does not normally need to go into the drafting.

There are some exceptions. When asking the court to act under a power that it has only because of a specific statutory section and not for any other reason, the statute should be pleaded. But note that this is a limited exception; a statute does not need to be mentioned merely because it is relevant, but only where it is the exclusive authority for the court to act. For example, the Trustee Act 1925 confers some specific powers on the court to make orders in connection with the administration of a trust, and it should therefore be mentioned when asking the court to act under those powers, see *Re Gonin* [1979] 1 Ch 16. If a statute merely modifies, extends or clarifies a legal principle, remedy or defence, it is not necessary to mention the statute itself, though all the elements required by the statute should be pleaded. For example, it is not necessary to plead the Misrepresentation Act 1967, but only the elements needed to establish a case of misrepresentation. Another small exception is that it is necessary to plead private Acts of Parliament where relevant, or to plead any appropriate point of foreign law. In *Ascherberg, Hopwood & Crew* v *Casa Musicale SNC* [1971] 1 WLR 173 there was an action regarding the copyright to two Italian operas, and it was held that the relevant Italian law should be pleaded.

Lastly, the rule is that it is not necessary to plead law rather than that it is wrong to plead law, so that although it would generally be bad pleading to put law in, there are some circumstances in which it would be justified. For example, if there is a point of law that may dispose of the whole case there may be good reason to plead it, to stop proceedings dragging on, see *Independent Automatic Sales* v *Knowles & Forster* [1962] 3 All ER 27. Alternatively, instructing solicitors can contact the other side informally to bring the point of law to their attention in the hope that they will withdraw the case, or at least negotiate.

(d) *Plead facts not evidence*

The pleading is there to set out the basic points of the case. It is not necessary to prove the case until it comes to court, and there is therefore no need to plead evidence. As with law, this is something that the lawyer will need to advise about in detail in an opinion or in conference, but it is not something that will need to go into the pleading to alert the other side to the evidence that you have. However, the relationship between the facts in the case and the evidence that will prove them is of necessity quite close, so again this is an area where some things are right or wrong, but where many are a matter of style or technique.

One point is that although evidence should not be pleaded, it will be necessary to prove every point at trial. Therefore, although the evidence itself does not go into the pleading, the lawyer should only plead a point which he feels he can prove, or at least will be able to prove when the case comes on for trial. The young lawyer should get used to considering what evidence he does have or will need for each point he pleads.

It can also be difficult, especially for the young lawyer, to distinguish between facts and evidence. One can only say that the ability to distinguish should come with time and practice, and that essentially the facts are the story of what happened, whereas the evidence is how you show the story was true. For example, 'a contract was made' is an allegation of fact, whereas the evidence is the written document on which it was set down, or the oral evidence of a party to the contract or a witness of what was said. Where something does rely on oral evidence, there may be no real distinction between fact and evidence at all. If a party to the action is a main witness then what he says is the allegation of fact, and the evidence by which it will be proved in court, so evidence will effectively be pleaded, because there is no choice. As with law, the rule is really that evidence should not be pleaded, rather than that it must never be pleaded, so there is no objection to this.

Again there is the point of strategy, that one does not want the other side to know more of one's case than is strictly necessary before trial. Therefore it is normally in the party's own interests not to plead evidence. On the other hand, some evidence, such as the existence of some written documents or some witnesses will be obvious from the pleading, and there is no harm in this. Perhaps the best way to summarise this rule is to say that generally evidence should not be pleaded, but that it is sometimes unavoidable, and that one should not get too worried about trying to make a complete distinction between fact and evidence, as sometimes the two are the same.

(e) *Plead facts not arguments*

A clear pleading is a series of statements that is not cluttered up with explanations and theories. The lawyer explains his arguments and conclusions to the client, and will put them into his speeches in court, but they have no place in the pleading, where they may confuse the issue and give the other side advance warning of arguments that they are not entitled to have. In telling a story to a child you might say that Kermit the Frog agreed to give Miss Piggy a diamond necklace, but Fozzie Bear persuaded him not too, but you would not go into great details of motivations and possibilities or the complexities will make the story incomprehensible. It is the same with pleading, that it is basic statements that are important rather than too many ifs and buts.

This does not mean that it is never necessary to give details, as there are areas where particulars must be given to make the situation clear, such as where an accident is alleged to have been caused by negligence. Where particulars are needed they should be pleaded as part of the case so that the other side will know the allegations against them and can prepare to deal with them. What one should not do is go beyond the facts to tie oneself down to a line of argument or a particular conclusion, as the purpose of the pleading is just to set out the facts.

(f) *Plead clearly and logically*

This should be an obvious rule. It should be possible to read through a pleading once, fairly quickly, and find out exactly what the case is about. This is the whole point of the pleading for the other side and for the judge. In fact it is worrying how often a pleading, even by an experienced lawyer, leaves you feeling in need of a strong cup of coffee before you go back and try to work out what it is all about.

The best approach to being clear and logical is to go back to RSC Order 18, rule 6, that a pleading must if necessary be divided into numbered paragraphs, and that each allegation should as far as possible be put into a separate paragraph. This goes back to the skeleton of a pleading discussed above, that you should begin by setting out briefly and in separate sentences the elements that you need for your case. Each of these separate points should then be expanded into a single paragraph, and this should be done strictly. Allegations that a representation was made, that it led to a contract, that it was false, and that damage resulted must have a separate paragraph each. If you are alleging more than one cause of action, either cumulatively or in the alternative, then each cause of action must also be in a separate paragraph. For example if you are alleging breach of contract as an alternative to misrepresentation, the allegation of breach must have a new paragraph for itself. Note also that if you are alleging that a contract was breached in more than one way, you should have a separate paragraph for each breach, as they are separate causes of action.

Usually the best way to be logical is to be chronological, that is that you set out what happened in the order in which it happened, but there is no rule to this effect, and there may be reasons for not following a strict time sequence, for example something relevant to the measure of damage may have happened at an early stage, but should go towards the end of the pleading when the damage suffered is dealt with.

(g) *Plead briefly*

This is the last and the least important of the principles. The words that you use in a pleading are very much a matter of personal style. However, while developing a style, it is good training to learn to draft as briefly as you reasonably can. An overall test of whether a particular allegation or a particular word is really needed, and what its purpose is will help in developing clarity, and in applying all the above principles. One would not wish to overstress this principle—there will generally be more problems in leaving something out so that you have to provide particulars or you are prevented from arguing it in court than there will be from putting something in, when at worst you have told the other side more than you need to or tied yourself down more than you should have.

Informal points of pleading

As well as these general principles of pleading, there are various other points that it may be useful to bear in mind. Firstly a couple of tests for the young lawyer learning how to plead. When you have drafted a pleading it is a good idea to leave it for a little while, if possible, and then go back to it when the mind is fresh and reread it, without any futher work on the case, just to see if the pleading on its own makes sense and says all the things that it should say. This is a good test to see whether points have been set out well and clearly. The second test is to read the pleading a second time (again after putting it aside for a little while if possible) pretending that you are representing the other side. The point is that the other side getting the pleading will have no other background information to go with the pleading, and therefore the pleading must make complete sense in its own right. Also of course the other side will be reading the pleading with a critical eye to see what information it gives them and what it does not. If an element of the case has not been pleaded it should be spotted, and if the other side may need to ask for particulars of a certain point this should be clear, and particulars may need to be added.

On the other hand, there are many tactical points in pleading and for example, one may choose not to give too many particulars, but may rather leave it to the other side to seek particulars if they wish to. You should of course give a little detail where particulars are needed or the pleading will clearly be insufficient, but you may get away with giving a little detail rather than full details. On the other hand there may be advantages in giving very full particulars, especially when giving particulars of negligence or damage, because you are then setting out formally how bad the other side is, which may well make your case look more impressive.

Another informal rule is never to anticipate too much—never leap a fence before you have to, or you may ultimately do yourself a disservice. When you read a brief you should try to anticipate what the other side may argue against you to see what the weaknesses in your case may be, but you should rarely do this in drafting. You may think of possible arguments for the other side that they do not think of themselves, so do not alert them to anything. Each pleading will usually only need to deal with facts as you allege they are at the time of the pleading, and anything raised by a pleading of the other side, and does not need to go outside that. There are only minor exceptions to this, where for example it is clear on the face of the pleading that the limitation period should have expired and the pleading should include the reason why the action should not be defeated.

Another general point that should help to create the right frame of mind for pleading is to think positively. That is that you should always put every allegation in the most favourable way from your client's point of view, which may well involve a careful choice of words. You should not overstate the case as this may well antagonise the other side, and you may have problems proving what you say at trial, but you should always try to put your client's case in the best possible way. There is a second element to thinking positively, which is that you should always try to build the pleading as far as possible on positive allegations rather than negative ones (though this will not apply so much to a defence). Negative allegations should not normally be needed, they may sometimes be confusing (especially where a pleading contains a double negative), and a negative allegation is much more difficult to prove.

A problem that will inevitably arise quite often is that the lawyer just does not have sufficient details to draft as he would like. He should try to avoid this by always collecting as much information as he can from the solicitor and client before starting to draft, by conference or telephone, but sometimes the situation is unavoidable. It may be that some information is not readily available from any source, or, especially in relation to damages, it is something that is not yet known, or that there is some good reason for issuing the pleading as soon as possible without waiting for certain information. There are not many good reasons for issuing a pleading in a rush if everyone works efficiently, but occasionally it may be that a time limit is about to expire and something does have to be done quickly.

If for any of these reasons all the information is not available for a draft, (but presuming of course that you do have enough information to sue), then the usual option is to draft wide, that is to draft in very general terms. As simple examples, if you do not know the date on which something happened you can say it was 'on or about' a certain date, or between one date and another. On a bigger scale, if you do not know exactly where an accident happened you can give a vague location, or if you do not know how an accident happened you can give the type of possible cause. However, the good pleader will only plead wide in this way if there is a real need to.

There are other lesser points of pleading style. The lawyer should always keep an open eye for good points, and remember them. One rare tactical point is that pleading can sometimes shift the burden of proof at trial, and therefore the right to begin at trial. In *Hunt & Winterbotham* v *British Road Services (Parcels)* [1962] 1 QB 617 the plaintiff claimed damages for parcels lost by the defendant. The defendant admitted the loss, but sought to rely on a term of contract that merely limited the damages payable. It was held on the facts that the burden of proof did not pass from the plaintiffs, though on slightly different facts it might have done.

The last general point on drafting is a fairly obvious one—one should always make every effort to get the draft as right as possible the first time. There is sometimes a tendency to think that you could always amend it later, or that you will leave it to the other side to apply for particulars. But unless there is a good reason for doing this, it is not only the mark of a bad pleader, but also irresponsible, as someone will end up having to pay for the extra paperwork, be it the client or the legal aid fund, and sometimes you may not get round to doing the amending and may lose the case. Also do not let familiarity weaken your attention to detail. If you do get used to doing pleadings in a particular type of work it can get easy just to do one like you have done before with little in the way of original thought, but this can lead to mistakes, and every case should have the right draft.

Wording and style

There is no magic in drafting with long words, antiquated phrases or bad grammar, though the young lawyer will sometimes get this impression from some of the drafting examples that he sees, and he must be careful not to pick it up. There is sometimes good justification for complicated constructions and special words, but they should only be used where there is good cause. Sometimes special legal terminology is needed, sometimes a phrase does have a particular legal meaning or is useful in a particular context, sometimes one has to deal with a very complicated situation or with a variety of conditions and exceptions, but the days of the incomprehensible and obscure legal document are now past.

The primary objective of drafting is to clearly communicate a case, and this should never be lost sight of. Some young lawyers do seem to be a little over-awed by the concept of pleading, but as long as they ensure that what they write contains the right elements, makes sense and is relatively easy to read they can refine their skills with experience to deal with more complicated cases. Some students learning to draft will get lost in sub-clauses and write sentences that do not even have verbs, and this is clearly to be avoided!

To get the feel of the style and wording to use, the young lawyer should try to read as many examples of different types of drafting as he can to become familiar with the sort of language that is appropriate, whether it is in precedent books or documents in cases that he comes across while in pupillage or in articles. He should read to learn, that is not just rushing through, but working out what elements there are in the draft, why they are there and how they are expressed. To some extent he should also read critically, to see if there might be a better or clearer way of dealing with something.

The language used should be ordinary English. Do not use a long word for the sake of it, but do not avoid using a long word where it is appropriate. Find the right word rather than the vague or impressive one. Do not use a complex tense for a verb when it is not needed, but do not use a simple tense where that is not really accurate. Colloquial expressions must be avoided, and so must abbreviations. They may be appropriate in an opinion, but they are out of place in a legal draft. Contrary to old practice, all dates, sums and other numbers in a pleading should be expressed in figures and not in words (RSC Order 18, rule 6). (This is not necessarily the case for documents other than pleadings, such as conveyances). For example, a sum of money should be '£10,000' and a date should be '10th June 1984', though there are still some variations on how a date is expressed, and you do sometimes still see 'the 10th day of June 1984'. It is important that the phraseology in a pleading should be consistent for the sake of clarity, even though it may make it more boring to read. For example, once you have referred to a document in a particular way you should not change the word you use. If you refer to a lease, you should not later refer to it as 'the contract', 'the agreement' or anything else, but always call it 'the lease'. In particular, the plaintiff in an action should be referred to throughout as 'the plaintiff' and should not in the body of the draft be referred to by name or in any other way, and the defendant should always be referred to as 'the defendant'. A person referred to in the pleading who is not a party should normally be called by their full name, e.g. 'John Smith' or 'John James Arbuthnot'.

Any references should be clear. For example it is often better to give someone's name again rather than just say he or she if there is any possibility of confusion as to who you are referring to. If something has a long title it may be useful to refer back to it as 'the said . . .', for example if the pleading refers to 'the property situated at 2, Railway Cottages, Romford, Essex' it is much quicker if referring to it again to say 'the said property' rather than give the full address again. However, do not overdo it. If there are two properties you cannot say 'the said property' or there may be confusion, you need to distinguish the two clearly. Also you sometimes see pleadings peppered with 'the said this' and 'the said that' without any reason, which should be avoided.

There are some occasions on which it is vital to be careful about the words in the drafting. A document or oral statement which is an essential element of a case must be referred to specifically, that is when it was made, who by, and if appropriate, where. Also any particularly vital part of what was written or said should be specifically pleaded. If any clause of a contract, trust, will etc. is vital then it should be set out in full in the appropriate paragraph, but the exact wording should only be set out if it is crucial to a particular issue, such as what is alleged to be a breach, or a claim for an injunction. If the wording is not crucial then it is not needed in the pleading, though the document itself can of course be evidence at the trial.

Actual words spoken may need to be quoted in, for example a defamation action or a misrepresentation action, though in anything other than a defamation action it will usually be enough to give the purport of the words used, for example 'the defendant orally represented to the plaintiff that the car was in perfect condition'.

There are some phrases that are particularly useful in pleading, having been used for a great many years, and having an accepted meaning that fulfils a particular purpose and does give a professional feeling to a pleading where they are used appropriately. The young lawyer should watch out for these types of phrases and remember them, but here are a few fairly common examples:

Further or in the alternative. This is a useful phrase where there are alternatives in a case, be it alternative causes of action, alternative breaches, alternative types of negligence etc. The phrase means that the allegation following it is either in addition to or an alternative to the allegation already made, giving the pleader the option of succeeding with one or the other or both.

As alleged or at all. This phrase is especially useful in a defence where one is denying how or why something happened, in that it can be used as a wide denial of any specific causation particularised by the plaintiff, or any other causation that might make the defendant liable.

If, which is denied. This is again a possibly useful phrase in a defence, that will effectively allow two alternative lines of argument. The first is that you deny an allegation, and the second is that, if it is found to be true, there is a further argument on the facts or the law that the defendant is not liable.

In the premises. This is a phrase to use when drawing a conclusion from allegations that have been made in previous paragraphs.

By reason of the matters aforesaid. An alternative to 'in the premises' with a similar meaning.

At all material times. A phrase to allege that a particular relationship or state of facts continued throughout the period covered by the pleading.

Things which must be pleaded

There are some specific details that must be pleaded by statute or by rules of court. For example, when pleading a claim under the Fatal Accidents Act 1976 it is necessary to plead appropriate details of the dependants, and this is dealt with in the section on tort drafting. It is also necessary to plead details of convictions, or findings of adultery or paternity which the party will wish to use in evidence at the trial, Civil Evidence Act 1968, ss.11, 12 and RSC Order 18, rule 7A. To rely on a conviction it is necessary to plead the actual offence of which the person was convicted, the date of conviction and the court convicting and the issue in the case to which the conviction is relevant. As regards a finding of adultery or paternity, it is necessary to plead the actual finding made, the court that made it, the proceedings in which it was made and the issue in the case to which the finding is relevant. If the other side wishes to deny the conviction, the finding or the relevance of it, they should plead that.

There are some other special areas in which particular things need to be pleaded, and as many of these are very specialist I will only give some examples here. In a mortgage action it is necessary to plead where the property is situated, and if appropriate whether it is a dwelling house and its rateable value, RSC Order 88, rule 3. In a probate action allegations as to interest should be specifically pleaded, as must any allegation that the will was not properly executed, or any reason why it might not be enforceable, RSC Order 76, rule 9. In proceedings against the Crown it is necessary to plead why the Crown is alleged to be liable, and the government department and officers involved, RSC Order 77, rule 3.

Defective pleading

There are a variety of ways in which a party can deal with defects in his own or the other side's pleading. There is also a variety of different types of defects—some will be fundamental because a vital part of the pleading has been left out or there is something basically wrong with the action, some will be important because they could have a real effect on the conduct or outcome of the case, and some will be trivial and unlikely to have any effect on the case.

Every lawyer should check for defects in his own pleading before he sends it out, and also as the case develops should check previous pleadings in the case to see if they are adequate or if they need to be added to or modified. Obviously he should also check every pleading he gets from the other side. If there is any defect, he needs to consider carefully what to do about it. It may be worth doing nothing at all if the defect is a minor one, or if it is a defect in the case of the other side that he may be able to exploit at trial, or if there is no point in doing anything as the expense might not justify what would be achieved.

On the other hand, there are a variety of things that can be done about defective pleading, such as amendment, seeking further and better particulars, or applying to have the pleading struck out, and the appropriate step should be taken if it is justified in the conduct of the case. The details of these steps are dealt with in books on civil procedure, but they will be mentioned in outline here as they are an important part of the development of the pleadings in a case.

Amendment

This is largely covered by RSC Order 20. If reasonable care is taken with the original draft it should not normally be necessary to amend it, but even with careful drafting, amendment may still be needed if new evidence comes to light or if new arguments are developed. Alternatively, it may be that one lawyer takes over a case in which a pleading was drafted by another and he feels the need to modify it. In any event, it is wise to check the pleadings before the case comes to court to ensure that they are in order. A further preliminary point is that you must not only decide what you wish to amend, you must also take care deciding what the amended wording should be, as amending is a positive process that needs as much care as drafting the original pleading.

Generally speaking, in the modern system of pleading, amendment is relatively easy provided that the party seeking it is prepared to pay the costs, and the other side is not prejudiced by the amendment.

The first possibility is in RSC Order 20, rule 1, that in an action begun by writ, the plaintiff may amend the writ once before pleadings are closed without the leave of the court. Unless there is any direction to the contrary, the amended writ must be served on each party. The following things cannot be done under this rule once the writ has been served: adding, omitting or substituting a party, altering the capacity of a party, adding or substituting a new cause of action, or the amending of a statement of claim indorsed on the writ. Thus this rule does not permit major amendments.

The second possibility is in RSC Order 20, rule 3, which is wider in providing that any party may amend any pleading of his once at any time before the pleadings are deemed to be closed without the leave of the court, and that he must then serve the amended pleading on the opposite party. If the statement of claim is amended then the defendant may amend his defence within 14 days, or if the defence is amended the plaintiff may amend his reply within 14 days, otherwise existing pleadings will stand, and similar rules apply to a counterclaim and a defence to counterclaim. If the other side objects to the amendment, they have the right to apply to the court for it to be disallowed, RSC Order 20, rule 4.

The third possibility is in RSC Order 20, rule 5, which provides that at any stage in the proceedings, the court may allow any party to amend a pleading on such terms as to costs or otherwise as may be just, and in such manner as the court may direct. An application for leave should be made by summons to a master. An amendment may be allowed after the expiry of the limitation period in the action if the court thinks just, provided the writ was issued in time. The name of a party may be amended even if the effect is to join a new party provided there was a genuine mistake, and the capacity in which a party sues may be amended. An amendment may also be allowed to add or substitute a new cause of action provided it arises out of the same or substantially the same facts as the original claim.

The above rules apply to writs and actions begun by writs. However, RSC Order 20, rule 5, allowing amendment at any stage with leave also applies to originating summons, a petition or an originating notice of motion. There is also a general power in RSC Order 20, rule 8 for the court to order the amendment of any document at any stage in the proceedings, on such terms as to costs or otherwise as may be just, where this is necessary to determine the real question in controversy between the parties or to correct any defect or error in the proceedings. By RSC Order 12 rule 12, a pleading may be amended by agreement in the Chancery Division at any stage, if the parties agree in writing. Since these rules are wide enough to permit amendment at any stage in the proceedings, it is quite possible to amend even at the hearing itself. But this is obviously to be avoided as the party seeking the amendment will almost inevitably have to pay the costs of it, and he will need leave, which may well not be forthcoming if there is any real prejudice to the other side, or if he is seeking a substantial amendment.

It is virtually impossible to amend to add a party or a cause of action at a late stage, so these must be correct at the beginning. In *Loutfi* v *Czarnikow* [1953] 2 Lloyd's Rep 213 it was said that there must be a strong justification for allowing an amendment at a late stage, though an amendment could be made even late in the trial itself if a pont had come out in the trial in evidence or in argument from counsel. In *J. Leavy & Co.* v *George H. Hirst & Co.* [1944] 1 KB 24 there was an action for breach of contract, and the defendant wished to raise the possibility of frustration at trial. It was held that if they wished to depart from their pleadings in this way they should consider applying to amend their pleadings.

Although the possibilities of amendment are wide, there are limitations where amendment is not possible. For example, although you can plead facts that have arisen since the writ, you cannot amend so as to add a totally new cause of action that has arisen since the writ, *Eshelby* v *Federated European Bank* [1932] 1 KB 254 (though you may of course begin a new action and if appropriate apply to have the two consolidated). Also you cannot amend a pleading after a hearing at first instance so as to raise a new cause of action on appeal. In *Williams* v *Home Office (No. 2)* [1982] 2 All ER 564 the plaintiff brought an action for false imprisonment in that he had been kept in a control unit in prison. He lost, and on appeal sought leave to amend to allege breach of statutory duty, but it was held that this was not possible, and these matters should have been pleaded for the original trial.

The way to amend a pleading, having got leave if necessary, is to use red ink to delete any words that have been removed and to write in any words to be added. If the pleading is amended more than once then a different colour ink should be used for each set of amendments. Also the pleading should be indorsed with a statement that it has been amended, stating the date on which it was amended, and the name of the judge, master or registrar who gave leave for the amendment, or if no leave was given, the rule under which the amendment was made. If the amendments are so numerous or lengthy that they would make the document difficult to read then a fresh document should be prepared and if necessary re-issued, RSC Order 20, rule 10.

Further and better particulars

Whilst you will normally be seeking amendment to deal with a defect in your own pleading, you may seek further and better particulars to remedy a defect in your opponent's pleading. You should not seek particulars just because the pleading from the other side has been drafted badly—that is their problem—but only if you need to know something that the pleading does not tell you. The point of further and better particulars is to help in the defence against allegations, not to cure bad drafting. There may well be tactical points in deciding whether or not to seek particulars, for example if you seek them it may show the other side that you mean to fight the case tooth and nail, but on the other hand if you seek particulars it may push the other side into preparing their case better.

The type of particulars that should be pleaded were discussed earlier in this chapter. In practice the most common types of particulars are of negligence, damage, breach of duty and the like. Particulars would normally only be needed of a positive allegation. Particulars may be required as to why a particular situation or mental state is alleged to exist. In *Bruce* v *Odhams* [1936] 1 All ER 287 the plaintiff claimed that she had been defamed in an article, and it was held that she should give particulars of why she alleged it referred to her. In *Stapeley* v *Annetts* [1970] 1 WLR 20 a policeman was arrested for theft, but the case against him was dismissed and he brought an action for wrongful imprisonment. It was held that although the burden was on the policeman to prove malice, he was entitled to particulars of why he was thought to be a thief.

However the party is only entitled to be given more details of the allegation against him that should have been in the original pleading. He is not entitled to be told any more than that, and he is not entitled to particulars of evidence, *Re Dependable Upholstery* [1936] 3 All ER 741. The party drafting the original pleading will have considered what amount of detail to include, but it may be that he has given no details at all of a general allegation, or that he has given insufficient detail for the other side to see what the case is that they have to meet. Decisions must be made as to whether to ask for particulars, and what to ask for particulars of. This is bound up with how you wish to conduct your case, and is often a policy decision more than a strictly legal one. It may be better to leave a weak pleading and argue at trial that the case should fail rather than seek particulars and tighten it up. It is only if you feel that you really do need to know more to prepare your own case properly that you should seek particulars.

The way to seek particulars comes from RSC Order 18, rule 12, and the first step should normally be to ask the other side by letter to provide the required particulars, as the court may refuse to order particulars unless there are sufficient reasons for seeking an order from the court first. If the appropriate particulars are not forthcoming then the court may order one party to serve on any other party particulars of any claim, defence or other matter stated in a pleading on such terms as the court thinks just. An order will normally be made before the service of the defence unless an order is desirable to enable the defendant to plead, or there is some other special reason. It may be convenient to wait until the summons for directions when the need for further particulars can be considered, but otherwise an application may be made.

The application for further and better particulars is set out in a formal document, and is answered in a formal way, therefore it is important to consider the wording carefully. (An example of an application and a reply is given.) You should ensure that you ask for exactly the right particulars so that the other side cannot avoid the issue. The particulars sought and the answers given must be set out together in the same document. Since the need to seek particulars normally means that the orignal draft was inadequate, it is the party preparing the original draft that will normally have to pay the costs.

Striking out pleadings

This is clearly the most radical way of attacking a pleading, because either the whole case or the pleading itself is misconceived. As with other matters of pleading, there may be tactical matters to consider. There is normally little point in applying to have a pleading struck out unless you have a really good argument

EXAMPLE 1 BASIC APPLICATION FOR FURTHER AND BETTER PARTICULARS

IN THE HIGH COURT OF JUSTICE 1985.B.No.1234

DIVISION

BETWEEN A. B. *Plaintiff*

and

C. D. *Defendant*

REQUEST FOR FURTHER AND BETTER PARTICULARS OF STATEMENT OF CLAIM

(Raise each point that is not clear in a separate numbered paragraph, making it as clear as possible what details are sought. The following are examples of possible paragraphs that may be adapted for use.)

1. Of '(quote the part of the statement of claim of which particulars are sought)'. State with proper particularity of the alleged , specifying:
   (a) When______
   (b) How______
   (c) In what manner______
2. Of '(quote the part of the statement of claim of which particulars are sought)'.
   (a) Specify______
   (b) Explain______
3. Of the allegation that , give full particulars of stating
4. Of the allegation that , give full details of all facts and matters relied on in support of this allegation.

Served the day of (Signed)
etc.

(As an alternative to numbered paragraphs, each point may be raised as 'Under paragraph 3'
'Under paragraph 4' etc., referring to the paragraphs of the statement of claim.)

EXAMPLE 2 BASIC REPLY TO AN APPLICATION FOR FURTHER AND BETTER PARTICULARS

IN THE HIGH COURT OF JUSTICE 1985.B.No.1234

DIVISION

BETWEEN	A. B.	*Plaintiff*
	and	
	C. D.	*Defendant*

FURTHER AND BETTER PARTICULARS OF THE STATEMENT OF CLAIM SERVED PURSUANT TO A REQUEST DATED __________

1. (Copy the wording of the first request.)
   (Set out the answer to the request, dealing with each separate point raised in order, and giving the correct amount of detail.)
2. (Copy the wording of the second request.)
   (Set out the answer to the request, in the same way as above.)

etc.

Served the day of (Signed)
etc.

as the court is slow to strike out a pleading, so you will only end of up having to pay the costs of a failed application, and warning the other side that they need to draft better. It is a matter of professional courtesy to warn the other side informally before you apply to have their pleading struck out, normally by the barrister who will make the application telephoning the barrister who did the pleading.

An application to strike out should be made under RSC Order 18, rule 19, which provides that the court may at any stage in the proceedings order any pleading or indorsement in the action to be struck out or amended on one of four grounds, and the action may be stayed or dismissed or judgment entered accordingly. This applies to any pleading and also to an originating summons or a petition. The application to strike out should be made as soon as possible after the pleading is served.

The grounds on which an application may be made are firstly that the draft contains no reasonable cause of action or defence as the case may be, which may be a matter of law or fact: for example in *Blackburn* v *Attorney-General* [1971] 1 WLR 1037, there was a claim for a declaration that the signing by the government of the Treaty of Rome was illegal being a surrender of sovereignty, which was struck out as containing no reasonable cause of action. Secondly, the pleading or part of it may be struck out if it is scandalous, frivolous or vexatious. Thirdly, it may be struck out if it may prejudice, embarrass or delay a fair trial of the action, and lastly it may be struck out if it is otherwise an abuse of the process of the court, for example if there is a bad motive in bringing the action.

Note that under the rule the court has a discretion to order that the pleading be amended or the action be stayed, and it is rare for a pleading to be struck out completely; if the case is capable of being argued on the face of the pleading then it should be allowed to continue even if it will almost certainly fail. The court also has an inherent jurisdiction to stay an action which may be used if appropriate. An application to strike out should specify exactly what is alleged to be wrong with the pleading, not just show general dissatisfaction, *Carl Zeiss Stiftung* v *Rayner & Keeler* [1970] 1 Ch 506. In *Wenlock* v *Moloney* [1965] 1 WLR 1238 the plaintiff claimed that the defendants conspired to put him out of business, but the original statement of claim was so vague that a second one had to be issued, which in turn was so bad that the defendant sought further and better particulars and applied to have it struck out. It was held that this would not be done as it was not a matter of looking at the evidence to see if the plaintiff's claim was justified, but just seeing if there was a cause of action in the pleading, which there was. By way of illustration, in *Thorne* v *University of London* [1966] 2 QB 237 the plaintiff was a law student who sued the University of London for negligence in marking his LLB examination papers as a result of which he failed the examination. This was struck out as being frivolous and vexatious because it was a matter of internal university regulation and not for the court. In *Drummond-Jackson* v *British Medical Association* [1970] 1 WLR 688 there was an action for libel over an article in the British Medical Journal, and it was held that this would not be struck out as there was a possibility of defamation, and the test was not whether the action was likely to succeed. In *Commission for Racial Equality* v *Ealing London Borough Council* [1978] 1 All ER 497 there was an action alleging a discriminatory education policy, and it was held that since there was a reasonably arguable case on the pleadings it should not be struck out; the test was only whether it was arguable, not whether it was 'the forensic equivalent of a mouse or a lion'.

Other procedural points connected with pleading

Admissions and denials are a special aspect of pleading, and are dealt with in RSC Order 27. It is of course a basic part of any pleading after the statement of claim that one can admit or deny something alleged by the other side, but there is specific provision for making admissions, as an admission may well limit the matters at issue between the parties so that the matter admitted does not have to be proved in any further way or argued about. In preparing a case, especially with costs in mind, each side should consider whether they can usefully make admissions or seek them from the other side.

The general provision is in RSC Order 27, rule 1, that a party to a case may give notice, by his pleading or otherwise in writing, that he admits the truth of the whole or any part of the case of any other party. Before the case goes to trial the possibility of admissions should be specifically considered, and rule 2 provides that a party may within 21 days of a case being set down for trial serve any other party with a notice requiring him to admit such facts or part of his case as is specified in the notice. Any admission made can only be used in the case in which it was sought by the party who sought it.

If admissions are made, whether by pleadings or otherwise then a party may apply to the court for judgment on the admissions, and the court may give judgment or make such order as it thinks just, RSC Order 27, rule 3. There can only be a judgment on the admissions if the whole case or all the elements of it are admitted, which will of course be quite rare. In *Blundell* v *Rimmer* [1971] 1 All ER 1072 there was an action for negligence in which the defendant admitted negligence but denied the alleged damage, and it was held that there could not be judgment on the admission as the plaintiff could only succeed if he showed that the negligence led to damage. In *Murphy* v *Culhane* [1977] QB 94 the defendant had pleaded guilty to the manslaughter of the plaintiff's husband, and she sued him for damages under the Fatal Accidents Act. The defendant admitted his plea, but denied that he was liable in tort. It was held that the plea could not be decisive in the civil action so there was no judgment on the admission. Lastly, in *Rankine* v *Garton Sons & Co.* [1979] 2 All ER 1185 the plaintiff slipped on glucose spilt at his place of work. In a letter his employers admitted negligence but asked for a medical report before they would settle the action, and again it was held that there could be no judgment on the admission as it was necessary to show not only that there was negligence but that it led to proved or admitted injuries.

One point to bear in mind is that if you do admit a point then it is no longer in issue, so no evidence can be given on it. In *Pioneer Plastic Containers* v *Commissioners of Customs & Excise* [1967] Ch 597 the plaintiffs claimed that some of their plastic products were not liable for purchase tax, the defendants admitted all the facts alleged, but said that in law they were chargeable. It was held that since all the facts were admitted no evidence could be heard. However it is possible to withdraw an admission that has been made with the leave of the court.

Interrogatories

This is another way of dealing with insufficient pleading, which is dealt with in RSC Order 26. You can seek further and better particulars of something raised in your opponent's pleading, or you can use interrogatories if there is no specific allegation in the pleading. A party can apply to the court for an order giving him leave to serve on any other party interrogatories relating to any matter in question between the applicant and that other party in the case. The order, if made, will require the other party to answer the interrogatories on affidavit within the period specified in the order.

The court will only make an order if it considers that the interrogatories are necessary to dispose fairly of the cause or matter or to save costs, and that will take into account any voluntary offer a party makes to make an admission or disclose a document. The test is not merely whether the proposed matter might be admissible, or could be put in a pleading. In *Jones* v *G.D. Searle & Co.* [1978] 3 All ER 654 there was an action for negligence, the plaintiff alleging that she had developed thrombosis having been prescribed a contraceptive pill. It was an issue whether the case was statute barred, and it was held that therefore there could be interrogatories about the legal advice the plaintiff had got earlier, although this would not normally be proper.

It is important to word the interrogatories very carefully to get the information that you want, and a copy of the proposed interrogatories must be served with the application. As with seeking further and better particulars, there are some policy considerations, as seeking interrogatories may well force your opponent to improve his preparation of his case or alert him to something he had not thought of, so it is usually only valuable to seek interrogatories if you really need them to prepare your case properly. The other side has to answer the interrogatories in the form of an affidavit, and this may of course be used in evidence at the trial, RSC Order 26, rule 7, and although it is possible to put in only some of the answers given, the court is entitled to look at them all. An example of an application for interrogatories is given.

A person is entitled to object to answering an interrogatory on the ground of privilege, and his objection should be set out in his answering affidavit, RSC Order 26, rule 4. Otherwise he should give full answers, as he would have to in court, of everything within his knowledge. Interrogatories may be served on a body or company in the same way as on an individual, and the person answering should make all reasonable inquiries within the company to answer the questions, and should put a statement in the affidavit that he has done this, *Stanfield Properties* v *National Westminster Bank* [1983] 2 All ER 244. If any answer given is insufficient then the court may order the party to give a further answer, either by affidavit or an oral examination, RSC Order 26, rule 5. If there is any failure to comply with the original order for interrogatories or with any further order, the court may make such order as it thinks just, and in particular it may order that the action be dismissed, or that the defence be struck out and judgment entered. Alternatively, the party failing to comply may be committed to prison, or his solicitor may be committed to prison if he has failed to give his client notice of the interrogatories without reasonable excuse, RSC Order 26, rule 6.

EXAMPLE 3 BASIC REQUEST FOR INTERROGATORIES

IN THE HIGH COURT OF JUSTICE 1985.B.No.1234

DIVISION

BETWEEN A. B. *Plaintiff*

and

C. D. *Defendant*

INTERROGATORIES

On behalf of the above-named Plaintiff for the examination of the above-named Defendant, delivered pursuant to the order herein dated
(Raise each question in a separate numbered paragraph. Each question must of course relate only to something the party asking for the interrogatory is entitled to know.)

1. Have you ever______ ?
2. Did you______ ?
3. If the answer to the preceding interrogatory is yes, state______

Delivered this______
etc.

Judgment in default of pleading

This is again a final resort in pleading tactics, where your opponent has failed to serve a pleading at all, and is contained in RSC Order 19.

Firstly, if the plaintiff fails to serve a statement of claim within the appropriate time after the issue of the writ the defendant may apply to the court for the action to be dismissed, and the court may dismiss the action, or may make such other order on such terms as it thinks just, RSC Order 19, rule 1.

Secondly, if the plaintiff's claim is for a liquidated sum and the defendant fails to serve a defence within the appropriate period, the plaintiff may seek judgment for a sum not exceeding that which he has claimed, plus costs, RSC Order 19, rule 2. If the plaintiff's claim is for an unliquidated sum he may only get an interlocutory judgment for damages to be assessed and costs, RSC Order 19, rule 3. There are further rules to cover claims for detention of goods, possession of land or mixed claims. It is also possible to apply for judgment in default of a defence to counterclaim, RSC Order 19, rule 8.

Any default judgment made may be set aside or varied on such terms as the court thinks just, RSC Order 19, rule 9, and it must be said that the court will be relatively slow to make an order for judgment in default unless there is very good reason. There is little point usually in giving judgment in default of a statement of claim if the limitation period has not expired, as the plaintiff can just begin a new action. Also, since the strict time limits for serving pleadings are so often ignored in practice there will have to be a substantial delay without any good reason before the court will be prepared to act.

8 *The writ and the statement of claim*

The writ is the most common method of commencing an action in the High Court. There are some cases where the writ is the compulsory way to commence an action, and many more where it may be used. Generally the writ is suitable to commence an action where the parties are in dispute rather than seeking the assistance of the court, especially where there is a substantial dispute of fact, and this will include almost all tort actions, many contract actions and some trust actions. By RSC Order 5, the writ is compulsory where there is a claim in tort (other than for trespass), where there is an allegation of fraud, or where there is a claim in respect of a death, personal injury or damage to property.

This chapter will deal specifically with preparing a writ and a statement of claim, though many of the general points about drafting made in the previous chapter will be relevant. (There are examples of statements of claim in particular actions later in the book.) Although a printed form is normally used for a writ, care should be taken to use it properly, putting in all the necessary information, and crossing out clearly those parts which do not apply in the particular case.

Distinguishing the writ and the statement of claim

The writ is the formal document which must be used to commence the action (RSC Order 6, rule 1) but although it must state the nature of the plaintiff's claim, the full statement of claim does not have to be indorsed on it, but can be a separate document, served at any time before the expiry of 14 days after the defendant gives notice of intention to defend (RSC Order 18, rule 1). This will mean that if it is not indorsed on the writ, the statement of claim should be served within 28 days of the writ's being served.

The technical distinction (though the terms are not actually used in the Rules of Court now) is that the writ may either be 'generally indorsed' with a brief general statement of the sort of case the plaintiff is bringing, or 'specially indorsed' with a full statement of claim (RSC Order 6, rule 2).

As to whether the statement of claim should be indorsed on the writ, the choice is for the plaintiff to make. If it is indorsed on the writ, it will save the costs of a separate document, and since the statement of claim should normally be served within 28 days of the writ, the work of drafting it will have to be done, and it might as well be put on the writ. However in practice a writ may well be issued before the statement of claim is drafted, and there may be good legal reasons for doing this, if for example the limitation period is about to expire. There may also be practical reasons for issuing a writ without a full statement of claim, for example to show the other side that you do intend to pursue the case seriously, especially if negotiations have gone on for some time and you hope to force a settlement.

If there is to be a general indorsement on the writ rather than a full statement of claim, there are no set words to be used, the rule being only that there must be a concise statement of the nature of the claim or the relief or remedy required (RSC Order 6, rule 2). This will generally consist of just a few sentences that give basic details of the type of action and what is claimed. If the claim is for a debt or liquidated demand, there must be a statement of the amount claimed (and that the proceedings will be stayed if that amount is paid to the plaintiff or his solicitor or agent within the time limited for appearing). If the action is for the possession of land there must be a statement of whether the claim relates to a dwelling house and, if it does, its rateable value. If the action is to recover possession of goods there should be a statement of the value of the goods.

A few simple examples of general indorsements are as follows:

(a) 'The plaintiff's claim is for damages for breach of a contract made in writing on 1st January 1985 for the sale of a painting, and for interest thereon'.

(b) 'The plaintiff's claim is for work done and materials supplied by the plaintiff to the defendant in accordance with an oral contract made on 1st February 1985

Particulars

Work done __________

Materials __________

(c) 'The plaintiff's claim is for:

(i) Damages for personal injury and loss caused to the plaintiff by the negligence of the defendant his servants or agents on 3rd January 1985 at 4, Grays Inn Place, London.

(ii) Interest thereon pursuant to s.35A Supreme Court Act 1981.'.

(d) 'The plaintiff's claim is as administratrix of the estate of Tybalt Capulet deceased for:

(i) Damages under the Fatal Accidents Act 1976 for the death of the said deceased caused by the negligence of the defendant in that__________;

(ii) Damages under the Law Reform (Miscellaneous Provisions) Act 1934 for the benefit of the estate of the deceased for the loss caused to the deceased by the negligence of the defendant;

(iii) Interest on the said damages'.

(e) 'The plaintiff's claim is for:

(i) Execution of the trusts of the above-mentioned settlement dated 1st April 1977 and made between Regan Lear and Goneril Lear.

(ii) Such other accounts, inquiries, directions and relief as may be just.

(iii) Costs'.

(f) 'The plaintiff's claim is for:

(i) An inquiry whether any of the funds of the above-mentioned will have been invested by the defendants in unauthorised investments, and if any, and if so what sums have been lost to the estate subject to the trust by reason of the unauthorised investment.

(ii) An account of all moneys due to the said estate by reason of any such loss.

(iii) Payment of the amounts found due on the taking of the said account.

(iv) Further or other relief.

(v) Costs'.

Although the general indorsement is brief, it is part of the pleading in the action, and is legally binding. The statement of claim cannot contain a claim or cause of action which is not mentioned in the writ or does not arise from the facts in it (RSC Order 18, rule 15) though subject to that, the statement of claim may alter, modify or extend any claim made in the writ. Thus the general indorsement should be drafted so that it does not inhibit the statement of claim, and, if the writ has been issued before the statement of claim, the general indorsement on it should be read before the statement of claim is drafted.

A problem is most likely to arise if different lawyers are involved, for example if the solicitor issues the writ before he sends the brief to a barrister for a statement of claim to be drafted, or if for some reason the client changes his lawyers during the case. The lawyer drafting a statement of claim should make sure that there is no existing generally indorsed writ to limit him, though if he is not sent a copy of the writ and no writ is referred to in instructions it is usually safe to assume that no writ has yet been issued. If the general indorsement is wrong or restrictive it is possible to amend it.

To illustrate this point, in *Sterman* v *E.W. & W.J. Moore* [1970] 1 QB 596 the plaintiff issued a writ claiming damages for injury at work but after the end of the limitation period sought to amend it to add claims for negligence and breach of statutory duty. It was held that while amendment might be possible, the original writ should be indorsed with the nature of the claim and the relief sought, and if it was not this could not be remedied by the statement of claim. In *Graff Brothers Estates* v *Rimrose Brook Joint Sewerage Board* [1953] 2 QB 318 the writ claimed damages for the wrongful removal of support, and the statement of claim went on to claim damages for negligence. It was held that this was acceptable as the statement of claim was within the general allegations made in the writ. Finally in the case of *Pontin* v *Wood* [1962] 1 QB 594 it was held that if the writ itself was for some reason a nullity the statement of claim could not cure it, though the statement of claim could possibly remedy a lesser defect.

Drafting the formal parts of a writ

Whether the writ is issued with a general indorsement, or with the full statement of claim indorsed on it, basic decisions must be made in the drafting of the formal parts of the writ. Every writ must be in the form set out in RSC Order 6, rule 1. Although this form is mass produced, proper care should be taken in completing it, to adapt it to the case in hand, filling in blanks and striking out any parts which are not appropriate.

The rules of court specify certain things which must be contained in a writ, and many of these are provided for in the basic form. By RSC Order 6, rule 2 the writ must, before it is issued, be indorsed with the statement of claim or a general indorsement. Other things must be indorsed specifically on the writ, which are dealt with as appropriate below. By RSC Order 6, rule 7 a writ is issued by being sealed by an officer of the Central Office in the High Court in London or at a District Registry. It is necessary to take a copy as well as the original writ and also a form of acknowledgment of service for each defendant. This will normally be done by someone from the solicitor's firm. The staff at the office will normally check to see that the form has been filled in properly, and are helpful in advising if any difficulty arises.

The heading

The heading must follow specifically the form of the prescribed form of writ, and RSC Order 18, rule 6 provides that every pleading must bear on its face the following information:

(a) The year in which the writ in the action was issued and the letter and number of the action.
(b) The title of the action.
(c) The division of the High Court to which the action is assigned and the name of the judge (if any) to whom it is assigned.
(d) The description of the pleading.
(e) The date on which it was served.

The High Court has three Divisions, now governed by the Supreme Court Act 1981, and it is for the person bringing the action to decide which Division to use. Each of the Divisions has equal powers and may grant the same remedies, but certain types of action must or should be brought in a particular Division.

Firstly there is the Queen's Bench Division, which is the largest, and which is appropriate for any type of case which is not specifically assigned to another Division. In particular it is appropriate for most tort and contract actions. The Queen's Bench also has a general supervisory jurisdiction, to deal with judicial review and most types of appeals from lower courts and other bodies, and for applications for habeas corpus. There are also two specialist courts within the Queen's Bench, the Commercial Court and the Admiralty Court.

Secondly there is Chancery Division, used basically for those matters specifically assigned to it, which of course are generally those matters requiring more detailed and specialist examination of documents. There is a basic list of those matters assigned to the Chancery Division in the Supreme Court Act 1981, Schedule 1 which include all causes and matters relating to the sale of land, redemption and foreclosure of mortgages, the execution of trusts and the administration of estates, bankruptcy, partnerships, the rectification of written instruments, contentious probate and all matters relating to companies. The rules of court also assign other matters to the Chancery Division: patents (RSC

Order 103 (the Patents Court is part of the Chancery Division)); proceedings relating to charities, (RSC Order 108) that is proceedings relating to the administration of a charity, not just a case in which a charity happens to be involved; many types of revenue proceedings (RSC Order 91); proceedings brought under the Trustee Act 1925 (RSC Order 93, rule 4) that is proceedings asking the court to use a power under that Act, not just where that Act happens to be relevant. Finally various types of proceedings under specific Acts are assigned to the Chancery Division, (RSC Order 93, rule 10) relating to building societies, trade unions, friendly societies etc.

The Chancery Division is generally more appropriate where the case will be a matter of reading or interpreting documents and of legal argument rather than one of disputed fact and the examination of witnesses. It will be appropriate for any matter connected with a trust, and for some contract actions. If the plaintiff does have a genuine choice of Divisions he should weigh up the practical differences between them. For example, pleadings in the Chancery Division tend to be longer and more detailed, which may be an advantage if the plaintiff's case is complicated. Also the Chancery Division is prepared to make more complicated orders at the end of a case and to enter into more complicated investigations into damages. It is rarely possible to get summary judgment under RSC Order 14 in the Chancery Division, though there is a procedure for getting summary specific performance (RSC Order 86). Though it will not usually be relevant, there is no jury trial in the Chancery Division as there is in the Queen's Bench, see *Stafford, Winfield, Cook & Partners* v *Winfield* [1980] 3 All ER 759.

Finally there is the Family Division, which was originally set up in 1970, and is now provided for in Supreme Court Act 1981, s.61. The matters which are assigned to the Family Division include all matters ancillary to divorce or judicial separation, and relating to the property or children of a marriage. Also cases concerning wardship, legitimacy and adoption will be heard in this Division, as well as appeals in relation to magistrates' orders in family matters which come to the High Court. Finally, the Family Division deals with non-contentious probate matters, which will generally be a case of dealing with simple wills leaving property within the family. It may be appropriate for some cases which do not involve married couples but cohabitees to be heard in the Family Division too, as the principles to be applied may be similar. Conversely, a case between a married couple does not necessarily have to be heard in the Family Division, for example if there is a contract for maintenance, that can be enforced by an action on the contract in the Queen's Bench Division and, if appropriate, summary judgment obtained, *Temple* v *Temple* [1976] 3 All ER 12, though it will normally be most appropriate for actions of this sort to go to the Family Division.

If any cause or matter is begun in one Division, it may at any time be transferred to another by order of the court, Supreme Court Act 1981, s.65 and RSC Order 4, rule 3. Thus the wrong choice of Division should not of itself be fatal to a case, though there may well be a waste of time and costs if a change is necessary.

Normally the correct decision should be made before the writ is issued, but in a case that is not specifically assigned to one Division, it is possible that it will only become apparent later in the case that the number and complexity of documents may make it more suitable for the Chancery Division rather than the Queen's Bench.

The writ should be marked with the Division which has been chosen for the case. Until recently, if the case was in the Chancery Division it was also necessary to mark it with the group of judges to whom it was assigned, but this is no longer necessary, *Practice Direction* [1982] 3 All ER 639. If the writ is issued in a District Registry this should also be marked. This is a matter of choice for the plaintiff, there are District Registries in major towns and cities and this may be more convenient for the plaintiff. A writ may be issued anywhere in the United Kingdom, wherever the cause of action arose, but it may be more convenient to have it tried locally since the circuit system does ensure that High Court judges sit in more than 20 places in the country, and Chancery judges in major commercial cities.

An action may be assigned to a particular judge, in which case this will be marked on the writ, but this is something to be dealt with by the court office, and not something for the pleader to deal with.

The reference number, on the right, consists of three elements, the year in which the writ is issued, and a letter and a number used to identify the action. These last two are a matter for the court office, but generally the letter for the action will be the initial letter of the plaintiff's surname (or otherwise the initial letter of the first surname to appear on the writ) and numbers are issued consecutively from the beginning of the year, each letter beginning with one and going on. Thus if Mr John Smith is the first person with a surname beginning with S to issue a writ in 1985, the reference number will be '1985.S.No.1'. Since this is a matter for the court office rather than the person drafting the pleading and is not subject to strict legal rules it is best if blanks are left on the draft to be filled in when the writ is issued.

There is a recent practice, though it is not a matter of strict rule, for the letters 'Ch.' to be placed before the reference number of an action begun in the Chancery Division, to distinguish it from a Queen's Bench action, so that if Mr Smith's action were being brought in Chancery the number would be 'Ch.1985.S.No.1'.

An 'in the matter of' title is only needed if the case is concerned with the interpretation of particular types of documents, and since this will normally be a matter for an originating summons rather than a writ, the matter of titles is dealt with in the chapter on originating summonses. However the rules are similar for all drafts, and a writ should have a title if necessary.

The full names of the parties should be set out properly, as a simple example,

BETWEEN

	Cedric Albert Arbuthnot	Plaintiff
	and	
	Elsie May Brown	Defendant

The full name should be given if known, without abbreviations, and without 'Mr' or 'Mrs'. The case will of course normally be referred to using the name of the first plaintiff and the first defendant, so that this case will be *Arbuthnot* v *Brown*. It is important to get the name of each party right with no doubt or confusion or the action may not be binding on them. Formerly further descriptions were added, for example a woman would be described as 'married woman' or 'spinster' as appropriate, but this is now no longer necessary, and the tendency is to keep titles as simple as possible. However, a relevant description may still be added if any doubt might arise about the sex or description of a party, *Practice Direction* [1969] 2 All ER 1130.

There have been some variations in the way in which the names of the parties to an action are set out, but as always clarity and simplicity are most important. In *Re Brickman's Settlement* [1982] 1 All ER 336, Megarry VC made observations on the headings of pleadings in the Chancery Division which are generally useful. If there are numerous people involved then the names of the plaintiffs and then of the defendants should be set out one beneath the other with numbers in brackets before each. The words 'Plaintiffs' and 'Defendants' should each appear just once, not 'First Defendant' etc. the word 'and' should not appear between the individual names, but just once between the plaintiffs and the defendants, and again if there are third parties. For example:

BETWEEN	(1) Archibald Anderson	Plaintiffs
	(2) Bertram Brown	
	and	
	(1) Clarence Clore	Defendants
	(2) David Donaldson	
	and	
	Ermintrude Eade	Third Party

It is of course vital to join the right parties, and the lawyer should give positive consideration to this—if you do not sue the right person you may fail altogether or you may not recover the damages sought. Sometimes the parties will be obvious and there will be no choice, but there may be an alternative to be considered. The general rule is in RSC Order 15, rule 4, which allows two or more people to be joined as plaintiffs or as defendants where there is some common question of law or fact that might otherwise be raised in separate actions, or where all the rights to relief claimed arise out of the same transaction or series of transactions, or with the leave of the court. There may need to be more than one plaintiff if more than one person wishes to obtain a remedy from what has happened. It is sometimes possible for one person to be a plaintiff on behalf of others. This concept of the representative action will be considered in the chapter on originating summonses because it is most often needed there.

As for defendants, it is important to consider whether more than one person may be liable for what has happened, especially in tort actions, where more than one person may have contributed to an accident, or have been responsible for something in different ways, for example one making a defective item and another selling it.

There may also be different people liable legally because of agency or vicarious liability. Of course if more than one person is made a defendant you must state clearly in the body of the pleading the different ways in which you are alleging each is liable, either pleading the facts on which each is liable or the legal relationship, such as that one employs the other.

There may be practical as well as legal reasons for joining more people in the action, for example if you are seeking damages, where it may well be that one person will be able to afford to pay them and another will not. One should not take this too far—there is no point in joining someone just because he is rich if the legal claim against him is virtually non-existent. There are other reasons for joining someone as a party, for example if you wish to get discovery of documents against them, but one should be very slow to join a person for purely strategic rather than genuine legal reasons. If there is the possibility of joining different people in the action the various alternatives should be discussed between the lawyers and with the client in conference or in an opinion; only the conclusion will appear in the draft.

Just a few special points about parties, most of which are pretty straightforward. If a person has died, his executors or personal representatives may sue or be sued in his place, RSC Order 15. It is those with direct legal rights and obligations who will normally be parties, so that for example it will normally be the trustees who are parties to an action involving trust property rather than the beneficiaries. Where a party is insured the basic action is still between those involved in the accident, but if the insured party is held liable to pay damages it will be the insurance company which actually pays them. Sometimes a special party needs to be added, for example in an action concerning the potential validity of a charity, the Attorney-General should be made a party to represent the public interest. This will be dealt with in more detail later in connection with trust actions.

Being a separate legal entity, a company can of course be a party to an action, using the correct full name of the company. It is also possible to sue people using a trade name, even if it is not an incorporated body, by using the trading name, and it is usual to add the words 'a firm' at the end, such as 'Easiphix Plumbers (a firm)'. RSC Order 81, rule 1 provides that two or more people claiming or alleged to be entitled as partners within the jurisdiction can sue or be sued in the name of the firm in which they were partners at the time the cause of action accrued. An unincorporated body may also be involved in an action, the normal method being to join an officer of the body, such as the Treasurer or Secretary, to represent it.

Proper consideration as to the parties should be given before the writ is issued. Although the misjoinder or non-joinder of a party should not of itself prove fatal to an action (RSC Order 15, rule 6), the court is not so ready to allow a change of parties as it is to allow an amendment to pleadings. Rule 6 does allow the court to order that a party should cease to be a party or should be added as party at any stage in the proceedings on such terms as it thinks just, but this power will rarely be used at a late stage in the proceedings if there will be any prejudice to the party. A party cannot normally be joined after the end of the limitation period.

It is important to name the party correctly or the action will not bind them. However a minor mistake in the name will not normally defeat the action if there is no real mistake as to identity and no-one has been seriously prejudiced or misled, *Alexander Mountain & Co.* v *Rumere* [1948] 2 KB 436. The same rule applies to a genuine mistake in the name of a company, *Simpson* v *Norwest Holst Southern Ltd.* [1980] 2 All ER 471. The real test is whether there has been a genuine mistake in the name but there is no real doubt about the identity of the party, *Evans Construction Co.* v *Charrington & Co.* [1983] 1 All ER 310.

There are special rules for a person under a disability being a party to an action, coming from RSC Order 80. These rules apply to a patient with a mental disability within the meaning of the Mental Health Acts or an infant, that is a person under 18 years of age. Such a person does not have the capacity to sue alone, but must sue by a 'next friend' and defend by a 'guardian ad litem', and they must have a solicitor. It is not necessary to have any court order for this, but appropriate documents under the Order must be lodged with the court. Normally the person used will be someone close to the patient or minor, such as a parent, but it must be someone with whom there is no possible conflict of interest in the case.

If the patient or minor is the plaintiff then the next friend should be decided on and named in the writ. However if the patient or minor is the defendant then only the name of the patient or minor need be given by the plaintiff in the writ, as the guardian ad litem will be decided on by the other side. The form of heading used in this type of case does not seem to be completely standardised, but should be similar to the following:

Minor plaintiff	'Alexander Allen, a minor, by Alexis Allen his next friend'
Minor defendant	'Belinda Brown, a minor, by Brian Brown her guardian ad litem'
Patient plaintiff	'Ronald Rogan, by Samuel Eagle his next friend'
Patient defendant	'Margaret Thrasher, by Frances Pimm her guardian ad litem'

There are other special rules in actions involving patients and infants which cannot be discussed in detail here.

The formal parts of the writ do not vary, and do not need writing out in full in a draft. The words warn the defendant that he should acknowledge service, which is merely a question of filling in the name and address of the defendant, and when and where the writ is issued, then, after the general indorsement or the statement of claim, the name and address of the plaintiff or his solicitor. RSC Order 18, rule 6 provides that every pleading must be indorsed with the party's name and address if he sues in person, or otherwise by the name or firm and business address of the solicitor by whom it was served, and if the solicitor is an agent for another, the name and firm and business address of the principal. RSC Order 6, rule 5 extends these provisions in the case of a writ, in that if a plaintiff sues in person and has no place of residence, or none within the jurisdiction, he should give an address within the jurisdiction where documents for him may be delivered. Finally, RSC Order 18, rule 6 provides that every pleading of a party must be signed by counsel if settled by him, by the party's solicitor or by the party himself if he sues in person.

If the statement of claim is not indorsed on the writ, then it will have to be served as a separate document, with the heading and formal parts being the same as on the writ.

The statement of claim

Whether the statement of claim is indorsed on the writ or served as a separate document, the principles for drafting it are the same, and many of them were examined in the chapter on principles of drafting. The formal parts must be filled in correctly, and the rest is a matter of telling the story simply and clearly. An example of an outline statement of claim is given here (Example 1), and examples of statements of claim in particular types of actions are given in the later sections of the book.

Pleading the cause of action

The principles here were dealt with in the chapter on principles of drafting. It is a matter of using numbered paragraphs to set out the facts of the case alleged in a logical order as concisely as possible.

Pleading remedies

The statement of claim must state specifically the relief or remedy which the plaintiff claims (RSC Order 18, rule 15). There is little point in pleading the cause of action well if you do not state fully and clearly the things that you want to get if you win. The client does not only want to win the case, but to get the right things out of it, and he should be advised on appropriate and possible remedies so as to make a decision as to what should be sought. There may be an obvious remedy, such as damages, but if there are alternatives, they should be considered fully.

The remedies sought are normally listed at the end of the pleading, in the part referred to as the prayer, beginning 'AND the plaintiff claims' followed by a list of the remedies sought, with each one stated briefly and numbered separately. It is generally a good policy to ask in the prayer for everything that might possibly be granted, and to pitch each claim as high as is reasonably possible, on the basis that there is no possibility at all of getting something that has not been asked for, so one might as well try. Once the remedies sought are specified it is then for the other side to argue whether what has been sought should in fact be granted.

It is quite possible to ask for different types of relief in the alternative if it would not be possible to claim both. If there is more than one defendant, it should be made clear whether all remedies are sought against both or whether some remedies are sought against one and some against another, which can be done either by having a separate numbered list against each defendant, or by making it clear in each numbered point against whom the remedy is sought. In the Chancery Division, 'Further or other relief' and 'Costs' should normally be sought in addition to other remedies, though this is not necessary in Queen's Bench.

Some suggestions of examples of remedies that may be sought apart from damages where appropriate, which are by no means exhaustive, are as follows. A remedy which may be useful in a variety of cases is a declaration, which is a statement by the court of a legal right or position. This will only be appropriate where there is some doubt or dispute about a right or legal position, and some other order may be needed in addition to the declaration to enforce the right. The declaration should be asked for in the pleading, giving the wording of the declaration sought, which should be as specific as possible, though it does seem that it is possible for the court to grant a declaration even if it is not specifically sought, *Harrison-Broadley* v *Smith* [1964] 1 WLR 456.

EXAMPLE 1 BASIC STATEMENT OF CLAIM

IN THE HIGH COURT OF JUSTICE 1985.B.No.

DIVISION

(Writ issued)

BETWEEN A. B. (Name in capitals) *Plaintiff*
and
C. D. (Name in capitals) *Defendant*

STATEMENT OF CLAIM

1. (Establish as far as is relevant to the action who the parties are and what they do.)
2. (Plead any relevant facts prior to the cause of action arising.)
3. (Plead the basic relationship from which the cause of action arises, e.g. the contract, duty of care, trust. Give all appropriate details, such as dates.)
4. (Plead any relevant details, e.g. relevant terms of the contract.)
5. (Plead the cause of action, e.g. breach of contract, negligence, breach of trust.)

PARTICULARS OF ____________

(Plead all appropriate details of the breach, negligence etc.)

6. By reason of the matters aforesaid the plaintiff has suffered loss and damage.

PARTICULARS OF DAMAGE

(Set out the details of special damage with figures, that is any loss which is already quantifiable.)

7. (Plead the basic facts of any type of loss or damage which you wish to claim for, but which is not an obvious result of the facts already pleaded.)

AND the plaintiff claims:

1. (List in separate paragraphs all remedies sought, including a claim for interest if that is sought and a claim for costs.)
2. (If the action is brought in the Chancery Division there should be claims for costs and for further or other relief.)

Served the day of Signed
etc.

An injunction is another remedy that may be useful in many situations, being a flexible and practical possibility. However in many cases it will be more useful to seek an injunction as an interlocutory remedy before the action comes on for trial. This was discussed in the chapter on preparing a case for trial. Where a permanent injunction is sought as well, it should be sought in the statement of claim, with the exact wording of the injunction sought.

It may be appropriate to ask for the return of a specific asset. If a chattel has been improperly detained, there may be an order for the delivery up of the chattel. Alternatively, if the plaintiff shows that he is entitled to possession of land he may seek an order for delivery up of possession of the land.

Some remedies are suitable for particular types of action. In an action in contract the plaintiff may ask for an order of specific performance to have the contract put into effect, and the pleading should make it clear whether specific performance of the whole contract or a particular term is sought. Another contractual remedy is rescission, where it is suitable and available, and the parties can be returned to the position they were in before the contract was made. In a trust action it may be appropriate to ask for specially appropriate remedies like the removal or appointment of a trustee. In either a contract or a trust action it may be appropriate to ask for an account, if there is any uncertainty as to the money due from one party to another. An account is a detailed written list of the sums due between the parties, and is useful where the remedy sought is money owed rather than damages. Once an account is taken, the money found due can be ordered to be paid.

A final general remedy that will be required in almost all actions is an order for costs. This is a matter for the discretion of the court, and does not have to be specifically pleaded (RSC Order 18, rule 15), though it is normal to ask for an order for costs in the Chancery Division.

Pleading a claim for damages

Although the actual claim for damages in the prayer is usually in the simple form 'And the plaintiff claims damages', because the figure to be paid is for the court to assess, it is necessary to put sufficient thought to what else should be put in the pleading in this regard. The lawyer should advise the client fully as to what heads of damage are recoverable, and what sum he can hope to get, and although most of this detail does not need to go into the pleading, he should plead sufficient to at least raise each head of damage.

There is a distinction between pleading a claim for liquidated and unliquidated damages. A liquidated claim is a claim for a specific sum and nothing else, where the sum is already known or can already be ascertained exactly. Where there is a claim only for a liquidated sum the exact figure should be claimed specifically, and there are special procedural rules under which the action can be dealt with quickly. The claim is for unliquidated damages where no exact figure can be given, and the amount due has to be left for the judge to decide, as in personal injuries cases and many contractual actions. In an unliquidated claim more detail may have to be pleaded. The overall principle that the pleading should be as brief as possible still applies, but it is necessary to plead the basic facts giving rise to each head of damage. Damage which flows directly and foreseeably from the facts giving rise to the cause of action will normally be presumed, but if there is a type of damage that is not obvious it should be raised in a separate paragraph or it may take the other side by surprise and not be recoverable. For example, if the defendant's negligence leads to a machine breaking down in a factory it will be obvious that some production and profits may be lost and that the machine will have to be repaired, and these things can just be listed under the particulars of loss and damage without further facts, but it is not obvious that a particular contract with another party may be lost, so that basic facts as to that would have to be pleaded if the plaintiff sought damages for that.

Facts in mitigation of damage may be pleaded as well as facts aggravating damage, but there is no strict rule here, and this will to some extent be a matter of judgment in each case. A plaintiff may plead facts which do obviously and irrefutably reduce his loss so as to give the defendant a more exact view of his claim, but he does not have to if there is any real doubt as to the extent to which his loss is mitigated. A defendant does not have to plead in detail to allegations of damage, as such allegations are deemed to be denied unless they are expressly admitted, but if the defendant does wish to make a strong point on the damages recoverable he may choose to make his position clear in his pleading.

To illustrate the type of detail that should be pleaded, there are a number of cases in which the plaintiff has failed to recover something he has lost because it was not pleaded. In *Perestrello E Companhia Limitada* v *United Paint Co.* [1969] 1 WLR 570 there was an action for breach of contract in which the plaintiff pleaded wasted expenditure, but not loss of profit. It was held that he could recover nothing under the second head—he should have raised the point with precise figures if appropriate and it was too late to amend his pleading at trial. In *Ilkiw* v *Samuels* [1963] 1 WLR 991 the plaintiff was injured at work, and the statement of claim alleged a specific loss of £77, but said nothing about a continuing loss of £200 p.a. It was held that therefore nothing was recoverable for this continuing loss. In *Domsalla* v *Barr* [1969] 1 WLR 630 the plaintiff fell off a steel erection at work and suffered continuing dizziness. He claimed that as a result he had had to turn down a job he had hoped to get in Nigeria, and was no longer fit enough to set up his own business eventually as he had hoped. It was held that he could not recover damages for these things because they were not pleaded, and because he could not provide sufficient evidence that these things would have happened. A final and similar example is *Ashcroft* v *Curtin* [1971] 3 All ER 1208, where a man was injured in a car accident and alleged that as a result he was no longer lively and dynamic enough to carry on his one man business. It was held that he could not get damages for this because there was insufficient evidence to show it was true.

There is a general principle of just pleading the basic facts, so all that is necessary is a paragraph or two giving sufficient detail to alert the defendant to the basic type of loss alleged. It will then have to be proved and argued about at trial. If too much detail is given, it may tie the case down unnecessarily. The only figures that need to appear in a pleading are those for special damage. General damage remains at large, and total figures need not be given, though it may still be useful to provide some basic figures from which the loss can be computed.

To illustrate the distinctions, if someone is injured at work it may well be that his clothes are damaged. You can find out immediately the cost of replacing them, so this should be listed as special damage, and the actual value given. He may well have to be off work while he recovers and will lose wages. If he has already gone back to work this can be pleaded as special damage because you know how many weeks he has been off work and what his weekly wage is, but if he has not yet returned to work you cannot put an exact figure on the loss, so that all that is necessary is to plead that he has not yet been able to return to work, and it is also helpful to plead the weekly wage that he is losing. Although you can advise the client what sort of figure he is likely to be awarded for his injuries, this figure will remain as general damages for the judge to assess.

Some cases illustrate the type of figures which it is useful to plead. In *Hayward* v *Pullinger & Partners* [1950] 1 All ER 581 there was an action for wrongful dismissal, and it was held that figures for lost salary and commission lost due to the dismissal were special damages and details should be pleaded. In *Monk* v *Redwing Aircraft Co.* [1942] 1 KB 182 again in an action for wrongful dismissal, it was held that the defendant was entitled to know whether the plaintiff had found a new job and, if so how long it was for and what the salary was, as this was all directly relevant to the quantification of damage. If such information is available it may therefore be useful to plead it, although this is not strictly necessary. Finally, in *Phipps* v *Orthodox Unit Trusts* [1957] 3 All ER 305 it was held that the defendant was entitled to know something of the plaintiff's tax position where this was relevant to the quantification of damage, although it would not normally be suitable to put this type of detail in the statement of claim.

In a few cases it may be possible to claim exemplary damages in addition to compensatory damages, but this is only where there is alleged to be oppresive, arbitrary or unconstitutional conduct by a servant of the government, or the defendant's conduct is calculated to produce a profit for him in excess of any damages he may have to pay, *Rookes* v *Barnard* [1964] AC 1129. If exemplary damages are to be sought they should be pleaded, RSC Order 18, rule 8.

It has now become possible to claim damages in a currency other than sterling, if this is appropriate, for example if a foreign law is the proper law of the contract, and the price in the contract is specified to be payable in a foreign currency, *Miliangos* v *George Frank (Textiles)* [1975] 3 All ER 801. It is also possible to get damages in a foreign currency in a tort case if that is necessary to fairly compensate the plaintiff, for example if negligence causes damage to a foreign ship which is repaired abroad, *The Despina R* [1979] AC 685. If a plaintiff does wish to have damages awarded in a foreign currency he should specifically plead this, giving the reason, *Practice Direction* [1976] 1 All ER 669, he should specify the currency requested and why it is appropriate, *Practice Direction* [1977] 1 All ER 544 and *Federal Commerce* v *Tradax Export S.A.* [1977] QB 324.

Pleading a claim for interest

Where there is a claim for the payment of a sum of money or damages, the plaintiff may well wish to claim interest too. In recent years, with relatively high rates of interest and inflation this has become an important part of many claims, and there have been changes in the way that claims for interest should be pleaded, which are now largely contained in the Supreme Court Act 1981, s.35A, RSC Order 18, rule 8 and *Practice Direction* [1983] 1 All ER 934.

Essentially an award of interest is at the discretion of the judge. A High Court judge can award interest in any action for the recovery of a debt or damages, at such rate as he thinks fit or the rules of court provide, on all or any part of the debt or damages, for all or any part of the period between the date the cause of action arose and the date of payment or of judgment in the case. If interest is claimed it should be pleaded, and although there are slightly different requirements depending on the interest claimed, the essential rule is that the claim should be pleaded in full, with all the details of rates, dates and so on that are relevant in assessing the amount of interest to award. These details should be pleaded in the body of the draft, and not just in the prayer, though there seem still to be some variations in practice as to how this is done.

The judge has to decide not only whether interest should be awarded and for what period, but also what rate is appropriate. Different rates are used for different purposes, and this may be something to be argued in court. If a rate is specified in an agreement, that rate will normally be used, otherwise the court will often use a rate 1% or 2% above bank rate or base rate. The court may in its discretion use a higher rate where there has been fraud or breach of a fiduciary duty. For personal injury actions the short term investment account rate is used, that is the rate of interest paid on money in court. If rates have varied over the relevant period then different rates may be used for different periods, or an average rate taken. One can only give general guidelines here, and the lawyer in practice will become aware of the current practice of the courts.

There are various circumstances in which interest can be awarded. The details to be pleaded will be slightly different for each, but the principle of the need to plead all the appropriate details for assessing the interest to be awarded applies to all.

Firstly, interest may be awarded as an inherent part of damages. This may happen for example in a contract case where the contract specifies that a rate of interest will be payable in specified circumstances. The term itself gives rise to the right to interest, and should be pleaded with details of the agreed rate and period, and the amount of interest due when the writ was issued, see *Bushwall Properties* v *Vortex Properties* [1975] 2 All ER 214. Even if a contract does not specify that interest will be payable, interest on a debt can normally be claimed if it is not paid and an action is commenced. However, it will not be payable prior to the commencement of the action, *President of India* v *La Pintada Cia Navegacion SA* [1984] 2 All ER 773.

Even if it is not specified in an agreement, interest may still be an inherent part of damages on the facts. For example, if a sum of money is not paid when it is due, and the defendant should have foreseen that as a result of his non-payment the plaintiff would have to borrow money, then the interest that the plaintiff has had to pay on borrowed money may be recoverable as part of his damages, *Wadsworth* v *Lydell* [1981] 2 All ER 401. This may also happen in a tort action, as in *Tate & Lyle Foods* v *Greater London Council* [1981] 3 All ER 716 where the plaintiff was deprived of the use of a jetty by the defendant's negligence which caused the river to silt up, and it was held that since the plaintiff had been deprived of profit he was entitled to recover theoretical interest on the money he was deprived of at a commercial rate.

The court has a general equitable discretion to award interest in a suitable case where the facts merit it. In *Wallersteiner* v *Moir (No 2)* [1975] 1 QB 373 it was held that a court could award interest where the defendant had improperly benefitted from a fiduciary position. Similarly, it may be appropriate for the court to award interest, possibly at a high rate, where a trustee has acted in breach of trust, *Bartlett* v *Barclays Bank* [1980] Ch 515. In *B.P. Exploration Co. (Libya)* v *Hunt* [1983] 2 AC 352 it was held that it might also be appropriate for the court to award interest to the extent that seemed just where a contract had been frustrated.

In an action seeking damages for personal injury or death, the court should normally award interest unless there are special reasons to the contrary, but interest will be calculated differently for different parts of the damages, *Jefford* v *Gee* [1970] 2 QB 130. For special damages, interest is awarded at half the appropriate rate from the date of the accident to the date of trial (the appropriate rate coming from the average rate for the short term investment account for the relevant period). On damages for pain and suffering, interest is normally awarded at 2% from the date of the writ to the date of trial, though the plaintiff may get no interest if he is slow in pursuing his action, *Birkett* v *Hayes* [1982] 2 All ER 70 and *Wright* v *British Railways Board* [1983] 2 AC 773. There will be no interest on damages for loss of future earnings or future earning capacity, as those damages do not relate to money that has been withheld from the plaintiff, see *Joyce* v *Yeomans* [1981] 2 All ER 21.

9 *Drafting other pleadings in a writ action*

The basic principles for drafting the later pleadings in an action begun by writ are broadly similar to those for the writ. However, there are some difficulties in that the later pleadings do not just logically tell the story in the way that the statement of claim does, but are designed rather to reply to earlier pleadings—the defence does not set out the defendant's version of events, but rather replies to the allegations made by the plaintiff. This emphasises the importance of the statement of claim in setting the stage for the entire action, but also shows that one does need slightly different skills for the later pleadings. The major pleadings are the defence, to which a counterclaim may be added, and the reply, which may if appropriate have a defence to counterclaim added. These will be dealt with in detail. Later pleadings are now rare, and will only be mentioned briefly. The third party notice is not an essential pleading, but may of course be issued if appropriate, so this will also be included.

Later pleadings will of course take their heading, including the number, parties etc. from the statement of claim, unless an extra party is added, in which case they will be added to the title.

The defence

The defence will normally be a shorter document than the statement of claim, and there is sometimes a tendency to see it as being less important. The defence is intended to set out all the basic lines of argument that the defendant will be using and to alert the plaintiff to them. The defence is of course the basic pleading for the defence case, and must be carefully drafted as such (see Example 1). It is more difficult to plead the defence as a coherent and logical document because it is a reply to allegations. It is not just a question of denying everything alleged, but is rather more subtle, making careful distinctions between reactions to the various allegations made and the various courses that can be taken, and pleading new positive allegations if necessary.

The basic approach to drafting a defence is to begin by examining the statement of claim in great detail, and getting the client's reaction to its contents. For the young lawyer learning to draft it may be useful to take a piece of paper, list on it the numbers of the paragraphs in the statement of claim, and write against each number your client's reaction to the allegation, such as 'Client admits this', 'Client denies this', 'Client admits the accident but says it did not happen this way' and so on. After this you go on to list at the bottom any separate points which your client wishes to argue. This is then the skeleton of a defence.

The lawyer should of course advise the client fully on every possible line of defence, and every possible way of restricting what he may be liable for but, as with any other pleading, it is only the essence of the main points that goes into the drafting. It is quite possible to plead more than one line of defence either cumulatively or in the alternative, even if your lines of argument conflict, but this is a matter of policy and may ultimately weaken your case as it may look as though you are scraping the barrel to find something rather than sticking to one clear argument.

A few general points should be noted before the elements of a defence are examined in detail. The defence does not need to plead to anything in the statement of claim which should not be there. For example if the statement of claim is badly drafted and contains passages of evidence you do not need to plead to that. Neither is it necessary to plead to an allegation of law, such as the legality of a contract, open for argument before the judge at the trial. Nor to anything said in the prayer rather than in the body of the statement of claim, nor to any allegation of damage, as these are all matters which remain at large until the trial. However, all these may be pleaded, and tactically it may be a good idea to do so. Indeed if you have a basic legal argument, for example that the action has been brought outside the limitation period, it really should be pleaded because it is fundamentally important to the action itself, and may well save time and costs by stopping the action continuing.

There may be defects in the pleading of the statement of claim. If the defect is minor and presents no real difficulty it can be ignored, but if it prevents the defendant pleading or preparing his own case properly something should be done about it. The defendant may seek *further and better particulars* or *interrogatories* or, in an extreme case, could seek to have the statement of claim struck out. However, if the bad pleading will just be a problem for the plaintiff there is no need to point out his failings to him, as his bad pleading may irritate the judge at trial, even if it does not prove a difficulty for him in presenting his case.

The form of a defence is fairly straightforward, as can be seen from Example 1. As with the statement of claim, each separate point or allegation should be contained in a separate paragraph, numbered successively. It is normally better to follow the order of the statement of claim in dealing with the allegations in it, but this is not essential. Several paragraphs from the statement of claim can be dealt with together, for example 'Paragraphs 1 to 3 of the statement of claim are admitted'. The main point is to make it clear in each paragraph what one is reacting to and what the reaction is. Any counterclaim may be added to the pleading, and this is dealt with later.

Possible courses in the defence

There are a variety of possible courses to take in responding to allegations, but the main thing is to react clearly to each and every one, especially allegations of fact. In doing this it is better not just to be generally negative and evasive, but to show exactly what the defendant's reaction is and how his case is founded. Wherever necessary it is better to get extra information from the client rather than pleading in a vague way.

For each and every allegation made in the statement of claim it is possible to adopt one of the following positions, or to have more than one reaction which is pleaded in the alternative:

(a) Admitting allegations. One should admit any allegations made by the other side which the client agrees are true. There is no point in denying something that is true and can easily be proved as this will just waste time and money. The Summons for Directions will review what admissions should be made, and if a party refuses to admit something which he should admit, he may end up paying the costs of proving it.

However, an allegation should only be admitted if it is agreed that every part of it is true, because every admission made will be binding at trial. If there is any reservation on a point, that can be pleaded, for example 'Save in that. . . the defendant admits paragraph 3 of the statement of claim'.

If any paragraph in the statement of claim, or any allegation, is not pleaded to, it will be deemed to be admitted, RSC Order 18, rule 13, so the defendant must ensure that he has pleaded to every allegation against him.

(b) Refusing to admit. This is a specific reaction which is different from a denial. If one refuses to admit something, the effect is to put the other side to prove. If something may have happened, but the client was not there or does not have sufficient knowledge to know about it, the best course is to refuse to admit it. Then one is not saying that the allegation is not true, just that it might not be, and that it is for the other side to show what happened.

(c) Denying an allegation. If an allegation is not admitted it should be 'traversed', either by refusing to admit it, or by denying it, RSC Order 18, rule 13. Care must be taken in denying allegations to distinguish clearly between those things which are denied and those which are not. There are some useful phrases for making these points, for example 'the defendant denies each and every allegation in paragraph 2 of the statement of claim' or 'The defendant denies each and every allegation in paragraph 2, save in that. . .'.

Some things should not be denied, for example one should not normally deny an allegation of law, especially if it is completely correct! It is surprising how often this can be done by someone pleading in a general way. Also there is little point in denying something which can be easily proved, as this just wastes time and money. The good pleader should also avoid denying something in order to raise some argument on the point, for example, denying the wording of a contract in order to argue that it is not legally binding. If the words are there in black and white there is no point in denying them. The proper course in this type of case will be to confess and avoid, which is discussed below.

It is important to take care in denying a negative allegation, because of course the result will be that the double negative makes a positive. If part of a paragraph in a statement of claim alleges that the defendant did not do something and the defendant denies the whole paragraph, then he is alleging that he did do the thing specified. Since a double negative does create an affirmative allegation, further and better particulars of the allegation may be required if necessary, *Pinson* v *Lloyds & National Provincial Foreign Bank Ltd* [1941] 2 All ER 636.

Lastly, a pure denial may in fact be misleading, in that it may not be clear what is being denied. For example, if the plaintiff alleges that he slipped on a sheet of ice on the defendant's premises and broke his hip, a simple denial is not sufficient.

A mere denial may mean that you deny there was ice, deny that it was on the defendant's premises, deny that the plaintiff slipped, deny that he broke his hip or all or any combination of these. Of course, the plaintiff should not put all these matters in one paragraph anyway, so the defendant should be able to plead to them clearly and separately, but if there is a paragraph in the statement of claim which contains more than one point the defendant should take care to plead to it specifically. Wide phrases may be helpful, for example, 'The defendant denies that the plaintiff slipped by reason of ice or for any other reason', 'the defendant denies that there was ice in the part of his premises alleged, or any other part', 'The defendant denies that the plaintiff was injured as alleged or at all'. This element of pleading a defence needs careful and clear thought, and perhaps consultation with the client as to exactly what his case is. A useful exercise for the student may be to go through each paragraph dividing it into separate allegations with quotation marks, and making sure that he does deal with each separate point.

(d) The general denial. This is a particular point of pleading on which lawyers hold quite strong and widely differing views. Because of the rule that every allegation which is not traversed is deemed to be admitted, some pleaders seek to avoid any difficulties by putting in a general paragraph to deny everything that they may not have dealt with specifically. The wording varies, but it is along the lines of 'Save as hereinbefore specifically admitted or not admitted, the defendant denies each and every allegation contained in the statement of claim as though the same were set out herein and separately traversed'. The effect of this is to deny every word of the statement of claim that is not expressly admitted.

Against the general denial, it must be said that it should not be necessary at all if the person drafting the defence has gone through the statement of claim in detail and has pleaded properly and clearly to every allegation in it, because there is just nothing else to add. Also the general denial alone is not good pleading, in that RSC Order 18, rule 13 provides that every allegation of fact made in the statement of claim should be specifically traversed in the defence, and that a general denial of the allegations, or a general statement of non-admission is not a sufficient traverse.

However, rule 13 does only mean that a defence consisting of a paragraph denying everything is not sufficient. It does not mean that the general denial as such is improper, and there may well be cases where a general denial is suitable. For example it may be used where the statement of claim is long and complicated, so that the defendant may be in genuine doubt whether he has been able to sufficiently plead to everything, or where the statement of claim is very vague so that the defendant has difficulty pleading to it, but in a simple case the general denial is really just a sign that the pleader has been lazy or is unsure of his case.

As with the simple denial, the general denial should be used with care. One should still admit everything that should be admitted rather than just denying everything, see *Warner* v *Sampson* [1959] 1 QB 297. A general denial may be appropriate where there are general allegations, but the defendant should still plead specifically to each allegation if he can, and may still be liable for costs if he denies anything unnecessarily, *John Lancaster Radiators* v *General Motor Radiator Co.* [1946] 2 All ER 685.

(e) Confession and avoidance. This is a very useful tool in drafting a defence, which the young lawyer should learn to use as soon as possible. The point is to admit all or part of an allegation and to add extra facts or arguments which shed a different light on things. In simple terms, to say 'Yes, but. . .', for example 'Yes I drove my car into him, but only because he walked out without looking'. This can be useful for many lines of defence, either to add further facts, or specifically to argue justification, provocation, self-defence, or some other variation on the facts.

Although confession and avoidance is very useful, some care should be taken with it, as the defendant is pleading extra facts or issues in the case and should take care not to tie himself down more than is necessary on a particular argument. Also he should be slow to put in something which he does not actually need to plead or he will be giving the other side information on his case which he does not have to give. The only thing that the pleading has to do is to deal with points raised by the plaintiff, and alert him to broad lines of argument so that he can prepare his case and is not taken completely by surprise on a major point at the trial.

(f) Objections on points of law. It is not actually necessary to plead points of law, but in practice it is useful to plead a fundamental point of law that may be decisive in the case, such as whether the action is alleged to be outside the limitation period. Any legal argument can always be raised in court whether it is pleaded or not, and the decision whether or not to plead should balance the fact that it may be useful to alert the other side to a major legal point that will be taken, but if there is a clever legal argument it may be best to keep it until the trial.

A further possibility is the plea formerly known as the demurrer where the defendant admits all the allegations made by the plaintiff, but still argues that he has no legal claim, because for example the court has no jurisdiction.

(g) Pleading positive allegations. The primary purpose of the defence is to reply to the allegations made in the statement of claim, but there are circumstances in which the defendant may wish to raise new points, and so positive pleading is sometimes needed. RSC Order 18, rule 8 sets out those things which should be positively pleaded in any pleading subsequent to the statement of claim, that is:

(i) Any matter which he alleges makes any claim or defence of the opposite party not maintainable (which will normally, though not exclusively, be points of law).

(ii) Any matter which, if not specifically pleaded, might take the opposite party by surprise and which might necessitate an adjournment if kept secret until trial.

(iii) Any matter which raises an issue of fact not arising out of the preceding pleading, which clearly includes any factual point the defendant may wish to raise to put a different complexion on the plaintiff's allegations.

The rule does give some examples of things which should be positively pleaded, such as performance, release, the limitation of an action, fraud, or any fact showing illegality. The general point is that if the defendant does want to raise a new point that was not in the statement of claim he should do so, normally in a separate paragraph after he has pleaded to the plaintiff's allegations. Other examples of things that may be positively pleaded in a defence are contributory negligence, see *Fookes* v *Slaytor* [1979] 1 All ER 137, estoppel, a lien, a release, an agreement ending the right of action, or a tender of the amount alleged to be owing.

(h) Objection to a drafting point. Although it is rarely done, it is possible to plead a defect in your opponent's pleading if he has not pleaded an element which is essential to his case, for example 'Paragraph 2 of the statement of claim discloses no consideration for the alleged contract'. In practice, if a pleading has this kind of defect it is more usual to seek to have it struck out or to seek further particulars.

(i) Pleading on remedies. It is not necessary to plead to the prayer of the statement of claim which lists the remedies sought. It is for the judge to make orders at trial, and it is completely open to the parties to argue at trial what remedies are appropriate. It is necessary to plead to any allegation made in the body of the statement of claim, but there is an exception when it comes to remedies, in that any allegation that a party has suffered damage or as to the amount of that damage is deemed to be traversed unless it is specifically admitted (RSC Order 18, rule 13). Therefore the defendant does not have to plead at all on allegations as to damage unless he specifically wishes to admit something, which is rarely done. Although the defendant will need to consider arguments as to the measure of damage he does not have to plead them. However, in practice there is no rule that one should not plead on damages, and it may be a good idea to plead major arguments on causation or mitigation to make the defendant's position clear at an early stage.

A counterclaim

Until the last century, each action had to be brought to court separately, so that if a defendant had a claim against a plaintiff he had to go to the expense and trouble of bringing a separate action. It is now possible to save time and costs by hearing the actions together, and this is the purpose of the counterclaim. When the defendant drafts his defence he will deal with the allegations made against him in the statement of claim, but if in addition he has a positive cause of action against the plaintiff he can add that as a separate section of the draft, the entire pleading then being a 'Defence and Counterclaim' rather than a 'Defence' (see Example 1).

Anything that may be a separate cause of action may be raised in a counterclaim (RSC Order 15, rule 2), which provides that a defendant in any action who alleges that he has any claim or is entitled to any relief or remedy against a plaintiff in any action may, instead of bringing a separate action, make a counterclaim, and that if he does so he must add it to his defence. The principle of the separate claim runs right through the procedure. That is, the rules for drafting a counterclaim are the same as those for the statement of claim. The counterclaim continues in its own right, and the defendant may get judgment even if the plaintiff's action is stayed, discontinued or dismissed (RSC Order 15, rule 2). The court may well give separate judgments with separate orders for costs on the statement of claim and the counterclaim, though if both claims are for damages the court may just give judgment for the balance, using its discretion as to what order to make for costs.

Although a counterclaim may be any cause of action, in practice it may well be in some way linked to the plaintiff's case. For example in a contract case one party may sue for breach of contract and then the other side may counterclaim alleging other breaches. This must be done by counterclaim if the defendant is alleging positive breaches for which he himself wants a remedy, rather than simply by raising a defence. For example, in *Hanak* v *Green* [1958] 2 QB 9 there was an action for breach of a building contract, but the builder counterclaimed for quantum meruit for the work he had done, and for trespass to his tools by the plaintiff, the result being that the court gave judgment for the builder for £10, the difference between the values of the claims of the two parties.

It is important to remember that if the defendant does wish to make positive allegations against the plaintiff and obtain remedies he must actually raise these matters as a counterclaim in his pleading, he cannot bring them up informally or later. His only option then will be to bring a separate action as plaintiff. In *Impex Transport Aktielskabet* v *AG Thames Holding* [1982] 1 All ER 897 the plaintiff sought summary judgment for freight owed, but the defendant swore an affidavit which included facts amounting to a counterclaim. It was held that this was insufficient, and as the matter had not been formally pleaded as a counterclaim it could not proceed. In another case the plaintiff got summary judgment on a dishonoured cheque and the defendant then sought to file a counterclaim, but it was held that this was not possible as the action was now over, *C.S.I. International Co.* v *Archway Personnel (Middle East)* [1980] 3 All ER 215.

The rules for drafting a counterclaim will not be discussed further as they are the same as the rules for drafting a statement of claim.

The set-off

This is another alternative for the defendant to consider when he is drafting a defence. It is again a positive allegation that can be raised by the defendant, and is an allegation that even though the plaintiff may have a case against the defendant, the plaintiff owes the defendant something, and this should be taken into account. If there is a claim by the defendant for a sum of money (whether or not the amount of money is ascertained) which relates to the whole or part of the claim by the plaintiff, this may be included in the defence as a set-off against the plaintiff's claim (RSC Order 18, rule 17). (See Example 1).

The court will deduct the amount of the set-off from the sum found due to the plaintiff, and give judgment for the balance. A set-off is in no way a separate action, and therefore cannot be judged if the plaintiff's action is withdrawn. A set-off can only be a claim for money and not for any other remedy for which there will have to be a counterclaim. A set-off will normally arise from the same facts as the plaintiff's claim, but does not have to. The possibility that there may be a set-off should be explored with the client.

To illustrate what can amount to a set-off, in *Nadreph* v *Willmett & Co.* [1978] 1 All ER 746 a firm of solicitors were sued for negligence for failing to renegotiate a lease for a client and the solicitors sought to set off financial advantages that could accrue to the plaintiff because there had been no renegotiation. It was held that this might be a set-off but on the facts was really a matter of mitigation of damage. In *British Anzani (Felixstowe)* v *International Maritime Management*

EXAMPLE 1 BASIC DEFENCE (WITH SET-OFF AND COUNTERCLAIM)

IN THE HIGH COURT OF JUSTICE 1985.B.No.1234

DIVISION

BETWEEN A. B. (Name in capitals) *Plaintiff*

and

C. D. (Name in capitals) *Defendant*

DEFENCE

(Plead to all the allegations in the statement of claim in separate numbered paragraphs. The following are examples of possible paragraphs that may be adapted for use.)

1. The defendant admits paragraph of the statement of claim.
2. The defendant denies paragraph of the statement of claim, save in that ....
3. The defendant denies that he was guilty of any........ as alleged in the statement of claim or at all.
4. The defendant denies that the plaintiff has sustained loss and damage as alleged in the statement of claim.
5. Further or in the alternative, the defendant denies that the alleged loss and damage were caused by the defendant as alleged in the statement of claim.
6. Save as is herein specifically admitted or not admitted, the defendant denies each and every allegation contained in the statement of claim as though the same were set out herein and specifically traversed.
7. The defendant claims to be entitled to set off against the plaintiff's claim the sum of £ , in that........ (set out the facts on which set-off is based).

COUNTERCLAIM

8. (Plead the facts giving rise to the counterclaim in separate numbered paragraphs as if pleading a statement of claim.
9.
10.

AND the defendant counterclaims:

1. (Set out in numbered paragraphs the reliefs sought due to the counterclaim.)
2.

Served the day of etc. Signed.

(U.K.) [1980] QB 137 the plaintiff agreed to build a warehouse for the defendant to lease, and eventually there were claims for rent arrears by the plaintiff and for defects in the building by the defendant. It was held that the defendant's claim on the defects might be a set-off, but that although the set-off did not need to come from the plaintiff's cause of action, it should be factually connected with it. Here it was not, so the defendant should have argued a counterclaim rather than a set-off. Only money which is already legally due to be paid by the plaintiff to the defendant can be a set-off, see *Business Computers* v *Anglo African Leasing* [1977] 2 All ER 741.

It may not be easy for the young lawyer to distinguish between a set-off, a counterclaim and a matter of mitigation of damage. There may certainly be an overlap between these things, and the cases quoted show how difficult it can be to tell one from another. To try to draw a few broad lines of distinction, a matter of mitigation of damage is a purely factual argument on how much should be awarded to the plaintiff in damages, and whether anything did or should have reduced the loss suffered by the plaintiff. Therefore it must arise directly from the facts of the plaintiff's claim. Points of mitigation do not have to be pleaded, though they may be.

The set-off has been defined, and the important elements are that it must be a sum of money that is actually said to be due from the plaintiff to the defendant, rather than just relating to what loss the plaintiff has suffered, though again it should arise from the same facts as the plaintiff's claim. The set-off will have to be pleaded, but is essentially a matter of arithmetic.

The counterclaim is a full cause of action against the plaintiff that may relate to money but can relate to anything. It does not have to be related to the plaintiff's claim in any way. A counterclaim must of course be fully pleaded. It is quite possible for a set-off to amount to a counterclaim if it does come from an independent right of action, and the defendant will then have to decide which he wishes to treat it as. A relatively small claim is probably better left as a set-off, but if the claim is for a relatively large amount it should be pleaded as a counterclaim so that the claim can continue even if the plaintiff drops his action. If the claim may be for an amount exceeding the plaintiff's claim it should certainly be pleaded as a counterclaim, because if it is only pleaded as a set-off, the court can only deduct it from the amount awarded to the plaintiff and cannot give judgment for the excess.

The set-off should be pleaded as a separate paragraph at the end of the defence, after dealing with all the allegations made by the plaintiff, as in Example 1. It should set out the facts giving rise to the set-off, and if possible the amount claimed.

The reply and defence to counterclaim

In many relatively straightforward cases it will not be necessary to have further pleadings after the defence. The plaintiff has set out his case in the statement of claim and the defendant his in the defence and it just remains to be argued at trial. However, in some cases, especially more complex ones, further pleadings may be needed to define the issues between the parties further. Note that this is the main purpose of a further pleading; with few exceptions, further pleadings are not there for the raising of new issues which should have been put into earlier pleadings, or can be inserted into them by amendment. The purpose of any pleading after the defence is to deal with any points raised for the first time by the previous pleading from the other side, and to raise any new matters that are relevant purely because of something that has been raised by the other side.

The defence is the last essential pleading in the action, and if no reply to the defence is issued within the appropriate time, there is an implied joinder of issue on the defence (RSC Order 18, rule 14). This means that the plaintiff is deemed to deny every material allegation of fact in the defence, unless any allegation is excepted from the joinder and is stated to be admitted. Thus the plaintiff does not have to serve a reply, and there is no point in his doing so if he would only wish to deny the allegations made by the defendant anyway.

There are various circumstances in which the plaintiff might choose to file a reply. He may wish to add to his pleadings in the light of something raised in the defence. It may be that an implied denial of everything in the defence is not sufficient and it would be useful to plead to the defence in more detail, perhaps making some admissions or dealing with an allegation by confession and avoidance. Lastly if the defence is quite long or complicated it may be advisable or useful to serve a reply to deal with the points raised in it in some detail, to help to clarify the issues before trial.

For the actual drafting of a reply see Example 2. It should again be set out in separate numbered paragraphs, and it is often useful, though not necessary, that it should follow the order of the defence. The approach is similar to that for drafting a defence, in that the pleader should decide for each allegation whether he admits it, denies it, wishes to confess and avoid etc., and should clearly plead his choice on each allegation. In practice a reply need not deal specifically with everything in the defence but will just deal with those matters which the pleader does wish to admit or confess and avoid, and will then conclude with a general denial of everything else in the defence.

There is one limitation on the pleading in a reply in that by RSC Order 18, rule 10, which says that a party shall not in any pleading make an allegation of fact, or raise any new ground or claim which is inconsistent with a previous pleading of his (though he is free to amend a previous pleading to put in the new allegation). A reply cannot be used to allege a totally new cause of action—again this should be done by amending the statement of claim if appropriate, or by commencing a new action. In *Herbert* v *Vaughan* [1972] 1 WLR 1128 the plaintiff alleged undue influence by one person, but then in his reply tried to allege undue influence by a totally different person, and it was held that this was a new cause of action which should not be raised in a reply.

Another circumstance where the plaintiff should issue a reply is where the defendant has pleaded a counterclaim. The point is that just as a counterclaim is like a statement of claim, so it needs defending in the same way. Therefore, if there is a counterclaim attached to the defence, the plaintiff will need to attach a defence to counterclaim to his reply. The rules for drafting a defence to counterclaim are exactly the same as those for a defence. As with the defence, anything in the counterclaim which is not denied is deemed to be admitted, so that detailed pleading is needed, and a general denial may be appropriate.

EXAMPLE 2 BASIC REPLY (WITH DEFENCE TO COUNTERCLAIM)

IN THE HIGH COURT OF JUSTICE 1985.B.No.1234

DIVISION

BETWEEN A. B. *Plaintiff*

and

C. D. *Defendant*

REPLY

(Plead to any allegations in the defence that you wish to deal with, in separate numbered paragraphs. The following are examples of possible paragraphs that may be adapted for use.)

1. As to paragraph of the defence, the plaintiff denies that........
2. As to paragraph of the defence, the plaintiff says that........
3. By reason of the matters aforesaid, the plaintiff says that........
4. Save insofar as the same consists of admissions, the plaintiff joins issue with the defendant on his defence.

DEFENCE TO COUNTERCLAIM

5. (Plead to all the allegations in the counterclaim in separate numbered paragraphs in the same way as pleading a defence.)
6.
7.

Served the day of Signed.
etc.

Further pleadings after the reply

The Rules of Court do provide for further pleadings after the reply, but extra pleadings are now rare. The further pleadings which may be filed are called the rejoinder, the surrejoinder, the rebutter and the surrebutter, but the leave of the court will be needed before any of these pleadings may be issued (RSC Order 18, rule 4). There will rarely be any need for these pleadings, because if a party wishes to add anything to the pleading it can usually best be done by amending an existing pleading rather than by issuing a new one. There will be an implied joinder of issue on the reply and defence to counterclaim so that the defendant is deemed to deny everything in it. It is open to either party to make admissions without issuing further pleadings, so it is only if there is a need to define issues further that further pleadings will be needed, where the facts are very complicated or where further matters came to light at a late stage.

Some of the rules mentioned in the pleading of a reply also apply to the pleading of later pleadings. By RSC Order 18, rule 14 there will be an implied joinder of issue on the last pleading served after the defence, so that every allegation of fact in the last pleading will be deemed to be denied unless expressly admitted. Therefore a further pleading does not need to be served, and if it is it need only deal with specific points and can join issue expressly on the rest. By RSC Order 18, rule 10 a party cannot in any pleading make an allegation of fact, or raise any new ground or claim which is inconsistent with a previous pleading of his, though he may of course amend any previous pleading.

If a further pleading is issued it only needs to deal in numbered paragraphs with any points in the previous pleading that the party issuing the pleading specifically wishes to answer, and may well contain a general denial of everything else in the previous pleading.

Third party notices

Although the third party notice is not an essential document in an action begun by writ, it is a document in a case that a lawyer may need to draft from time to time. When issuing the writ the plaintiff will decide who he should join as defendants. If he wishes to add a further party later then he should apply to amend the writ to add a further party, and the court will have to decide whether it is proper to allow this.

However, the defendant receiving a writ will have had no choice over the parties to the action, and he may wish someone else to be made a party, in which case he will need to issue a third party notice, under RSC Order 16. The grounds on which this may be done are where:

(a) The defendant claims any contribution or indemnity from a person who is not already a party to the action. That is essentially that he alleges that someone else is wholly or partially responsible for the action complained of by the plaintiff.

(b) The defendant claims against the person who is not yet a party some relief or remedy relating to or connected with the original subject matter of the action.

(c) The defendant requires that any question or issue relating to or connected with the original subject matter of the action should be determined not only between himself and the plaintiff but also between either or both of them and someone who is not yet a party to the action.

The details of when a third party notice is appropriate will not be examined here, as they are more a matter of procedure and substantive law than a matter of drafting, but the lawyers advising the defendant should always consider whether there might be anything to be gained from joining a third party.

The third party notice can be issued in an action begun by writ before the defence is served on the plaintiff, otherwise the leave of the court will be needed. Once a third party notice is served, the person on whom it is served has the same rights as regards any claim made against him as any other defendant would have (RSC Order 16, rule 1).

As for the drafting of a third party notice, see Example 3. Specific forms are laid down by the rules of court and must be used. There are two different forms, the usual one being where the claim is for a counterclaim, indemnity or other remedy or relief, and the alternative being where there is a question or issue to be determined rather than a specific claim. The heading of the third party notice will be taken from the writ, adding the name of the third party after that of the defendant. There are gaps in the form to be filled in to state the nature of the plaintiff's claim against the defendant, the nature of the defendant's claim against the third party, and the grounds for the claim. These gaps should be filled in following normal drafting principles, stating the basic elements of the case clearly and concisely.

Since the third party becomes a defendant as regards the claim against him he may serve a defence and there may be further pleadings following the ordinary rules already outlined.

EXAMPLE 3 BASIC THIRD PARTY NOTICE

IN THE HIGH COURT OF JUSTICE 1985.B.No.1234

DIVISION

BETWEEN A. B. *Plaintiff*

and

C. D. *Defendant*

and

E. F. *Third Party*

THIRD PARTY NOTICE

(Issued pursuant to the order of Master dated)

To E. F. of (address)

Take notice that this action has been brought by the Plaintiff against the Defendant. In it the Plaintiff claims against the Defendant (state briefly the type of claim made) as appears from the writ of summons, a copy whereof is served herewith, together with a copy of the statement of claim.
The Defendant claims against you (state briefly the nature of the claim against the third party e.g. an indemnity or a contribution) on the grounds that:

1. (Plead the facts giving rise to the claim against the third party in
2. separate numbered paragraphs as if pleading a statement of claim.)
3.
4.

And take notice (warning of the need to acknowledge service) etc. Signed.

10 *The originating summons action*

The whole procedure and purpose of an action begun by originating summons is different from that of an action begun by writ. Broadly the difference is that the writ action is designed as an adversary action where both sides prepare their cases with witnesses and evidence on disputed matters of fact, whereas in an originating summons action all parties are essentially asking the court the same questions of construction, and arguments will tend to be on law rather than on fact. The point of the drafting is different in that the statement of claim is designed to tell the basic story and the later pleadings go on to define the issues between the parties, while the originating summons sets out the questions which the parties would like the court to deal with, and there is no need for further pleadings.

There are basic procedural differences, not only in that there are fewer formal drafts in an originating summons action, but also that many procedural steps in a writ action, such as automatic discovery, do not apply in the originating summons action. There are some types of action where the originating summons is compulsory, and others where it is optional and it is for the plaintiff to decide on the most suitable way of beginning the action. It is most suitable in actions concerned with trusts or wills or similar actions concerned with documents, which are usually heard in the Chancery Division, so the tendency is for Chancery practitioners to use an originating summons if there is a choice, and for the Queen's Bench barrister to use a writ.

The originating summons is not strictly speaking a pleading, so the rules for pleadings do not apply unless they are expressly extended. However, many of the general rules for drafting, such as the need to be concise and clear, do apply.

The use of the originating summons

This was mentioned briefly in the chapter on basic principles of drafting. The main rules are that an originating summons must be used to commence an action where any application is made under any Act, unless the rules of court expressly require or authorise some other means of beginning the action, or the proceedings are already pending (RSC Order 5, rule 3). This means an action where the court is required to use a power that it only has by reason of an Act, not merely where an Act happens to be relevant. For example, there are various sections in the Trustee Act 1925 which authorise the court to make certain orders in connection with a trust, and in such a case the action should normally be begun by originating summons. This is dealt with further in the section on drafting for trust actions.

More generally, the originating summons is appropriate if the sole or principal question at issue is, or is likely to be, one of the construction of an Act or of any instrument made under an Act, or of any deed, will, contract or other document, or some other question of law, or in which there is unlikely to be any substantial dispute of fact (RSC Order 5, rule 4(2)). This is where the plaintiff has the choice how to begin the action.

If the case may fall within one of these categories the lawyer must decide what to do. The sole or principal question in the case must fall within these categories, so that if the meaning of a document is only a subsidiary issue in a case that is really about something else, the originating summons would not be appropriate. If the case does basically fall within one of the categories, then the next question is whether there is going to be a substantial dispute of fact, where the test is whether they will dispute facts rather than words or legal issues. If the fight is over the words of one of the clauses of a trust deed and whether they create a valid trust an originating summons should be used, also if facts are not really in dispute but there is a question whether a resulting trust has arisen. If alternatively the trust concerns a house where a couple were living together and there are substantial disputes of fact as to who paid for what, who built the extension etc., then a writ will be more appropriate.

The last stage when deciding whether to use an originating summons to commence an action is to consider the type of evidence you will be using, and any procedures you may wish to use in the course of the action. If the evidence is likely to be mainly documents and affidavits then the originating summons is appropriate, but if the parties are likely to wish to call a number of witnesses in court to give evidence of disputed points and the trial will consist largely of their evidence then a writ action is almost certainly more suitable. As for procedure, if the issues to go to the court can be clearly and immediately formulated into questions of construction then an originating summons will be appropriate, but if full pleadings may be needed to fully define the issues between the parties, a writ may be more suitable. Also procedural steps such as summary judgment and automatic discovery are by and large only available in a writ action, so that if these steps may be useful in the case the action should probably be begun by writ.

It is not always easy for the young lawyer to decide which originating application to use, but it is something that he will get the feel of in practice. In most cases the answer is quite clear but there are some difficult borderline decisions on which he may ask help from older practitioners. It should of course not be crucial if the wrong choice is made as it is possible to change from an originating summons to a writ action and vice-versa, but it may inhibit proper preparation for the trial.

Some cases help to illustrate the proper use of the originating summons. In *Re Sir Lindsay Parkinson & Co. Settlement Trusts* [1965] 1 WLR 372 the beneficiaries of a trust took out an originating summons to seek the removal of the trustees. It was held that such an action could be begun by originating summons or writ, but that since there was an allegation of breach of trust the writ was more appropriate as there would no doubt be disputes of fact and discovery would be available. In *Re 462 Green Lane, Ilford* [1971] 1 WLR 426 the plaintiff issued an originating summons to decide whether a caution registered on the property should be removed, but it was held that since the basic case involved an allegation of fraud, the case must be begun by writ under RSC Order 5. In *Re Deadman* [1971] 1 WLR 426 the plaintiff issued an originating summons to decide whether a gift in the will of the deceased was valid. There was later an amendment to include an allegation of undue influence, and it was held that therefore the action should continue as though it had been begun by writ.

Finally, there are certain specific cases in which an originating summons is appropriate by rules of court or statute, for example:

(a) Proceedings for possession of land (RSC Order 113).
(b) Actions under the Charities Act 1960 (RSC Order 108).
(c) Various proceedings under the Companies Acts (largely concerned with the technical running of the company) (RSC Order 102).
(d) Approval of a settlement on behalf of a person under a disability.
(e) Property disputes between husband and wife as to the matrimonial home.
(f) Applications under the Inheritance (Provision for Family and Dependants) Act 1975.
(g) Applications for variation of a trust.

Although originating summonses are most common in the Chancery Division, they may occasionally be appropriate in the Queen's Bench.

The procedure in an originating summons action

The procedure in an originating summons action comes from RSC Order 28, and is much simpler than the procedure in a writ action. This is because once the questions for the court have been formalised there is little else to do except prepare the arguments for the court. The basic stages are as follows:

(a) Originating summons issued.
(b) Originating summons served. This should happen within 12 months of its being issued.
(c) Acknowledgment of service. This should be done by the defendant within 14 days of his receiving the originating summons. It is possible for the defendant to make a counterclaim against the plaintiff if he alleges that he is entitled to any relief or remedy against the plaintiff, but this is not as formal as in a writ action, and may be dealt with as the court directs (RSC Order 28, rule 7).
(d) Plaintiff files affidavits. Within 14 days of the acknowledgment of service, the plaintiff should file at the court office the affidavit evidence on which he intends to rely, and copies must be served on the defendants (RSC Order 28, rule 1A). (This is a relatively new rule, giving a more detailed timetable for an originating summons action.)
(e) Defendant files affidavits. If a defendant wishes to adduce affidavit evidence he should file it within 28 days of receiving copies of the plaintiff's affidavits. He should serve copies of his affidavits on the plaintiff (RSC Order 28, rule 1A).
(f) Plaintiff files affidavits in reply. If the plaintiff wishes to adduce further affidavits in reply, he should file them within 14 days of receiving the defendant's affidavits, and send copies to the defendant (RSC Order 28, rule 1A).
(g) Fixing appointment for hearing. Within one month of the end of the time within which copies of affidavits may be served the plaintiff should make an appointment for the attendance of the parties at court. This is often referred to as

a 'Masters Appointment' as the hearing is by a Master or in Chambers. The purpose of the hearing is similar to a summons for Directions, and various orders on the conduct of the action can be made. In a simple case it is possible for this hearing to be treated as a trial. It is possible for an order to be made for the action to continue as though the case had been begun by writ and for the affidavits to stand as pleadings (RSC Order 28, rules 2 and 4).

(h) Order for trial. When the court is satisfied that the matter is ready for determination it can make an order for hearing or trial (RSC Order 28, rule 9).

This is a skeleton of the procedure. It is less formal than the writ procedure, and has fewer stages, though the courts have wide powers to make orders on the conduct of the case. There are less interlocutory procedures available than there are in a writ action, but orders on discovery etc. may be made if they would help in the conduct of the case. Such applications may be made to a judge in Chambers in the Queen's Bench, or by Notice of Motion to a judge in the Chancery Division. The rules for a writ action are applied flexibly in an originating summons action, *Re Caines* [1978] 2 All ER 1.

Clearly the affidavits are the basis of the action, though the court may make orders for the taking of oral evidence. If a party wishes to use affidavits other than those he has filed he needs the leave of the court. The drafting of the affidavits is therefore very important, and this is dealt with in a later chapter.

This chapter will deal with the normal form of originating summons, but there are alternative forms of expedited or ex parte originating summonses which may be used where appropriate.

Drafting an originating summons

The purpose of the originating summons is not to tell the story of what has happened. This will be done in the affidavits filed by the parties, which may be ordered to stand as pleadings if the action is ordered to continue as a writ action. The purpose of the originating summons is to define clearly those matters which the court is being asked to deal with. This is done in two main ways in the numbered paragraphs in the main part of the document, the first being to formulate questions for the court to answer, and the second to ask the court to exercise a particular power that it has to assist the parties.

Since the originating summons action is not really adversarial in the way that the writ action is, the main purpose of the drafting is not so much to put the client's case in the best possible light, but rather to be reasonably objective, and to draft the problems as clearly as possible. It is in court that there will be argument for any particular conclusion that the client hopes the court will reach, and in the drafting of the affidavits. In an originating summons case one will often be advising an executor, a personal representative or a trustee who will probably not have a personal interest in the property under dispute anyway but merely wants to know what he should do with it, and this helps the sense of objectivity. However, your client will sometimes have strong views on the case, and this will be considered in the section on advising in trust cases.

The young lawyer learning to draft originating summonses will often take one of two fairly extreme views. He may find them relatively easy, because it is only necessary to isolate two or three areas of difficulty in the case and put them in the

EXAMPLE 1 BASIC ORIGINATING SUMMONS ASKING QUESTIONS OF CONSTRUCTION

IN THE HIGH COURT OF JUSTICE Ch.1985.B.No.

CHANCERY DIVISION

IN THE MATTER of........

BETWEEN (1) A. B.
(2) C. D. *Plaintiffs*
and
(1) E. F.
(2) G. H.
(3) I. J.
(4) K. L. *Defendants*

TO (1) (name of first defendant) of (address of first defendant) who (state briefly his interest in the case, e.g. because he claims to be a beneficiary.)
AND TO (2) (name of second defendant) of (go on to state address and interest as with (1).)
AND TO (3) (name of third defendant) of (go on to state address and interest as with (1).)
AND TO (4) (name of fourth defendant) of (go on to state address and interest as with (1).)

Let the Defendants........ (directions as to acknowledgment of service)

By this summons, which is issued on the application of the Plaintiffs (1) (name of first plaintiff) of (address of first plaintiff) and (2) (name of second plaintiff) of (address of second plaintiff) the (state briefly their interest in the case, e.g. that they are trustees and executors of the will), the Plaintiffs seek the determination of the Court on the following questions and the following relief, namely:
(Set out in separate numbered paragraphs the points which you wish the court to construe. The following are examples of possible paragraphs that may be adjusted for use.)
1. Whether upon the true construction of clause of the said will and in the events which have happened, the sum of £ is held on trust for:

(i) (Set out separately all the possible options)
(ii)
(iii)
(iv) on any other, and if so what, trust.

2. If the answer to question 1 is in the sense (i), that it may be determined whether the said sum of £ is held on trust for:

(i)
(ii)
(iii) on any other, and if so what, trust.

3. That it may be determined whether on the true construction of clause of the said will, the residuary estate of the deceased is held on trust for:

(i)
(ii)
(iii) on any other, and if so what, trust.

4. If the answer to question 3 is in the sense (i), and it is considered impracticable to carry out the charitable purpose with the funds available, that the Court may approve a scheme for the application of the funds (if the approval of a cy pres scheme may be needed.)
5. That the second defendant, or some other fit and proper person, be appointed to represent...... (e.g. a group of minors) (to be used if a representation order is needed).
6. Insofar as may be necessary, administration of the estate.
7. That provision may be made for the costs of this application.
8. Further or other relief.

If the defendant does not......
etc.

Settled by: (Signed).

EXAMPLE 2 BASIC ORIGINATING SUMMONS ASKING THE COURT TO EXERCISE POWERS E.G. OF APPOINTMENT OR APPROVAL

IN THE HIGH COURT OF JUSTICE Ch.1985.B.No.

CHANCERY DIVISION

IN THE MATTER OF........

BETWEEN
(1) A. B.
(2) C. D. *Plaintiffs*
and
(1) E. F.
(2) G. H.
(3) I. J.
(4) K. L. *Defendants*

TO (1) (name of first defendant) of (address of first defendant) who (state briefly his interest in the case, e.g. because he claims to be a beneficiary)
AND TO (2) (name of second defendant) of (go on to state his address and interest as in (1))
AND TO (3) (name of third defendant) of (go on to state his address and interest as in (1))
AND TO (4) (name of third defendant) of (go on to state his address and interest as in (1))

Let the Defendants...... (directions as to acknowledgment of service)

By this summons, which is issued on the application of the Plaintiffs (name of first plaintiff) of (address of first plaintiff) and (name of second plaintiff) of (address of second plaintiff) the (state briefly their interest in the case, e.g. that they are trustees of the trust), the Plaintiffs seek the following relief, namely:
(Set out in separate numbered paragraphs the things which you wish the Court to do. The following are examples of possible paragraphs that may be adapted for use)
1. That the Court may approve...... (set out exactly what you wish the court to approve).
2. That the Court may appoint X. Y. to be a trustee of the said trust. (where the appointment of a new trustee by the Court is sought).
3. That provision may be made for the costs of this application.
4. Further or other relief.

This application is made under section 57 and section 41 of the Trustee Act 1925 (as appropriate)

If the defendant does not......

draft, rather than having to summarise the whole case as is needed in a statement of claim. Also it can feel easier in that one is 'passing the buck' to the court to make decisions. The alternative is to find the originating summons very difficult because of the care that is needed in drafting the questions accurately to define exactly what the problem is, and to suggest all the possible answers. The truth is inevitably somewhere between the two—that the originating summons is just a different drafting skill. The statement of claim needs clear and concise thinking; the originating summons needs clear and logical thinking. The real art of drafting questions in an originating summons is something that can only come with practice, and with as much experience as possible of your own and other lawyers' pleadings. However, a good beginning for the young lawyer is to make brief notes before he begins drafting, making a numbered list of the points which he wishes to ask for guidance on, and what the possible answers are.

Drafting the formal parts of the originating summons

The general form for an originating summons is specified in the rules of the High Court (RSC Order 7, rule 2), and it is for the plaintiff to complete it as appropriate. As with the writ, blank forms are issued for completion by the lawyer in the case. Since the originating summons is not technically a pleading many of the technical rules that apply to writs do not apply, but some do, for example the need to indorse the name and address of the plaintiff or his solicitor on the summons before it is issued (RSC Order 7, rule 3). Examples 1 and 2 illustrate an originating summons asking questions of construction, and asking the court to exercise powers. There are actual examples of originating summonses in the section on drafting for trust actions.

The heading

The originating summons should begin by stating the Division of the High Court in which the action is to proceed, and if the summons is issued through a District Registry this should also be stated. The reference number of the action should also appear at the top of the summons. In practice the rules for the writ are followed for all these things.

There were formerly quite complicated rules as to the heading of an action, under which it was necessary to head an originating summons to be 'In the Matter of......' each and every document that the court was required to interpret and each and every statute that the court was required to act under. These complex headings served no particular purpose, and the rules have now been considerably simplified, *Practice Direction* [1983] 1 All ER 131, which applied to all proceedings in the Chancery Division, as follows:

> The general rule is that the title should contain only the parties to the proceedings, but there are two exceptions; (1) where the proceedings relate to the administration of an estate or a probate action they should be entitled 'In the estate of AB deceased'; and (2) where the proceedings relate to the construction of a document they should be entitled 'In the matter of (describe document briefly) dated   between AB and CD'. Parties should be

> named by their initials and surnames only; and if there are numerous parties, it will usually suffice to state that the document is made 'between AB and others'. If there is more than one document, only the main or first document need be referred to.
>
> If proceedings are under an Act of Parliament, the Act no longer need be mentioned in the title but should be referred to in the body of the writ or originating summons.

There have been some minor variations in the way that this rule has been interpreted in practice, but the present position can be summarised fairly simply by saying that in an action in the Chancery Division there should be an 'In the Matter of......' heading where the proceedings do relate to the administration of an estate or the construction of a document, but not in any other case. If there is more than one document, there should still only be a single 'In the matter of......' heading relating to the main document.

The heading should be correct under these rules, but there are variations in practice among different practitioners, and it will not be crucial in the action. To give examples of headings complying with these rules, if the case relates to the construction of a clause in the will of Mr Julius Caesar the heading should be 'In the estate of Julius Caesar deceased'. If the proceedings relate to the construction of a clause in a lifetime settlement then the heading should be 'In the matter of the settlement dated 13th February 1982 between J. Caesar and B. Brutus'. If the action is purely to ask the court whether a trust has arisen on a set of facts where there is no written document, or is purely to ask the court to exercise its powers under a statute then no heading is needed except for the names of the parties.

As with a writ, the full names of the parties should be set out properly. However there are some special points to consider when deciding on the parties to an originating summons action. In beginning an action by writ the plaintiff has a complete choice of who to sue, and if there is more than one person that he could sue he may choose to sue one rather than another because his case against one is stronger, or because one can better afford to pay any damages awarded. In an originating summons one is often asking the court to make decisions as to the distribution of assets, and therefore it is necessary to join all those who may have a claim to the assets, because only then will they be bound by any decision that the court makes. If they are not made parties, they will not be bound, and are quite free to make claims in the future.

Thus the objective in an originating summons is not to make strategic choices as to who to make parties, but to join everyone who may have a claim to the assets in question. The person or persons taking out the summons will be the plaintiffs, and anyone else with a possible claim should be made a defendant (RSC Order 7, rule 2). Having said this, it does not mean that the draft should join as parties everyone mentioned in instructions who has the remotest possible connection with the case. This will produce an unnecessarily long list of defendants and will waste money. The test is whether the person or body in question does have a direct potential claim to any part of the assets in dispute. Consider each asset about which there is any possible doubt and list those who may have a legal or equitable interest in it, and that should give a basic list of defendants.

This list should take into account every possibility, for example if a gift in a will fails the property may go instead to the next of kin, in which case the closest member of the next of kin should be joined. If property is left to someone with remainder to their children then it may be necessary to join someone to represent the children, even if they are not yet born, so that their claim may be argued if necessary. On the other hand, it is not necessary to join someone who does not have a direct claim to the assets, for example if money is left 'to John Smith to help teachers in Northampton learn to use computers' it is only John Smith who needs to be made a party to the action, as it is him who may get the money; the teachers in Northampton are just a description of the purpose of the gift, and it is not necessary to join one of them as a party.

It is not always easy to know where to draw the line as to who should be a party. Some experienced lawyers will join everyone who may have any possible claim, whereas others will only join those parties that they strictly have to. The young lawyer will get the feel of how to take decisions with practice.

It may well be that several people will have exactly the same type of claim to property, and that it would just make the action more complicated and expensive to join all of them, when they will all have exactly the same legal argument. To avoid this unnecessary expense it is possible to join one of the group as a party to represent all those with the same type of interest. These rules apply equally to writ actions, but since a representation order is more likely to be helpful in an originating summons action the rules are discussed here, as are the various types of representative action in RSC Order 15.

The general rule for representative proceedings is in RSC Order 15, rule 12, which provides firstly that if numerous persons have the same interest in any proceedings, the proceedings may be begun by or against any one or more of them, representing all, or all except one or more of them, unless the court orders otherwise. Secondly, the plaintiff may apply to the court at any stage in the proceedings to appoint one or more of the defendants (or some other person who will then be made a defendant) to represent all or all except one or more of numerous persons who have the same interest as defendants in the proceedings, and the court may make an order on such terms as it thinks fit. One defendant can only represent a group of people if the plaintiff gets an order to that effect from the court, and this order should be asked for at the end of the draft.

Once there is a representative in the proceedings, any judgment or order will bind everyone represented, though the order can only be enforced against them with the leave of the court, and it is still open to the person represented to dispute his liability before the order is enforced.

There are cases illustrating where a representative action is appropriate. The basic test was discussed in *Smith* v *Cardiff Corporation* [1954] 1 QB 210, where the council increased rents by differing amounts and a tenant wished to bring a representative action to object. It was held that the people represented must have a common interest, arising from a common grievance to produce a remedy beneficial to all, and that this did not apply in the case as different tenants had suffered differently. In *John* v *Rees* [1969] 2 WLR 1294 there were various disputes in a local Labour Party, and the local M.P. for Pembrokeshire was expelled. It was held that a member of the Labour Party could bring a representative action within the rules of the party. In *Prudential Assurance Co.* v *Newman Industries* [1979] 3 All ER 507 it was held that a shareholder could bring a representative action against company officials, provided that no shareholder got a benefit they would not otherwise have had. It was held in *Moon* v *Atherton* [1972] 2 QB 435 that not only could one leaseholder in a block of flats bring an action representing the others, but that another leaseholder could take over when she dropped out.

However, for one person to represent others there must be a complete identity of interest, both legal and factual, and for example you cannot have a representative action for libel, as proof of damage to each plaintiff is an essential part of the case, *E.E.T.P.U.* v *Times Newspapers* [1980] 1 All ER 1097.

A second and separate type of representative proceedings comes from RSC Order 15, rule 13, where members of a group of people with a similar interest cannot easily be ascertained or found. This rule only applies to proceedings concerning the estate of a deceased person, or property subject to a trust, or the construction of a written instrument of statute, and will therefore clearly be most likely to apply in an originating summons action. The rule applies to three classes of people:

(a) Where a person, class or some member of a class cannot, or cannot readily, be ascertained.

(b) Where a person, class or some member of a class, though ascertained, cannot be found.

(c) Where, though the person, or the class and the members of it can be ascertained and found, it appears to the court expedient to make an order to save expense.

In any of these cases the court may appoint a person or persons to represent any person (including an unborn person) or class of people who has or may have an interest in any thing (whether present or future, contingent or unascertained), or who may be affected by the proceedings. Any person so represented will be bound by the outcome of the proceedings. The court also has a power to approve a compromise on behalf of any person so represented in the action.

The third separate type of representation comes from RSC Order 15, rule 14. This allows that any proceedings may be brought by or against trustees, executors or administrators without having to join as well any beneficiaries of the trust or estate. Any order made in the proceedings will then bind the beneficiaries unless the court orders otherwise. This is perfectly reasonable, as all the beneficiaries would otherwise have to be joined, and the trustees will of course be under a duty to act in the best interests of the beneficiaries in bringing or defending the action.

Following the title and the names of the parties there is a formal section in the originating summons which should be completed carefully by the person drafting. This formal part falls into three sections, and each will be considered in order.

'To......' This section should list the defendants that the originating summons is being sent to, giving the name of each, the address of each, and the type of claim that he has or may have that has led to his being made a party. For example 'To Joseph Aloysius Bloggs of 3, Acacia Avenue, London SW50, who claims to be interested as a beneficiary under the said will'. The full name and

address of each defendant should be relatively straightforward, but it is necessary to take care in specifying what type of claim he has. The description of the existing or potential interest should be as brief and specific as possible, for example distinguishing whether it is a beneficial interest or an equitable interest, and whether it is under a will or a settlement or in specific property as the case may be, or whether it is an interest as next of kin. If two or more defendants are alleged to have exactly the same type of interest then the names and addresses of all of them can be given together, followed by a single description of the interest, for example:

'To Calpurnia Caesar of 3, New Road, Milton Keynes, who claims to be beneficially entitled under the terms of the said will and as next of kin to the deceased',

'To Regan Lear and Goneril Lear, both of 3, Old Mews, London SW3, who claim to have an equitable interest in the property known as The Manor, Lower Codswallop, Gloucestershire'.

'Let the defendant......' This is a formal paragraph warning the defendant of the need to acknowledge service. It is a set form of wording needing no drafting.

'By this summons......' This section deals with the plaintiff or plaintiffs who have taken out the summons, and should give the name of each, the address of each, and the capacity in which they bring the action. Again it is necessary to take care to define properly the capacity of the plaintiffs. They may for example be trustees of a settlement, or trustees and executors of a will. An example of the wording of this section is, 'By this summons, which is issued on the application of the plaintiffs, Viola Knight of Gable House, Updean, Surrey and Sebastian Knight of The Manor, Updean, Surrey, trustees and executors of the said will, the plaintiffs seek the determination of the court of the following questions, and the following relief, namely......'.

The body of the originating summons follows these paragraphs. The other formal parts follow the body of the drafting and follow a set pattern of a warning of the effects of failure to acknowledge service, and an indorsement of the name or firm and business address of the solicitors of the plaintiff in the same way as on the writ (RSC Order 6, rule 5).

Since the originating summons is not technically a pleading, it does not need to be signed by the person drafting it, though it is common for the person doing the drafting to acknowledge that it is his work by signing the backsheet of the draft, or signing the draft in a place different from the normal signature.

The body of the originating summons

There are two main things that the body of the originating summons may seek to do. One is to ask the court questions, where for example a point of construction is in doubt, and the other is to ask the court to exercise a power to assist the plaintiffs.

RSC Order 7, rule 3 provides that every originating summons should include a statement of the questions on which the plaintiff seeks the determination or direction of the High Court or, as the case may be, a concise statement of the relief or remedy claimed in the proceedings begun by the originating summons with sufficient particulars to identify the cause or causes of action in respect of which the plaintiff claims the relief or remedy.

This is the basis for the principles of drafting the originating summons. Like a writ, it should be in numbered paragraphs, each paragraph dealing with a separate point that the court is asked to deal with. Each of these paragraphs should ask the court one question, or ask the court for a single type of relief or remedy. Each paragraph should be concise, just giving the elements of the problem because the affidavits supporting the summons are the place to go into detail. However, the paragraphs should contain sufficient information for the court to be able to understand what they are being asked about. The originating summons should make sense when read on its own, even though it is just the skeleton of the problem.

Before beginning to draft the originating summons it is useful to make a brief numbered list of the basic points that are to be raised in each paragraph, that is each issue that you wish to ask a question about and every relief or remedy that you want from the court. This will normally arise quite easily from the opinion in the case. If the advice in the opinion is that the law is clear and that something is either valid or invalid then the point does not need to go to court, but if your legal advice is that the point is in doubt then the matter must go to the court in the draft. This initial list should make it clear for each paragraph whether it is to be phrased as a question or to ask for a remedy or relief.

If you wish to ask the court what the meaning of a particular wording or action is or whether it is valid, this should be done in the form of a question. There must be a separate question for each separate issue. If an issue is complicated it may be necessary to ask more than one question about it and to put different alternatives into the questions, but there should be as few questions as is reasonably possible. The questions must be phrased in a way that allows the court to give a simple answer, that is you should not effectively ask the court 'please can you tell me what this means?', but the draft should give the court the various alternative meanings so that the court only needs to say yes or no, or to say simply which alternative it chooses. This purpose should help the lawyer as well as the judge, because it helps him to clarify the issues and possibilities in his own mind ready to argue them in court.

To prepare for the draft, note briefly all the various alternative meanings of the words that the court is to interpret, or all the possibilities of what may happen to property if there is any uncertainty about the disposition of it. For example, if a clause in a will is in dispute the possibilities may be:

(a) It is valid in one way.
(b) It is valid in another way.
(c) It is invalid and falls into residue.
(d) It is invalid and passes to the next of kin on intestacy.

Also it may be possible for something to be invalid in one way but valid in another, for example a trust may not be valid as a charitable trust but it may be valid as a private trust. All the different alternatives of validity and invalidity should be thought of as far as possible, and this is examined in more detail in the section on trust actions. It is difficult to think of every possibility, and it is common to add as a final alternative something general to allow for something that has not occurred to you, such as 'some other, and if so what trusts'.

As far as possible all the different alternatives for one problem should be contained in one paragraph, or the draft tends to get too long and confusing, but sometimes the facts lead to so many alternatives that it is more convenient and clear to divide the possibilities up into separate paragraphs. For example, one might have one paragraph listing the primary alternatives, and then a further one dealing with the alternatives if the court should make a particular choice in the first paragraph.

Each alternative should be given as briefly as possible, preferably in a single phrase or sentence. Although the rules for drafting statements of claim do not strictly apply to originating summonses, there is still no need to plead law, evidence, or background facts. However the young lawyer learning to draft does need to take care that each paragraph does make sense. Some students in listing the alternatives seem to lose sight of the need for grammar and proper sentences, because it does take time and practice to learn how to phrase the alternatives properly, but as with any other draft, it is useful to put it down when it is finished and then go back later to reread it.

There is a substantial art to drafting questions in originating summonses, and it does take some time to develop the ability. One needs to think logically and to take a great many possibilities into account at the same time, and to be able to simplify a mass of possibilities into a few basic propositions. Also there are a variety of styles in the drafting of originating summonses, and of dividing up the matter to go in the summary. It is useful when looking at the drafts of others to note any particularly useful phrasing or way of dealing with alternatives and remember them for future use. This is dealt with further in the chapter on advising and drafting in trust actions.

Asking the court to use a particular power to grant relief is an alternative use of an originating summons, though it is quite possible to combine it with asking questions so long as different things are put in separate paragraphs. It may be that there is no difficulty about the meaning or validity of something, but that the plaintiff wishes to ask the court to exercise a particular power that it has to help him with a difficulty. In this case there is clearly no need for questions and alternatives, you simply ask the court to exercise its power.

The drafting here is relatively straightforward, in that all that is needed is a paragraph literally just asking the court for the relief sought. The draft does not need to say why there is a difficulty or to give any factual background, as again this will be done in the affidavits. The thing that is important is to take care that the words in the draft do clearly ask for exactly what you want. For example, if you are asking the court to approve something you must specify exactly what it is that you want the court to approve, because if the wording is slightly wrong then the approval that the court gives may not in fact cover the situation and protect your client.

It is of course only possible to ask the court to exercise a power that it has. One cannot ask the court to do something purely because it would be useful, but only if the court does specifically have the power under a statute, a rule of court, or because of its inherent jurisdiction. To give a few examples, the court has various powers under the Trustee Act 1925 to appoint or remove trustees, to approve various transactions in connection with the trust and so on and by RSC Order 85 the court has the power to deal with questions in connection with the administration of an estate.

If the court is being asked to exercise a power that it has under a statute or due to a rule of court, then that statute or rule should be quoted in the draft. It is no longer necessary to put the statute in the heading, following the 1983 Practice Direction mentioned above, so earlier precedents which did this should now be ignored. Instead the statute or rule should be referred to in the body of the draft. This is normally done by putting it at the end, after the numbered paragraphs in a separate un-numbered sentence, such as, 'This application is made under section 57 of the Trustee Act 1925', or 'This application is made under Order 85, rule 2'. It is only necessary to do this if you really are asking the court to use a power which it only has because of that section or rule. It is not necessary if the section or rule merely happens to have some relevance to the action, or if the court has an inherent power and does not need to act under the section. For example the court has an inherent power to approve a cy pres scheme for a charity which is merely widened by the Charities Act 1961, s.13 and it is therefore not really necessary to quote the section when you are asking the court to act under its inherent power, though one does see it done sometimes in practice.

It is necessary to specify in the originating summons every remedy or relief that is asked from the court, with a separate paragraph each, or the court will not have a power to grant it. Although there is no strict rule, in practice the lesser remedies and reliefs should be put in the last paragraphs, after the main paragraphs asking questions, and for particular reliefs that are needed. The reliefs are sought in separate paragraphs, not in a separate part of the draft, as in a statement of claim.

For example, ancillary orders may be required in the action. If a representation order for one of the defendants to represent a particular group of people is needed, this should be requested, for example, 'That the fourth defendant be appointed to represent all the adult children of the deceased'.

One of the final paragraphs should of course seek an order for costs.

Since all the reliefs and remedies sought should be specified, it is common to put in a final paragarph asking for 'further or other relief' or words to that effect, in case the person doing the draft has forgotten to include anything. However, this can only be used to give some relief or remedy similar to that already claimed, and will probably not cover the case where an important point that should have been pleaded is not in the draft at all.

11 *Drafting affidavits*

Almost any lawyer will have to draft affidavits frequently, as they play a part in many types of civil action. Having said that, the affidavit is a chameleon that turns up in many different forms for many different purposes, and the drafting will need to be approached in different ways for these different purposes. Some affidavits are very short and are just a necessary part of a minor procedural step, whereas others are long and complicated and may be the basic evidence on which a case is decided. This chapter will look at the rules for drafting affidavits, the circumstances in which affidavits are needed, and the approach to different types of affidavits.

The affidavit is essentially a written sworn statement of evidence. It is a form of evidence that may be used either because that form of evidence is usual in the action, for example originating summons actions are usually conducted on affidavit evidence, or used with the agreement of the parties, or used in certain other circumstances allowed by statute or by the Rules of Court. Affidavits are also often required by the Rules of Court to support certain types of applications to court, especially interlocutory applications, where it is not really convenient to take oral evidence from witnesses. Of course at the trial of most actions oral evidence will be preferred.

Although the affidavit is the sworn evidence of a particular witness, it will not be written by that witness himself, or take his exact words in the way that a statement in a criminal case will normally do. Instead it will be drafted by a lawyer, using the facts supplied by the witness, but adapting them to the form that will be most useful to the court. A reasonably straightforward affidavit in support of a court application will normally be drafted by a solicitor. Even if the barrister has advised on the application and has done other drafting in the case, the affidavits in support will normally be done by the instructing solicitor. However, if the affidavit is likely to be particularly complex, or if it may be of basic importance in the decision in the case then the barrister will normally draft it. This is because once a barrister has been instructed, he is in charge of the conduct of the case, and an affidavit may well be an important part of the way the case is put to the judge. If there may be any doubt as to who should draft the affidavit it should be made clear in the instructions in the brief, or by agreement between the barrister and the solicitor.

The uses of affidavits

The use of affidavits varies according to the type of proceedings and the stage reached. There are limited circumstances in which affidavits can be used as evidence at the trial of an action, though there are some types of case that are normally conducted on affidavit evidence, especially actions begun by originating summonses, and there are some types of proceedings where affidavits can be important in the conduct of the case, such as in applications for ancillary relief on divorce. Affidavits are often required to support applications for interlocutory applications, as provided by the rules of court. This does give a wide variety, from complex affidavits that may be the basis of a case to short, formal affidavits that are straightforward.

The general rule for admitting affidavit evidence at the hearing of a case comes from RSC Order 38. Every fact at issue at the trial should normally be proved by the examination of a witness orally in open court (RSC Order 38, rule 1), but in an action begun by writ the court may order at any time at or before the trial that the affidavit of any witness may be read at the trial, if in the circumstances of the case it thinks this is reasonable. The order may be made on such terms as the court thinks fit as to the filing of the affidavit, giving copies of it to other parties and producing the deponent for cross-examination, but otherwise the deponent will not then have to attend the trial or be cross-examined. Such an order may be made where there may be a difficulty in the witness being available for the trial or where their evidence is not substantially in dispute or is only of minor importance. The possible use of affidavit evidence should be considered at the summons for directions (RSC Order 25, rule 3).

In an action begun by originating summons, petition or originating motion, or on an application to court on a summons or motion the emphasis is different and evidence may be given by affidavit unless the court directs otherwise (RSC Order 38, rule 2), though a court may order a deponent to attend for cross examination, and there are some exceptions to this in the rules of court.

In addition to these general rules, there are many special provisions in the Rules of Court and in statute requiring the use of affidavits or prescribing their contents in particular cases. Affidavits in applications for ancillary relief on divorce are dealt with in the Matrimonial Causes Rules 1977, rules 68–85. To give some other examples, an application under the Inheritance (Provision for Family and Dependants) Act 1975 must be supported by an affidavit, and the personal representatives of the deceased must and other defendants may also file affidavits. The contents of such affidavits are prescribed by RSC Order 99, rules 3 and 5. Applications under the Maintenance Orders Acts 1950, 1958 and 1968 or the Attachment of Earnings Act 1971 should also be supported by affidavits giving appropriate details (RSC Order 105). As a different example, in contentious probate proceedings, every party should file an affidavit as to any testamentary scripts that he knows of (RSC Order 76).

Particular types of application to the High Court or to a single judge of that court also need to be supported by an affidavit, for example an application for judicial review (RSC Order 53), or an application for bail (RSC Order 79). An application for habeas corpus must be supported by an affidavit as to the nature of the restraint by the person restrained or someone acting on his behalf (RSC Order 54).

These are just a few examples of cases where affidavits may be needed that will be necessary for the action, and may be an important foundation for the case.

The lawyer in practice will come to know of other cases where affidavits are needed in the areas of law he works in.

In addition there are many procedural steps that need to be supported by an affidavit under the Rules of Court. This is quite practical, as before the case comes to trial it will be difficult or inconvenient to get witnesses to attend court, and they may not be appropriate for a procedural application. Sometimes a rule merely specifies that an application must be supported by an affidavit, and sometimes it goes on to give details of what the affidavit should contain. Many of these affidavits will be fairly formal and straightforward, but some will be more complex and important. The following is a list of some of the procedural steps where affidavits may be needed, but it is in no way exhaustive:

(a) An application for leave to serve a writ out of the jurisdiction must be supported by an affidavit stating the grounds on which the application is made, that there is believed to be a good cause of action, and where the defendant is believed to be (RSC Order 11, rule 4).

(b) An application for summary judgment under Order 14 must be supported by an affidavit verifying the facts on which the claim is made, and stating that in the deponent's belief there is no defence to the claim except as to the amount of damages claimed. Such an affidavit may contain statements of information or belief provided the sources and grounds for belief are given. The defendant has no obligation to file an affidavit in reply, but in practice he may well do.

(c) An application for an ex parte interlocutory injunction should be supported by an affidavit verifying the facts on which the injunction is sought (RSC Order 29, rule 1).

(d) An application for leave to issue a third party notice must be supported by an affidavit stating the nature of the claim made by the plaintiff, the stage the proceedings have reached, the nature of the claim made by the applicant, the facts on which the claim against the third party is based, and the name and address of the proposed third party (RSC Order 16, rule 2).

(e) A party under a duty to make discovery of documents may be required to make an affidavit verifying the list of documents for discovery, which must be in a specified form (RSC Order 24, rules 2 and 3).

(f) Applications for disclosure of documents under the Supreme Court Act 1981, ss.33 and 34 must be supported by an affidavit stating the grounds for the application, specifying the documents sought and saying how they are likely to be relevant to an issue in the proceedings, and why the person against whom the order is sought is likely to have them, (RSC Order 24, rule 7A).

(g) Applications for the inspection of property under the Supreme Court Act 1981, ss.33 and 34 should be supported by an affidavit specifying the property in respect of which an order is sought, and why it is or may become relevant to proceedings (RSC Order 29, rule 7A).

(h) An application for an interim payment must be supported by an affidavit verifying the damages or other sum to which the application relates, the grounds for the application, and exhibiting any relevant documentary evidence (RSC Order 29, rule 10).

(i) An application for summary judgment under RSC Order 86, for specific performance of an agreement etc., must be supported by an affidavit verifying the facts, and stating that in the deponent's belief there is no defence to the action. It may contain statements of information or belief with their sources or grounds.

(j) A claim for summary possession of land under RSC Order 113 must be supported by an affidavit stating the plaintiff's interest in the land, the circumstances of the occupation of the land, and that the plaintiff does not know the name of any person occupying the land who is not named on the summons.

(k) An application for a garnishee order to enforce a judgment must be supported by an affidavit identifying the judgment and the amount unpaid, and stating the grounds for the belief that the person named does owe money to the judgment debtor and is within the jurisdiction, with his bank if known (RSC Order 49, rule 2).

Drafting an affidavit

Since there are so many types of affidavits for so many different purposes, this section can only deal with basic principles. As always, the barrister or solicitor will learn in practice to modify his approach to the type of affidavit needed, where he can run off a short affidavit in a common form and where he will need to do careful work on what to include and how to phrase it. He will also learn where the rules do require specific points to be dealt with in the affidavit.

As for the general approach to drafting affidavits, there is perhaps even more room for variations of technique and style here than in other areas of drafting. Sometimes an affidavit will need to be filled with formal and legalistic phrases because it deals with a technical and difficult point, but in that most affidavits will normally be sworn by a party in the case rather than by the barrister or solicitor who drafts them, they should as far as possible be written in the ordinary English that the witness would use. The lawyer's skills are needed to advise that an affidavit is needed, to check what needs to be included in it, and to sort the information given by the witness to include only those matters which are relevant in a suitable order, but beyond that, the affidavit should be as clear, simple and easy to read as possible.

The heading

The heading of the affidavit should be the same as that of the cause or matter in which it is sworn (RSC Order 41, rule 1). That is, it should have the same heading as other drafts as regards the court or Division of court, the same reference number and the same parties. However, if there are a great number of parties, it is sufficient to state the name of the first plaintiff or the first defendant, as appropriate followed by the words 'and others'. If there is an 'In the matter of......' heading, this should also appear on the affidavit.

The body of the affidavit

There are some main rules on the contents of affidavits. RSC Order 41, rule 1 provides that:

> Every affidavit must be expressed in the first person, and, unless the court

EXAMPLE 1 BASIC FORM OF AFFIDAVIT

Sworn on behalf of the Plaintiff
(or the Defendant)

IN THE HIGH COURT OF JUSTICE 1985.B.No.1234

DIVISION

BETWEEN A. B. *Plaintiff*
and
C. D. *Defendant*

I, (full name of deponent) of (address of deponent) a (occupation of deponent) make oath and say as follows:
(Set out in numbered paragraphs the facts which the deponent knows which are relevant to the purpose for which the affidavit is filed).
1.
2.
3. There is now produced and shown to me marked 'X.Y.1' a ...... (to be used when the deponent refers to an exhibit).
4. I have been informed by (give name) and believe that ...... (to be used when the deponent is permitted to include matters of information and belief, and must therefore give his source).

Sworn at ...... Signed (by deponent)

Before ......

otherwise directs, must state the place of residence of the deponent and his occupation or, if he has none, his description, and if he is, or is employed by a party to the cause or matter in which the affidavit is sworn, the affidavit must state that fact. In the case of a deponent who is giving evidence in a professional, business or other occupational capacity, the affidavit may, instead of stating the deponent's place of residence, state the address at which he works, the position he holds and the name of his firm or employer, if any.

To comply with this, an affidavit will begin with a concise statement of the required information, for example:

I, Julius Caesar, the plaintiff in this action, of 3, The Landing, Dover, a self-employed writer, make oath and say as follows:

I, Albert Einstein, a research scientist employed by Big Bang Enterprises, of The Trading Estate, Greenham Common, Berkshire, make oath and say as follows:

Following this statement, the main part of the affidavit will set out the appropriate information that the affidavit is to deal with. The affidavit should be divided into paragraphs, numbered consecutively, each paragraph being as far as possible confined to a distinct portion of the subject matter (RSC Order 41, rule 1). The other rules are that dates, sums and other numbers should be expressed in figures rather than words. Also, an affidavit should contain only such facts as the deponent is able to prove of his own knowledge, except where a specific exception is provided by the rules of court (RSC Order 41, rule 5). The reason for this is clearly that an affidavit is just another form of evidence, so that hearsay should not appear in an affidavit any more than in oral evidence. The most general exception is that affidavits to be used in interlocutory proceedings may contain statements of information or belief, provided the sources and grounds for the belief are given, using a phrase like, 'I have been informed by Ignatius Iago and verily believe that......'.

Again on the basis that the affidavit is a form of evidence, it should not contain any matter which is scandalous, irrelevant or otherwise oppressive (RSC Order 41, rule 6), and the court may order any such matter to be struck out of the affidavit. Clearly this means that no affidavit should contain allegations which are needlessly offensive or unfounded, or any matter which is not really relevant to the purpose of the affidavit. An affidavit may be seen as oppressive if it is unjustifiably long or complex, or may unfairly prejudice the other side in the preparation of their case.

These elementary rules do leave a wide scope for the contents of an affidavit, and thus a wide scope for the skill of the person drafting the affidavit. The rules can essentially be summarised as saying that an affidavit should contain in a concise and logical form the relevant information known to the deponent which is admissible. Although it is essentially a form of evidence, an affidavit may sometimes contain things that are not normally evidence such as legal submissions by counsel, where these are necessary.

In preparing to draft an affidavit, the lawyer needs to have its purpose clear in his mind. If the affidavit is to support a relatively minor interlocutory application then he will only need to deal in a straightforward way with a few points, almost as if he were filling in a form. If the affidavit has a very specific purpose, as where a witness needs to deal with a particular issue, then the lawyer will have to isolate and organise all that is known on that point. If it is a major affidavit in support of the whole case of the party then the affidavit will have an importance similar to the drafting of a statement of claim, and will need consideration of the aims of the whole case, the issues in it, and the strategy to be followed.

Having a clear concept of the purpose of the affidavit, the lawyer will need to identify the elements needed to fulfil that purpose, that is the points that will be necessary to give the appropriate relevant details of the situation, and what points will be directly relevant to the issues that the judge will have to deal with in court. To do this, he will have to ensure that he has all the relevant information for the affidavit. A short and formal affidavit may well be done from the papers that the lawyer already has in the case, but a more complicated affidavit will need a full statement from the witness who is to swear the affidavit for the lawyer to work with. This will normally mean that the solicitor will have to interview the witness with the purpose of the affidavit in mind so that he can cover all the necessary points, and it may also necessitate collecting other information to be included in the affidavit. In addition to the statement, it may sometimes be necessary to have a further meeting to clear up any matters that are not clear.

Sometimes an affidavit will have to be prepared quickly, especially if it is in support of an interlocutory application, but if there is time to get all the relevant information together, the effort should be made to make the draft as full as possible. No lawyer ever knows if a witness will come up to proof when he gives oral evidence in court, but in drafting an affidavit the lawyer does have the chance to organise the presentation of the evidence, and he should not waste it!

Once the lawyer does have all the information he needs, he should sift and arrange it before he begins the draft to ensure that the finished result really will be clear, concise and well-structured. A statement from a client or witness will inevitably contain material that is not relevant to the case at all, or at least is not relevant to the subject of the affidavit, and the solicitor or barrister will have to weed out all the things that are not really needed for his purpose.

Having isolated the relevant information, the lawyer must take care with the structure of the affidavit, especially if it needs to be quite long. The affidavit must not ramble from one issue to another and back again as a statement may, but must have a logical basis that builds up the points in sequence and is easy for the judge to read and follow. A well drafted affidavit is a good way for a lawyer to get the main elements of his case across to the judge.

There are no rules as to the structure that should be followed. Often it is best to set out facts and issues in chronological order, using a separate paragraph for each separate event, but sometimes it may be better to deal with one issue completely and then go to another issue. The lawyer will have to judge which is most suitable in the circumstances. It is a good idea to note briefly the order of things to be covered before beginning to draft.

As for the style of the affidavit, it has been said that this will be as much as anything a matter of the style of the individual lawyer. For a short, procedural affidavit the style may well be quite formal. If the affidavit is to be sworn by an expert witness then the language may well be fairly technical. However, for most affidavits the language should be straightforward, and certainly does not need the complicated phraseology or the quasi-legal terminology that one sometimes encounters. The language used should not be stilted or colloquial, but everyday English written well enough to impress the judge.

Sometimes an affidavit is not just a list of objective facts but also contains arguments on behalf of a party in a case, because it is intended to help the client as much as possible. This must be done with care. The lawyer should never put arguments into an affidavit gratuitously, but only where they have a real purpose to serve, as in an affidavit applying for financial provision. If the affidavit is purely evidence, the arguments should be kept for court. In addition, the lawyer should never invent anything to go into an affidavit, even if he is only making what he thinks is a reasonable conjecture to fill up a gap in the information he has. Everything in the affidavit must come from the information or instructions that the lawyer has been given, and must be something that the deponent would accept. He will have to swear that the affidavit is true, and it must be so.

However, having stated these principles, the affidavit will not always have to be a purely objective summary of facts or an anaemic view of the case, if it is a vital affidavit in the case. The affidavit is the evidence of the person who signs it to be true, and it should express their views. If they have strong views on the issues in the case, or what they want to achieve in the case, these may be included in the affidavit where appropriate. If the views are so strong that they might harm the case, the lawyer can advise on leaving them out or toning them down, and that is a matter of taste and feel.

The affidavit may be structured to promote the interests of the client, whether or not they have strong views. As examples, in an affidavit in support of an application for financial provision on divorce there may be points to make as to the origin of assets and who paid for them, and also as to what assets can really be available to make provision. Alternatively, in an affidavit applying for custody the client may have strong views as to why the other spouse should not have custody, and these points should be included, suitably expressed.

The jurat

The final part of the affidavit is the jurat, which must be properly completed for the document to be valid. The jurat is a short formal section that must be signed by the deponent of the affidavit in the presence of an authorised person, that is a Commissioner for Oaths or a proper officer of the court (RSC Order 41, rule 1). The affidavit should not be sworn before the solicitor of the party on whose behalf the affidavit is to be used, or his agent, partner or clerk (RSC Order 41, rule 8). The jurat will consist of the names and signatures of these people together with the date and place where the affidavit was sworn.

Defects in affidavits

Once the affidavit has been drafted, it will be typed up in the proper form and sworn, and then filed as appropriate for use in court. If there is any defect in the wording, then the appropriate words can be altered, erased or added at any stage, but the person who swore the affidavit should initial the alteration and rewrite in the margin any words or figures written on the erased part (RSC Order 41, rule 7), and if this is not done the affidavit can only be used with the leave of the court.

If there is any other defect in the affidavit, including any failure to comply with the technical rules as to how it should be prepared, then the defective affidavit may still be filed or used, but only with the leave of the court (RSC Order 41, rule 4). If there are defects in the affidavits of a party, the other side can object to the affidavit's being used, but they should object as soon as possible, and not at a later stage when they have filed their own affidavits in reply, *Langdale* v *Danby* [1982] 3 All ER 129.

Technical rules on the preparation and use of affidavits

Not only should the affidavit be properly drafted, but it should be well presented, and filed according to the rules for use in court. There has in recent years been a tendency to be rather lax in the preparation of affidavits, perhaps because they are not actually pleadings in the case, but proper care must always be taken. No judge will be impressed by a badly presented affidavit, and there have been comments to this effect by various judges. To improve and standardise the presentation of affidavits, there was a *Practice Note* [1983] 3 All ER 33 for all affidavits in the High Court and the Court of Appeal beginning with a warning that any affidavit which does not comply with the rules of court and the Practice Note may be rejected, or may be made the subject of an order for costs.

Like other documents to be used in the High Court, an affidavit must be on A4 paper of a durable quality, with a margin not less than 1½ inches wide on the left hand side of the face of the paper and on the right hand side of the reverse. It may be printed, typewritten, or in clear and legible handwriting (though preferably not the last), and a clear photocopy with no blemishes is acceptable (RSC Order 66). This Order also gives details of the size of type and the processes for copying the affidavit which are acceptable. The affidavit should be in book form, and use both sides of the paper (RSC Order 41, rule 1).

The Practice Note says that the affidavit should not be held together with a thick plastic strip down the spine, or anything else which would hamper filing, but by some firm method which is not bulky. The traditional way is to use a fabric tape threaded through holes made down the left hand side.

For easy reference, the top right hand corner of the first page of every affidavit and also the backsheet should be marked in some clear, permanent way in dark blue or black ink with the party on whose behalf it is filed, the initials and surname of the deponent, the number of the affidavit in relation to the deponent, and the date when it was sworn. These elements will be abbreviated, as in '2nd Dft: S. Shylock: 3rd: 15.9.83'.

The affidavit may refer to other documents or objects, and where appropriate, if these items are available they should be exhibited to the affidavit. For example, the maker of the affidavit may have in his possession letters, formal documents, diagrams, plans or reports that are relevant, and they should be exhibited rather than just being attached to the affidavit (RSC Order 41, rule 11). However something that would not normally be admissible or used as evidence by the court should not normally be exhibited, such as articles from legal periodicals, *Gleeson* v *J. Whippell & Co.* [1977] 1 WLR 510 (where there were dicta that the affidavit should contain evidence rather than sources of inspiration!)

Any item that is exhibited must be specifically referred to in the body of the affidavit, and must there be given an identification number, which consists of the initials of the maker of the affidavit, and a consecutive number relating to the number of exhibits that there are. For example, in the affidavit by S. Shylock the numbers would be 'S.S.1', 'S.S.2' and so on. In a second affidavit by the same person in one case the numbers continue rather than starting again.

The 1983 Practice Note deals in detail with the presentation of exhibits. They should not be bound up with the affidavit itself, but should be presented with it with a certificate identifying the exhibit that has the same title as the affidavit. There are slightly different rules for different types of exhibit. As for documents, the original should be used, or a photocopy which really is fully and clearly legible. Documents that are before the court anyway, such as pleadings, do not need to be exhibited. A number of documents may be exhibited together, but there should be a front page to the bundle of documents listing what documents are there and the date of each. The bundle should be securely fastened, but easy to use, with numbered pages. Documents which the court is being asked to interpret or enforce should always be exhibited separately.

Any letters should normally be exhibited as a bundle rather than separately, with the earliest on top, firmly fastened and with the pages numbered. Any other types of exhibits must be clearly marked as such, and if the thing cannot be marked directly, it must be marked in a way that cannot easily be removed (that is, with something more than a piece of Sellotape). Each part of the exhibit should be marked if it comes apart, and any container that it is in should be marked.

Although the possibilities of exhibiting documents and objects to affidavits are wide, they should be used with care. A thing should always be exhibited if it is relevant, and the lawyer should always consider possible exhibits. On the other hand, only items which are genuinely directly relevant should be exhibited, and not items which are mere background, or which can more properly be put in evidence in some other way. An affidavit will not magically turn something into admissible evidence if it is not so otherwise, such as hearsay statements, *Re Koscot Interplanetary (U.K.)* [1972] 3 All ER 829. If the affidavit refers to a document which is not exhibited, the other side can ask to see it (RSC Order 24, rule 10).

The rules for the actual use of an affidavit in court proceedings will vary with the type of case. One can only say generally that affidavits should normally be filed at the appropriate court office at the correct time before the actual hearing (RSC Order 41, rule 9). Where an affidavit is required under an Act or rule of court there will often be directions as to when it should be filed. The original affidavit with exhibits should be filed, and there are rules for supply of copies to other parties in the case and use of copies which again vary according to the purpose of the affidavit. If the affidavit has not been filed as it should be, it can still be used with the leave of the court, though there will usually have to be an undertaking to file it as soon as possible. Although an affidavit is sworn evidence, it can normally only be used in the proceedings in which it is filed and not in any other case, as in *Medway* v *Doublelock* [1978] 1 All ER 1261, where a husband swore an affidavit in a maintenance action and it was held that it could not be used in a separate action where his company was being sued.

There have been particular problems with the preparation and use of affidavits to support interlocutory applications, in that they are not properly drafted and not available in sufficient time. A *Practice Note* [1983] 1 All ER 1119 relates to these problems and lays down quite detailed rules. If the hearing of an application is likely to last more than 30 minutes, it will be put on a list of special appointments, and the affidavits should be lodged in advance of the hearing so that the judge has chance to read them, at least 24 hours in advance, or more if the parties have longer warning of the date. The approach must be to begin to draft the affidavits as soon as the decision is made to make the application, and not when the application is due to be heard.

The Practice Note also deals with procedure for ex parte applications, where the judge's clerk should be provided with the relevant documents including the affidavit in support and a draft of the order sought by 3.00 p.m. on the day preceding the hearing. If the case is so urgent that this is not possible, the papers should still be lodged with the judge's clerk before the hearing unless the case is exceptional. There are details as to what the affidavit in support should contain:

> The affidavit in support should contain a clear and concise statement (a) of the facts giving rise to the claim against the defendant in the proceedings, (b) of the facts giving rise to the claim for interlocutory relief, (c) of the facts relied on as justifying application ex parte, incuding details of any notice given to the defendant or, if none has been given, the reasons for giving none, (d) of any answer asserted by the defendant (or which he is thought likely to assert) either to the claim in the action or to the claim for interlocutory relief, (e) of any facts known to the applicant which might lead the court not to grant relief ex parte, (f) the precise relief sought.

On an ex parte application, the affidavit may well be the only evidence before the judge, so it is even more important than usual to see that it contains the proper things and is well expressed.

12 *Advising and drafting for civil appeals*

If, after all the advice and preparation, the case is lost at first instance, then the possibility of an appeal arises. There are various different routes of appeal from interlocutory decisions and different types of hearing by courts and tribunals which are dealt with fully in books on procedure. This chapter will deal with the principles of advising on an appeal, drafting grounds of appeal, and preparing for the hearing of the appeal where there is an appeal from the High Court to the Court of Appeal, though many of the points that are made have a wider application.

The procedure for appeals to the Court of Appeal has been reviewed and substantially modified in the last few years. Because of concern over delays in the hearing of appeals, and over shortcomings in the way that some appeal cases were prepared for hearing, a committee under the chairmanship of Lord Scarman was set up in 1978, and as a result of the comments of that committee there have been changes in the rules of court, and several Practice Notes on the way that cases should be prepared. The *Practice Note* [1982] 3 All ER 374 is a useful summary of the main changes that have been made, the reasons for them, and what they hope to achieve.

Jurisdiction and procedure for appeals

The lawyer will have to check the route for appeal in any particular type of case, but the basic framework, as derived from the Supreme Court Act 1981, is as follows:

(a) An appeal from a decision of a Master or Registrar will generally go to a judge of the High Court, though it may go to the Court of Appeal if for example the Master has given judgment on an issue.

(b) An appeal from a judge in Chambers may go to the Court of Appeal, though in the Chancery Division and the Family Division it will go first to a judge in open court.

(c) An appeal from a final decision of a judge of any Division of the High Court will go to the Court of Appeal.

An appeal from a final decision of the High Court will be as of right, but an appeal on an interlocutory matter will usually need leave, Supreme Court Act 1981, s.18. There are some further limitations. It will be necessary to get leave to appeal from a consent order, and there are a few special cases where it is not possible to appeal at all; there is no appeal against the decision of an official referee (though you can against a special referee), there is no appeal against a decree absolute of divorce if there was an opportunity to appeal against the decree nisi which was not taken, and it is not possible to appeal against an order refusing a vexatious litigant leave to bring an action.

The procedure for appealing is governed by RSC Order 59, and the main stages are as follows:

(a) A notice of appeal must be served by the appellant. This should be done within four weeks, of the date that judgment was signed (RSC Order 59, rule 4). There were formerly a variety of different time limits for appealing, but these have now gone, the only exception being social security cases, in which the time limit is six weeks, *Practice Note* [1982] 1 WLR 1312. If leave to appeal is needed, it should be sought initially from the High Court judge who heard the case. If he refuses, leave may be sought by motion to a single judge of the Court of Appeal (RSC Order 59, rule 14). It will still be necessary to serve the notice of appeal within four weeks even if leave has to be sought. If the four week time limit has expired, it is possible to apply for leave to appeal out of time, the application being to a single judge of the Court of Appeal, who will only grant leave if there was a good reason for the delay.

(b) The notice of appeal must be served on all the parties concerned with the appeal.

(c) A respondent who is served with a notice of appeal may serve a notice in reply, within 21 days of being served with the notice of appeal (RSC Order 59, rule 6). He should serve a notice in reply if he wishes to argue that the decision of the court below should be affirmed on different grounds from those relied upon by the judge, to argue that the decision of the court below should be varied in some way, or if he wishes to cross-appeal and argue himself that the decision of the court below was wholly or partly wrong.

(d) Within 7 days of serving the notice of appeal the appellant should apply to have it set down for trial (RSC Order 59, rule 5). The application should be made to the proper court officer, providing him with a copy of the judgment or order appealed from, two copies of the notice of appeal, and a list of any exhibits used at the trial. The officer has a discretion to extend the 7 day period for setting down, and should set the case down in the appropriate list of appeals. The appellant should inform all the parties within 2 days that the case has been set down.

(e) Any necessary interlocutory applications may be made while the parties are waiting for the case to come on for hearing. Such applications are normally made by motion to a single judge of the Court of Appeal. For example, a party may wish to apply to have execution of the judgment stayed pending the hearing of the appeal (this will not happen automatically), to be allowed to adduce fresh evidence at the hearing of the appeal (which can only be done with leave), or to get security for costs.

(f) Within 14 days of the case appearing in the List of Forthcoming Appeals, the appellant must lodge all the appropriate documents with the clerks to the Lords Justices of Appeal (RSC Order 59, rule 9). The time it will take for the case to appear in this list will depend on the number of cases waiting to be heard at the time and various other factors, but the appellant should begin to prepare all the appropriate documents well in advance to ensure that they are ready in time. In particular, transcripts of appropriate parts of the original trial should be applied for as soon as possible. Normally three copies of each document will be needed (one for each judge), but the number may vary in some special types of case, such as Admiralty cases.

The documents needed are:

(i) The notice of appeal (and any notice amending it).

(ii) Any notice in reply by the respondent (and any notice amending that).

(iii) The judgment or order of the court below.

(iv) The writ or other process by which the proceedings in the court below were begun, with any pleadings, and any interlocutory process which is being appealed against.

(v) The transcript of the official shorthand note of the judge's reasons for his decision, or if there is none, the judge's note of his reasons, or counsel's note of the reasons, approved if possible by the judge.

(vi) Such parts of the transcript of the official shorthand note or other record of the evidence given in the court below as are relevant to any issue on the appeal. If there is no such record, the judge's note may be used.

(vii) A list of any exhibits used at the trial.

(viii) Such affidavits or exhibits as were evidence in the court below and are relevant to a question or issue on the appeal.

The appellant should also try to give an estimate of how long the hearing will last. Once the documents have been lodged, the registrar can give directions relating to the documents to be produced at the appeal, the manner in which they are presented, and other matters incidental to the conduct of the appeal as appear best for the just, expeditious and economical disposal of the appeal.

(g) The hearing. The appeal will be heard when it reaches the top of the appropriate list of appeals, though some care will be taken to try to avoid existing commitments of counsel. The hearing in the Court of Appeal is by way of rehearing (RSC Order 59, rule 3) which means that the court may totally reconsider any matter in issue at the original trial. However, the Court of Appeal will only actually reconsider those matters raised in the notice of appeal and any notice in reply, and the hearing will normally be conducted entirely on the basis of affidavits and transcripts of evidence rather than oral evidence. The judges will usually have read in advance the documents lodged, or at least the most important parts of them, and they may also have read the basic arguments of counsel which are now often submitted in advance in a written form (this will be examined in detail later). This means that although there is a rehearing the atmosphere will be totally different from the original hearing because it will usually be entirely a matter of written documents and legal argument, and because the judges will immediately be able to focus on the central issues without a prolonged introduction to the case.

Because there is a rehearing, the Court of Appeal may take into account matters which have arisen since the original trial, and may draw its own inferences of fact, though it will be slow to depart from the conclusions of the judge who saw the witnesses giving evidence.

(h) The decision. The Court of Appeal may give its decision at the end of the hearing, or it may reserve judgment. The court has a wide range of powers open to it (RSC Order 59, rule 10). It has all the powers and duties of the High Court, and can therefore give any judgment or make any order that that court could have given or made. It is possible for these powers to be used even if a point was not specifically pleaded in the notice of appeal or the respondent's notice, and the court can make such order as it thinks just for the determination on the merits of the real question in controversy between the parties.

Although the Court of Appeal does have all the powers of the High Court as regards remedies and may substitute different remedies for those granted by the judge at first instance, there are some limits on what the Court of Appeal will be prepared to do. It will be slow to grant a remedy that is not sought in the notice of appeal or the respondent's notice, and it will be slow to depart from an inference of fact or an exercise of discretion of the judge at first instance. It will also be slow to vary an assessment of damages, unless the judge made an assessment that was wrong in principle, was clearly based on a misunderstanding of the facts, or fresh evidence has come to light which is relevant to the assessment of damages.

It is possible for the Court of Appeal to order a new trial (RSC Order 59, rule 11), though it will be slow to do so, unless there is a very good reason not least because of the time it will take and the costs involved. For example there may be a new trial if there is substantial new evidence which should be heard with the existing evidence. The court is not bound to order a retrial merely because there has been a misdirection or an improper admission or rejection of evidence unless some substantial miscarriage of justice has occurred as a result. A retrial of part of the case rather than the whole case may be ordered.

The Court of Appeal has a discretion as to the order for costs, and the order will usually include the costs of the original hearing as well as of the appeal, the winner of the appeal getting the costs of both. This may well not be the case if the appeal is only partially successful.

Advising on an appeal

Obviously you do not appeal merely because you lost the case before the judge at first instance. Equally, you may consider appealing even if you won if the judge did not grant all the things that your client sought. The decision whether to appeal from all or part of a decision involves the balancing of all the appropriate factors to make a realistic and practical decision.

The lawyers should give the client full information as to the possible advantages and disadvantages of an appeal, and the final decision should be the client's, though the lawyers may make strong recommendations to him according to what they feel the real chances of success are. The possibility of appealing may well be discussed immediately after the judge has given his decision, or even before if it is clear that the client is likely to lose, but it may well be necessary to arrange a conference with the client for a full discussion and for a decision on an appeal to be taken. Obviously the decision must be taken quickly because of the need to serve the notice of appeal within 4 weeks of the judgment. Although it is possible to ask for leave to appeal out of time, this will only be granted if there is good reason for the delay.

As for the grounds of appeal, the main possibilities are an appeal on a matter of law, an appeal on a matter of fact, or an appeal on a procedural irregularity. Of these, an appeal on a matter of law will usually be the strongest, provided the lawyer has a coherent argument supported by authority. An appeal on a matter of fact will usually have to show a clear misunderstanding or mistake by the trial judge to succeed. This is because the Court of Appeal will only have affidavits and transcripts of evidence, whereas the trial judge will have seen the witnesses giving oral evidence, and may have been able to form impressions of them which are not easily transmitted on the written page. An appeal on a matter of fact is more likely to succeed if fresh evidence has come to light which was not available at the time of the trial, and the Court of Appeal can also take into account changes in the facts since the trial. These principles apply to the facts on which the measure of damages is based as well as the facts of the case itself, and as was said above, the Court of Appeal will be slow to change the award of damages made by the trial judge without good reason. In *McCann* v *Sheppard* [1973] 1 WLR 540 a 26 year old man was injured in a car accident. He was awarded £41,252 in damages, but while an appeal was pending he committed suicide, probably due to his depression at the injuries he suffered. It was held that this should be taken into account, and the part of the damages for loss of future earnings was substantially reduced.

An appeal on a procedural defect will depend on the type of defect, whether it was likely to have had a real effect on the outcome of the trial, and whether anything could and should have been done about it at the time. If there is any procedural irregularity at the trial the lawyer should normally object at the time, and it is only if he does and the judge does not accept his submissions or objections that there is a possible ground for appeal. Once the judge is summing up or giving judgment, it will normally be too late for the lawyer to object to anything said, or at least inappropriate, so something said by the judge at that stage may be the basis for an appeal.

The seeds of the appeal often come from the original trial and the preparations for it. The purpose of the appeal is to remedy any defect in the original trial, not to give the lawyer a second chance to get it right. Therefore every cause of action and major argument of fact should be properly prepared and presented at the trial, and a new cause of action or an important new argument cannot normally be raised for the first time on appeal. In *Williams* v *Home Office (No.2)* [1982] 2 All ER 564 the plaintiff brought an action for false imprisonment, having been kept in a control unit in a prison. The action failed, and he sought leave after the trial to amend his pleading to add breach of statutory duty. It was held that this could not be done as it should have been pleaded and argued as part of the case at the first trial. In *Lloyde* v *West Midlands Gas Board* [1971] 1 WLR 749 the plaintiff was injured by an explosion in an outhouse where he kept his moped, and where the gas meter was. He sued the gas board, pleading res ipsa loquitur, but did not argue it at trial. Damages were awarded on the grounds that the meter was defective, but on an appeal the plaintiff sought to argue the res ipsa loquitur point as well. As he had pleaded it the court did not prevent this, but held that as the defendant had not expected it to be raised on appeal there should be a new trial to be fair to both sides.

Thus the lawyer should plead and argue his case fully or he will be limited as to what he can argue on appeal. The other thing that he should do is keep a note at trial with a possible appeal in mind. If there are procedural problems, he should raise them at once, and only bear them in mind for an appeal if the judge's decision goes against him. As to the evidence, he will have copies of all the documents, but a note of oral evidence should be taken. The barrister may do this himself, but this may be done by his pupil, or by someone from the solicitor's office who attends court. This does not need to be a full note, and need not include basic information which is not in dispute, but it should contain the major questions and answers on examination-in-chief and cross-examination. These notes may be useful as a source for later questions to that witness or another witness, or for references in a closing speech. They may also be useful on an appeal, both for finding grounds of appeal, and for identifying those parts of the evidence of which you will need transcripts. Some barristers evolve a useful system of using different coloured pens in their notes, with one colour for points they may need in cross-examination, another colour for points that may be useful in their speech at the end, and a further colour for points that may be useful if there is an appeal. It is necessary, and probably most useful, to take these notes by hand, as tape recorders may only be used with the leave of the court, Contempt of Court Act 1981, s.9, *Practice Direction* [1981] 3 All ER 848.

The first stage of advising on an appeal must be to list the possible grounds of appeal of all types, on law, fact or procedure. These points must then be classified to decide whether an appeal might be against the judge's findings or the remedies granted by him, and whether the appeal would be against the whole or part of the judgment. The next stage is then to decide whether it is in fact worth appealing, which begins with evaluating the chances of success of the possible grounds of appeal. This may well involve intuition or guesswork on the part of the lawyer as to the view that the Court of Appeal will take, and it may well be best explained to the client by giving him the odds or the percentage chance of winning ('Well, I'd have thought there was a 60% chance of success'). In favour of an appeal, the case may be very important to the client, with a big point of principle or a large amount of money at stake, so that he will be prepared to appeal even if the chances of success are not good. Also the appeal may be relatively cheap, since all the evidence has already been collected for the trial at first instance, but this will not necessarily be so. If the point is important for the client he may wish to retain a Q.C. for the appeal even if he did not for the trial, and this will of course add to the costs.

Against appealing, there is of course the principle that there is no point in throwing good money after bad, and if the appeal fails the client will end up not only losing the case, but probably also paying the costs of both sides, which is something that should be made completely clear to him. If the client is on legal aid there will be the question whether the chances of success of the appeal really justify the extension of legal aid for it. There is also the point that if you appeal it may result in a cross-appeal from the other side, and this could result in your getting less from the appeal than you did from the original trial if, for example, the Court of Appeal reduces an award of damages.

The client's lawyers will consider all these matters, the barrister and solicitor may well confer, and they will no doubt reach a provisional decision as to whether there should be an appeal. Their views will be passed on to the client, in conference or in a written opinion, and the client can then decide what to do. Although he will probably follow the advice of the lawyers, the final choice should be his. Sometimes the client feels very strongly and may want to appeal even if the chances of success are negligible, in which case the lawyers should of course try to dissuade him. Conversely, a client may be so exhausted and dispirited by the trial itself that they may not wish to bother to appeal (this can happen particularly in matrimonial cases where emotional strain is added to the strain of the trial). If the chances of a successful appeal are good then the lawyers should of course strongly encourage the client to go on. With the appeal as much as with the original case, at the end of the day the lawyer has no right to be too paternal and take the decision for the client. The client may well have to pay for the case and will certainly have to live with the consequences, so the lawyer can only advise.

The possibility of an appeal is something for both sides to consider. Even if you do not wish to appeal, the other side may do so, in which case you are not limited to defending the judge's decision. It is possible not only to argue that the decision should be upheld, but that if necessary it should be upheld on grounds other than those given by the judge. The respondent to an appeal may also himself argue that the decision of the court below should be varied in whole or in part, or may himself cross-appeal if he did not get all he wanted from the original hearing. If it is clear that the other side may appeal, you should begin to consider your own position immediately.

Drafting a notice of appeal

The notice of appeal is a form of notice of motion. Beyond that, there is no prescribed form for it, though the form that appears in the Rules of Court is normally followed in practice (see RSC Order 59, rule 3). See Example 1 for an outline notice of appeal.

As for the contents of the notice of appeal, rule 3 specifies that it may relate to the whole or a specified part of the judgment or order of the court below. If it is in respect of only a part, it must be clear which part. It must specify the grounds of the appeal, and the precise form of the order which the appellant wishes the Court of Appeal to make. At the hearing of the appeal, the appellant will not be entitled to rely on any grounds of appeal or to apply for any relief which is not specified in the notice of appeal unless the Court of Appeal gives leave.

Since it is therefore vital that the notice be specific and comprehensive, the best preparation for drafting is to make brief numbered notes of all the grounds of appeal to be raised, and all the orders which the Court of Appeal will be asked to make. It is important to have clear in your mind exactly what you are appealing against and what you hope to get out of it, as well as the reasons for the appeal.

The heading

Many elements of the heading, including the number of the action and the names of the parties, come from the existing pleadings in the action. However, the case will now be in the Court of Appeal. The form of the title can be seen from Example 1.

EXAMPLE 1 BASIC NOTICE OF APPEAL IN A CIVIL CASE

IN THE COURT OF APPEAL 1985.A.No.1234

ON APPEAL FROM THE HIGH COURT OF JUSTICE

DIVISION

BETWEEN A. B. *Plaintiff*

and

C. D. *Defendant*

NOTICE OF APPEAL

Take notice that the Court of Appeal will be moved as soon as Counsel can be heard on behalf of the above-named (plaintiff or defendant) on appeal from the (judgment or order) herein of the Honourable Mr Justice (given or made) on the day of 1985 whereby it was (adjudged or ordered) that (set out briefly the essence of the judgment or order made). (If the appeal is only against part of the judgment or order then say instead 'on appeal from so much of the judgment as adjudged that...... etc., setting out that part of the judgment or order from which you wish to appeal.)

For an order that the said (judgment or order) be set aside and that...... (set out briefly but exactly the orders that you wish the Court of Appeal to make, including any order as to costs. If you wish several orders to be made, it may be clearer to set them out in separate numbered points).

And further take notice that the grounds for this appeal are that:

(Set out the grounds of appeal in separate numbered points. The following are examples of possible paragraphs that may be adjusted for use.)

1. That the Learned Judge was wrong in law in holding that......
2. That the Learned Judge misdirected himself in that......
3. That the Learned Judge wrongly admitted the evidence of......
4. That there was no evidence to support the finding of the Learned Judge that......
5. That the Learned Judge's finding that...... was wrong in law and against the weight of the evidence.

And further take notice that the (plaintiff or defendant) proposes to apply to set down this appeal in the List.

Dated etc. Signed

The body of the pleading

This consists of two sections, the first setting out the details of the judgment appealed against and the judgment which the appellant hopes to get to replace it, and the second setting out in numbered paragraphs the grounds for the appeal.

'Take notice that......' Here it is necessary to fill in correctly the details of the existing judgment. It should be clear whether the appeal is against the whole judgment or only part of it, and if so, precisely which part.

Following this, the appellant sets out precisely the order or orders which he wishes the Court of Appeal to make. In that the Court of Appeal has the same powers as the High Court, the court can make any order that the judge at first instance could have made, but this is subject to the normal rules that you must put in the pleading the relief sought, and that you cannot seek on appeal something radically different that was not raised at the original trial. An application for costs will normally be part of the relief sought.

'And further take notice that the grounds of appeal are:' Here are set out the grounds of appeal, each ground of appeal being a separate numbered point. If there is to be an appeal at all, it is usual to put in every possible ground of appeal, as even if some of them would have no chance of success alone, this will give the full picture. On the other hand it is not usually a good idea to put in a vast number of petty points as this may just irritate the judges and waste time in court. The grounds of appeal need not be in any particular order, but they should be in some logical order, for example grouping together similar grounds of appeal or grounds of appeal on a particular point.

Each separate point must be raised in a separate numbered paragraph. The notice of appeal should just raise each point as briefly as possible. The details will be argued at trial, though in fact the practice has arisen in the past few years of putting in writing skeleton arguments that are handed in for the judges to read just before the hearing. Each ground of appeal must be specific and clear, not just a general expression of discontent. The case of *R* v *Morson* [1976] Crim LR 623 involved a criminal appeal, but the comments in it would apply equally to a civil appeal—that a general allegation that the summing-up as a whole was unfair was not sufficient, but that specific points about what the judge said should be made.

The conclusion of the notice

At the end of the notice of appeal should appear the List of Appeals in which it is proposed that the case will be set down, this being necessary under the rules of court. There should also be the signature of the solicitor of the appellant and a warning to the respondent, as in the example in this chapter.

The respondent's notice

The respondent who is served with a notice of appeal has a choice what course to take, and this should be fully considered by his lawyers. The possibilities come from RSC Order 59, rule 6, which provides that a respondent must serve notice if he wishes:

(a) To contend on the appeal that the decision of the court below should be varied, either in any event or in the event of the appeal being allowed in whole or in part.
(b) To contend that the decision of the court below should be affirmed on grounds other than those relied upon by that court.
(c) To contend by way of cross-appeal that the decision of the court below was wrong in whole or in part.

For any of these courses the respondent must serve a notice specifying his grounds and the precise form of order which he proposes to ask the court to make. If the respondent does not serve notice, or does not serve a full notice, he will not be entitled on the hearing of the appeal to apply for any relief not specified, or to rely in support of any contention on any ground which was not specified in his notice or relied on by the court below, unless he has the leave of the court. Thus the drafting of the respondent's notice may be as important as the drafting of the notice of appeal.

Even if the respondent is basically content with the decision of the judge at first instance, he may still need to serve a notice if for example he feels that the appeal may have some chance of success as the grounds relied on by the judge at first instance were open to criticism and he wishes to argue that the decision should be upheld on other grounds. Equally if the respondent is basically content with the existing decision but wishes to argue that it should be varied in some way, this should be pleaded in his notice. The alternative is for the respondent to serve a notice of cross-appeal, if he himself wishes to argue that the decision of the court below was wholly or partly wrong. In such a case the grounds of cross-appeal should be pleaded in the same way and in as much detail as the grounds of appeal themselves.

In that the notice of appeal and any respondent's notice will have to be drafted relatively quickly, it is possible that something may be left out, or that extra information may come to light after the notice has been served. In such cases it is quite possible for the notices to be amended (RSC Order 59, rule 7). Firstly, a supplementary notice may be served by either side before the day when the case first appears in the list of forthcoming appeals. Otherwise, the notice of appeal or the respondent's notice may be amended at any time with the leave of the Court of Appeal, a single judge of the court, or the registrar.

Preparing for the appeal

The first steps towards preparing for the appeal will be taken during the original hearing, when the lawyer will note anything that may be a possible ground of appeal. In any event, the decision whether or not to appeal will have to be taken as soon as possible after judgment, and preparations will need to begin forthwith. The lawyer should also decide whether any interlocutory applications will be needed for orders pending the hearing of the appeal, for example to prevent the judgment given from being executed, as there will be no automatic stay of execution.

The next step is to prepare the evidence and documents for the hearing of the appeal. It is the responsibility of the appellant's lawyers to ensure that the affidavits and exhibits from the trial are made available for the Court of Appeal, together with any necessary transcripts of evidence or of the judgment given. It is necessary to apply for the transcripts, and in doing so to specify exactly which parts of the evidence will be needed. If unnecessary transcripts are asked for they may prolong and possibly confuse the appeal hearing, and will certainly increase the costs. The costs of unnecessarily long transcripts may not be allowed, so the client will have to pay for it himself. If a note of evidence was kept during the trial, it should be possible to specify what is needed. In the High Court a shorthand note or a tape recording is made of most proceedings, and it is a transcript of this that should be used wherever possible (RSC Order 68).

In addition to this written evidence, there are some circumstances in which the Court of Appeal will be prepared to hear fresh evidence (RSC Order 59, rule 10). There is a power to receive further evidence on questions of fact by oral examination in court, or by affidavit, but where the appeal comes after a full trial or hearing on the merits of the case, further evidence will only be admitted on special grounds. Leave will be needed to admit the evidence, which should be obtained from a single judge of the Court of Appeal, and which will only be given if the evidence could not with reasonable diligence have been obtained for the original trial, if it is such that it would have had an important influence on the outcome of the case, even though it would not necessarily have been decisive, and if the evidence is apparently credible. Evidence of things which have happened since the date of the trial or hearing is admissible without leave, and the lawyers on both sides should consider whether there is any material change in the facts that should be brought to the attention of the court, for example matters relevant to the quantification of damages.

The proper preparation of cases for the Court of Appeal has been a matter of great concern in recent years. The notice of appeal and the respondent's notice should define clearly the issues which the Court of Appeal is being asked to consider, and the purpose of having to lodge the papers in the case in advance is so that each judge can have the opportunity of reading them before the hearing. Therefore the hearing of an appeal should be much more efficient and incisive than a trial at first instance, because the issues are clear, most hearings will be conducted entirely on paperwork, and everyone will be aware of the background in advance. This means that the lawyers must be fully and properly prepared, because normally no prolonged introductory speeches will be needed, and there will be few pauses where the lawyer can collect his thoughts as there might be at a trial. Since the judges have already read some if not all of the papers, they may already feel that some of the points of appeal lack merit but that they would like to hear argument on some of the others, and therefore the lawyer for the appellant may well be asked to deal with a particular point in detail soon after the hearing has begun.

Thus the lawyer must have his arguments in order and background research must be done well in advance. The judges of the Court of Appeal are themselves concerned that there should be proper preparation so that appeal hearings may be as efficient as possible, and there have been several recent Practice Notes to make suggestions about and encourage proper preparation.

The *Practice Note* [1982] 3 All ER 376 commented on many changes that were introduced to streamline the appeal procedure, some of which have been incorporated into RSC Order 59, such as the single four week time limit for appealing. The Practice Note also sought the assistance of barristers and solicitors, especially in two areas—the proper preparation of documents, and the presentation of skeleton arguments for the court.

As for the preparation of documents, the importance of collecting and preparing these and lodging them all with the court at the appropriate time was stressed in the *Practice Note* [1983] 2 All ER 416. In particular, the Practice Note emphasised the need to use official transcripts of evidence or of the judgment rather than some form of unofficial note, and the need to apply for these transcripts as early as possible so that they would be ready in time. If an official transcript is not available then the rules of court should be followed, and the judge's note of the judgment should be used, or in default of that, an agreed note by counsel.

In addition to these transcripts, the other documents should also be properly prepared for the hearing so that they may be easily referred to and used. A bundle of the documents needed for the appeal should be prepared, with the contents agreed by both sides. The pages of the bundle should be clearly numbered, with an index on the top of the bundle so that each document can be easily found. All the documents that will be needed except for the transcripts should be included in this bundle, which should be put together in a folder, or firmly fastened.

As for the preparation of skeleton arguments mentioned in the 1982 Practice Direction, the idea here is that the lawyer should prepare and hand into the court shortly before the hearing a written note of the main arguments that he intends to put forward. The idea of conducting appeals on the basis of written submissions, as happens in some countries, has been rejected as being contrary to the British tradition of oral hearings, but the idea of a basic summary of the points in the appeal has been found attractive. These written summaries should be helpful to the judges and the lawyers in clarifying the hearing in that everyone can get to grips with the case quickly.

More detail on the preparation of skeleton arguments was given in the *Practice Note* [1983] 2 All ER 34. The skeleton argument is not a compulsory part of procedure on an appeal, but should be used where it is suitable. It is a summary in numbered paragraphs of the arguments to be raised so that judges do not have to spend time making notes, but it is in no way a formal pleading, and will not take the place of oral argument in court.

The Practice Note sets out what the skeleton argument should be:

> It should contain a numbered list of the points which counsel proposes to argue, stated in no more than one or two sentences, the object being to identify each point, not to argue it or elaborate it. Each listed point should be followed by full references to the material to which counsel will refer in support of it, i.e. the relevant pages or passages in authorities, bundles of documents, affidavits, transcripts and the judgment under appeal. It should also contain anything which counsel would expect to be taken down by the court during the hearing, such as propositions of law, chronologies of events, lists of dramatis personae and, where necessary, glossaries of terms. If more convenient, these can of course be annexed to the skeleton argument rather than being included in it.

The case of *M.V. Yorke Motors* v *Edwards* [1982] 1 WLR 444 included comments on the preparation of written arguments (though in this case for the House of Lords), saying that they were to enable everyone to concentrate on the main arguments and to read the background in advance, not to take over from argument in court, and that therefore they should not be too lengthy. In the case a written summary of 39 foolscap pages was said to be much too long.

The skeleton argument should be prepared shortly before the hearing of the appeal, so as to be completely up to date and contain the lawyers' current thinking on the case. It should be supplied to the Court of Appeal before the hearing to give the judges sufficient time to read it. If there is a difficulty, the summary may be handed in at the beginning of the hearing, with enough copies for all the judges. A copy should also be provided for the other side. Skeleton arguments should be prepared wherever they may be useful, but even in those cases where they are not really appropriate, it may still be helpful to provide written notes of the main arguments for the use of the court. Preparing the notes should help the lawyer in clarifying his thoughts, as well as helping the judges.

Appeals to the House of Lords

If either side is dissatisfied, an appeal may lie from the Court of Appeal to the House of Lords. There is no appeal as of right, but leave is needed (see the Administration of Justice (Amendment) Act 1934, s.1). Leave may be sought from the Court of Appeal or, if they refuse, from the House of Lords within one month. If leave is still refused, no further application is possible. Leave may be given subject to certain conditions, for example as to security for costs. Because the appeal will add substantially to the costs of the case it will normally only be permitted if something important is at stake, such as valuable property or an important point of principle or law. If there is an important point at stake which one party wishes to have settled authoritatively they may agree to pay the costs of the other party whatever the outcome of the appeal so as to get a decision.

Once leave has been given, the notice of appeal should be lodged within 3 months of the date of the judgment appealed against. The principles for drafting the grounds of appeal are similar to those for drafting appeals to the Court of Appeal. It is necessary to specify exactly what the appeal is against, what the grounds are, and what is being sought from the House of Lords. Fresh evidence may be admitted if relevant, but as with the Court of Appeal, it will not be possible to bring in arguments not used below. The former practice of reversing the name of the case on appeal no longer applies, *Practice Direction* [1974] 1 WLR 303.

As with the Court of Appeal, the current practice is for the parties to lodge a succinct statement of the arguments and authorities in the appeal, which is settled by counsel. This may be a little more detailed than the skeleton argument for the Court of Appeal, but it should not be too detailed, and will not be a substitute for the arguments of counsel before the court, *M.V. Yorke Motors* v *Edwards* [1982] 1 WLR 444. The statement of arguments should conclude with a numbered summary of the reasons on which the appeal is founded.

As an alternative, there is the leap-frog procedure introduced by the Administration of Justice Act 1969. This is appropriate where there is some good reason for going directly to the House of Lords without first appealing to the Court of Appeal, that is, if the case relates wholly or mainly to the construction of an Act or statutory rule that has been fully argued in the proceedings and on which an authoritative ruling is needed, or where the case is one in which the judges will be bound by an existing decision of the Court of Appeal, or of the House of Lords in a fully considered judgment in earlier proceedings.

The leap-frog procedure can only be used if the trial judge gives a certificate (which should be sought within 14 days of the judgment) and the House of Lords gives leave. There must be a sufficient case to justify going directly to the House of Lords, and the parties must consent. It will again be necessary to draft grounds of appeal similar to those outlined in this chapter.

13 *Advising and drafting for county court actions*

Although the volume of work means that county court actions are important in practice, the advising and drafting skills needed are essentially a modified version of those for the High Court so that only the more important differences in procedure need be mentioned. A number of the High Court rules are specifically made to apply in the county court, and where there is no rule for the county court then the appropriate High Court rule, modified as appropriate, will apply.

The main difference is that the procedure in the county court is simpler, and many steps are effectively taken by the court office rather than by the parties themselves. This is especially important for small claims, where the parties may not have legal representation. The statutory basis for county court jurisdiction and procedure is contained in the County Courts Act 1984, the County Court Rules 1981 and the County Court (Forms) Rules 1982.

Advising the client

The basic approach to interviewing the client and getting information from him was discussed in Chapter 2. After the initial interview with the client, decisions will have to be made as to which court the action should be brought in, and what legal representation will be needed. These decisions will of course be based on the jurisdiction of the county court, but there are also some practical points to take into consideration.

The county court has jurisdiction under the County Courts Act 1984 to hear the following types of cases:

(a) Actions founded on tort or contract where the amount claimed does not exceed £5,000 (CCA 1984, s.15). In deciding whether the limit is exceeded, any set-off can be taken into account, and the plaintiff can in writing agree to abandon part of his claim so as to bring it within the county court limit.

(b) Actions for the recovery of money due under any enactment, so long as the amount claimed does not exceed £5,000 (CCA 1984, s.16).

(c) Actions for the recovery of land or in which the title to land comes into question where the net annual value of the land for rating purposes does not exceed £1,000 (CCA 1984, s.21).

(d) Actions for the administration of an estate, an execution or declaration or variation of trust, for the foreclosure or redemption of a mortgage, for maintenance or advancement, or various other equitable actions where the amount in dispute does not exceed £30,000 (CCA 1984, s.23). Also probate actions where the estate is within this limit (CCA 1984, s.32).

(e) Admiralty proceedings where the value in dispute is less than £5,000, in salvage proceedings where the value of the property saved does not exceed £15,000 (CCA 1984, ss.26–31).

(f) Various special jurisdictions by statute, e.g. under the Inheritance (Provision for Family and Dependants) Act 1975, (CCA 1984, s.25), under certain sections of the Settled Land Act 1925, the Law of Property Act 1925 (CCA 1984, s.24), and in landlord and tenant actions.

(g) The parties may by written consent agree that the county court should have jurisdiction, but not in cases that should be brought in the Chancery, Family or Admiralty jurisdictions of the High Court (CCA 1984, s.18).

These jurisdictional limits are not decisive as to where the case should be brought. Even if the case is within the county court jurisdiction, it will normally be possible to bring it in the High Court too (with a few statutory exceptions) as that court has no lower limit. Therefore the lawyer must consider and advise on where the case should be brought. The most relevant factor will usually be costs; not only will it normally be much more expensive to bring an action in the High Court, but there may also be a penalty in costs if a case within the county court limit is taken to the High Court (CCA 1984, ss.19–20). If the plaintiff recovers less than £3,000 in the High Court he will only get costs on the county court scale, and if he recovers less than £600 he will get no costs at all, unless it was reasonable for him to bring the action in the High Court, or there were reasonable grounds for believing that he would recover more.

The next important factor will be the complexity of the law involved, which may well justify going to the High Court, even if the case is within the county court limits. This is especially the case with proceedings that would go to the Chancery or Admiralty Division of the High Court. If the case is complex enough to justify the briefing of a barrister, he may well feel that the extra expertise and procedural possibilities in the High Court should be used, especially if he is a specialist barrister who does most of his work in the High Court.

If a case is within the county court jurisdiction, the judge has the power to grant any relief or remedy in law or in equity that a High Court judge can grant, (CCA 1984, ss.38–39). However, there are limitations, in that for example an injunction or specific performance can only be granted in the county court if it is directly ancillary to a case (though see *Hatt & Co (Bath)* v *Pearce* [1978] 2 All ER 474 where there was only a claim for £1 damages but it was held that an injunction could be granted ancillary to it). Although most procedural steps that are available in the High Court are also available in the county court, they may be modified or limited. For example, the rules for payments into court are slightly different, and there is no automatic general discovery, although discovery may be sought. While there are basic drafts for claims in the county court, as will be seen, there are fewer and shorter pleadings than in a High Court action. For all these reasons, if preparation before trial and interlocutory and procedural strategy may be important in the case, it should probably be brought in the High Court rather than the county court.

There are also other practical points, such as pure convenience. Outside the major cities it may well be much more convenient and quicker for the case to be brought in the local county court, rather than for everyone concerned to wait and have to travel to a centre where a High Court judge sits and this should be considered. This decision is not necessarily final, as a case can be moved from the county court to the High Court or vice versa if this becomes desirable for some reason (CCA 1984, ss.40–42). The decision must be made for the whole case, and it is not possible to split a cause of action and bring two separate actions within the county court limits (CCA 1984, s.35).

Allied to the decision of where to bring the action is a decision as to legal representation. If the case is within the county court jurisdiction then the client may represent himself, or be represented by a solicitor or barrister (CCA 1984, s.60). If the solicitor feels that he can deal with the case himself, then of course he should do so. If he feels the need for the opinion of Counsel, then counsel will advise on where he feels the case should be brought, bearing in mind all the factors outlined above. At the other end of the scale, if the case is very small the client may be able to represent himself. If the claim is for less than £500 then the solicitor may advise the client on the use of the Small Claims Court.

Preparing the case for court

The details of the procedural steps for bringing a case in the county court can be found in the County Court Rules or the County Court Practice. Most steps will be similar to or a modified version of the procedural steps in the High Court.

There is a basic division between default actions for the payment of a sum of money, and other actions called fixed date actions. The main stages in a fixed date action will be as follows:

(a) The plaintiff requests the County Court Office to issue a summons. This is done by the plaintiff himself or his solicitor handing in the appropriate form with two copies of the particulars of claim. The court staff will then prepare the summons and issue it, normally by post.

(b) The defendant will receive with the summons a form on which he can state whether he wishes to defend the action, admit the plaintiff's claim, or bring a counterclaim. He should return this within 14 days. The plaintiff may get judgment if the defendant admits his claim or fails to appear, or there is a procedure for getting summary judgment if there is no real defence (CCR Order 9).

(c) The pre-trial review. A date for this will be set, at least 21 days after the summons was issued. At the review the registrar can give all directions that are necessary for the just, expeditious and economic disposal of the action (CCR Order 17). It is vital for both parties to give proper thought in advance as to what directions they would like to enable them to prepare and present their case at trial. For example, they may seek directions as to how evidence should be presented at trial, whether any admissions may be made, and whether there should be any inspection and discovery, given that this is not automatic.

Interlocutory applications may be made pending the hearing, normally to the registrar on notice (CCR Order 13). The things that may be applied for are similar to the High Court, but the rules are in some cases slightly different, and the lawyer should check to be sure of the details. For example:

(i) Interim payments (CCA 1984, s.50).
(ii) Provisional damages for personal injury (CCA 1984, s.51).
(iii) Discovery and inspection prior to action (CCA 1984, s.52).
(iv) Disclosure and inspection in cases of personal injury or death (CCA 1984, s.53).
(v) Payment into court (CCR Order 11).
(vi) Discovery and interrogatories (CCR Order 14).

(d) The hearing of the case. The registrar may hear the case if the claim does not exceed £500, with the leave of the judge, or if the parties give their consent. Otherwise the case will be heard by a county court judge. Costs will normally be given on set scales according to the work done, though there is a discretion to award more if the case is particularly complicated.

If the action is for a debt or for a liquidated or unliquidated sum of money, then the case will be a default action and the above procedure will be modified. The plaintiff will apply for the summons to be issued, but when it is served there will be served with it a notice warning the defendant that the plaintiff may get judgment in default if he does not within 14 days pay the sum due with costs, or enter a defence to the action. The action will only proceed, with a date being set for the pre-trial review, if the defendant does enter a defence or counterclaim, or if the plaintiff has reason for not accepting the money tendered. This procedure is clearly an effective way of getting judgment for a sum of money within the county court limit.

Drafting for the county court

Although the basic principles for drafting in the county court are very similar to those for the High Court, the actual requirements of drafting are rather different. There is a much greater reliance on forms issued by the court, which only need to be completed by the party or his lawyer. The set forms for summonses and for many other applications are in the County Court (Forms) Rules 1982, set out in the *County Court Practice* (Butterworths, annual), otherwise known as the Green Book.

In addition to this, there is less reliance on drafting in preparing a case in the county court. The plaintiff should give appropriate particulars of his claim, and the defendant appropriate particulars of his defence and any counterclaim, but no further document is needed (though further particulars of the plaintiff's or the defendant's case may be ordered if necessary). The actual pleading in the particulars of claim or the defence will tend to be shorter and simpler than in the High Court pleading because a case with complex law or facts would normally go to the High Court anyway.

However, these points do not mean that drafting for the county court will necessarily be easy, as it will still require skill and practice to reduce the case to a reasonably short and straightforward draft. All the rules discussed in earlier chapters as to what should go into a draft, how it should be expressed and what particulars should be given will essentially apply. This section will just deal with a few special points to bear in mind when drafting for the county court rather than the High Court.

Whenever the object of the proceedings is to obtain relief against any person, or to compel any person to do or to abstain from doing any act, then the case should be begun by a summons with particulars of the claim made by the plaintiff (CCR Order 3). Alternatively, in particular cases provided for by statute or by the Rules, the case should be begun by an originating application (such as an application under the Inheritance (Provision for Family and Dependants) Act 1975, or an application for a business tenancy) or by a petition (such as an application for a divorce).

As for the particulars of claim, CCR Order 6 provides that when he commences an action, the plaintiff should file particulars of claim specifying his cause of action and the relief or remedy that he seeks, and stating briefly the material facts on which he relies (see Example 1). The heading for the particulars of claim should state the county court where the summons is taken out and where the case will be heard, and this must be a court that has jurisdiction to hear the case (CCR Order 8). This differs according to the type of case, but essentially the court should be the court within whose district the defendant resides or carries on business, or where the cause of action wholly or partly arose, or where any land in dispute is situated. The heading should also state the number of the action and the names of the parties. If the action is brought under a statute, the statute should be specified.

The actual particulars of claim should set out in numbered paragraphs the basic elements of the claim that the plaintiff is making. As in a statement of claim, these paragraphs should plead facts rather than law or evidence and should be set out with separate points in separate paragraphs, and in a suitable order. Particulars of breach, negligence, damage etc. should be given as appropriate. There is a tendency for particulars of claim to be much briefer than a statement of claim, but the lawyer should ensure that this is so only if it is justified by the relatively straightforward nature of the case, and that nothing is left out which should be pleaded.

Certain things must be pleaded in particular types of action, for example there are specified details that must be pleaded in actions for the recovery of land, in connection with a mortgage, or in a hire-purchase action, and these are set out in CCR Order 6. If the plaintiff abandons part of his claim so as to bring it within the county court limits, this must be pleaded.

All the remedies claimed by the plaintiff should be pleaded, again as in the statement of claim, and appropriate particulars of damage should be given. As in the High Court a claim for interest must be pleaded with all appropriate detail (CCA 1984, s.69). Simple interest may be awarded at such rate as the court thinks fit on all or part of the damages for all or part of the time since the cause of action arose until the time of payment or judgment. However, it seems that the rules are not necessarily entirely the same as for the High Court, and for example exemplary damages do not have to be specifically pleaded, *Drane* v *Evangelou* [1978] 2 All ER 437.

The particulars should be dated and signed at the end as shown in Example 1.

The rules for drafting a defence (CCR Order 9), a counterclaim, and a third party notice are again similar to the rules for the High Court, only details of form being different (see Examples 2 and 3). There will be no further pleadings in the county court.

Particulars of any pleading may be ordered by the court if necessary, though as in the High Court, a written application should be made before a court order is sought (CCR Order 13). Pleadings may also be amended if necessary with less formality than in the High Court, by serving the amended pleading, though the court may disallow the amendment if they do not feel it is just (CCR Order 15).

Affidavits may be required to support an application under the County Court Rules. Also, affidavit evidence may be accepted at trial on a more general basis than in the High Court (CCR Order 20). Affidavit evidence may be accepted if one party gives notice to the other that he wishes to use it at least 14 days before the hearing, and the other side does not object within 7 days of that, or if the judge thinks that it is reasonable to admit it. This may be considered at the pre-trial review. The rules for the drafting of an affidavit are the same as for the High Court, except that an affidavit can generally contain a matter of information and belief, provided the source is given.

Appeals

An appeal from the decision of a registrar will normally lie to a county court judge (CCR Order 37). An appeal from a decision of a county court judge will normally lie to the Court of Appeal, and the procedure for that will be similar to the procedure already outlined for an appeal from the High Court to the Court of Appeal (CCA 1984, s.77). This appeal will normally be as of right for either side, but leave will be needed if the claim was for less than half the limit for the county court jurisdiction, or if the judge was deciding a matter that came to him on appeal from a decision of a registrar (except where the matter involved an injunction or the custody of a child). There will be no right of appeal if the parties have agreed in writing that the judge's decision would be final.

The drafting, procedure and preparation will be the same as that for an appeal from the High Court to the Court of Appeal. If no transcript is available it is possible to ask the judge to make a note of any point of law or evidence in the case, or of his decision (CCA 1984, s.80). The Court of Appeal will have powers to wholly or partly allow the appeal, to make an order determining on the merits the real question in issue between the parties, or to order a new trial (CCA 1984, s.81).

EXAMPLE 1 BASIC PARTICULARS OF CLAIM FOR THE COUNTY COURT

In the *County Court* *Case No.*

BETWEEN A. B. *Plaintiff*

and

C. D. *Defendant*

PARTICULARS OF CLAIM

(Set out in numbered paragraphs the basic facts on which the claim is founded, as in pleading a statement of claim.)

1.
2.
3.
4.

AND the Plaintiff claims

(Set out in numbered paragraphs each relief sought.)

1.
2.
3.

Dated...... etc. Signed

EXAMPLE 2 BASIC DEFENCE FOR THE COUNTY COURT (with set-off and counterclaim)

In the *County Court* *Case No.*

BETWEEN A. B. *Plaintiff*

and

C. D. *Defendant*

DEFENCE

(Set out in numbered paragraphs your response to every point raised in the Particulars of Claim, as in pleading a Defence in the High Court. The following are examples of possible paragraphs that may be adjusted for use.)

1. Paragraph of the Particulars of Claim is admitted.
2. Paragraph of the Particulars of Claim is not admitted.
3. Save in that......, paragraph of the Particulars of Claim is denied.
4. The Defendant claims the right to set-off £ against the Plaintiff's claim, in that......

COUNTERCLAIM

(Set out in numbered paragraphs the facts of any counterclaim, in the same way as pleading Particulars of Claim.)

5.
6.
7.

AND the Defendant counterclaims:

(Set out in numbered paragraphs the relief sought on the counterclaim.)

1.
2.
3.

Dated...... etc. Signed.

EXAMPLE 3 BASIC THIRD PARTY NOTICE FOR THE COUNTY COURT

In the County Court *Case No.*

BETWEEN	A. B.	*Plaintiff*
	and	
	C. D.	*Defendant*
	and	
	E. F.	*Third Party*

To E. F.

TAKE NOTICE that this action has been brought by the Plaintiff against the Defendant and that the Defendant claims against you:

(a) that he is entitled to contribution from you to the extent of......
or (b) that he is entitled to be indemnified by you against liability in respect of......
or (c) that he is entitled to the following relief or remedy relating to or connected with the original subject matter of the action, namely......
or (d) that the following question or issue relating to or connected with the subject matter of the action should properly be determined as between the Plaintiff and the Defendant and the third party, namely......
(Choose and complete the appropriate one.)

The grounds of the Defendant's claim are:
(Briefly state the grounds.)

If you dispute the Plaintiff's claim...... (warning of need to give notice)

AND TAKE NOTICE that you should attend at on at o'clock when directions will be given for the further conduct of these proceedings.

If you fail to attend you may be deemed to admit:...... (warning that he may be deemed to admit all claims against him and liability, and will be bound by the judgment).

Dated

14 *Advising and drafting in criminal cases*

Some of the general principles for advice and drafting in civil cases will also apply to criminal cases. However, the fact that the criminal case is essentially between the state and the individual and that the reputation or liberty of the individual may be at stake means that there are some basic differences in advising and deciding on strategy. It will not be possible to cover all the problems that can arise, but the practical problems that may come up most often in advising the defence or the prosecution are included, together with the principles for drafting indictments and grounds of appeal.

The details of criminal procedure will not be covered, only those points in procedure which may need special consideration and advice.

Advising for the defence

There may be special problems in having contact with the client in a criminal case. The client may be able to make an appointment to see the solicitor for advice on an actual or potential charge against him and discuss the case thoroughly, but often the first meeting will be in more difficult conditions. The client may meet the solicitor shortly before he goes into court under the duty solicitor scheme, so only immediate issues can be dealt with. Most difficult, the client may be at the police station so that things must be dealt with quickly and under pressure. Although the importance and immediacy may vary, there are three basic things that the lawyer will need to consider when he first sees the client—bail, legal aid, and what line the client should take with the police and the prosecution.

Bail and the freedom of the client If the client has not yet been charged there should normally be no difficulty about his freedom—if he is merely 'helping the police with their inquiries' he is free to leave the police station at any time, though the Police and Criminal Evidence Act 1984 has introduced greater powers for the police to detain a suspect prior to charging him and will extend the Duty Solicitor Scheme to the police station. It remains to be seen how these will work in practice. As soon as the client has been charged the possibility of bail arises, and can be sought from the police. A station sergeant or an officer not below the rank of an inspector may grant bail, and must consider doing so if the accused cannot be brought before a magistrates' court within 24 hours, Magistrates' Courts Act 1980, s.43. The policeman should grant bail unless he considers the offence to be serious, and if he does grant it he may ask for sureties. If the accused was arrested on a warrant, bail will depend on whether the warrant was indorsed for bail when it was issued, and not on the policeman's discretion.

In any event, the accused must be brought before the magistrates' court as soon as possible and that court will consider bail. The essential point here is that the accused has the right to bail until he is convicted, Bail Act 1976, s.4, unless one of the exceptions in Schedule 1 of the Act applies. The lawyer for the defence must make the most of the application for and right to bail. If the client is kept in custody his life will be totally disrupted—his relationship with his family and friends may be strained, every element of his daily life may be upset, he may even lose his job, and it may be more difficult for him to prepare his defence properly. Only in a small proportion of very serious cases is bail totally out of the question, so the lawyer should prepare and present a proper application. Even an alleged murderer may get bail if there is no likelihood of his absconding or committing further offences, *R* v *Vernege* [1982] 1 WLR 293.

The solicitor, or the barrister if one is involved at this stage, must take care to get all the relevant information from the client, asking about his work, home and financial circumstances, his health, and anything else that may be affected by his being kept in custody. Inquiries should also be made as to whether the accused would be able to find sureties and for what amount. It is important that the first application for bail be made properly, as once bail has been refused once there is less chance that it will be granted later. It is useful to discuss matters with the officer in charge of the case. If the police are prepared to accept bail then the magistrates' will almost certainly grant it, whereas if the police oppose bail the lawyer will have to develop good positive arguments to get it. Since the court can impose conditions on the grant of bail it is often useful to negotiate with the police as to what conditions they would regard as appropriate, such as regularly signing on at the police station, depositing a passport or not going to a specified place while on bail.

Even if the magistrates do not grant bail on the first application, the accused can only be remanded for up to 8 days at a time unless he consents to a longer period, Magistrates Courts Act 1980, s.128, so the application for bail can be made again when he reappears in court. If there was not time to get full information for the first application for bail, it is vital to get it for the second, as once the magistrates have heard two full applications for bail, they will not normally hear another full application unless there is a change in circumstances *R* v *Nottingham Justices ex p. Davies* [1981] QB 38, so that the client will stay in custody at least until he is committed, and probably until trial. If magistrates do refuse bail having heard full argument, it is possible to appeal to a Crown Court judge. The alternative is to apply to a High Court judge, who has an inherent power to grant bail, but legal aid is not available for this, and the Crown Court judge will usually be more convenient.

The cost of the defence The vast majority of criminal cases have legal aid, and this should be discussed with the client as soon as possible. If the client needs legal aid the solicitor should ensure that it is applied for, either helping the client fill in the forms, or applying to the magistrates in court. As with civil cases, the lawyer should always check the legal aid certificate in the case to see that it does cover what is being done, and should be sure to apply to extend legal aid where necessary, for example if there is an appeal.

What the client should tell the police Police questioning is a difficult issue, not made easier by media comment, and a number of rather exaggerated fictional series about police practice on television. There is an inevitable conflict. The first reaction of the solicitor must be to tell the client to say nothing, or only to answer questions with the lawyer present, because of the danger that he may, even unintentionally or on the spur of the moment, say something that could be used against him at trial. Conversely the police will quite properly want to find out as much about the offence as they can, to get information about anyone else involved in the offence, or to recover stolen property. To get the information that they need to prove who committed an offence, the police may well feel the need to apply some pressure or to discourage someone from leaving the police station. There is an inevitable conflict between the need to solve crime and the interests of civil liberties.

This is not the place to discuss where the bounds for police questioning should lie. Suffice it to say that for the defence lawyer the line of advice will basically have to be that the client should say nothing, unless his lawyer is present. But of course there is nothing to be gained from being completely uncooperative. If the client can give information to the police without prejudicing his position the police will normally respond by being helpful on issues such as bail. Also a line of defence may well be strengthened if the client tells the police his version of events at the earliest opportunity and maintains it right up to trial.

Once the preliminary issues have been dealt with, the next step for the defence lawyer is to get full details from the client of what he says happened. This will normally involve two stages, getting the client to give his version of events, and his reaction to every allegation against him in the statements from the prosecution witnesses. It is normally best to begin by asking the client to say what happened in his own words, to assess whether what he says is really convincing, and possibly to obtain a full picture where asking specific questions might have left something out. Once the basic statement has been made the lawyer can fill in any gaps by questioning the client. Even if the solicitor sends a good and full statement as part of the brief, it is useful for a barrister to ask the client to tell him what happened again, so that he has the chance of assessing what is said.

There is a real art to asking the client questions in a criminal case, which may take years to build up, and requires an ability to assess a person and a situation. In a civil case a client may over-emphasise or twist facts a little, but he will rarely lie to his lawyers, whereas in a criminal case the client has a very strong motivation for lying, and the lawyer will inevitably wonder if he really did commit the offence. This needs to be dealt with carefully. On the one hand one needs all the details that the client can give to be able to conduct the case properly, and in finding these out it is necessary to turn over every stone to see what is underneath and to ask awkward questions. If the defence lawyer doesn't, the prosecution certainly will, and it may well ruin a line of defence if something unexpected comes out at trial for the first time. Thus the defence lawyer must press his client to tell him everything in advance in his own interests. On the other hand, there is also a danger in letting the client say too much, as those who have read or seen the Rumpole series of stories will know. Once the client has told the lawyer something, he cannot say anything to the contrary in court. At the extreme, if the client admits that he committed the offence charged, the lawyer cannot defend him on a plea of not guilty. He must either plead guilty or be represented by another lawyer (the first lawyer should not tell the second of the confession). It is therefore not advisable to ask a direct question which may encourage a confession, let alone 'Did you do it?'. If the client does admit the offence this is not necessarily the end of the matter, as the lawyer should certainly examine whether the client is guilty in law by running through the elements of the offence—many people think they are guilty of theft if they take something without realising that you need an intention to steal—if one element is missing then of course the client can plead not guilty.

This is not a legal rule, but a matter of professional practice to be enforced by the appropriate professional body. It applies to each lawyer separately, and if for example the client confesses his guilt to the solicitor but not to the barrister, it seems that it is proper for the solicitor not to tell the barrister and for the barrister to go on with the defence. The rule can present difficulties, if for example the client does not actually confess his guilt but the lawyer is still pretty sure in his own mind that the client is guilty, and the client knows this. The lawyer can quite properly defend the client because there is no confession of guilt, but the client may think that the lawyer defended him although he believed him to be guilty.

The rule applies not only to full confessions of guilt, but also to admissions to particular facts. There is no positive duty to tell the court of the admission, just not to contradict it. If for example there is a charge of burglary and the client admits stealing something but denies entering the property as a trespasser, the lawyer can represent the client on a plea of not guilty to burglary, but he cannot positively assert that the client did not steal anything. (Alternatively there may be a plea of guilty to the lesser offence of theft.)

Once the defence lawyer has the basic facts from the client, he should go on to fill in as many details as he can, thinking of all the other possible witnesses or sources of evidence that may be available. This is very much an imaginative process of trying to work out what did or might have happened—to try to visualise the events to think of weaknesses in the prosecution case and possible lines of defence. Any ideas should be followed up with the client, and the client should be encouraged to tell the lawyer if he remembers anything more.

It is often difficult to establish a good working relationship with the client in a criminal case. The client may well be under a considerable stress just because of the criminal charge, even if it is not relatively serious. A charge of shoplifting can cause real mental distress to someone who is elderly or who regards it as undermining their social status. The client may be in real fear of the threat of the possible sentence to his life and family, especially if there is a danger that he may go to prison. There is also often tension from the lawyer if he wonders whether the client is telling him the whole truth, and the client wonders whether the lawyer believes him. In a civil case the lawyer and the client may well come from a similar professional type of background, but in a criminal case they may well have totally different types of background which may make it difficult for there to be any real rapport between them.

All these things can make communication difficult, but it is vital, and the lawyer must make a conscious effort to overcome any problems. The client may not be very articulate, he may well be worried or angry about what is happening, but he should always be able to feel that his lawyer has a full grasp of the case.

In addition to the initial consultation with the client, the lawyer should see him to explain and deal with any outstanding matters just before the trial, and must always make a point of seeing him after the trial, especially if he is convicted, as a matter of professional courtesy even if there will not be an appeal.

Communication may be particularly difficult if the client is in custody. Of course the lawyer will have access to the client in the prison, or in the cells at the court, but the client in prison cannot just pick up the telephone when a new point or a question occurs to him, so it is especially important that the barrister and the solicitor should ensure that everything is covered when they do meet that client, and that he is given time to say anything he wants to or ask questions. When the client could only be remanded for up to eight days at a time he might see his lawyer once a week, but now that remands can be up to 28 days with consent, it may be a month between one time that the client sees his lawyer and the next.

Having gathered all the information about the alleged offence that he can from the client, the lawyer will have to advise him how to plead, though this decision will not have to be finally taken until the start of the trial, and it may well be that the lawyer will also wish to assess the strength of the prosecution case before a final decision is taken. Sometimes this will be easy—if the client says he did not commit the offence then he should plead not guilty, and if he freely admits the offence he should plead guilty, but sometimes the lawyer will have to advise the client carefully. The lawyer must remember that it is for the accused person to plead personally in court and that the final decision how to plead must be his—the lawyer can give clear advice, but he must not put undue pressure on the client to plead one way or the other.

If the client says that he is guilty the lawyer cannot represent him if he pleads not guilty, but he should go through all the elements of the offence with the client to see if he really is guilty or if there is some possible line of defence. He should also investigate motives; someone on a shoplifting charge may wish to plead guilty just to get the case over with, although they did not intend to take the item, in which case the lawyer must advise them that they should plead not guilty to avoid having a criminal record. However, if the client still wishes to plead guilty, he cannot be prevented from doing so. The plea must be unequivocal—if the client does insist on pleading guilty the lawyer cannot say in mitigation that they did not intend to take the item! Conversely, a client may insist on pleading not guilty despite the weight of evidence against them, and they must be allowed to do so.

There may be an alternative of pleading guilty to a lesser offence to consider, if the elements of the crime charged include the elements of a less serious offence, for example an allegation of robbery necessarily involves an allegation of theft. There is no obligation to plead guilty to a lesser offence, the accused can just plead not guilty to the offence charged, but the choice is open to him and the lawyer must advise. If there is a real chance of acquittal it may be best to plead not guilty, but if there is a real danger of conviction it may be better to plead to the lesser offence and hope to get a lower sentence.

Even if the defendant does decide to offer a plea to a lesser offence, it will only be effective if the prosecution and the judge accept it. The prosecution should be contacted for their view before the trial, and they will consider the public interest. If they feel that the evidence they have justifies the more serious charge they should not accept the plea to the lesser one, but if there is any real doubt whether they will get a conviction for the more serious charge they should accept the plea to save the time and expense of a trial. The judge should be consulted before or at the start of the trial and he will apply a similar test. He will normally agree with the prosecution decision, but he may not, *R* v *Broad* (1978) 68 Cr App R 281. When Peter Sutcliffe was prosecuted for the 'Yorkshire Ripper' murders the prosecution were prepared to accept a plea of guilty to manslaughter in the light of the reports on his mental state, but the judge was not, and the jury did eventually return verdicts of guilty to murder. If the plea to the lesser offence is not accepted it will lapse, unless the prosecution seek to add the lesser offence to the indictment, or ask the judge to direct the jury on the possibility of convicting of a lesser offence at the end of the trial.

The possibilities of 'plea bargaining' are often commented on and criticised, and the lawyer should take care to behave properly here. The term has no strict meaning, but is used to cover any negotiations as to how the defendant should plead and what he may get in return. This can include pleading guilty to a lesser offence, pleading guilty to the offence charged to get a lower sentence, or agreeing to give evidence for the prosecution in another case to avoid being charged with a serious offence. One can only say briefly that the lawyer must take great care to act openly and properly in the interests of his client and the public. Some general rules for plea bargaining come from *R* v *Turner* [1970] 2 QB 321; the lawyer should act in the client's best interests, giving strong advice if necessary but without undue pressure, and the accused must be given free choice as to how to plead. He should not feel the prosecution or the judge are forcing him to plead guilty. Counsel should avoid consulting a judge in private, but if he does go counsel for both sides should see the judge together. A judge should not make specific promises as to what sentence he will give for a guilty plea, but should only give general indications of the type of sentence that may be appropriate.

One final point about pleas is the practice of taking offences into consideration (often referred to as t.i.c.s). This means that in addition to the offences actually charged the defendant admits informally that he has also committed other offences, which are taken into account when he is sentenced. The advantage to the defendant is that no further proceedings will be taken against him for the other offences, and although he will get a higher sentence than he would otherwise have for the offence charged, it will be much lower than if he had been separately charged with the other offences. It is an advantage to the prosecution that liability for the other offences is decided without further investigation or expense. This is not a formal procedure, but just a matter of agreement between defence and prosecution that may be initiated by either side.

If the defendant is to plead guilty the lawyer will have to investigate possible matters of mitigation, but if he is to plead not guilty the lawyer will have to make further inquiries and decide what line to take. It is not for the lawyer to invent a line of defence (though some clients seem to think it is), but only to advise on what lines of defence may be open. The basic possibilities, which are not mutually exclusive, are as follows:

(a) Leaving the prosecution to prove its case. This will be a part of most defences, as the burden of proof, beyond a reasonable doubt, is on the prosecution. The lawyer should examine whether the prosecution have evidence on all the points that it needs to prove, and whether the evidence they have is admissible. Without offering any evidence or other argument itself, it is open to the defence to submit that there is no case to answer either at committal or at trial, or to argue at the end of the trial that the defendant should not be convicted on the evidence available.

(b) Saying the defendant was not at the scene of the crime and had nothing to do with it. This will involve two elements—alibi evidence to prove where the defendant was at the time (notice of which must be given to the prosecution, Criminal Justice Act 1967, s.11), and challenging any identification evidence that the accused was at the scene of the crime. There are strict rules for the carrying out of identification parades.

(c) Agreeing the defendant was at the scene of the crime, but denying either that a crime was actually committed or that the accused was involved in it if it was. Here the case will often turn on disputes of fact, and the defence lawyer will have to challenge prosecution evidence and seek evidence of the accused's innocence. It will be necessary to take care in challenging prosecution evidence where the accused has previous convictions, as he may lose his 'shield' and they will go in, Criminal Evidence Act 1898, s.1. The admissibility of a confession may be challenged if the accused says it was got by unfair means, but arguments will need to be strong to have the confession ruled inadmissible. Short of that the accused may say that he has been 'verballed', that is that the police say that he said things which he did not in fact say. This is often done on the basis that the alleged statement contains things that the accused would not have said, such as 'Its a fair cop, guv', or by showing that the notes of events made by policemen are identical and must therefore have been agreed by them, although they were supposed to have made their own notes separately.

The lawyer must use judgment in challenging prosecution evidence. Allegations against the police and prosecution witnesses should only be made if the lawyer reasonably believes that they are true, and that they can form a useful part of the defence case. In several recent cases judges have severely criticised the making of allegations that are mere 'mudslinging'.

(d) There may be legal arguments why the accused has not committed the offence charged, and these will have to be developed with authorities.

There may be particular problems for the defence in deciding what line to take if there is more than one accused, and decisions as to tactics and evidence may be complicated. One lawyer can represent more than one accused if they have similar lines of defence, but they should be separately represented if there is any conflict of interest. If the defendants do tell different stories the decision for each as to what line to take may be difficult, and it must be remembered that previous convictions can go in if one co-accused gives evidence against another.

Advising for the prosecution

The majority of prosecutions are brought by the police, with a different system for each police area, each tending to use particular solicitors and barristers. There are proposals at present before Parliament for a unified prosecution system and it remains to be seen how this will work in practice, though many principles for conducting a case for the prosecution will remain the same. In certain circumstances the prosecution may be in the hands of someone other than the police, such as the Director of Public Prosecutions. In any event, prosecution work is normally in the hands of specific solicitors and barristers who regularly do this type of work. It is the duty of the prosecution to prosecute the case fairly, not to get a conviction at any cost. As it is sometimes put, he is there to prosecute, not to persecute. There is a public interest in convicting those who commit crimes, but not in convicting the innocent.

Firstly, there is the decision to prosecute, much criticised in the *Ponting* case. Then there is the actual conduct of the case when the prosecution should be thoroughly pursued if the evidence justifies it. The burden of proof beyond a reasonable doubt is on the prosecution, so complete preparation of evidence and arguments on facts and on law is essential. If the accused wishes to plead guilty to a lesser offence, or to have offences taken into consideration the prosecution should only agree if they do feel that this is in the public interest. It is not in the public interest to let someone who has committed a serious assault get away with a plea to a less serious offence, unless there is a real doubt about the evidence and the chances of securing a conviction.

On the other hand, the prosecution must be open. While the defendant is entitled to keep his case secret until the trial (except for disclosing any defence of alibi), the prosecution should disclose theirs. If there is to be a Crown Court trial, this will happen at committal, and if the prosecutor wishes to use evidence at trial that was not in the committal papers, he should give notice to the defence with a copy of the evidence. If the prosecution comes to know of any evidence that may favour the defence, they should disclose that to the defence in any event. Even if there is to be a summary trial without committal proceedings, the prosecution should let the defence have copies of any statements in advance of the trial.

The Attorney-General has given guidelines on this duty of disclosure [1982] 1 All ER 743. The general duty is to disclose all witness statements and documents which are not in the committal papers, unedited versions of any statements which have been edited, as well as statements of witnesses to be called at committal. All these should be made available to the defence solicitor as early as possible if they have some bearing on the offence charged and the circumstances surrounding the case. If the documents are short the defence should be given a copy, but if there are more than 50 pages they may just be made available for inspection, see *R* v *Penfold* (1979) 71 Cr App R 4.

There is a discretion not to disclose documents, which should be exercised on the advice of counsel if there is any doubt. The first ground for refusing disclosure is that it may lead to attempts to get a witness to retract or change his statement, or to intimidate him. The second ground is that the statement is made by someone close to the accused, such as a relative, which is believed to be wholly or partly untrue, and which the prosecution may use in cross-examination. The third is that the statement favours the prosecution, but that it is believed that the witness may have said something different to the defence, so that again the prosecution may wish to use the statement in cross-examination. If the statement is neutral or negative and there is no reason to doubt its truth there is no need to disclose it, though the name and address of the witness should normally be given. Lastly, the statement need not be disclosed if it is so sensitive that this would not be in the public interest, for example on grounds of national security, because it discloses offences by someone other than the accused, or because it contains details of private delicacy. The question is to balance the sensitivity of the document with its possible value to the defence. If necessary a sensitive part of a document may be blanked out.

If the prosecution do know of evidence that is positively favourable to the defence, they should disclose that, *Dallison* v *Caffery* [1965] 1 QB 348. If this is not done it may be a ground of appeal, as in *R* v *Shadrack* [1976] Crim LR 55, where a document on the police file supported the defence of one of the defendants but was not made available to him, so his conviction was quashed. There was a similar result in *R* v *Leyland Justices ex p. Hawthorn* [1979] QB 283, where the prosecution did not tell the defence that they knew of two witnesses who could give evidence in favour of the accused.

When it comes to sentence, the prosecutor has no duty to press for a heavy sentence, and indeed he will often not be involved at the sentencing stage, as the sentence is a matter for the judge based on a plea in mitigation. At most the prosecution should give objective help as to the type of sentences available. One thing the prosecution should do if appropriate is to seek a compensation order where someone has suffered personal injury, loss or damage as a result of the offence charged or of an offence taken into consideration, Powers of Criminal Courts Act 1973, s.35. It is normal practice for the police to ask the victim if he would like to seek compensation, and for the prosecution then to raise the matter if there is a conviction. It is necessary to show a clear case for compensation, and if possible to give evidence of the value of the damage suffered. By statute, compensation should now take priority over a fine if the defendant is unable to pay both, which emphasises the point that the victim must be given proper consideration. Compensation can be given for anxiety and distress if it is directly connected with the offence, *Bond* v *Chief Constable of Kent* [1983] 1 All ER 456.

Recent cases have held that the police may get an injunction to freeze money in a bank account, or may keep money found on the defendant's premises in police possession if it is traceable from an offence, and especially if it is evidence. However, the money may not be kept just for possible compensation or fine, see *Malone* v *Metropolitan Police Commissioner* [1979] Ch 344 and *Chief Constable of Kent* v *V* [1983] QB 34.

The mode of trial

Many minor offences, including for example many of the more minor motoring offences, are purely summary and can be tried only by the magistrates' court, and some very serious offences are triable only on indictment at the Crown Court. However many criminal offences, including many of the offences under the Theft Acts and many types of assault are triable either way. Therefore the lawyer will have to consider and advise as to which type of trial is more appropriate. The procedure for deciding the mode of trial comes from the Magistrates' Courts Act 1980 ss.18–22, which allows both prosecution and defence to make representations on the matter. Since a person over 18 has the right to a jury trial where the offence is triable either way, his choice may often be decisive, but the accused has no right to insist on a summary trial, and the prosecution may ask for a trial in the Crown Court if they feel that the offence is serious.

The main factors in deciding on mode of trial, most of which will be more important for the defendant, are as follows:

(a) The seriousness of the offence. This is a question of the facts of the alleged offence, and the value of property stolen or the seriousness of injuries inflicted may be crucial. There are no set limits, but if the value of the property stolen is in the thousands of pounds or the injuries inflicted are likely to take some time to heal the case should normally be heard in the Crown Court. Peripheral facts may make the case more serious, for example, the theft of a relatively small sum from an employer or while in a position of trust may merit a Crown Court trial.

(b) The possible sentence for the offence. Magistrates have limited sentencing powers, generally not being able to impose fines of more than £2,000 or prison sentences of more than six months, unless some other limit is set by statute for the offence. The magistrates should only try the case if they feel that, should they convict, these sentencing powers will be adequate. When this point is being considered, it should be remembered that if something in the character or antecedents that comes out at a later stage makes the magistrates feel that their sentencing powers are inadequate, they may commit the accused to the Crown Court for sentence. It is the full sentencing powers of the magistrates that should be taken into account in each case—if there are two or more offences triable either way the magistrates may impose a prison sentence of up to 12 months, or they may for example impose orders for compensation and costs in addition to a fine.

(c) The cost of proceedings. A summary trial will inevitably be much cheaper, because there will be less time in court, less expensive preparation, and the case may well be done by a solicitor with advocacy skills, without the extra expense of briefing a barrister to act as well. If the defendant does elect trial by jury he must accept that a much larger costs order may be made against him, *R* v *Boyesen* [1982] 2 All ER 161.

(d) The time factor. Most people on a criminal charge will express the wish to get it all over with as soon as possible, and undoubtedly a summary trial will be quicker. If there is a jury trial, there will have to be commital proceedings first, and then the wait for the Crown Court trial to come on. If the accused is on bail the time factor should not be crucial, but if he is in custody it may be that the offence is too serious to be tried summarily anyway.

(e) Knowing the prosecution case. If the trial is at the Crown Court there will be committal proceedings first, which will enable the defence to know the details of the prosecution case well in advance. This will also give the defence the chance to ask for a long form of committal, and use it to challenge prosecution evidence, and perhaps to submit no case to answer, or that the case should not be committed. If there is a summary trial the defence should normally still get the prosecution statements in advance, but they may not get them a long time in advance to be able to prepare their case fully.

(f) Complex legal or evidential points. If there are complex legal or evidential points, the usual view is that the case should go to the Crown Court. This is not necessarily true, as the magistrates' clerk will always have legal training and will be able to explain points, and so will a stipendiary magistrate if the case comes before him. However, there is something in the argument. The atmosphere of a Crown Court tends to be more suitable for a legal argument than a busy and often noisy magistrates' court where people are continually slipping in and out. Also the Crown Court judge will normally hear an argument on a legal point or the admissibility of evidence in the absence of the jury, so that if it is inadmissible the jury will never hear it, whereas magistrates will hear the evidence to decide, and even if they hold that it is inadmissible, it may be impossible for them to totally ignore it.

(g) The chances of acquittal. There is a general feeling that an accused is more likely to be acquitted by a Crown Court jury than by magistrates. Different research has come up with different conclusions as to whether this is really true, and it does depend on what basis statistics are drawn up. It can only be said that magistrates in a busy court hearing dozens of similar cases with similar lines of defence may jusifiably get a bit cynical, whereas people only sit on juries once or twice in their lives, and they may therefore be rather more prepared to give the accused the benefit of any doubt.

(h) Publicity. This is sometimes thought to be a relevant factor. The argument is that a quick hearing at a magistrates' court may pass unnoticed, whereas a full trial at a Crown Court might attract attention. There may be some truth to this, but the local press may have a reporter at the magistrates' court who will pick up the case anyway, and if someone well known is charged with an offence, it will probably attract publicity wherever it is tried.

At the end of the day it is a matter of balancing all these factors, and of deciding which of them are more important. For example, someone on a shop-lifting charge may well want to get it dealt with quickly and cheaply and get a low sentence, but they may wish to argue about the admissibility of evidence and hope to be acquitted by a jury. In each case it will be necessary to decide where the balance lies.

There is a special rule where the charge is of criminal damage, in that the offence will be triable either way if the value of the damage is more than £400, but purely summary if the value of the damage is less than £400. The magistrates will have to make a decision on the value of the damage, and there is no right of appeal against their finding, so it is important for the lawyers to prepare arguments on valuation in advance, supported by evidence as far as possible.

The place and mode of trial for a juvenile are subject to different rules which cannot be covered in detail here. The juvenile will normally be tried in the juvenile court with a few specific exceptions. He may be tried in the Crown Court if the charge is homicide, if he is over 14 and the offence is punishable with 14 years or more imprisonment, or if he is jointly charged with an adult for an indictable offence and it is in the interests of justice that they be tried together, Magistrates' Courts Act 1980, s.24. The juvenile may be tried in the adult magistrates court if he is jointly charged with an adult, or he aided and abetted the adult in the offence (or vice-versa), or if the charges against them arise from the same or connected circumstances, Children and Young Persons Act 1933, s.46. There is a discretion in many of these cases, where the lawyer should consider the possibilities and advise fully.

Summary trial

The procedure for trial at the magistrates' court is very well dealt with in other books, and I will only raise a few brief practical points here. The accused will normally be represented by a solicitor who does criminal advocacy work, though a barrister may be brought in. A young barrister may be briefed to appear at a summary trial if there is no suitable member of the firm of solicitors available to do the work, and this will give him good experience. Legal aid will not cover the briefing of a barrister for a summary trial unless there is good reason, so a certificate for counsel should be sought.

It is not always easy to prepare properly for a summary trial. Although it is now the practice for the prosecution to provide in advance copies of the statements of the witnesses that they intend to call, they may not be provided until a late stage and a great deal of work may have to be done at the last moment. In any event, preparation of the defence must be done quite quickly for a summary trial, normally within a few weeks. The basic lines of defence, with supporting evidence, can be prepared, but it may be difficult to prepare lines of cross-examination. Even if the prosecution statements are available, they may well be short, and only give a rough idea of what the witness will actually say. This means that the defence lawyer at a summary trial will have to listen especially carefully to everything that is said, and think and react quickly. It may also be difficult for him to arrange for someone to take a note of what is said by the witnesses, so he will have to do this himself as he goes along. The summary trial may thus be quite a challenge to the lawyer, who may have to improvise in a way that is not normally necessary in the Crown Court. If anything comes up that is a complete surprise for the defence it is of course possible to seek an adjournment.

It is important to use any period of waiting before going into court profitably. Although longer cases will usually be listed for a set date and time, shorter cases will normally be called with several at one time, so that there may well be a wait before one is called into court. This time can be used talking to the client, to get his views on any prosecution statements that you have, and to ask questions to clarify anything that is still not clear. If there is a real likelihood of conviction, you should also find out anything relevant to sentence, such as what level of fine he could reasonably afford to pay, and warn him what the possible sentence may be. Although it is important to talk to the client for all these reasons, it may not be easy. Many magistrates' court buildings are Victorian, cramped and not entirely salubrious, to the extent that however worried the client is about the case, he may well comment on the surroundings. Any discussion may well have to take place in the corridor, it may not be possible even to sit down, and it may be difficult to take notes. There may well be people and policemen standing around waiting for their cases to come on, which is distracting, and does not help the client to think clearly or communicate.

Despite the surroundings, it is important for the lawyer to remain completely calm and collected, and to give this feeling to his client. Despite the fact that the court may be busy, this atmosphere should go with you into court. It may be particularly difficult for the young lawyer who has not had a lot of experience, but he should not let the fact that there may be a list of cases to be heard and that people may be popping in and out of court all the time rush him. He should take time to make his points clearly and fully for his client's sake.

There are various methods of appeal from a magistrates' decision, and the lawyer will have to consider and advise on which is appropriate if necessary, and ask for any appropriate extension of legal aid. The most common type of appeal will be to the Crown Court. There is a right to appeal without leave, and there will be a rehearing of the case, or of matters relating to sentence if only the sentence is appealed against. Because there is a complete rehearing, it is not necessary to draft grounds of appeal, but only to give notice. The Crown Court will only have the sentencing powers that the magistrate had, but within that limit, the sentence may be increased.

The alternative, if appropriate, is to go to the Divisional Court for judicial review of the magistrates' decision. For this it will be necessary to state in detail what sort of remedy is sought and on what grounds. If there is a choice between appeal to the Crown Court and judicial review, the former should normally be preferred as being quicker, cheaper and more convenient (separate civil legal aid will need to be sought for judicial review). The final alternative, only to be used where strictly appropriate, is to appeal by way of case stated to the Divisional Court, where the point at issue is solely the interpretation of a legal provision.

Committal proceedings

If the accused is to be tried on indictment, there will normally be committal proceedings first. The basic purpose of the committal used to be to check that there was sufficient evidence to justify sending the accused for trial, though this is no longer really the case with the growth of the short form of committal. In any event, the accused is in no way on trial, and does not have to plead at committal proceedings. It is no longer strictly necessary for a lawyer to be present if there is a short form of committal, though he should attend if there are any applications to be made. The committal may be attended by a solicitor or a young barrister. If it is to be a long form of committal then it is desirable for the barrister who will appear at the trial to conduct the case for the defence so he can see the witnesses, but in practice this is not always done. For example, in the Jeremy Thorpe case his solicitor, Sir David Napley, conducted the committal although he could not appear at the trial.

There is a basic choice for committal proceedings, which the lawyer must consider and advise on. The first, and by far the most common, is the short form of committal without consideration of the evidence, Magistrates' Courts Act 1980, s.6(2). This is essentially a formality and will only last a few minutes, as the court will merely ascertain that the conditions for a short form of committal exist and the prosecution statements will be handed in without being read. The conditions are that all the evidence should be in the form of written statements, that the accused should have a legal representative, and that the defence do not wish to submit that the case should not be committed for trial. Only matters relating to bail, legal aid and witness orders will need to be dealt with. The short form of committal is quick, cheap, and allows the defence not to reveal their case at all until the trial. Therefore it should always be chosen unless there is a good reason for a long form of committal.

The alternative is the long form of committal, with consideration of the evidence, Magistrates' Courts Act 1980, s.6(1), where the magistrates will actively consider the evidence to see if it justifies sending the case for trial. Since the prosecution will be content with the short form of committal, this is essentially a choice for the defence, who again will have to balance factors to see if a long form of committal is really justified. The following factors are most likely to be important:

(a) A submission of no case to answer, or that the case should not be committed. There must be a long form of committal if the defence wishes to make either of these submissions to stop the case proceeding any further. The first submission can be made at the end of the prosecution case if their evidence is weak, or if there is no evidence at all on a crucial element of the offence, and the latter submission can be made at the end of the committal on the basis that the evidence as a whole does not justify committing the case. If either submission succeeds, the case will go no further and the client will go free. However, there is only any point in making either submission if it does have a real chance of success, otherwise it is a waste of time and money, and gives the prosecution practice and shows them the weaknesses in their case so that they can be better prepared for the trial. Also, the accused is not actually acquitted, so a new prosecution for the offence can be brought, so it may be better to let the weak case go to the Crown Court and get an acquittal.

(b) Challenging prosecution evidence. There is no point in having a long form of committal just to challenge some parts of the prosecution evidence, because again you are just bringing defects to their attention so that they can be properly prepared at trial. However, if the credibility or admissibility of a substantial element of the prosecution evidence can be challenged it is worth having a long form of committal so that the evidence can be challenged and the case may not then be committed. The odd bit of hearsay can be allowed to pass and can be challenged at trial, but if the prosecution depends on a confession that may well not be admissible, it should be challenged. Also if identification is in issue, there should normally be a long form of committal to check the identification evidence, following several cases in which weak identification evidence may have led to the conviction of the wrong person.

The prosecution should in fact take out any inadmissible evidence before they send the statements to the defence, *R* v *Colchester Stipendiary ex p. Beck* [1979] QB 674, but if the defence do object to something that has been left in which they do not raise at committal, they should still draw the matter to the attention of the prosecution, who may agree to withdraw that part of the evidence voluntarily, or at least will not mention it at trial until the defence have had chance to object.

(c) Getting more details about the case. The prosecution statements may well be short or unclear, and this may be at least partially remedied by having a long form of committal at which the defence can cross-examine prosecution witnesses.

This will enable the defence to see what the witness is like and how convincing he is, and to ask him questions to get more detail. This may also be helpful if the defendant's lawyer feels that he is not being very communicative, so he wishes to find out more rather than be surprised at trial, or if he wants to try out a line of defence. The committal does give the lawyer some opportunity to ask questions that he would prefer not to ask in front of the jury at trial, though of course all the witness's answers will be taken down in a written deposition, and could be used later, so this must be done with care.

It is sometimes possible to make tactical use of these depositions, as happened in the Jeremy Thorpe case, where discrepancies between what the witnesses said at committal and what they said at the Old Bailey were used to argue that they were at least inconsistent, if not unreliable. Despite these possible advantages, it is not wise to get a prosecution witness to give evidence at committal unless there is good reason. Giving evidence will give them practice, which means that they will inevitably be less nervous and more convincing at trial. Also the questions asked by the defence may well reveal lines of defence that could otherwise be kept secret until trial. However, the fact that there is a long form of committal does not mean that all the witnesses have to give oral evidence, and in practice the defence can indicate to the prosecution those witnesses whom they would like to give oral evidence at the committal, and the statements of the rest may be read out and handed in. The defence can thus choose which witnesses they cross-examine at this stage, but they cannot force the prosecution to call any particular witness, *R* v *Grays Justices ex p. Tetley* (1979) 70 Cr App R 11.

(d) Publicity. There are strict reporting restrictions on committals, so that the trial itself will not be prejudiced, Magistrates' Courts Act 1980, s.8. Normally the accused will want this for his own privacy, but he may want to have the committal reported, for example if he knows that there may be witnesses who could support his defence, and he wants to get them to come forward for the trial. He can do this by asking for a long form of committal, and asking for reporting restrictions to be lifted so the details can go into the papers.

Once they have the prosecution statements, the defence lawyers should weigh up any of these factors that are relevant, and if there is a good reason for wanting a long form of committal they should let the court know so that the case can be listed appropriately. The defence should let the prosecution know which witnesses they would like to have at the committal and which ones they will be prepared to accept statements from at this stage. If the prosecution decide that they will want to call a witness at trial whose statement was not given to the defence before the committal, they must tell the defence and supply them with a copy of the witness' statement. The only evidence of which the defence has to give notice to the prosecution is an alibi—he must let the prosecution know the essence of the alibi within 7 days of the committal, with the name and address of any witness who can support it. This notice does not need to be detailed.

At the end of the committal any appropriate applications for bail and in connection with bail should be made. If bail is refused by the magistrates it can be sought from a Crown Court judge or a High Court judge. The committal papers will be sent to the appropriate Crown Court officer for the indictment to be drawn up.

There is an alternative to committal proceedings that may be used in special circumstances, and which has been used in some well-publicised cases in recent years, such as the case where policemen were accused of causing the death of Barry Prosser while he was in custody, namely the voluntary bill of indictment, Administration of Justice Act 1933, s.2. A voluntary bill may be granted by a High Court judge where committal proceedings have proved abortive or incomplete, for example if the accused continually interrupted the committal proceedings, or one person alleged to be involved in an offence is arrested after others have already been committed, and it is desirable all be tried together. The prosecution should send the statements in the case together with the proposed indictment to the judge in Chambers, and he may grant the voluntary bill without hearing representations from the lawyers. The voluntary bill is very unsatisfactory for the accused, as he has no right to be heard on whether it should be granted or not, and he has no chance to choose a long form of committal if that might be useful to him, *R* v *Raymond* [1981] QB 910.

Drafting an indictment

The indictment is normally drawn up by a court officer rather than by the prosecution barrister, unless the case is particularly complex or important. In any event the prosecution and the defence lawyers should check the indictment to see if they have any possible problem or objection as regards the wording, the offences and the people charged. The indictment should be drawn up and preferred within 28 days of the committal proceedings, though this time limit may be extended, and it is not necessarily fatal if it is not preferred within the time limit, *R* v *Farooki* [1983] Crim LR 620. The indictment must be based on the evidence from the committal proceedings, and may include any offence that arises from the facts in those papers, and not only an offence for which the magistrates committed the accused for trial.

The contents and form of the indictment come from the Indictments Act 1915 and the Indictment Rules 1971, and the present form of the indictment is relatively simple (see Example 1). The problem in practice is to decide what offences to charge, and when offences and offenders may be joined in the same indictment. The basic form of the indictment comes from the Act and the rules and must be followed, but the wording for the counts for different types of offence is not mandatory, though from time to time the courts do approve particular forms of words for particular offences as being useful. The best source of information on this is *Archbold's Criminal Pleading, Evidence and Practice* (Sweet and Maxwell), which gives a form of wording for most criminal charges from murder to interrupting a clergyman who is giving a sermon.

The first part of the indictment is the heading, which will consist of the court where the case is to be heard and the names of the parties. The prosecution is normally brought in the name of the Crown and will therefore be 'The Queen', but it may be brought by someone else where appropriate, such as the Director of Public Prosecutions. The full name of the defendant should be given, and if there is more than one defendant, their names should be put on separate lines and numbered. It is not fatal to the indictment if the name of a defendant is not correctly stated so long as there is no mistake as to his identity. A company may be a defendant to a criminal action in appropriate circumstances.

EXAMPLE 1 BASIC INDICTMENT

IN THE CROWN COURT AT No.

THE QUEEN v A. B. (Name of defendant in capitals)

A. B. is charged as follows:
(Set out each separate alleged offence as a separate count. These are examples of possible counts, with many more being given in the section on criminal drafting.)

Count 1. Statement of Offence

Theft, contrary to section 1 of the Theft Act 1968.

Particulars of Offence

A. B. on the day of 1985 at (state where the offence took place) stole a (state property stolen), the property of (state who owned the property).

Count 2. Statement of Offence

Burglary, contrary to section 9(1)(*a*), of the Theft Act 1968.

Particulars of Offence

A. B. on the day of 1985 entered a building known as (give the address of the place burgled) with intent to steal therein.

Date. Signed
Officer of the Crown Court.

The body of the indictment contains the charges, Indictments Act 1915, s.3:

> Every indictment shall contain, and shall be sufficient if it contains, a statement of the specific offence or offences with which the accused person is charged, together with such particulars as may be necessary for giving reasonable information as to the nature of the charge.

This means that each charge consists of two parts, the statement of the offence and the particulars. The indictment rules provide that if more than one offence is alleged, the statement and particulars of each should be in separate numbered paragraphs, called counts. Each count must allege only one offence or it will be void for duplicity, but if two or more people are alleged to have committed the same offence together, they can be put in the same count.

The first part of a count is the statement of offence. This is normally a single sentence which just states the type of offence, and if the offence is created by a statute or an instrument made under the authority of a statute, the section of the statute or the relevant instrument should be stated. A simple allegation of 'theft' or 'murder' together with the appropriate statutory section is sufficient. Some examples are given in the section on criminal cases.

The second part of the count is the particulars of offence. This should give the essential elements of the offence so that the defendant knows exactly what charge he has to answer, but it is not necessary to include all the legal elements of the offence. Normally the particulars will state who is alleged to have committed the offence, when and where, and who or what the offence was against, as far as is relevant. The wording of the particulars will often come from the wording of the section creating the offence, though a charge of theft may simply allege that the defendant 'stole' without including all the elements of the Theft Act 1968, s.1.

The particulars should be as specific as possible to be fair to the defendant, but if there is any doubt, for example as to the date when an offence was committed, the point may be pleaded wide, for example 'on a day between . . . and . . .' or 'on or about . . .'. It is normal though not essential in an allegation of theft to state what was stolen and it's value, and again this should be as specific as possible rather than just 'a quantity of . . .'.

If an offence may be committed in more than one way, the particulars should include which way is alleged. For example, although handling is a single offence, it has been held that it can be committed in two completely different ways, *R* v *Sloggett* [1972] 1 QB 430, and therefore the indictment should make it clear which is alleged, receiving or dishonestly helping to dispose of the goods. If a section merely gives alternative words rather than alternative ways of committing the offence, the alternative words can be put into the count without stating which is alleged, so the second type of handling can be charged as 'dishonestly undertook or assisted in the retention, removal, disposal or realisation of the stolen goods by or for the benefit of another' without necessarily choosing between the words. If there are by statute various exceptions of defences to an offence, these do not have to be negatived in the indictment.

If there is more than one count in an indictment, they should be put in a logical order, either chronological, or with the more serious charges before the less serious ones. If there is more than one defendant it should be made completely clear which defendant or defendants each count is against. Alternative charges may be put in alternative counts.

Deciding what charges to put in an indictment may be difficult. If there is any doubt then every possible charge arising from the committal papers should be noted down, together with the elements of each possible charge. For example, if there is a possible charge of theft under the Theft Act 1968, s.1 the elements are dishonesty/appropriation/property that can be stolen/that property belonging to someone other than the accused/the intention of permanently depriving the owner of the property. The next stage is to read through the committal papers and to tick every element on which there is evidence. If every element is ticked then the offence can be charged, but if there is no evidence on any element then the offence should not be charged (unless evidence on the point can be found for the trial). If there is more than one offence of which all the elements are present they can all be charged, but a choice may have to be made.

The following general principles should be taken into account when deciding what offences to charge:

(a) An indictment should not be overloaded. If too many offences are charged together the trial will be long and complicated and the jury may get confused, *R* v *Novac* (1977) 65 Cr App R 107. Either a choice should be made, or the charges be put into two separate indictments leading to two separate trials.

(b) The most serious offence justified on the evidence should be charged, in the public interest. The defendant may offer a plea of guilty to a lesser offence and this can be considered if it arises. However, the more serious offence should only be charged if it really is justified, following the principle of prosecution not persecution.

(c) If an indictment alleges a serious offence it should not include something trivial too. This will just add to the cost and length of trial without any real purpose. For example, if there is a charge of murder there is little to be gained from adding a relatively trivial allegation of criminal damage, see *R* v *Ambrose* (1973) 57 Cr App R 538. If the defendant is acquitted on the serious charge the prosecution may proceed with the smaller offence if they see fit.

(d) If the same facts give rise to more than one offence, normally only one should be charged. If someone steals something and then sells it, it is normal to charge him with theft rather than theft and handling. This will depend on the facts and is a matter of discretion, for example both theft and handling may be charged if they take place some time apart in totally different circumstances, or may possibly be charged in the alternative if the evidence is not clear.

It is a matter of fact whether a series of events gives rise to one or more charges. If a person goes on a shop-lifting spree it must be decided if this is one continuing theft or a series of thefts. In *R* v *Wilson* (1979) 69 Cr App R 83 it was held correct in such a case to have one count alleging thefts in a branch of Boots and another alleging thefts in a branch of Debenhams.

(e) Two offences should not normally be charged where one is 'included' in the other. If the evidence shows that the accused entered property and stole something, he should normally be charged with burglary and not burglary and theft. Again this is a matter of the facts and discretion, and there may be reasons for charging both, probably in the alternative, if the evidence is not clear.

This point includes any decision whether to charge a complete offence or some other degree of involvement. A charge of a complete offence includes in itself a charge of attempt to commit an offence, but other involvement, such as a conspiracy, or aiding and abetting another to commit an offence will have to be charged in a separate count if appropriate.

(f) If there is a string of similar offences, only some representative counts may be charged, to save the time and expense of trying them all.

(g) The strength of the evidence is important, and should always be borne in mind when deciding what offences to charge. If there is strong evidence on one charge but relatively weak evidence on another, it may be better to put the first in the indictment and not bother with the other.

Having decided what offences should be charged, it is necessary to decide whether they can be put in the same indictment. The test comes from the Indictment Rules, rule 9, which provides that 'charges for any offence may be joined in the same indictment if those charges are founded on the same facts, or form or are a part of a series of offences of the same or a similar character'. This test was discussed in detail by the House of Lords in *Ludlow* v *Metropolitan Police Commissioner* [1971] AC 29, where it was held that an attempted theft in one pub in Acton and a robbery of a small amount of money in another pub in Acton 16 days later were properly joined in the same indictment.

The test is a matter of whether on the facts the offences are in some way linked, and there is no great lapse of time between one and another. It has been held that offences of assault, possession of an offensive weapon and possession of a prohibited drug were properly joined where the drug was taken to build up courage to take the weapon to commit the assault, *R* v *Conti* (1974) 58 Cr App R 387. It has also been held that various offences connected with putting pressure on witnesses as to the evidence they will give can properly be joined, *R* v *Barrell and Wilson* (1979) 69 Cr App R 250. However, charges of stealing a car and then raping a girl in it may not properly be joined, *R* v *Thomas* (1949) 33 Cr App R 74.

Even if the offences are properly joined under this test, the accused may apply for the counts to be severed at the judge's discretion if he might otherwise be prejudiced or embarrassed in his defence if they are tried together, or if it is for some other reason desirable, Indictments Act 1915, s.5(3). The defence may wish to apply to have the indictment severed as a matter of policy in the hope that if the defendant is tried on each count separately, he is more likely to be acquitted on both. The judge may order severance if for example there are so many counts that the jury may become confused, if one of the counts is particularly scandalous or prejudicial, or if evidence is admissible on one count but not on another (though this point may be complicated if there is similar fact evidence, *R* v *Scarrott* [1978] QB 1016.

It will also be necessary to decide who to charge if more than one person is involved in the commission of the offences. The test is one of 'nexus', that is whether the offences and offenders are so related by time and other factors that it is in the interest of justice that they be tried together, i.e. whether the accused were both effectively involved in the same incident, as in *R* v *Assim* [1966] 2 QB 249 where two men were charged in connection with a fight in the entrance to a club and it was held that the charges against them were properly put in the same indictment, although it was alleged that each had assaulted a different person. There are some specific circumstances in which offenders may be joined in the same indictment, as under the Theft Act 1968, s.27, by which all people alleged to have stolen or handled the same goods may be joined in one indictment.

The judge has a discretion to order that the offences be tried separately, even if they have been properly joined, if one of the accused will otherwise be prejudiced in his defence. This may be ordered if for example evidence is admissible against one accused but not another, or if the jury may be confused by the number of defendants. It will not normally be sufficient for separate trials that the accused have conflicting defences, *R* v *Lake* (1978) 68 Cr App R 172, and it must be said that the current tendency is to refuse separate trials unless there is very good reason, because of the expense, and the feeling that it is normally better for all the evidence to go together before a single jury, *R* v *Moghal* (1977) 65 Cr App R 56. It is possible that the prosecution may wish the accused to be tried separately, because one co-accused cannot be called to give evidence against another, in which case they will draft separate indictments.

If there is more than one possible defendant it will be necessary to decide not only whether they can be joined in the same indictment, but also whether they can properly be put in the same count or should be in different counts.

If there are any defects in the indictment they can normally be solved by amendment, as with civil pleadings. An application can be made to a judge to amend an indictment at any time before or during a trial, and the application will usually be granted provided there is no injustice to the accused, Indictments Act 1915, s.5. The accused may be granted an adjournment if necessary to deal with the amendment, and the need for amendment may be relevant to costs. If necessary amendments may be made even after the jury has retired if there is good reason and no injustice is caused, *R* v *Collison* (1980) 70 Cr App R 249. If an amendment is allowed, it must be indorsed on the indictment.

If there is a fundamental defect in an indictment, such as the fact that the court does not have jurisdiction, or the indictment is against someone who cannot be prosecuted because they have diplomatic immunity, an application may be made to the judge to quash the indictment, and this should be done as soon as possible.

Preparing for the trial

This section sets out a few practical points to be considered when preparing for trial at the Crown Court. Many of the appropriate procedural points came from the Crown Court Rules 1982. The prosecution will have done the basic preparation for the committal proceedings, but they will need to research any legal points and prepare references to authorities. Also they will have to consider any extra evidence that will be needed for the trial, especially if there was a long form of committal that revealed weaknesses in their case. Notice of any extra evidence that is to be called will of course have to be given to the defence.

Probably the defence will have most preparation to do. Many criminal trials turn on disputes of fact and evidence rather than legal argument, so that is what they should concentrate on. Firstly they should examine all the prosecution evidence that they have, deciding whether its admissibility can be challenged and seeing what the defendant says about the allegations made. If any of the evidence appears to be inadmissible then the prosecution should be told, so that they can either drop it voluntarily, or they will not lead it at trial until the defence have had chance to challenge it. Basic lines of cross-examination for each prosecution witness can be prepared in advance from their statements.

The next stage for the defence is to gather their own evidence. This should include the solicitor's finding any possible witness to see if he should be called, but also assembling any other evidence that may be useful, such as plans and photographs, though the preparations must be reasonable as any excessive or unduly expensive preparations may not be allowed when it comes to costs. One particular point that will need consideration is whether the defendant himself should give evidence. He may choose to give sworn evidence or not to give evidence at all. Factors to take into account when making a decision are the sort of impression that the defendant may make on the jury, whether he should give evidence to explain certain points that are vital to his defence and on which there is no other evidence, and whether he has previous convictions, because if he does and he loses his 'shield', by for example attacking a prosecution witness, then his convictions will go in if he gives evidence. This is also a matter of tactics—the lawyer may decide that it is best not to call the client but just to make a closing speech saying that the prosecution has not proved their case.

It is important to think of the possible sentence, especially if the defendant intends to plead guilty. The defence lawyer should make full investigations as to the circumstances of the client as this is one of the main foundations for a good plea in mitigation. He should try to anticipate what sentence the court might feel appropriate and try to argue for something that is as low as is reasonably possible, though if there are serious aspects to the offence these must be accepted or the sympathy of the judge will be lost. Both sides should also consider whether any procedural applications should be made before or at the beginning of the trial. Bail and legal aid points were mentioned earlier, but it may be suitable to apply for the indictment to be amended, or for the charges against co-accused to be severed.

With the trial in view, some problems about potential jurors have arisen in recent years. In some countries such as the United States it is possible to question potential jurors before the trial to see if there are any possible grounds for challenging them, but this is not possible here. Generally a juror will only be challenged for what he looks like in court—for example the defence may challenge a man in a pin-striped suit carrying the Daily Telegraph if they are defending a long haired teenager charged with possessing cannabis purely because he might be more likely to convict. The prosecution may ask a potential juror who has difficulty reading the oath to stand by in a complex fraud case if they feel he may not be able to understand the case fully. In any event, challenges will normally only have a minimal effect. It is not possible for example for a woman to insist on a female jury, or a black person to insist that their jury should consist of blacks. The most one can normally do for the defence is to tell the client to let you know immediately if he knows any of the potential jurors.

In recent years it became clear that in some cases the prosecution were making further inquiries about potential jurors. Whether this was desirable was hotly debated, and the Attorney-General issued guidelines on the subject in 1980. It is proper for the prosecution to check police records to see if a potential juror does have previous convictions, but they should only go beyond that in a few special cases, for example where there is an issue of national security or the defendants are alleged to be terrorists. The consent of the Attorney-General should be sought before the further inquiries are made, and the results of the inquiries should be sent to the Director of Public Prosecutions for a decision. The prosecution should only ask a juror to stand by as a result if the information reveals that the potential juror is likely to be a security risk, or may be susceptible to improper approaches. The defence do not have the right to know any details of what the prosecution find, though the prosecution should tell them of anything indicating that a potential juror may be inclined against the accused, for example if he is related to a policeman on the case, *R* v *Mason* [1980] 3 WLR 617.

Another difficulty which has come to light recently is so called 'jury nobbling', where an attempt is made to bribe or threaten a juror on a case. Now several trials a year are stopped because this had or may have happened, especially in London, in large drugs or robbery cases at the Old Bailey. The time taken by and expense of a re-trial must be avoided, so steps are taken where possible to protect jurors, such as obscuring the members of the jury so that they cannot be seen from the public gallery, or giving them police protection during the trial. This is a real threat to the jury system, and although the lawyers in the case should have no contact with the jury directly, they should be aware of the problem, and bring any relevant matters to the attention of the police or the judge immediately.

Advising and drafting for an appeal

Although the systems for civil and criminal appeals are separate, they do have many points in common when it comes to advising and drafting. There is a separate Division of the Court of Appeal to hear criminal appeals, and the procedure for appealing from a Crown Court trial comes largely from the Criminal Appeal Act 1968 and the Criminal Appeal Rules 1968. As with civil appeals, the practical working of the appeal system has been under review in recent years to make hearings more efficient. A guide to the present procedure called 'A Guide to Proceedings in the Court of Appeal Criminal Division' (1983) 77 Cr App R 138 is available from the Registrar of the court.

The first step is to decide whether there are any possible grounds of appeal against conviction or sentence or both, and whether those grounds are based on matters of law or of fact. The lawyer should try to give a view orally immediately after the trial, and should in any event see the client. Normally a brief will then be sent by the solicitor to the barrister to give a written advice on a possible appeal. Because of the time limit for appeals, the written advice should normally be sent back to the solicitor within 14 days if possible, so that he has time to consult with the client and file the notice of appeal.

The advice on appeal should review every possible ground of appeal, clearly separating grounds of appeal against conviction and against sentence. The basic legal or factual background to each point should be given and its chance of success weighed, but because of the speed needed and the fact that transcripts will not be available at this stage, the advice may well deal with the appeal in outline rather than in great detail.

The grounds of appeal should be lodged within 28 days. The grounds are usually lodged by solicitors, together with forms N and G as appropriate. It must be clear whether the appeal is against conviction or sentence or both, and the grounds should be as full as possible, though inevitably it may not be possible to put in all details until transcripts are received.

Leave to appeal may well be needed. There is a right to appeal against conviction on a matter of law, but an appeal on the facts or mixed law and fact, or an appeal against sentence needs leave. It is not always easy to decide whether an appeal is purely on a matter of law, but basically it is only where the appeal is purely a matter of interpreting a statute or case law that leave will not be needed. Most arguments on evidence or procedure will normally involve some question of fact so leave will be needed. Leave can be sought first from the trial judge, but perhaps understandably he may not grant leave. Therefore leave must be sought from a judge of the Court of Appeal Criminal Division within the 28 day period, with an appeal from him to a full three-judge court if necessary. As with civil appeals, leave to appeal out of time will only be given if there are good reasons for the delay.

Again as with civil cases, various applications may have to be made pending the hearing of the appeal. If the client has legal aid, this will cover basic advice on the appeal, but it will need to be extended to cover the appeal itself. It is also possible to apply for bail, but as the appellant has been convicted he has no right to bail, so it will only be granted in a few cases if there is a sentence of imprisonment. If transcripts of any part of the trial or of the judge's summing up or judgment are needed, they should be sought as soon as possible, and again as with civil cases, the lawyer should specify as clearly as possible which parts he needs. The Registrar of the Court of Appeal Criminal Division has general duties and powers to ensure that the necessary transcripts and documents are collected and made available for the hearing.

Fresh evidence can only be admitted with leave, Criminal Appeal Act 1968, s.23. Leave should be sought from a single judge of the Court of Appeal Criminal Division. Leave will only be granted if the evidence is admissible, credible, and there is a good reason why it was not available for and used in the trial.

It is now common practice to lodge perfected grounds of appeal shortly before the hearing in any case where it is useful. This is a fresh document that sets out each ground of appeal in more detail, giving the basic argument of each ground, supported by specific references to and quotations from the transcripts or other documents in the case. There should be specific references to any cases relied on, the Criminal Appeal Reports being preferred if the case is in them. As with the skeleton argument in a civil appeal, the perfected grounds should help the judges to come to grips with the case quickly.

The appeal may be dismissed summarily if there is no good ground for appeal, Criminal Appeal Act 1968 s.20. Otherwise the hearing will consist of legal argument on documents and transcripts. The judges will normally have read the grounds of appeal in advance, and may indicate to counsel which grounds they feel have most merit and which they would like to hear argued in detail. If after argument the judges do not find any of the grounds of appeal meritorious the prosecution will not even be called upon to reply. If the appeal is purely against sentence the prosecution will usually not even appear as they have no interest in the severity of the sentence.

The Court of Appeal Criminal Division has wide powers. As regards conviction, it may allow the appeal, as a whole or in part, or dismiss it. Alternatively, the court may substitute an alternative conviction. This will include any lesser offence. The court can order a retrial, if there is fresh evidence and it is in the interests of justice that it should be put before a jury, Criminal Appeal Act 1968, s.7, but because of the expense and the extra time this will take it will only be ordered if there is very good reason, *R* v *Rose* [1982] 2 All ER 731. Apart from this, the court does have an inherent power to order a retrial as a venire de novo, though again this will only be used in limited circumstances, *R* v *Inns* (1974) 60 Cr App R 231. The lawyers for the appellant should be clear which objective they hope to achieve.

The fact that one of the grounds of appeal is found to be justified does not necessarily mean that the appeal will succeed. The court may choose instead to apply the proviso, Criminal Appeal Act 1968, s.2. This can be applied if the court feels that despite the ground of appeal, no miscarriage of justice has actually occurred.

As regards an appeal against sentence, if the appeal is allowed in whole or in part, then the Court of Appeal Criminal Division can impose any sentence that the Crown Court could have passed for the offence, but not so as to impose a sentence which is overall more severe than that imposed by the court at trial. Any time spent in prison pending the appeal will count as part of the sentence, unless the court directs otherwise.

Drafting grounds of appeal

Having put together a list of the potential grounds of appeal in the case, they should be put into an appropriate order for drafting. Any logical order is acceptable, but it is best either to follow the events of the trial in order, or to put the strongest grounds first (see Example 2). Often all the possible grounds of appeal are listed, even if some of them are unlikely to succeed on their own, but if there are a large number of possible grounds of appeal then the relatively trivial ones should be left out. If the grounds of appeal are too lengthy and elaborate the court may not find them easy to follow, and false hopes of success may be raised in the client, *R* v *Pybus* (1983) *The Times* 23rd February.

The heading for the grounds of appeal is taken from the case, and it is followed by the grounds of appeal against conviction and the grounds of appeal against sentence, as appropriate, with each separate ground of appeal in a separate numbered paragraph. The form for the initial grounds of appeal and the perfected grounds of appeal is similar, the only difference being that the latter contains more detail.

Although an appeal may be allowed on the ground that the conviction is unsafe and unsatisfactory, it is wrong to make a general allegation like this as an actual ground of appeal. Each ground should be specific, and should refer to a particular point of evidence or procedure as appropriate, *R* v *Morson* (1976) 62 Cr App R 236. If an objection is made to specific words, for example in the judge's summing up, then those words should be quoted and not just referred to, *R* v *Cogan* [1975] 3 WLR 316.

The following are suggestions of possible grounds of appeal against conviction:

(a) A misdirection by the judge, that is any misdirection made by the judge when he sums up as to any matter of law or fact, or as to the burden or standard of proof or any other aspect of the case. There are forms of words on matters like the standard of proof which are commonly used by judges. If the judge does not make use of one of these he must take great care.

(b) A failure by the judge to give a direction or an adequate direction on an essential part of the case. When the judge sums up to the jury he must cover all the main elements of the prosecution case and the defence case, both legal and factual, and also any background legal matters, such as a possible need for corroboration. If he fails to remind the jury of any of these points, this may be a ground of appeal.

(c) Some improper comment. The judge's summing up should of course be impartial, and if he includes any comment showing his personal views on the case or any prejudice against the defendant, it may be a ground of appeal.

(d) A wrongful admission or exclusion of evidence. The appellant may have grounds for objecting to the judge's decision to admit prosecution evidence or to exclude evidence offered by the defence. However, it must be said that any argument about the admission or exclusion of evidence should normally be raised at the trial, and the Court of Appeal will be slow to accept any argument on evidence that was not raised at the trial.

(e) Some other improper decision on the part of the judge. Some other decision by the judge on a procedural matter may be objected to, for example a decision that there is a case to answer following a submission of no case to answer. Again, any objection to a procedural matter should be raised at the time in the trial, or the court may not be prepared to accept it as a ground of appeal.

(f) A material irregularity. Anything else that did or did not happen at the trial may also be a ground of appeal, for example if it comes to light that one of the jury members left the jury room after the jury had retired.

Possible grounds for appeal against sentence are as follows:

(a) That the sentence passed is not permissible by law. If the sentence passed is by law not available, or exceeds a maximum limit then the appeal must succeed, though the Court of Appeal may of course substitute any other sentence that the Crown Court could have given.

(b) That the sentence is excessive. Although there is a maximum sentence for each offence laid down by statute, the convicted person will of course rarely be given the maximum, unless there is only one sentence available as in the case of murder. There is a tariff system which relates the severity of the facts in the case to the maximum available, and the lawyer will come by experience to know how this tariff system operates. If the sentence given in a particular case exceeds what would normally be expected in that type of case then it is a ground of appeal that the sentence is excessive.

(c) That the sentence is wrong in principle. There is a wide range of different types of sentence that a judge at the Crown Court can pass, and it may be a ground of appeal that he has selected the wrong type of sentence. For example, it would normally be considered wrong to send a person who has no previous convictions to prison for a relatively minor theft or assault.

(d) That wrong matters were taken into account when deciding sentence. Counsel for the defendant will of course raise various matters that he feels should be taken into account in deciding on the sentence when he makes his plea in mitigation. When the judge passes sentence it may become obvious that he has either failed to take into account something raised in the plea in mitigation, or that he has chosen to take into account something that should be irrelevant to the sentence, and this may be a ground of appeal.

(e) Disparity of sentence. There is often more than one person involved in committing a criminal offence. Whether or not they are tried together, if more than one person involved in an offence is convicted then the sentence passed on each of them should take into account their relative involvement in the case. If this does not happen, the one who has received the disproportionately high sentence can appeal. Sometimes disparity may be justified, for example a defendant who pleads guilty may properly get a lower sentence than one who pleads not guilty and is convicted.

The grounds of appeal should be signed by the person who drafts them.

Appeals to the House of Lords

These are relatively rare in a criminal case, and will only be mentioned briefly. Either side may appeal to the House of Lords, but only if a point of law of general public importance is involved, and if leave is given, Criminal Appeal Act 1968, s.33. An appeal can only be made with the leave of the Court of Appeal or the House of Lords, and a certificate from the Court of Appeal that a point of law of general public importance is involved. It is not common for a criminal case to turn on a point of law, especially one of particular importance, so there are few cases where this sort of appeal can be considered at all.

Leave should be sought from the Court of Appeal within 14 days, and if leave is refused, should be sought from the House of Lords within 14 days of the refusal. Bail may be sought pending the hearing, but there is no right to bail. The defendant will have no right to attend the hearing, which will be purely a matter of legal argument. The House of Lords has all the powers of the Court of Appeal Criminal Division when dealing with the case.

EXAMPLE 2 BASIC GROUNDS OF APPEAL IN A CRIMINAL CASE

THE QUEEN v A. B.

GROUNDS OF APPEAL

The grounds of appeal against conviction are:
(Set out the grounds of appeal in separate numbered paragraphs. The following are examples of possible grounds which may be adapted for use.)

1. The Learned Judge wrongly allowed......
2. The Learned Judge wrongly refused to admit the evidence of......
3. The Learned Judge in his summing up misdirected the jury in that......
4. The Learned Judge failed to give the jury any direction as to......
5. The Learned Judge wrongly commented on...... in saying that......
6. There was a material irregularity at the trial in that......
7. In all the circumstances of the case the conviction is unsafe and unsatisfactory.

The grounds of appeal against sentence are:
(Set out the grounds of appeal in separate numbered paragraphs. The following are examples of possible grounds which may be adapted for use.)

1. The Learned Judge failed to give any or any proper weight to......
2. In view of the fact that...... the sentence was too severe.
3. In passing sentence the Learned Judge was wrongly influenced by......
4. The sentence was too severe in all the circumstances of the case.

Signed.

Advising and drafting in particular types of cases

The purpose of the second part of this book is to apply the general principles of giving advice and drafting to particular types of case. For this purpose the general principles will be extended to show how they apply in some basic areas of law with which almost any young solicitor or barrister will be familiar. These sections will presume the basic knowledge of the law in each area that the lawyer will have to have to be able to spot the type of case that he is dealing with and the main issues in it. Having seen how the principles apply in main areas of law, the young lawyer can go on from there to adapt the skills to other areas of law that he may be asked to deal with, such as sale of goods or landlord and tenant, developing his technique as he goes.

In each area guidelines will be given as to the particular points that should be taken into account when giving advice, the range of remedies that should be considered, and any points that may be particularly important to the lawyer or the client in practice. Examples of the basic types of draft that a lawyer dealing with a case in each area might need to do are set out at the end of the relevant chapter.

The examples of drafting are general and must be approached with care as examples rather than as things to be copied. When he has to draft a pleading a lawyer will take one of two courses—either he will produce a draft similar to something that he has done before or he will try to find something to copy, quite possibly using a reference work. In either case it is essential that he should make sure that the draft he produces really is suitable for the case in hand and does comply with all the rules for good drafting, rather than just being something that has been adapted to be vaguely right for the case in hand.

In doing a draft similar to something one has done before, the danger is of falling into something easy rather than bothering to make the necessary effort. The experienced practitioner who constantly deals with a particular type of case and has developed his own style will quite properly draft pleadings that tend to follow a set pattern because he has developed a good way to do things, but the young lawyer must always take great care that he produces the right draft for the case rather than just reproducing something because that is easiest. It will be very useful for him generally to build up a collection of drafts for particular types of case. This should include not only drafts of each type that he may have to do, but should also be kept critically to note good and bad ways of doing things, alternative ways of doing things and different types of personal style. This collection of examples is best if it is ordered in some way, either by the areas of law involved such as 'tort' and 'contract', or as to the type of draft, such as 'statements of claim' and 'defences'. This sort of collection of things to look at, whether they come from textbooks, a professional course or other practitioners will often be of more use than any reference book of precedents in developing an ability to draft.

As was said earlier, in looking at examples of drafting provided by practitioners, the young lawyer should try to distinguish those things in the draft which have to be done in the way they are and those things which are just a matter of personal style. If he is in doubt he may have the chance to ask the lawyer who did the draft about this. The experienced practitioner should avoid telling the young lawyer that one thing must be done in a certain way when it is only a matter of his own personal style.

Using reference works for precedents

Many lawyers especially young lawyers, will find that they need to use reference works to find precedents for drafting in some cases. Such works must be used with care and discrimination to get a good result, and must never be thought of as an easy way out as they will never give an answer but will at best give suggestions, so the lawyer will have to use his skill to make the right choice and adapt as necessary. The young lawyer should learn to use such books intelligently as soon as he can. If a precedent is taken from a book without being properly adapted the case may be lost, or at best the pleadings will have to be amended, which may prove expensive if it happens at a late stage. In *Brickfield Properties* v *Newton* [1971] 1 WLR 862 the statement of claim for negligence and breach of statutory duty was copied from *Atkin's Court Forms* but it was held that it should have been pleaded differently as a failure to supervise was involved, though the plaintiff was allowed to amend.

There are two types of reference works for pleadings. Firstly, there are books which give the basic form for pleadings without actual examples. These give examples of forms prescribed by court rules and also approved forms that may be used where they are suitable, such as *The Supreme Court Practice* (The White Book, Sweet and Maxwell) and *The County Court Practice* (The Green Book, Butterworths). If there is any doubt as to the type of pleading or application that should be drafted, this is a good starting point. Secondly, there are books which actually do precedents for pleadings and other drafting in particular types of case. The main one is *Atkin's Court Forms* (Butterworths), which comes in 42 volumes with indexes, and is regularly updated with new volumes. Atkin contains notes and examples of general areas of pleading, such as county court actions and Appeals, in general areas of law, such as contract or negligence, and also in specific areas of law, from charities to plant breeders rights! Each of these has an explanatory text, as well as many precedents with notes.

A smaller book, which comes in a single volume and deals largely with statements of claim and defences in tort and contract cases is Bullen, Leake and Jacob's *Precedents of Pleadings*. This has chapters on the basic rules of pleading, and also many precedents for particular types of case. The other single volume work is *Chitty and Jacob's Queen's Bench Forms*, which gives many examples of all the different types of pleading and drafting that may be needed for an action in the Queen's Bench. The existing 1969 edition is very out of date, but a new edition is in preparation.

When using any of these reference works it is essential to make decisions as to the type of case, the causes of action and the remedies sought before opening the book at all. These can even be noted down, for example 'Statement of claim. Tort. Negligence or breach of statutory duty. Damages', or 'Defence, Contract, Misrepresentation. Damages or recission'. The danger is that if these points are not clear in the mind, it will be all too easy to adapt the case to fit the drafting precedent that is found, rather than the other way round. The best that one can ever hope to find from a precedent book is an example vaguely like the actual case that can be adapted to fit. The precedent itself must never be allowed to take over.

Having made basic decisions, the next step is to use the index intelligently. This means looking for the right type of draft (it is quite common for students to confuse general and special indorsements on a writ) and the right type of case, for example 'Breach of trust—statement of claim' or 'Misrepresentation—general indorsement'. It is also important not to look at the index just once, but to look up every element in the case for which there might be a precedent. It may be possible to find a single precedent for the case, but often it is necessary to put two or three precedents together, taking different elements from each—the outline of the statement of claim may come from one, the way to plead particulars from a second, and the remedies sought from a third. The final stage is to adapt the precedent properly to fit the case. This is not only a matter of changing a few words and filling in the right dates, which will rarely give a full and accurate result. The best approach is to identify the essential elements of the precedent, to see the way that particular points are expressed and to get the feel of the thing. This can be done by noting the basic order and contents of each paragraph to get a skeleton outline of what should be pleaded and how, and also noting any good way in which a part of the pleading is set out or worded. Once these elements have been found, the precedent book can be put away and the pleading drafted by the lawyer who now has an idea of what to include, but can also use his own judgment and style to suit the case.

In the following sections on particular types of case examples are given of various different drafts, trying to choose ones for basic types of action that the young lawyer is most likely to come across. The examples should only be used as basic guides to the things to include and the way to set things out rather than as exhaustive precedents. Each draft should be read as though it had been written on 1st April 1985.

Advising and drafting in contract cases

This is just a short guide to some of the things to bear in mind when meeting a client, reading a brief or preparing a case for court in a contract case. The detailed law can be researched where necessary, but the important thing for the young lawyer is to concentrate on identifying the main points in the case—the details of the contract itself, what causes of action arise from it and what remedies are sought. Also he needs to do everything he can to take a realistic view of the case before him—what things he can and cannot prove, and what is the most practical way to deal with it.

The contract

The first step is to establish the details of the contract and to see if there are any difficulties with it—is it oral or written, when was it made, where was it made, and by whom? If the contract is written or evidenced in writing then the lawyer will of course wish to see it, and once a contract has been reduced to writing that will normally be conclusive as to its terms, and rarely will parol evidence be admitted as to further terms. There are few circumstances where the contract has to be in writing, basically where it relates to the sale of land or the disposal of an existing equitable interest, Law of Property Act 1925, ss.40, 53. If the contract is not in writing, the lawyer will want to have full details of everything that was said when it was made, which will probably involve getting a full statement from the client and anyone else who was there at the time. If a contract is oral there may of course be problems in proving its terms, especially if the evidence amounts to one person's word against another's.

It will be necessary to decide exactly who the contract was between to decide who should be made parties to the action, which may be a crucial decision. It may be necessary to decide whether to sue an individual or a company, and to consider whether someone acts as an agent for someone else. If more than one person contracted with the client, their liability will probably be joint and several, but it may be necessary to decide whether to sue one or more of them (not least in looking to see which could pay damages).

A person may not have had the capacity to make a contract if they were under a disability or a minor.

Even if there is a contract, it may be possible to sue someone who was not a party to it—the mere fact that there is a contract should not limit the mind to contractual causes of action. For example, it may be possible to sue the other party to the contract or someone else for negligence, or some other tort. One particular possibility is the tort of inducing breach of contract, where someone else knew of the contract and positively encouraged a party to it to breach it, see *Merkur Island Shipping Corporation* v *Laughton* [1983] AC 570 (see Example 9).

It may be necessary to decide on other details about the contract, such as when it was made if there were protracted negotiations. This may involve analysing offer and acceptance to decide when the terms were agreed. There will in practice rarely be a problem about whether there was consideration for a contract, but the consideration should be pleaded to show that the contract is enforceable.

Finally, there may occasionally be a problem depending on the type of contract if it is for some reason void, voidable or illegal.

The terms of the contract

Having identified the contract, the next stage is to identify all its terms to see which are relevant to the case. This is not just a question of the obvious terms, but any terms that may have a bearing on the case, in arguments for or against the client. A written contract will need reading with care for the possible meanings of the terms, and perhaps to consider whether some of the terms are not enforceable, for example because they are penalties or improperly in restraint of trade. If the contract was oral, this will again require a detailed discussion with the client and any witnesses as to what was said, and the difficulty that the other side may dispute what was said. Even if the contract was written it may be necessary to try to argue that something that was said should still be a term of the contract and the contract should be rectified.

If there is no express term on which to base the client's case, it may be necessary to try to find an implied term. This needs care not vagueness—there must be a clear legal basis to imply the term, not just the feeling that it would be fair. It may be necessary to ask the client if there has been any previous course of dealings, any normal business terms in this type of contract, any term that can be implied for proper business efficacy, or that the officious bystander would say went without saying. It is necessary not only to decide that a term could be implied, but the exact wording of the term to be implied, as this will have to be pleaded and should favour the client as much as is reasonably possible.

The contract may be undermined

Something may have undermined the purpose of the contract. The most common possibility is misrepresentation (see Example 5). This will involve establishing that something was a representation rather than a mere 'puff', and that it was relied on in making the contract. The details of exactly what is alleged to be the representation, and when it was made and to whom will have to be pleaded. Often the representation will be purely oral, so again difficulties of proof will have to be considered, as the defendant is quite likely to deny that he said what is alleged.

As an alternative, which is not all that common in practice, the contract may be undermined by mistake (see Example 11). It may have to be made clear to the client that it is not enough that he may have made a mistake, but that generally there will have to be a mutual mistake on a material matter to affect the contract.

Another possibility that is not all that common is that the contract may have been undermined by duress or undue influence, depending on the relationship between the parties and the facts so that the contract is not enforceable.

Problems with performance

A common cause of action will be that the other party has not fulfilled his obligations under the contract. As a general point, if this is what the client says, it may be worth asking him whether he has really fulfilled his part to check whether there is a real possiblity of a defence or counterclaim in any possible action. As far as drafting is concerned, it will normally be presumed that the party pleading has performed his own obligations, but if there is any special obligation or important condition precedent to liability arising it is probably a good idea to plead that it has been fulfilled.

In an extreme case, there may be total failure of consideration (see Example 4), if on the facts the other side have really done nothing to fulfil the contract. In such a case the contract can be rescinded if it is possible to put the parties back to the position they were in, see *Finelvet A.G.* v *Vinava Shipping Co.* [1983] 2 All ER 658.

Alternatively it may be possible to argue that the contract has been frustrated (see Example 7). Recent cases have shown that the courts will be prepared to look at the factual situation to see if a contract has been frustrated, but the argument of frustration does in fact rarely succeed, see *National Carriers* v *Panalpina (Northern)* [1981] AC 675 and *B.P. Exploration Co. (Libya)* v *Hunt* [1983] 2 AC 352. It really will be necessary to show that a legal or factual situation really has undermined the whole point of the contract, which will be rare. Because of the difficulties of showing frustration, and the limited remedies available it will often be better to use another cause of action, unless the real desire of the client is just to get out of his obligations under the contract.

The most common problem with performance will of course be breach (see Examples 2, 3 and 10), and the important thing here is to identify clearly what term has been breached, when, how and by whom, as this detail will have to be pleaded, and a wrong identification of the breach may result in losing the case. If there is more than one breach, it will be necessary to decide whether to allege them all, or only the most serious, and if more than one breach is relied on, each will have to be pleaded in a separate paragraph. The type of breach should also be identified; there may be an anticipatory breach before performance of the contract is due, but this must be distinguished from the case where there has not yet been a breach at all but only a threat of a breach, so that it is appropriate to negotiate or seek a quia timet injunction rather than commence an action.

The type of breach will also be relevant to whether the contract can be treated as over or not. This is an important point to explore with the client—does he just want to get out of the contract or continue with it? It can also be an important legal issue, in deciding whether any of the terms of the contract are still in operation or not. The point will be whether the breach has gone to the root of the contract, see *George Mitchell (Chesterhall)* v *Finney Lock Seeds* [1983] 2 AC 803, or whether the contract has been repudiated and it is open to the plaintiff to accept or reject the repudiation.

Remedies in a contractual action

It has been stressed time and again that remedies will be one of the most important factors in any action, and that all possibilities should be considered and discussed with the client to see what he hopes to achieve. Being practical, the best first step to getting what the client wants may well be to negotiate—there is no point in rushing off to get an injunction if being taken to court will only antagonise the other side rather than make him amenable to reason—but once an action is begun the remedies sought must be decided on.

The main possibility is damages, and much has already been said about advising on a drafting for damages claims, so only some particular points for contract cases. The first thing to consider and advise on is the basic purpose of contract damages, which is to cover all reasonably foreseeable loss, *Hadley* v *Baxendale* (1884) 9 Ex 341, to put the plaintiff where he would have been if the contract had been fulfilled. This measure will not cover things which are not foreseeable or which are too remote. For example, if the defendant's breach caused the plaintiff to lose a particularly valuable contract with someone else, he will only be able to recover if the defendant knew of the contract, *Victoria Laundry (Windsor)* v *Newman Industries* [1949] 2 KB 548. Another area where there may be problems with contract damages is getting money for distress or injured feelings, but arguments may succeed, *Jackson* v *Horizon Holidays* [1975] 1 WLR 1468.

It is useful to ask the client to produce a complete list of the things that he has lost so that the lawyer can advise whether they are recoverable or not, and put in the draft sufficient facts to raise heads of damage that may not otherwise be obvious, and such details as are known of special damage. If there is a possibility that something can be recovered it will generally be worth putting it in, and it will then be for the court to judge. The plaintiff is entitled to the measure of damages that is most favourable to him, provided it is reasonable and should not have been mitigated, *Paula Lee* v *Zehil & Co* [1983] 2 All ER 390. It is important to look at the position that the client will be left in in a practical way to see that the damages will not leave him suffering any loss and will allow his business to continue, see *Bacon* v *Cooper Metals* [1982] 1 All ER 397.

There are alternative measures of damages that may apply. It seems that a claim under the Misrepresentation Act 1967 will attract the tort measure of damages, *Andre & Cie* v *Ets Michel Blanc et Fils* [1977] 2 Lloyds Rep 166 and *Howard Marine & Dredging Co* v *Ogden* [1978] QB 574, and if the representation is fraudulent the favourable measure of damages for fraud will apply, *Doyle* v *Olby* [1969] 2 QB 158. The other alternative measure of damages is 'reliance loss', which may apply where any expected profit from the contract is nebulous or difficult to assess but the plaintiff has spent substantial sums of money in reliance on the contract he made, *Anglia TV* v *Reed* [1972] 1 QB 60. It would seem that recovering reliance loss is a direct alternative to loss of profit and the plaintiff must choose between them and plead the appropriate heads of damage for the one he wants, *C.C.C. Films (London)* v *Impact Quadrant Films* [1984] 3 All ER 298.

Having advised on the measure of damages and what specific things are recoverable within that measure it will be necessary to consider the actual figures in the case. One should of course try to give the client a figure for what he is likely to recover, but only the figures that are already known for special damage; figures for assessing general damages such as salary lost will need to be pleaded. Where a figure for a loss of a chance or loss of future profits will be difficult to assess it is especially important for the lawyer to develop detailed arguments as to what his client should get. With the help of the client and possibly an accountant and other experts the lawyer must suggest some way of assessing what his client should get. This is his job, and he cannot just say that it is difficult and leave it for the judge.

It will be necessary to advise on what will be deducted from damages as well as what is recoverable, and an important point in many contract cases will be the possibilities for mitigation. The lawyer must advise the client at an early stage of his duty to mitigate and examine the real facts of the case to suggest ways in which this could be done. Some clients will naturally want to mitigate their loss but some will be angry at what has happened and may not wish to do so, and the legal duty must be made clear to them. It is possible to recover the reasonable costs of mitigation as part of the damages in the action.

Other things may also reduce damages and should be investigated, such as statutory benefits received by the plaintiff. If the plaintiff gets a lump sum earlier than he would otherwise have got it, for example because he had a fixed term contract which is terminated early, the damages he gets will be reduced because he has the money early and can invest it. Tax may also reduce damages, but only in limited circumstances. If a trader loses profits on which he would have been taxed and gets damages, those damages will go into his accounts and be taxed, and since one replaces the other, tax will not reduce the amount of damages awarded. However in awarding damages for loss of employment, statute provides that the first £25,000 will be tax free and there will be further tax relief above that. To ensure that the plaintiff is not overcompensated due to this, the court will reduce the damages awarded and calculate the sum that after deduction of tax will leave the plaintiff with his net loss, see *Shove* v *Downs Surgical* [1984] 1 All ER 7.

An alternative route to getting damages is an action for quantum meruit, where damages cannot be claimed under a contract because no sum was set for the work to be done, or the contractual work has not been finished through no fault of the plaintiff. The award made will depend on the facts of the case, see *British Steel Corporation* v *Cleveland Bridge Engineering* [1984] 1 All ER 504. The sum claimed in quantum meruit should be pleaded, (see Example 8).

As for alternative remedies, there may be an application for rectification where a written contract does not properly set down the terms agreed by the parties, but this can only be done if there is an error or mutual mistake, not just because one party was mistaken as to what was intended (see Example 9).

The plaintiff may claim rescission of the contract, but only where it is still possible to restore the parties to the position they were in before the contract was made, otherwise the plaintiff will only be able to get damages (see Example 4). If the contract is rescinded, the plaintiff may want to claim repayment of money paid. Restitution is a remedy to seek when one party has property belonging to the other.

As for equitable remedies, specific performance must always be a first choice of remedy where the subject matter of the contract cannot be adequately replaced by another item or damages, though whether it is available will depend on the terms of the contract and the facts of the case, see *Sudbrook Trading Estate* v *Eggleton* [1982] 3 All ER 1. A contract for the sale of land will need to be in writing to be specifically enforceable, *Cohen* v *Nessdale* [1981] 3 All ER 118. Specific performance will not be available for a contract of personal service, so tactics will be important in trying to negotiate or to get an injunction that might induce the other side to allow the contract to continue, if that is what the client wants (see Example 5).

The other type of equitable relief that may be useful in many contractual actions is the injunction, whether quia timet, interlocutory or final. It will normally be necessary to have an express negative term in the contract to base the injunction and it is important to prepare full arguments as to why the injunction should be granted and to contemplate possible objections rather than just rushing off to court. It may well be practical to try negotiating with the other side before seeking an injunction to get a practical agreement rather than possibly aggravating the situation.

Advising a defendant

Advising a defendant in a contract case will involve three main elements: firstly whether there is any defence to the plaintiff's cause of action, secondly whether the plaintiff is entitled to the remedies he claims (especially the types of damage he claims) and thirdly whether there is any possible counterclaim.

On the first of these there may be arguments on the facts alleged, as to what was said and done in the making or performing of the contract or the alleged breach, or there may be arguments on the law as to whether the defendant is legally liable on the facts alleged. There may also be independent legal arguments, that the defendant was not bound by the contract because of duress or undue influence, or that he could not fulfil the contract due to a mistake or because it was frustrated.

As to remedies, there may again be arguments on fact or law, or the defendant himself may wish to rely on a clause of the contract to avoid or limit his liability. An exemption clause may provide that the defendant will not be liable in particular circumstances, and whether this will protect him will depend on the construction of the words and whether they apply to what has actually happened, *Photo Production* v *Securicor Transport* [1980] AC 827. Alternatively there may be a penalty clause to limit liability and the effectiveness of this will depend on various factors such as whether it provides a genuine preestimate of damages, *Dunlop Pneumatic Tyre Co.* v *New Garage and Motor Co.* [1915] AC 79, and again the court will look to see if the clause actually applies to what has happened, *Export Credit Guarantee Dept.* v *Universal Oil Products Co.* [1983] 2 All ER 205.

Like the plaintiff, the defendant and his lawyer must look at the quantification of damages in detail to see if it is recoverable at all, what the plaintiff should get for it, and whether the plaintiff should have mitigated his loss. Even if the defendant is liable, there may still be substantial arguments as to what he should pay. It seems that it is not possible to argue contributory negligence in contract, *Basildon District Council* v *J.E. Lesser* (1984) *The Times*, February 15th.

The defendant should be specifically asked if he knows of a possible counterclaim, even if none is immediately obvious from the facts.

EXAMPLE 1 STATEMENT OF CLAIM—SALE OF GOODS—LIQUIDATED DAMAGES

IN THE HIGH COURT OF JUSTICE 1985.G.No

QUEEN'S BENCH DIVISION

Writ issued 10th March 1985

BETWEEN ANGELO GOLDSMITH Plaintiff

and

ANTIPHOLUS EPHESUS Defendant

STATEMENT OF CLAIM

1. By an oral contract made on 1 May 1984 the plaintiff agreed to sell and the defendant agreed to buy a pure gold necklace manufactured by the plaintiff for the sum of £25,000.

2. It was a term of the contract that the said necklace should be delivered to the defendant on or before 1 July 1984.

3. In pursuance of the contract, on 10 June 1984 the plaintiff delivered the said necklace to the defendant at the home of the defendant at 3, Comedy Court, Error Road, London SW37, where the defendant received and accepted it.

4. The defendant has wrongfully failed and refused to pay to the plaintiff the price of the said necklace, namely £25,000 and the same is still due and owing by him to the plaintiff.

5. Further, the plaintiff claims interest pursuant to section 35A of the Supreme Court Act 1981 on the said sum of £25,000 at the rate of interest payable on judgment debts current at the date of the writ herein from 10 June 1984 until payment or judgment, whichever is the earlier. The amount of interest from 10 June 1984 until 10 March 1985 is £1,875.

AND the plaintiff claims:

1. The said sum of £25,000.

2. The said sum of £1,875 for interest pursuant to section 35A of the Supreme Court Act 1981 and continuing at the rate aforesaid from the date hereof until payment or judgment, whichever is the earlier.

J. Mortimer

EXAMPLE 2 STATEMENT OF CLAIM—BREACH OF CONTRACT—EMPLOYMENT CONTRACT

IN THE HIGH COURT OF JUSTICE 1985.B.No

QUEEN'S BENCH DIVISION

BETWEEN IAGO BADDIE Plaintiff
and
OTHELLO MOORE Defendant

STATEMENT OF CLAIM

1. The defendant is and was at all material times an international businessman. The plaintiff is an experienced personal assistant and body-guard with training and qualifications in secretarial work and in the martial arts.

2. By an oral agreement made on 1 November 1981 the defendant agreed to employ the plaintiff as his personal assistant and body-guard for a period of ten years commencing on 13 November 1981, and an annual salary of £10,000, together with all travel and accommodation expenses.

3. It was an express term of the said agreement that after three years of satisfactory service the defendant would promote the plaintiff to the position of Manager and Chief Security Officer at an increased annual salary of £15,000.

4. On 13 November 1984, in breach of the said agreement, the defendant appointed one Michael Cassio as his Manager and Chief Security Officer, instead of appointing the plaintiff to this position, although the plaintiff had given satisfactory service.

5. By reason of the matters aforesaid, the plaintiff has suffered loss and damage.

PARTICULARS OF DAMAGE

Loss of increased salary of £5,000 per annum for a period of seven years £35,000

6. Further, by reason of the matters aforesaid, the plaintiff has suffered frustration, embarrassment, and severe depression.

7. Further, the plaintiff claims interest pursuant to section 35A of the Supreme Court Act 1981 on the amount found to be due to the plaintiff at such rate and for such period as the Court thinks fit.

AND the plaintiff claims:

1. Damages.

2. The aforesaid interest pursuant to section 35A of the Supreme Court Act 1981.

Ann O. Nimous

EXAMPLE 3 STATEMENT OF CLAIM—BREACH OF CONTRACT

IN THE HIGH COURT OF JUSTICE 1985.A.No .

QUEEN'S BENCH DIVISION

BETWEEN THESEUS ATHENS Plaintiff

and

PETER QUINCE PRODUCTIONS LIMITED Defendants

STATEMENT OF CLAIM

1. The plaintiff is and was at all material times the owner and manager of the Duke of Athens Theatre, Shaftesbury Avenue, London. The defendants present dramatic works which are written, directed and performed by working men and women on social and political themes.

2. By a written contract dated 1 April 1984 made between the plaintiff and Peter Quince on behalf of the defendants it was agreed that the defendants would present performances of the play 'Pyramus and Thisby go to the Wall' at the plaintiff's said theatre, giving one performance on each night from 17 June 1984 to 24 June 1984. The defendants were to receive a total fee of £30,000 for these performances.

3. In breach of the said contract, on 19 June 1984 Peter Quince orally informed the plaintiff that the defendants would give no further performances due to ideological differences between members of the cast. No further performances were given.

4. By reason of the matters aforesaid, the plaintiff has suffered loss and damage.

PARTICULARS OF DAMAGE

Money refunded to ticketholders	£ 5,000
Cost of programmes printed	£ 1,000
Wasted catering	£ 2,000
	£ 8,000

5. Further, the performance of the play on 24 June 1984 had been arranged by the plaintiff as a special promotion to be attended by Hippolyta Amazon, a leading film actress, to promote the theatrical and film interests of the plaintiff. This was made known orally by the plaintiff to Peter Quince on 1 April 1984.

6. By reason of the said breach of contract, the promotion on 24 June 1984 had to be cancelled, and the plaintiff has suffered loss and damage and loss of goodwill.

7. Further, the plaintiff claims interest pursuant to section 35A of the

Supreme Court Act 1981 on the amount found to be due to the plaintiff at such rate and for such period as the court thinks fit.

AND the plaintiff claims:

1. Damages under paragraphs 4 and 6.
2. The aforesaid interest pursuant to section 35A of the Supreme Court Act 1981.

Sue D. Nymm.

EXAMPLE 4 STATEMENT OF CLAIM—SALE—IMPLIED CONDITION—TOTAL FAILURE OF CONSIDERATION

IN THE HIGH COURT OF JUSTICE 1985.S.No

QUEEN'S BENCH DIVISION

BETWEEN	ROBERT SHALLOW	Plaintiff
	and	
	JOHN FALSTAFF	Defendant

STATEMENT OF CLAIM

1. By an oral agreement made on or about 1 May 1984, the plaintiff agreed to buy from the defendant a hunter horse named 'King Henry the Fourth', in consideration whereof the plaintiff agreed to pay the defendant the sum of £25,000.

2. On or about 5 May 1984, the plaintiff paid to the defendant the said sum of £25,000, and the defendant delivered the said hunter horse to the plaintiff.

3. It was an express or alternatively an implied term of the agreement that the said hunter horse was the lawful property of the defendant and/or that he had title or lawful authority to sell the same.

4. In breach of the agreement, the said hunter horse was not the lawful property of the defendant, but of one Edward Poins, and the defendant had no title or lawful authority to sell the same.

5. In the premises the plaintiff has suffered loss and damage, namely the value of the said hunter horse, £25,000.

6. Further or in the alternative, in the premises the consideration for the payment of the said sum of £25,000 has wholly failed, and the said sum is repayable to the plaintiff.

7. Further, the plaintiff claims interest pursuant to section 35A of the Supreme Court Act 1981 on the amount found to be due to the plaintiff at such rate and for such time as the court thinks fit.

AND the plaintiff claims;

1. Under paragraph 6, £25,000.
2. Further or in the alternative, damages under paragraphs 4 and 5.
3. The aforesaid interest pursuant to section 35A of the Supreme Court Act 1981.

Samuel Silent.

EXAMPLE 5 STATEMENT OF CLAIM—SALE—MISREPRESENTATION

IN THE HIGH COURT OF JUSTICE 1985.Q.No .

QUEEN'S BENCH DIVISION

BETWEEN URSULA QUICKLY Plaintiff
and
JOHN FALSTAFF Defendant

STATEMENT OF CLAIM

1. The plaintiff is and was at all material times the owner and manager of a public house known as The Boar's Head Tavern, Eastcheap, London WC1. The defendant is a dealer in wines, spirits and beers.

2. On or about 1 April 1984, in order to induce the plaintiff to enter into a contract with him for the purchase of wines and beers, the defendant orally represented to the plaintiff he could supply 'Falstaff Sack' and 'Falstaff Real Ale', both of which:

(a) Were in excellent condition for drinking
(b) Were already supplied to 50 public houses in the London area
(c) Were highly recommended in the publication 'Best Booze in Britain'
(d) Would be supplied to the plaintiff at a reduction of 10% from the normal price charged by the defendant.

3. In reliance upon the defendant's said representations, on 13 April 1984 the plaintiff entered into a contract with the defendant to purchase 300 crates of the said 'Falstaff Sack' and 500 barrels of the said 'Falstaff Real Ale' for a total price of £30,000, which sum was paid to the defendant forthwith. The said contract was partly oral and partly in writing, the amounts ordered and the price being noted on the reverse side of a laundry bill.

4. The defendant's said representations were false in that the said 'Falstaff Sack' and 'Falstaff Real Ale':

(a) Were not fit to be drunk, both having a bitter taste and cloudy colouring
(b) Were not supplied to 50 public houses in the London area, only 20 such public houses having been supplied, and the majority of those having returned their supplies to the defendant.
(c) Were not highly recommended in 'Best Booze in Britain', being mentioned therein only as 'veritable gnat's piss'.
(d) Were sold to the plaintiff at a price 20% in excess of the price

quoted in a written handbill produced by the defendant for his customers.

5. Further or in the alternative, the defendant's said representations were made fraudulently in that the defendant made them knowing that they were false, or reckless as to whether they were true or false.

6. By reason of the matters aforesaid, the plaintiff has suffered loss and damage.

PARTICULARS OF DAMAGE

Value of 'Falstaff sack' and 'Falstaff Real Ale' as represented	£30,000
Real value of 'Falstaff Sack' and 'Falstaff Real Ale'	£ 5,000
Difference in value	£25,000

7. Further, the plaintiff claims interest pursuant to section 35A of the Supreme Court Act 1981 on the amount found to be due to the plaintiff at such rate and for such time as the court thinks fit.

AND the plaintiff claims;

1. Rescission of the said contract on the ground of misrepresentation with all proper consequential directions.
2. Repayment of the sum of £30,000 paid by the plaintiff to the defendant pursuant to the contract.
3. Further or in the alternative, damages.
4. The aforesaid interest pursuant to section 35A of the Supreme Court Act 1981.

Lorde C. Justiss

EXAMPLE 6 STATEMENT OF CLAIM—SALE—SPECIFIC PERFORMANCE

IN THE HIGH COURT OF JUSTICE 1985.S.No

CHANCERY DIVISION

BETWEEN SAMUEL SHYLOCK Plaintiff

and

ANTONIO MERCHANT GALLERIES (a firm) Defendants

STATEMENT OF CLAIM

1. The defendants are and were at all material times dealers and specialists in modern prints and paintings.

2. By an oral agreement made on 1 September 1984, made between the plaintiff on the one part and Mr Basil Bassanio acting in the course of his employment as an assistant at a gallery owned and run by the defendants on the other part, it was agreed that the defendants would sell to the plaintiff a set of paintings by the modern Venetian artist Mercy Quality entitled 'Pounds of Flesh', for a consideration of £40,000.

3. The agreement was set down in writing signed by the plaintiff and the said Mr Basil Bassanio acting on behalf of the defendants on 13 September 1984.

4. In breach of the said agreement the defendants have refused and still refuse to deliver the said paintings to the plaintiff, despite repeated requests by the plaintiff, both orally and in writing, that they should do so.

5. Further, the plaintiff claims interest pursuant to section 35A of the Supreme Court Act 1981 on any amount found due to the plaintiff at such rate and for such time as the court thinks fit.

AND the plaintiff claims:

1. Specific performance of the said agreement.

2. Further or in the alternative, damages for breach of the said agreement.

3. Interest as aforesaid pursuant to section 35A of the Supreme Court Act 1981.

B. Brieffe.

EXAMPLE 7 STATEMENT OF CLAIM—FRUSTRATION

IN THE HIGH COURT OF JUSTICE 1985.G.No

QUEEN'S BENCH DIVISION

BETWEEN RICHARD GLOUCESTER Plaintiff
and
EDWARD PLANTAGENET Defendant

STATEMENT OF CLAIM

1. The defendant was the breeder and owner of a racehorse known as 'The Crown of England'.
2. By an oral contract made on 22 June 1984 the defendant agreed to sell the said racehorse to the plaintiff for a sum of £50,000.
3. On 24 June 1984 the plaintiff paid the defendant the sum of £50,000 as specified in the contract.
4. On 22 August 1984 the said racehorse died suddenly.
5. In the premises the contract has been frustrated, and the plaintiff is entitled to recover the sum of £50,000.

AND the plaintiff claims £50,000.

Thomas More.

EXAMPLE 8 STATEMENT OF CLAIM—QUANTUM MERUIT

IN THE HIGH COURT OF JUSTICE 1985.R.No .

QUEEN'S BENCH DIVISION

BETWEEN (1) REGINALD ROSENCRANTZ
(2) GILBERT GUILDENSTERN Plaintiffs
and
CLAUDIUS REX Defendant

STATEMENT OF CLAIM

1. The defendant is and was at all material times the managing director of Elsinore Enterprises plc. The plaintiffs own and operate a small detective agency from 13, Denmark Hill, London SW33.

2. By an oral agreement made on 1 March 1984 the defendant instructed the plaintiffs to keep full-time surveillance on one Hamlet Prince, a director of the said Elsinore Enterprises plc for a period of three months reporting all his movements and meetings.

3. It was an implied term of the agreement that the defendant would pay to the plaintiffs a reasonable fee for the said work on completion thereof.

4. A reasonable fee for the said work was £20,000, but the defendant has failed to pay to the plaintiffs that sum or any sum.

5. Further or in the alternative, the defendant prevented the plaintiffs from completing the said work in that on 23 May 1984 he sent the said Hamlet Prince to work abroad where the plaintiffs could no longer keep surveillance on him.

6. Further, the plaintiffs claim interest pursuant to section 35A of the Supreme Court Act 1981 on any amount found due to the plaintiff at such rates and for such time as the court thinks fit.

AND the plaintiffs claim:

1. £20,000 as the sum due on quantum meruit.
2. The aforesaid interest pursuant to section 35A of the Supreme Court Act 1981.

M. Marple.

EXAMPLE 9 STATEMENT OF CLAIM—INDUCING BREACH OF CONTRACT

IN THE HIGH COURT OF JUSTICE 1985.A.No .

QUEEN'S BENCH DIVISION

BETWEEN ARIEL ENTERPRISES plc Plaintiffs

and

CALIBAN'S CON-ARTISTS (a firm) Defendants

STATEMENT OF CLAIM

1. The plaintiffs are and were at all material times the inventors and manufacturers of magic tricks and illusions carrying on business at Summer Solstice House, Salisbury, Wiltshire. The defendants are wholesale sellers of games and toys to retail shops in southern England, carrying on business from Cave Chambers, Tempest Terrace, London E55.

2. Prior to the wrongful acts of the defendant complained of, the plaintiffs entered into a contract with Puck's Promotions Ltd on 21 June 1984 to suppy the said Puck's Promotions Ltd with magic tricks for a period of five years.

3. The defendants, who well knew at all material times that the said contract had been entered into by the plaintiffs, maliciously and wrongfully, and with intention to injure the plaintiffs, procured and induced the said Puck's Promotions Ltd to break their said contract with the plaintiffs, and to refuse to perform or further perform the same.

PARTICULARS

(i) On or about 1 October the defendants wrongfully informed the said Puck's Promotions Ltd that the trick 'Whispering Magic' manufactured by the plaintiffs did not work.

(ii) On or about 5 October 1984 the defendants wrongfully informed the said Puck's Promotions Ltd that the defendants produced more imaginative tricks of more interest to the public than the plaintiffs tricks.

(iii) On or about 5 October 1984 the defendants wrongfully informed the said Puck's Promotions Ltd that they could supply tricks more quickly and more cheaply than the plaintiffs.

4. In consequence of the aforesaid, the plaintiffs have lost the benefit of the said contract, and have lost the profit that they would otherwise have made, and have been injured in their business, and have thereby suffered loss and damage.

PARTICULARS OF DAMAGE

Loss of sales of new tricks in the account year 1984–85	£55,000

5. Further, the plaintiffs claim interest pursuant to section 35A of the Supreme Court Act 1981 on any amount found due to the plaintiffs at such rates and for such time as the Court thinks fit.

6. Further, the defendants threaten and intend unless restrained from so doing by this Honourable Court to continue to do the acts hereinbefore complained of.

AND the plaintiffs claim:

1. Damages.
2. An injunction to prevent the defendants by themselves, their servants or agents or otherwise, from doing or continuing to do anything to induce further breaches of the contract specified in paragraph 2, or any similar contract made by the plaintiffs.
3. The aforesaid interest pursuant to section 35A of the Supreme Court Act 1981.

Sugar Plum-Fairee

EXAMPLE 10 DEFENCE TO STATEMENT OF CLAIM IN 2— COUNTERCLAIM FOR BREACH OF IMPLIED TERM

IN THE HIGH COURT OF JUSTICE 1985.B.No1234.

QUEEN'S BENCH DIVISION

BETWEEN IAGO BADDIE Plaintiff

and

OTHELLO MOORE Defendant

DEFENCE

1. The defendant admits paragraphs 1 and 2 of the Statement of Claim.
2. The defendant denies that there was any term in the agreement as alleged in paragraph 3 of the Statement of Claim, or any similar term.
3. In the alternative, if, which is denied, there was a term in the agreement as alleged in paragraph 3 of the Statement of Claim, the conduct of the plaintiff in the course of his employment was not such as to justify his promotion as alleged in the Statement of Claim or at all.

PARTICULARS

(i) The plaintiff frequently argued with other employees of the defendant.
(ii) The plaintiff frequently failed to inform the defendant of important business matters which he should have brought to the attention of the defendant.
(iii) The plaintiff frequently took business decisions which should have been referred to the defendant for decision.

4. In the premises, the defendant denies that he was in breach of the agreement as alleged or at all.
5. The defendant denies that the plaintiff has suffered the alleged or any loss or damage.

COUNTERCLAIM

6. It was an implied term of the agreement that the plaintiff should keep secret all records, knowledge and information that might from time to time be communicated to him by the defendant in the course of his employment, and that he should not make use of it other than in the course of his employment with the defendant.
7. On or about 7 October 1984 the plaintiff gave to one Roderigo Venetian, a business competitor of the defendant a copy of a contract that

the defendant had made on that day with one Brabantio Senator, and technical plans and details connected therewith.

8. As a result of the matters complained of in paragraph 7, the defendant has suffered loss and damage in that he has lost the benefit of the rights that he obtained from the said contract with Brabantio Senator, full details of which will be served separately.

9. Further, the defendant claims interest pursuant to section 35A of the Supreme Court Act 1981 on the amount found to be due to the defendant at such rate and for such period as the court thinks fit.

AND the defendant claims:

1. Damages.
2. The aforesaid interest pursuant to section 35A of the Supreme Court Act 1981.
3. A declaration that the contract, technical plans and details referred to in paragraph 7 were confidential records and information communicated to the plaintiff in the course of his employment and were the sole property of the defendant.
4. An order for the delivery up by the plaintiff of all records and other written knowledge and information that the plaintiff received in the course of his employment with the defendant.

Mae O. Pinion

EXAMPLE 11 DEFENCE TO STATEMENT OF CLAIM IN 6—MISTAKE—COUNTERCLAIM FOR RECTIFICATION

IN THE HIGH COURT OF JUSTICE 1985.S.No.4321.

CHANCERY DIVISION

BETWEEN SAMUEL SHYLOCK Plaintiff

and

ANTONIO MERCHANT GALLERIES (a firm) Defendants

DEFENCE

1. Paragraph 1 of the Statement of Claim is admitted.

2. Paragraph 2 of the Statement of Claim is admitted, save in that it was agreed that the defendants would sell to the plaintiff not only the four paintings entitled 'Pounds of Flesh', but also a companion work by the same artist entitled 'A drop of blood', with an additional consideration of £10,000 for that painting.

3. It is admitted that on 13 September 1984 the plaintiff and the defendants signed a written contract which was intended to embody the agreement as set out in paragraph 2 herein, and not any other agreement.

4. The written contract was so signed by the plaintiff and the defendants in the belief that it embodied the agreement set out in paragraph 2 herein, but it does not in fact embody it in that it was understood by the parties that the said painting 'A drop of blood' was part of the series of paintings entitled 'Pounds of Flesh', whereas the artist had stipulated that the said painting 'A drop of blood' should be sold for a separate consideration. The said written contract was thus signed under a mutual mistake of fact, and the defendants have never agreed to the terms contained in it.

5. The defendants are now and always have been ready and willing to sign a written contract correctly embodying the agreement set out in paragraph 2 herein, but no such contract has been tendered to them.

6. In the premises, the agreement alleged in paragraphs 2 and 3 of the Statement of Claim is not binding on or enforceable against the defendants.

COUNTERCLAIM

7. Paragraphs 2, 3 and 4 of this Defence are repeated.

AND the defendants counterclaim:

1. An order that the written contract dated 13 September 1984 be rectified so as to embody the agreement actually made between the parties as set out in paragraph 2 herein, and that the said contract be treated as being so rectified.

2. Alternatively, that the said contract be rescinded.

Portia de Belmont.

Advising and drafting in a tort case

When advising a client who may have a case in tort, there are a few areas that are particularly important. Many tort cases will depend on allegations of fact, and special skills must be developed to establish fully the client's version of what happened, and to use the imagination to find any gaps or possible defects in this version that the other side may raise and exploit. A skill to grasp technical matters quickly will be needed where an accident has been caused for example by a machine, and also to grasp sufficiently a medical report describing injuries to the plaintiff, which may be very important when it comes to assessing damages. There will also be some development of basic skills in getting the feel of assessing damages for personal injuries, and in drafting particulars of negligence, injury and damage.

Clarifying the facts

Many tort cases will turn on allegations of fact, so it is particularly important for the lawyer to get clear in his mind what the client is telling him, and to be sure that he has the whole story. This can be done by asking the client to tell the story of what happened in his own words, and then asking him again at a later stage, watching on both occasions for anything left out and any contradictions. Bear in mind that what the client says may not be entirely objective—if he was injured he may not be able to remember things clearly, and in any event he may be angry at what has happened, or may have turned it over in his own mind so often that he has distorted his memory (especially to decrease his own responsibility and increase that of someone else—almost any driver involved in a car accident will do this). The lawyer will have to ask questions to fill in any gaps and to test any part of the case that seems weak. The client will rarely lie to his lawyer, but what he does say must be challenged and checked.

The lawyer must also understand any technical details of the case, not least to be able to explain them to the judge. For an industrial accident this may involve mastering the details of a mechanical process and special terminology. Expert evidence may be needed on this, and may have to be sought at an early stage to see whether there is a cause of action or not. For the facts of the case and the technical background, it will be a matter of proving as well as understanding, and all independent evidence and reports that are available should be sought, including maps, plans and photographs.

Choosing the cause of action

On the basis of full facts the lawyer will have to consider the possible causes of action. This may be obviously nuisance or trespass, but there are overlaps so that the same set of facts may give rise to an action in negligence, breach of statutory duty and occupier's liability, so a decision will have to be made. As outlined in earlier chapters, the best way of doing this is to write out the elements of each possibility and checking which can be most easily proved and has least legal difficulty, only bringing more than one if there is justification for the cost. For example, negligence will need a duty of care/that is owed to the plaintiff/that has been breached by the defendant/which breach has led to damage/for which damages are recoverable (see Examples 1 and 2). Alternatively, for breach of occupiers liability there would need to be a defendant occupier/of a specific building/the plaintiff is a visitor to whom a common duty of care is owed/the plaintiff is injured in the building (see Example 2).

If breach of statutory duty is a possibility, it will be necessary to get the exact wording of any relevant statute or regulation at an early stage to see if there is a breach, as argument may well turn on it. The solicitor or barrister who regularly works in this type of case will soon become familiar with the main provisions that he works with, but care and special research will always be needed with less common areas of regulation (see Example 3).

There may be a cause of action in an area other than tort, and the inter-relation of tort and contract has arisen in several cases in recent years, though the principles of the relationship are far from clear. A fraud action may be brought in tort or contract, *Yianni* v *Edwin Evans* [1982] QB 438. Alternatively the action itself can be brought on two bases, one in contract and one in tort, as in *Esso Petroleum* v *Mardon* [1976] QB 801 where the case was for breach of warranty and negligent misrepresentation, or *Howard Marine and Dredging Co* v *Ogden* [1978] QB 574 where the action was brought under the Misrepresentation Act 1967 and for negligence. Lastly, the facts may justify an action in contract and tort but the plaintiff may choose one, as in *Parsons* v *Uttley Ingham* [1978] QB 791 where the plaintiff chose to rely on breach of contract alone.

The plaintiff will again have to choose which of the possibilities has least problems in law and in evidence, but the measure of damages available will also be relevant. Lord Denning has said that the plaintiff should get the same damages for what he has lost whether he sues in tort or contract, *Parsons* v *Uttley Ingham* (above), but other cases have taken a stricter view. The purpose of damages in contract is looking forward to put the plaintiff where he would have been if the contract had been fulfilled, whereas tort looks back to put the plaintiff where he was before the tort was committed. There are also differences in what is covered, although the two measures of damage seem to be moving closer together, damages for hurt feelings are recoverable in tort but often not in contract, whereas damages for purely economic loss can be recovered in contract but still not always in tort and so on. In deciding whether to bring an action in contract or tort or both it will be necessary to examine whether everything lost will be recoverable in the actions possible.

The other decision to be made is whom to sue, as there will often be a choice. One may be able to sue the person who actually causes an accident or their employer, or the person who owns the building where an accident occurs, or to choose between the person who sells an item and the one who manufactured it. One should examine all the possibilities before deciding who there is the strongest factual and legal case against, and who is most likely to be able to pay damages. Costs should be kept down by not suing people unnecessarily, but if there is any real doubt several possibilities should be joined to avoid having to bring another action (if possible), and because the other option may well be made a third party anyway.

Damages and other remedies

The main remedy in most tort actions will be damages, so it will be necessary to consider fully and advise on the appropriate way of measuring damages, what things the plaintiff can recover for, and as closely as possible what figure the plaintiff can hope to get. The general test for tort is of course to compensate the plaintiff for all loss arising from the tort that is foreseeable and is not too remote. As with contract, the lawyer should ask the client to tell him all the things that he has lost, so that he can see if they come within this test, and can claim them in the pleading as special damage if a figure can already be given, or as general damage.

One problem in recovering damages in a tort action used to be that purely economic loss was not recoverable, but it seems that it now can be, provided that it is sufficiently proximate and within the scope of the duty owed by the defendant to the plaintiff, *Junior Books Ltd* v *Veitchi* [1983] AC 520. Another problem in assessing damages in a tort case will often be determining a figure for injuries received—the lawyer in practice will build up an ability to feel the right figure for a case, and looking up cases in *Kemp and Kemp* and *Current Law* for comparison was dealt with earlier. As with contract, it will be important to advise on what may be deducted as well as what is recoverable, finding out for example whether the plaintiff has received any statutory benefits, and whether there may be any tax effect on the damages, *BTC* v *Gourley* [1956] AC 185.

There are special principles for assessing damages for loss of future earnings, and for loss of dependency where there has been a death. It is worth putting effort into arguments here because exact arithmetic is impossible, and there may be good arguments on the promotion that might have been expected or the contribution that the deceased made to the welfare of his family. In any event, the financial background should be investigated almost as fully as the facts of the case. Where someone has been killed damages will be sought for the estate under the Law Reform (Miscellaneous Provisions) Act 1934, including special damage and damages for any pain and suffering prior to death, and there will also be a claim for damages for the dependants under the Fatal Accidents Act 1976, the rules being amended by the Administration of Justice Act 1982 for all deaths after 3 January 1983. The damages for the dependants will either take the salary of the deceased and deduct the money that he spent on himself, or add together the figures that the deceased spent on his dependants, multiplying the annual dependancy by a multiplier depending on the age of the deceased and the number of years he might have gone on working. There may also be damages for bereavement. The lawyer must deal with all the relevant figures in detail to prepare calculations for the court.

As for remedies other than damages, the plaintiff may seek an order for the return of a specific chattel where appropriate, or may seek a declaration or an injunction, for example to stop a nuisance. In a tort it is especially important to consider the position of the client in a practical way and make full use of all possible procedural steps and means of obtaining evidence. The discovery process may be particularly important to get hold of reports, and the client may be helped for example by seeking an interim award of damages.

Points on drafting

Because a tort case will often involve examining the factual details of an event it is particularly important, but particularly difficult for the young lawyer, to develop a drafting technique that is very clear and gives sufficient particulars without tying the case down too much or being too vague. Provided the essential elements of the case are pleaded in an appropriate order following the basic principles of drafting this should not be too difficult, but there is an art to pleading particulars of negligence, breach of statutory duty or injury well.

In practice there are many different approaches to pleading particulars in tort, from the basic to the over-ornate, and as always the young lawyer should look at every example that he comes across to develop his own style, remembering always that particulars of negligence or breach should cover every way that the accident could have occurred without being more wide and vague than they need to be. Particulars must never be copied straight from a precedent but must be based on the facts of the case, *Brickfield Properties* v *Newton* [1971] 1 WLR 862. For example, in *Waghorn* v *George Wimpey & Co.* [1969] 1 WLR 1764 the plaintiff sued his employers alleging that he fell while crossing a bank at the site where he worked. It came out in evidence at trial that he had in fact fallen some distance from the bank, so his action failed as this was a radical departure from the pleading in the case. Particulars of injury are normally taken straight from a medical report, but should be a brief and clear summary of the main points of the report rather than being taken verbatim from it. Medical particulars can be given as a paragraph or as numbered points under a 'Particulars' heading.

If the plaintiff is alleging res ipsa loquitur he should plead it, though it was held in one case that if a claim for negligence involved all the facts from which res ipsa loquitur could be implied, that would be sufficient, *Bennett* v *Chemical Construction (G.B.)* [1971] 1 WLR 1571. In a fatal accident case there are various particulars of the dependants and the deceased that must be pleaded by statute (see Example 4). In a personal injury action of any kind it is always necessary to give particulars of the injuries suffered, and the age of the deceased at the date of the accident, or his date of birth.

Advising a defendant

As in a contract case, there are various courses for those advising the defendant to take, and various things that they should consider. The first possible course is to deny that the plaintiff has a cause of action at all, either on a matter of law or because the defendant's version of the facts is different from the plaintiff's. The lawyer for the defence will have to investigate the facts and the evidence just as much as the lawyer for the plaintiff. It may be difficult for the defendant to deny that there was an accident (though he need not admit it), but he may deny that he owed a duty to the plaintiff, that he was responsible for the accident, or that he was responsible for the resultant loss, or all of these (see Example 7).

The second possibility, to use alone or in the alternative, is to argue a positive defence. This may be a legal or technical defence, such as the expiry of the limitation period, or a specific defence provided by the statute or regulations that give rise to his liability. Other positive defences depend on the facts, such as volenti non fit injuria, where the plaintiff voluntarily accepted any risk in the situation, or the slightly different argument that the plaintiff consented to what was done. Other possible lines of defence not so common in practice are necessity, that it was necessary for the plaintiff to do what he did, or self-defence. Finally, there is the possibility of novus actus interveniens, where some new event rather than the act of the defendant is said to be responsible for the injury or loss suffered by the plaintiff.

Another possible line, perhaps the most common in practice, is to argue, perhaps in addition to one of the above defences, that the plaintiff was partly responsible for what happened, and that therefore there is contributory negligence (this applies to other actions, not just negligence). If there is found to be contributory negligence it will reduce the damages payable. Such an allegation must be pleaded (an example is given in the examples of pleading), and the lawyer must prepare his arguments on the facts and his evidence to show contributory negligence. He must not only prove the contributory negligence, but also argue what effect this should have on damages, that is what extent the plaintiff was responsible and in what proportion damages should be reduced (there is a great difference between 20% and 40% in what the defendant will have to pay). The defendant should also consider whether anyone else could be argued to be responsible for what happened to the plaintiff, and if they are not already a party to the action he should consider making them a third party (see Examples 8 and 9).

EXAMPLE 1 STATEMENT OF CLAIM—NEGLIGENCE—RES IPSA LOQUITUR

IN THE HIGH COURT OF JUSTICE 1985.P.No

QUEEN'S BENCH DIVISION

BETWEEN PERCY PROSPERO Plaintiff

and

ANTONIO ALONSO'S FLYING FUNFAIR (a firm) Defendants

STATEMENT OF CLAIM

1. The defendants own and operate a funfair consisting of various mechanical rides, with various sideshows, at Sycorax Pleasure Island, Margate, Kent.

2. One of the mechanical rides at the said funfair is called 'Tempest Tossed', and in this members of the public are invited to sit in small model boats, each boat having seating space for two people. When the ride is activated, the said boats are mechanically propelled in varying directions at heights up to twenty feet above the ground.

3. On 13 August 1984 the plaintiff attended the said funfair, and took a seat alone on the said ride 'Tempest Tossed'. An employee or agent of the defendants fastened a safety bar across the front of the seat in which the plaintiff sat.

4. Shortly after the said ride was activated the plaintiff was propelled by the machinery in an upward direction with such force that he was ejected from his seat and fell to the ground from a height of approximately twenty feet.

5. The said accident was caused by the negligence of the defendants, their servants or agents.

PARTICULARS OF NEGLIGENCE

The defendants, their servants or agents were negligent in that:

(i) They failed to erect the said ride with any or any sufficient care as to the safety of those who might ride in it.

(ii) They failed to maintain the said ride adequately or at all.

(iii) They failed to provide any or any proper supervision of members of the public using the said ride.

(iv) They failed to ensure that members of the public would be safe in using the said ride.

(v) They failed to give any or any adequate warning as to the possible dangers of the said ride.

The plaintiff will further rely on the principle of res ipsa loquitur.

6. As a result of the said negligence the plaintiff sustained injuries.

PARTICULARS OF INJURIES

The plaintiff, who was aged 50 at the date of the said accident, suffered the following injuries:

(i) Concussion.
(ii) Shock.
(iii) Compound fracture of the right leg.
(iv) Cuts and abrasions to the right arm and the right side of the face.

As a result of the said injuries, the plaintiff was in hospital for 10 days. He suffers some residual stiffness in the right leg, and may develop arthritis in the near future. He has suffered frequent and severe migraines since the accident, and is likely to need a course of psychiatric treatment to help with these.

7. Further, as a result of the said negligence, the plaintiff has suffered loss and damage.

PARTICULARS OF SPECIAL DAMAGE

Damage to clothing	£150
Loss of watch	£100
Loss of personal cassette player	£120
	£370

8. Further, the plaintiff claims interest pursuant to section 35A of the Supreme Court Act 1981 on the amount found to be due to the plaintiff at such rate and for such period as the court thinks fit.

AND the plaintiff claims:
1. Damages.
2. The aforesaid interest pursuant to section 35A of the Supreme Court Act 1981, to be assessed.

M. Python.

EXAMPLE 2 STATEMENT OF CLAIM—OCCUPIER'S LIABILITY—NEGLIGENCE

IN THE HIGH COURT OF JUSTICE 1985.S.No .

QUEEN'S BENCH DIVISION

BETWEEN DUNCAN SCOTLAND Plaintiff

and

(1) MACDONALD MACBETH

(2) FLORA MACBETH Defendants

STATEMENT OF CLAIM

1. The defendants are and were at all material times the joint owners and occupiers of premises known as 'The Thane of Cawdor Hotel', Dunsinane Hill, Birnham Beeches, Berkshire.

2. On the 1 November 1984 the plaintiff entered the said premises as a lawful visitor and guest.

3. While the plaintiff was sitting on a couch in the lobby of the said premises, two ceremonial daggers which were part of the decoration of the lobby fell from their fitting on the wall and hit the plaintiff, severely injuring him.

4. The matters complained of were caused by the negligence and/or the breach of statutory duty under section 2 of the Occupiers Liability Act 1957 of the defendants, their servants or agents:

PARTICULARS OF NEGLIGENCE AND/OR BREACH OF STATUTORY DUTY

(i) Failure to affix the said daggers to the wall in an adequate manner.

(ii) Failure to give any or any sufficient consideration to the best manner of affixing the said daggers, and/or to the weight of the said daggers.

(iii) Failure to check adequately or at all whether the said daggers remained adequately affixed to the wall.

(iv) Failure to consider adequately or at all whether the said daggers were a safe form of decoration in the place where they were affixed.

(v) Failure to take any or any reasonable care to ensure that the plaintiff was reasonably safe in using the said premises as a visitor.

5. By reason of the matters aforesaid, the plaintiff, who was aged 38 at the date of the accident, sustained injuries and has suffered loss and damage.

PARTICULARS OF INJURY

The plaintiff suffered two severe stab wounds to the chest, one of which punctured his left lung. He sustained further minor cuts and bruising to his chest and his upper right arm. He remained in hospital for three weeks. He still has difficulty breathing on occasion, and as a result is no longer able to keep up his hobby of running in marathons.

PARTICULARS OF SPECIAL DAMAGE

Damage to clothing	£100
Loss of earnings	£700
Medical expenses	£500
	£1,300

6. Further, the plaintiff claims interest pursuant to section 35A of the Supreme Court Act 1981 on the amount found to be due to the plaintiff at such rate and for such period as the court thinks fit.

AND the plaintiff claims:

1. Damages.
2. The aforesaid interest pursuant to section 35A of the Supreme Court Act 1981, to be assessed.

Horace Rumpole.

EXAMPLE 3 STATEMENT OF CLAIM—BREACH OF STATUTORY DUTY

IN THE HIGH COURT OF JUSTICE 1985.B.No .

QUEEN'S BENCH DIVISION

BETWEEN NICHOLAS BOTTOM Plaintiff

and

THE MIDSUMMER-NIGHT'S DREAMY UNDERWEAR COMPANY LIMITED Defendants

STATEMENT OF CLAIM

1. At all material times the plaintiff was employed as a weaver by the defendants at their premises at Athens Court, Greek Street, London, which premises were a factory within the meaning of the Factories Act 1961.

2. On 24 June 1984 there was on the premises a power operated spin weaving machine, fitted with two sharp edged flying spindles. The said machine was a dangerous machine and contained dangerous parts, namely the said flying spindles.

3. On the said date, in the course of his employment, the plaintiff was operating the said machine to weave cloth when the said flying spindle became entangled in his hair when he bent forward, causing his head to be pulled violently into the said machine, in consequence whereof the plaintiff sustained severe injury.

4. The accident was caused by a breach of statutory duty under section 14 and section 16 of the Factories Act 1961 by the defendants, their servants or agents.

PARTICULARS OF BREACH OF STATUTORY DUTY

(i) Failing to fence securely the said flying shuttles, which were dangerous parts of the machine, as required by section 14(1) of the Factories Act 1961, or at all.

(ii) Failing constantly to maintain and keep in position any fencing or guard over the said flying shuttles while they were in motion or use, as required by section 16 of the Factories Act 1961, or at all.

5. Further or in the alternative, the accident was caused by the negligence of the defendants, their servants or agents.

PARTICULARS OF NEGLIGENCE

(i) Failing to take any or any adequate precautions for the safety of the plaintiff while he was engaged in the said work.

(ii) Exposing the plaintiff to the risk of damage or injury of which they knew or ought to have known.
(iii) Providing for use by the plaintiff a machine that was defective or unsafe.
(iv) Failing to provide an adequate system of maintenance for the said machine.
(v) Failing to provide and maintain a safe system of work in the said factory.

6. As a result of the breach of statutory duty and/or the negligence, the plaintiff sustained injury and has suffered loss and damage.

PARTICULARS OF INJURY

The plaintiff, who was born on 10 June 1953, suffered severe scalp damage and loss of hair. The hair may never fully grow back, and severe scarring may be left for some years. There were severe lacerations to both ears, which are likely to remain elongated and badly misshapen. Due to the need for continuing treatment to the scarred tissue, the plaintiff was off work for three months.

PARTICULARS OF SPECIAL DAMAGE

Damage to gold ear-ring	£100
Hairdressing treatment	£1,000
Lost wages	£2,500
	£3,600

7. Further, the plaintiff claims interest pursuant to section 35A of the Supreme Court Act 1981 on the amount found to be due to the plaintiff at such rate and for such period as the court thinks fit.

AND the plaintiff claims:
1. Damages.
2. The aforesaid interest pursuant to section 35A of the Supreme Court Act 1981 to be assessed.

Ann Summers

EXAMPLE 4 STATEMENT OF CLAIM—FATAL ACCIDENTS ACT CLAIM

IN THE HIGH COURT OF JUSTICE 1985.P.No .

QUEEN'S BENCH DIVISION

BETWEEN LAERTES POLONIUS Plaintiff
(Son and Executor of the estate of Herbert Polonius deceased)
and
HAMLET PRINCE Defendant

STATEMENT OF CLAIM

1. The plaintiff is the son and executor of the estate of Herbert Polonius deceased (hereinafter called 'the deceased') who died on 13 November 1984, probate of the will of the deceased having been granted to him on 1 January 1985 from the Elsinore District Registry. He brings this action on behalf of the estate of the deceased under the provisions of the Law Reform (Miscellaneous Provisions) Act 1934, and on behalf of the dependants of the deceased under the provisions of the Fatal Accidents Act 1976.

2. On 13 November 1984 the deceased was collecting wild flowers by a hedgerow in Arras Lane, Queen's Common, Essex when the defendant drove his Sword sportscar registration number EGO 111 in a southerly direction down Arras Lane in such a negligent fashion that he ran into the deceased, causing him fatal injury.

3. The defendant so negligently drove and controlled the said car that he caused or permitted it to run into the deceased.

PARTICULARS OF NEGLIGENCE

The defendant was negligent in that he:

(i) Drove at a speed that was excessive in the circumstances.
(ii) Failed to keep any or any proper look out for pedestrians.
(iii) Caused or permitted the said car to proceed on the wrong side of the road.
(iv) Drove the said car along a public highway without ensuring that it was in sound and safe mechanical order.
(v) Failed to brake and/or swerve adequately or at all so as to avoid the deceased.

4. Further, in reliance on section 11 of the Civil Evidence Act 1968 the plaintiff will adduce evidence at trial that the defendant was on 13 March 1985 convicted at the Elsinore Crown Court of careless driving contrary to section 3 of the Road Traffic Act 1972, as evidence of the negligence alleged in paragraph 3.

5. By reason of the matters aforesaid, the deceased, who was aged 60 at the date of the accident, sustained severe injuries from which he died on the same day.

PARTICULARS OF INJURIES

The deceased suffered a fracture to his skull, causing severe concussion, and also fractures to several of his ribs, and to his right arm and leg. He suffered severe loss of blood and substantial internal bleeding.

6. By reason of the matters aforesaid, the estate of the deceased and his dependants have suffered loss and damage.

PARTICULARS PURSUANT TO STATUTE

The claim herein under the Fatal Accidents Act is brought on behalf of the following persons:

(i) The plaintiff, now aged 19 years, son of the deceased.
(ii) Ophelia Polonius, now aged 16 years, daughter of the deceased.

At the date of his death the deceased was the sole support of the said children. He was employed as a Senior Civil Servant at an annual salary of £25,000, and allowed £100 per week for the support of the said children.

PARTICULARS OF SPECIAL DAMAGE

Damage to suit	£150
Destroyed brief case	£100
Destroyed umbrella	£ 30
Funeral expenses	£1,500
	£1,780

7. Further, the plaintiff claims interest pursuant to section 35A of the Supreme Court Act 1981 on the amount found to be due to the plaintiff at such rates and for such periods as the court thinks fit.

AND the plaintiff claims:

1. Damages for the estate under the Law Reform (Miscellaneous Provisions) Act 1934.
2. Damages on behalf of the dependants under the Fatal Accidents Act 1976.
3. The aforesaid interest pursuant to section 35A of the Supreme Court Act 1981 to be assessed.

Perry Mason.

EXAMPLE 5 STATEMENT OF CLAIM—WRONGFUL INTERFERENCE WITH GOODS

IN THE HIGH COURT OF JUSTICE 1985.K.No .

QUEEN'S BENCH DIVISION

BETWEEN	SEBASTIAN KNIGHT	Plaintiff
	and	
	ANTONIO CAPTAIN	Defendant

STATEMENT OF CLAIM

1. The plaintiff is and was at all material times the owner of a bag of Krugerrands to the value of £25,000.
2. On 7 January 1985 the plaintiff gave the said bag of Krugerrands to the defendant for safe-keeping.
3. By an oral request made on 1 February 1985 in the Market Place, Illyria, Yorkshire, the plaintiff demanded the return of the said bag of Krugerrands from the defendant, but the defendant failed and refused, and still refuses to deliver it up to the plaintiff.
4. In the premises the plaintiff has suffered loss and damage.

PARTICULARS OF DAMAGE

Value of Krugerrands	£25,000
Value of bag	£ 200
	£25,200

And the plaintiff claims:

1. An order for the return of the said bag of Krugerrands.
2. In the alternative, damages.

N. Lawson.

EXAMPLE 6 STATEMENT OF CLAIM—NUISANCE—*RYLANDS* v *FLETCHER*

IN THE HIGH COURT OF JUSTICE 1985.B.No .

QUEEN'S BENCH DIVISION

BETWEEN	BASIL BANQUO	Plaintiff
	and	
	THE THREE WITCHES SOUP COMPANY LIMITED	Defendant

STATEMENT OF CLAIM

1. The plaintiff is and was at all material times the owner and occupier of a dwelling house at 'Wee Nook', 1, The Heath, Ilkley Moor, Yorkshire. The defendants are and were at all material times the owners and occupiers of land and premises at 2–3, The Heath, Ilkley Moor, Yorkshire, adjoining the plaintiff's premises. At all material times the defendants have carried on the business at this property of manufacturing soup for sale in their chain of health food shops.

2. Since about March 1984 the defendants have wrongfully caused to issue and proceed from their land offensive smells and vapours, soot and other dirty matter which have spread and diffused over the plaintiff's land and dwelling, and the defendants have thereby committed a nuisance to the plaintiff.

3. As a result the plaintiff's house has been rendered unhealthy and uncomfortable to live in, and the plaintiff and his family have thereby been caused annoyance and discomfort and the plaintiff has suffered loss and damage.

PARTICULARS OF SPECIAL DAMAGE

Damage to paintwork of house	£1,000
Damage to plants and trees	£1,000
Loss in value of plaintiff's house	£10,000
	£12,000

4. Further or in the alternative, the matters complained of in paragraph 2 constituted a non-natural user of the defendant's land, and the defendants wrongly failed to prevent the escape of the said smells, vapours, soot and other dirty matter to the plaintiff's land.

5. The defendants threaten and intend unless restrained from so doing to continue to commit the said nuisance.

6. Further, the plaintiff claims interest pursuant to section 35A of the

Supreme Court Act 1981 on the amount found to be due to the plaintiff at such rate and for such period as the court thinks fit.

AND the plaintiff claims:

1. Damages.
2. An injunction restraining the defendants, their servants or agents from continuing the said nuisance.
3. The aforesaid interest pursuant to section 35A of the Supreme Court Act 1981, to be assessed.

Bran Flake.

EXAMPLE 7 DEFENCE TO 1—CONTRIBUTORY NEGLIGENCE—VOLENTI

IN THE HIGH COURT OF JUSTICE 1985.P.No 1234.

QUEEN'S BENCH DIVISION

BETWEEN PERCY PROSPERO Plaintiff

and

ANTONIO ALONSO'S FLYING FUNFAIR Defendant

(a firm)

DEFENCE

1. Paragraphs 1, 2 and 3 of the Statement of Claim are admitted.
2. Save in that it is admitted that the plaintiff fell from the ride to the ground, paragraph 4 of the Statement of Claim is denied.
3. It is denied that the defendants, their servants or agents were negligent as alleged in the Statement of Claim or at all.
4. Further or in the alternative, the alleged accident was caused wholly or in part by the negligence of the plaintiff:

PARTICULARS OF NEGLIGENCE

(i) On taking his seat on the ride, the plaintiff was wearing a personal cassette recorder, and was thus unable to hear any of the instructions given to him by the employees of the defendant operating the ride.
(ii) The plaintiff failed to read and/or pay proper attention to a written notice informing those using the ride of the need to take care.
(iii) The plaintiff failed to ensure that the safety bar over his seat was fastened properly or at all.
(iv) The plaintiff failed to sit properly in his seat so as to avoid being thrown out.
(v) In all the circumstances, the plaintiff failed to take any or any reasonable care for his own safety.

5. No admission is made as to the alleged or any pain, injury, loss or damage suffered by plaintiff, or as to the causation thereof.
6. Further or in the alternative, with full knowledge of the risk of injury or damage to himself in taking the ride referred to in paragraph 2 of the Statement of Claim, the plaintiff voluntarily agreed to accept such risk, and to waive any claim in respect of injury or damage that might be occasioned to him. The plaintiff is therefore not entitled to maintain his claim against the defendant.

Served etc. P. Parrot.

EXAMPLE 8 DEFENCE TO 2—ALLEGATION AGAINST THIRD PARTY

IN THE HIGH COURT OF JUSTICE 1985.S.No 1357

QUEEN'S BENCH DIVISION

BETWEEN DUNCAN SCOTLAND Plaintiff

and

(1) MACDONALD MACBETH

(2) FLORA MACBETH Defendants

and

HECATE'S HANDYMEN LIMITED Third Party

DEFENCE

1. The defendants admit paragraphs 1 and 2 of the Statement of Claim.

2. The defendants make no admission as to paragraph 3 of the Statement of Claim.

3. The defendants deny that the alleged accident was caused by negligence or breach of statutory duty on the part of the defendants as alleged in paragraph 4 of the Statement of Claim or at all.

4. The alleged accident was caused by the negligence of the Third Party, their servants or agents, who were independent contractors who were employed to affix the said ceremonial daggers to the said wall in the course of redecorating the hotel during October 1983, the defendants reasonably and entirely entrusting the said redecoration to them.

PARTICULARS OF NEGLIGENCE

(i) Failing to use an adequate adhesive and/or fixing for the said daggers.

(ii) Failing to take into account the weight of the said daggers in affixing them to the wall.

(iii) Failing to take into account the need to provide a long-term secure fixture for the said daggers.

(iv) Failing to consider adequately or at all the need for safety for those using the hotel when deciding to use the said daggers as decoration.

5. The defendants make no admissions as to any of the matters alleged in paragraphs 5 or 6 of the Statement of claim.

Served etc. R. Burns

EXAMPLE 9 THIRD PARTY NOTICE RELATED TO 8

IN THE HIGH COURT OF JUSTICE 1985.S.No 1357.

QUEEN'S BENCH DIVISION

BETWEEN DUNCAN SCOTLAND Plaintiff

and

(1) MACDONALD MACBETH

(2) FLORA MACBETH Defendants

and

HECATE'S HANDYMEN LIMITED Third Party

THIRD PARTY NOTICE

Issued pursuant to the order of Master Banquo dated 1 March 1985.

To Hecate's Handymen Limited of 13, Blasted Heath Industrial Estate, Birnham Beeches, Berkshire.

Take notice that this action has been brought by the Plaintiff against the Defendants. In it the Plaintiff claims against the Defendants damages for negligence and/or breach of statutory duty, as appears from the Statement of Claim, a copy whereof is delivered herewith, together with a copy of the Writ of Summons.

The defendants claim against you to be indemnified against the Plaintiff's claim and the costs of this action, or a contribution to the Plaintiff's claim on the grounds that:

1. By a written contract dated 1 August 1983 between you and the defendants, you agreed to undertake repairs and redecoration work at the Plaintiff's premises known as 'The Thane of Cawdor Hotel', Dunsinane Hill, Birnham Beeches, Berkshire, for a total cost of £7,777.

2. It was an express term of the said contract that you would choose appropriate decorations for the said hotel, and that you would guarantee the quality thereof, and would indemnify the defendants in respect of any liability, loss or damage that the defendants might incur or suffer arising out of or connected with any defect in the said repair or redecoration work, provided such defect was due to any negligence or omission of yourself, your servants or agents.

3. The matters complained of by the Plaintiff were caused wholly or in part or contributed to by the negligence of yourself, your servants or agents in carrying out the said repairs and redecoration.

PARTICULARS OF NEGLIGENCE

(i) Failing to use an adequate adhesive and/or fixing for the said daggers.

(ii) Failing to take into account the weight of the said daggers in affixing them to the wall.

(iii) Failing to take into account the need to provide a long term secure fixture for the said daggers.
(iv) Failing to consider adequately or at all the need for safety for those using the hotel when deciding to use the said daggers as decoration.

4. By reason of the matters aforesaid, the defendants have suffered loss and damage.

PARTICULARS OF SPECIAL DAMAGE

Damage to antique daggers	£500
Cost of redecoration	£1,000
	£1,500

And take notice.....

R. Burns.

Advising and drafting in a trust action

Although the basic principles of advising and drafting will apply in a trust case as much as any other, a slightly different approach and emphasis will sometimes be needed, and there are some areas of particular complexity. The young lawyer going into a Chancery practice will learn to deal with the more complex problems as he goes along, but this chapter gives a guide to some of the ways in which a trust case is different from other types of case.

There are broadly two types of action that may be brought in connection with a settlement or trust: the first is the originating summons type of action where there is some doubt as to the validity of the trust or the powers contained in it, the second is the statement of claim action, which will generally arise where a beneficiary wishes to challenge the actions of a trustee or of another beneficiary. Whether the trust arises from a will, a document coming into operation during life or on death or from something said or done, the lawyer will first have to decide which type of action is appropriate, and guidance for this was given in the chapters dealing with the use of the originating summons and the statement of claim.

In deciding which type of action is appropriate, the lawyer will have to identify very specifically what the problem or problems are—whether they relate to the validity of the trust as a whole or of terms of it, whether it is a matter of the use of a power given by the trust or by statute, or whether it is some particular action that is complained of. It is probably a good discipline for the young lawyer to make a point of listing the problems that arise in numbered order on a piece of paper, and also to note down exactly what the property in dispute is, and the role of any person mentioned in his instructions to identify them as a trustee, beneficiary or potential claimant. A trust action may involve more people and more complexities than other types of cases, and the lawyer must always keep the elements of the case clear in his mind.

A trust case may have a different feel to it from a contract or tort case because it will often not be adversarial in the way they are, and a case will often turn on the interpretation of words rather than facts. If the lawyer is acting for a trustee, the trustee will often not have a personal interest in the outcome of the case, but will just wish to have certainty as to what he should do with property. Therefore the lawyer will be asked for purely objective advice, generally paid for from the trust fund, but he will have to advise going to court if there is any real doubt about what should happen to any valuable part of the trust property to protect the trustee from personal liability.

If the lawyer is acting for a beneficiary, there will be a more adversarial approach in the need to build up arguments as to why a disposition favouring the client is valid, and why a disposition favouring anyone else is not. Even the lawyer representing a trustee will have to anticipate arguments that beneficiaries may raise as to what is valid—remembering that where substantial property is at stake potential beneficiaries may well argue very strongly, especially where there are personal feelings at stake as well, for example a wife arguing that a mistress should not be entitled to any provision. Some potential beneficiaries would rather litigate until a fund is exhausted rather than let anyone else get anything (though as in any other case the lawyer must keep the client informed of the costs position).

Although it may not be as important as in other types of case, procedural, evidential and practical matters should be born in mind. Evidence may be very important if a trust is alleged to have arisen from something said or done rather than from a document, and full statements from those present and other relevant evidence must be collected. Practical points may include the possibility of settling an action by agreeing a division of property (which may not be possible if for example there is a question whether a cause is charitable or not and this has to be decided on), or giving advice on the possible effects of tax when a trust is set up, when someone dies, or when property passes to a beneficiary.

Dealing precisely with property rights

One of the most important things in a trust action is giving specific advice as to what should happen to each item of property in dispute, as this will be the main thing that every trustee and beneficiary is interested in. If there is a clearly valid disposition in a document or because of what has happened then the lawyer can advise on that, but if there is any doubt as to what should happen to any part of the property involved then every possibility and alternative must be explored, and every possible recipient clearly stated, with what they might hope to get.

In doing this it may be useful to draw a 'family tree' or flow chart, dividing to trace each possibility of what may happen to the property. The diagram may get complicated, but if there is any possibility that any part of any disposition may fail it is vital to explore who the property may go to instead. Such a diagram giving all the options can form the basis for drafting a question in an originating summons.

If a disposition in a lifetime settlement may fail, there may be the following chain of possibilities in a diagram:

Specific disposition of property to person or body

↓

A further specific disposition to some other person or body in the settlement

↓

A resulting trust back to the settlor or his estate

↓

A further disposition of his property made by the settlor in life or on death.

If a disposition in a will fails, there may be a slightly different chain of possibilities, as follows:

Specific disposition of property to a person or body
↓
A further specific disposition to some other person or body in the will
↓
Falling into residue, the property may pass to the one entitled to the residue
↓
If it does not fall into residue, or there is no provision for residue, property may pass to the next of kin

Most of these possibilities will depend on the wording of a disposition or events which have happened, but some possibilities are imposed by statute, such as the rules on intestacy and the possibility of the court ordering provision for dependants. On death a person is entitled to leave all their property as they wish by will, but to the extent that there is no will, or it does not fully deal with all the property left by the deceased, the property will pass to the next of kin. The rules specify what relative will get what share of the property, and depend on what relatives the deceased leaves and the size of his estate.

(a) If the deceased leaves a spouse, but no children, parents, brothers, sisters, nephews or nieces, the spouse will take the whole estate.
(b) If the deceased leaves children but no spouse, then the children will take the whole estate in equal shares.
(c) If the deceased leaves a spouse and children, then the spouse takes all the personal chattels and the first £40,000 of the estate, with a life-interest in half of the estate above that figure. The children take the other half equally, taking the half in which the spouse has an interest on the spouse's death.
(d) If the deceased leaves a spouse and relatives other than children, the spouse takes the personal chattels and the first £60,000 of the estate, with half the excess above that, the rest of the excess going absolutely to the closest relatives equally.
(e) If the deceased leaves neither spouse nor children, his estate goes to his closest relatives equally.

If a relative has died before the intestacy, their share will go to their children, and there are other rules which the lawyer can research as they arise in practice. The figures for the entitlement of a surviving spouse are raised by order from time to time.

Whether property passes under a will or on intestacy, specific categories of people who were dependent on the deceased may apply for the court to order provision under the Inheritance (Provision for Family and Dependants) Act 1976. A lawyer advising on what will happen to property on death should bear in mind the possiblity of an application being made under this Act by anyone.

An originating summons action

Basically an originating summons action will be appropriate where there are doubts about the validity of a trust, or what can be done under the powers contained in it. Such an action should not be necessary if a will or trust document is drawn up with proper care in the first place, but it may arise where a trust depends on a document drawn up without proper advice, or on something done or said. As was said before, it is essential to identify clearly what property is at stake, who are the trustees and beneficiaries, and what all the possible alternatives are (see Examples 1 and 2).

The first point will be whether the trust is valid at all, that is whether it has complied with all the necessary requirements. It is of course quite possible to create a trust purely orally or by actions, the only problem then being proof, but a will has to comply with the requirements of the Wills Act 1837, and a trust in land or dealing with an existing equitable interest will have to be in writing, Law of Property Act 1925, ss.40, 53. A private trust will also have to have the necessary certainties, and the one that arises most in practice is the need for certainty of beneficiaries, *McPhail* v *Doulton* [1971] AC 424, and the lawyer may have to consider whether a relatively wide clause is valid, *Re Barlow* [1979] 1 All ER 296, or whether potential uncertainty may be resolved by giving someone a power to make decisions, *Re Tuck* [1978] 1 All ER 1047.

If the trust is possibly charitable, it will not have to comply with the need for certainty, nor will property have to vest within a perpetuity period, but it will have to come within one of the accepted heads of charity and have any necessary degree of public benefit. The lawyer will have to prepare his arguments on these points, not least because of the tax advantages available to charities, and because the public concept of what is charitable is not the same as the legal concept, for example it has been held that Amnesty International is not charitable, because of the political element in its aims, *McGovern* v *Attorney General* [1981] 3 All ER 493. If the trust is basically charitable but there is some difficulty such as too little money or that an intended beneficiary has ceased to exist, the lawyer will also have to consider and advise on the possibility of a cy pres scheme under the inherent power of the court or the Charities Act 1961, s.13. He should consider whether it will be necessary and possible to show a general charitable intent, and also make inquiries as to what kind of scheme would be possible.

In considering every possible way in which the trust may be valid, it is clearly best if it is charitable because of the tax advantages and the fact that the certainty and perpetuity rules do not apply, but if it is not charitable it may still be valid as a private purpose trust if it comes within one of the special categories of trusts for specific animals or for masses or tombs and satisfies the perpetuity rules. Alternatively, the trust may be valid as a purpose trust as in *Re Denley* [1969] 1 Ch 373 provided it satisfies the perpetuity rules, or as a private trust if the rules of certainty and perpetuity are satisfied.

The other area of validity of trusts that has increased in importance over recent years is that of implied, resulting and constructive trusts. Such trusts will often involve an interpretation of facts rather than documents. As examples, a resulting trust may arise where property is voluntarily transferred without directions as to how it should be used, or where property held on trust is not fully disposed of. Where a person in a fiduciary position gains an advantage from his position a constructive trust may arise, and when one person gains an interest in property legally owned by another an implied or constructive trust may arise. These types of trust were developed by Lord Denning, but now that he has gone from the Court of Appeal there may be more reluctance in the Court to hold that a trust has arisen, see *Burns* v *Burns* [1984] 1 All ER 244. The lawyer will have to advise not only on whether there is a chance that a trust has arisen, but also on the size of interest in the property each person has, and whether their interest is a set sum or a proportion of the value of the asset. It may be necessary to ask for the asset to be sold for the client to realise their interest.

There are some other special types of trust, which are not all that common in practice. A secret or half-secret trust may arise where there is the necessary communication and acceptance of terms. There are special rules for mutual wills, protective trusts and so on that the lawyer going into a specialist practice may have to deal with.

In looking at the different possibilities of how a trust may be valid the lawyer may need to develop arguments if his client has a particular interest in the trust being valid or invalid. For example it may sometimes be possible to persuade the court to strike out certain words that would make the trust invalid, though this will be done rarely, *Re Woodhams* [1981] 1 All ER 202.

An originating summons action may also involve a problem with the administration of the trust, if one is asking the court to construe whether there is a power in the trust to carry out a certain transaction or not, or where one is asking the court to approve a particular transaction that the trustees do not otherwise have the power to carry out. An example of this can be seen in the examples of drafting (see Example 3).

A statement of claim action

A statement of claim will normally be appropriate in a trust action where there is no doubt about the validity of a trust or the powers of the trustees under it, but where there has been some breach of powers under an existing trust by trustees. However, it may also be appropriate where there is a real dispute of fact, for example as to whether an implied, constructive or resulting trust has arisen. The approach to a statement of claim action in ascertaining facts and collecting evidence will be similar to tort and contract (for drafting, see Examples 4, 5 and 6).

The lawyer advising a beneficiary will have to advise on whether there has been a breach of trust, who to sue, and what remedies are appropriate. The first and last of these points will be considered in more detail later, but generally speaking a trustee will be strictly liable for any breach of trust and he should be sued unless the breach is technical, little will actually be recovered or negotiation is possible. Any beneficiary can sue, as the proceeds will go back into the trust, and generally all the trustees should be sued as they will be jointly and severally liable, unless this is not justified on the facts. It may be possible to sue someone other than the trustees. For example, a beneficiary of a trust may be liable for a breach and may have his interest impounded if he suggested the breach or consented to it in writing. An agent of the trustees or some other person may be open to an action in tort or contract, if for example they have given negligent advice. Alternatively such a person may be a constructive trustee if they have actually received trust property.

The lawyer representing a trustee will need to investigate whether on the law and facts there has been a breach, and should see what has happened to any property that left the trust. There is a statutory defence for a trustee who has acted honestly and reasonably in all the circumstances, Trustee Act 1925, s.61. It may also be possible that some other person who advised or helped the trustee should be made a party to the action, and held liable for what has been lost.

The administration of a trust

All sorts of problems can arise as to whether trustees have the power to carry out a particular transaction or the court will authorise it (a matter of interpreting the trust and statutory provisions, normally raised in court in an originating summons action), or as to whether trustees have abused their powers (a matter of interpreting those powers and looking at the facts, normally raised in court in a statement of claim). The details of the law on administering a trust will have to be researched for the individual case, but some of the most important areas are as follows. As well as statutory powers, the court has inherent powers to help with the administration of a trust, and under RSC Order 85 has wide powers to help with the administration of the estate of a deceased.

Trustees must be properly appointed and removed. The original trustees will be appointed by the trust instrument or will arise from the facts. New trustees can be appointed by the trustees themselves under the trust instrument or the Trustee Act 1925, ss.36, 39, and this should be done if necessary. If the help of the court is needed, the court can appoint new trustees under the Trustee Act 1925, s.41 or its inherent power. The trust property must be properly vested in the new trustees. If there is any problem with an existing trustee, his removal and replacement should of course be considered.

The trustees must invest the trust property properly, and in days of inflation, high interest rates and a wide variety of possible investments this can be a real problem. They will have any powers of investment given to them by the trust instrument, which will have to be read carefully, but otherwise their powers are restricted by the Trustee Act 1925 and the Trustee Investment Act 1961, because of the need to protect beneficiaries and stop the trustees speculating unwisely. The trustees will have to take proper advice and divide the trust fund if necessary, as well as investing in something proper. If the investment powers of the trust are too narrow, the courts may authorise a particular investment or a change in the trust under the Trustee Act 1925, s.57, and have recently shown that they are sympathetic to the need for wider investment powers in suitable cases, *Mason* v *Farbrother* [1983] 2 All ER 1078 and *Trustees of the British Museum* v *Attorney-General* [1984] 1 All ER 337.

Because of the strict limits on their powers of investment, trustees must be advised to act within their powers or get the approval of the court to avoid personal liability. A trustee must never get any benefit from his position as trustee, beyond any remuneration properly authorised, and must be advised on how strict this duty is. If a trustee does, for example, wish to purchase trust property, he should only do so with the consent of all the beneficiaries or the court, and must be completely open in seeking consent.

As for giving the trust property to the beneficiaries, the trustee must again act within the strict confines of the powers given to him by the trust instrument, or the statutory powers of maintenance and advancement provided by the Trustee Act 1925, ss.31, 32. The entitlement of each beneficiary must be checked properly, distinguishing clearly between entitlement to capital and income, and the rights of different types of beneficiaries such as a tenant for life and remaindermen. If the trustee has any discretion, it is open to him to exercise it, but otherwise if there is any doubt as to possible entitlement it must be referred to the court, to protect the trustee.

Normally a trustee must personally use the care and skill of the ordinary prudent man of business in exercising all his powers and duties (or a higher standard if he is a professional trustee) and will be personally liable if anything goes wrong. He may appoint an agent under the terms of the trust, or under the Trustee Act 1925, s.23, and if he does so, he should not be liable for the acts of the agent if he acts in good faith (though there is some doubt as to the inter-relation of s.23 and s.30 of the Act). Here, as in all other areas, the trustee must be advised to act carefully and within the limits of his powers to avoid possible personal liability.

Possible remedies

An originating summons may only wish to seek the determination of the court on various areas of doubt, but every possible type of relief sought should be specified, see the dicta in *Belmont Finance Corporation* v *Williams Furniture* [1979] Ch 250.

The court does have a variety of powers to make orders in connection with a trust by statute, the rules of court, and under inherent powers, and several of the main possibilities such as appointing and removing trustees, authorising transactions and approving cy pres schemes have already been mentioned. If any such order is sought it must be specifically asked for in the pleading, with the statutory section quoted if necessary.

More generally, a remedy that will often be sought for breach of trust is damages, that is, that an account be prepared of the loss to the trust and an order that the sum found due be paid back into the trust. Advice will have to be given on how damages will be quantified and what will be recoverable, trying to give as exact a figure as possible, as in any other action, and the appropriate facts and figures will have to be pleaded. The situation may be complicated if there has been an unauthorised investment or a misapplication of trust funds, and the lawyer may have to develop detailed arguments as to how loss should be quantified. Interest may be claimed, and a high rate of interest may be awarded in a case of fraud, or where the trust has been deprived of a commercial rate of interest, *Bartlett* v *Barclays Bank Trust Co. (No 2)* [1980] Ch 515.

If trust property has been misapplied, the best remedy may be tracing to recover the property itself, especially if it has gone up in value, or the trustee may be unable to pay damages (see Example 6). It is thus worth investigating what has happened to trust property if there is a chance that it has not been dissipated. Trust property may also be recoverable if a constructive trust has arisen, or in a case of fraud, see *Bankers Trust Co.* v *Shapira* [1980] 3 All ER 353.

A declaration may be made, for example as to whether a trust has arisen, or what property is subject to a trust. An injunction, especially an interlocutory one, may be useful to stop further breaches of trust, or to stop trust property being dissipated. An account may be sought where it is not clear what a trustee owes. Other remedies may also be appropriate in a trust action, for example an order for specific performance or the appointment of a receiver.

Drafting points

The young lawyer often finds drafting in a trust case more difficult than in contract or tort, not because the basic principles are very different, but because it can be more difficult to decide who should be parties and to produce a concise and logical draft that isolates the problem that has arisen, or gives all the alternatives in an originating summons. A real ability to do this can only come with practice, but it can be built up from clear thinking and careful analysis of whether there is a trust, what its terms are and so on. This approach in reading the brief and advising the client should result in a clear draft.

As regards parties, in any action concerning the validity of the trust or the administration of it, the trustees will normally be the plaintiffs, and any person or body with any possible interest in the trust property will need to be joined as defendants, whether their interest arises under the terms of the trust, because they are next of kin or otherwise. If people have slightly different interests, they must be joined separately, even though they may in fact choose to be represented by the same lawyer at trial, or not be represented at all.

The possibilities of representative orders were considered in the chapter on originating summonses. They should be used where possible to keep down costs, and applied for in the pleading. However, only people with a direct claim to property need to be joined, and if for example property is left to the trustee for him to distribute 'among the inhabitants of Stratford upon Avon', there is no need to appoint someone to represent the inhabitants as they are not a legal entity, and have no direct claim but are merely the objects of a purpose. However, this is an area where it is difficult to be categoric as different lawyers might well make different decisions as to who to join. A party should not be joined where there is no need as this will inflate costs, but if there is any real doubt as to whether they should be joined, they may be put in to ensure that they have a chance to be heard, and will be bound by the decision of the court.

An incorporated charity may be made a party in the same way as any company, but an unincorporated charity or association will have to be joined by making a treasurer or secretary a party to represent it. If there is any question as to the validity of a disposition to a charitable purpose, or some other purpose trust, the Attorney-General should be made a party to the action. This is not necessary where the property is left to a body which is clearly charitable, such as Oxfam, where the only question is whether the charity gets the money or not, and the charity itself should be a party.

The need for an 'In the matter of. . .' heading in a trust action and how it should be worded were dealt with in the chapter on originating summonses, as were the other formal parts of the draft of an originating summons. Some simple examples of originating summonses follow.

EXAMPLE 1 ORIGINATING SUMMONS—VALIDITY OF DISPOSITIONS IN A WILL—CHARITY

IN THE HIGH COURT OF JUSTICE Ch. 1985.C.No .

CHANCERY DIVISION

In the matter of the trusts of the will dated 15 March 1981 of J. Caesar, deceased.

BETWEEN(1) MARK ANTHONY
(2) CALPURNIA CAESAR Plaintiffs

and

(1) SOOTH SAYER
(2) ROMA PARVA DISTRICT COUNCIL
(3) MARCUS BRUTUS
(4) HER MAJESTY'S ATTORNEY-GENERAL
Defendants

TO (1) Sooth Sayer of 1, Forum Court, Town Square, Roma Parva, who appears to represent those persons living in Roma Parva who may be beneficially interested under the trusts of the will;

(2) Roma Parva District Council of The Town Hall, Roma Parva, who may be entitled to property as trustees under the will;

(3) Marcus Brutus of Orchard House, Roma Parva who may be beneficially interested or entitled to property as a trustee under the will;

And to Her Majesty's Attorney-General.

LET The Defendants. . . (directions as to acknowledgement of service).

BY this summons, which is issued on the application of the plaintiffs, Mark Anthony of 3, Bury Court, Roma Parva and Calpurnia Caesar of Tiber Manor, Roma Parva, the executors and trustees of the estate of Julius Caesar deceased, the plaintiffs seek the determination of the court on the following questions, and the following relief, namely:

1. That it may be determined whether in the true construction of clause 2 of the will the sum of £50,000 is held;

(i) On a fixed trust for the inhabitants of Roma Parva on the date of the death of the deceased.

(ii) On discretionary trust for the inhabitants of Roma Parva at the date of the death of the deceased.

(iii) On trust for those entitled to the residuary estate.

(iv) On any other, and if so what, trusts.

2. If the answer to paragraph 1 is in sense (i) or (ii), that such directions and inquiries as are necessary may be made to determine what persons may properly be considered to be inhabitants of Roma Parva at the date of the death of the deceased.

3. That it may be determined whether on the true construction of clause 3 of the will the property known as Tiber Manor, Roma Parva is held:

(i) On trust to be transferred to the second defendant on a valid charitable trust.

(ii) On trust to be transferred to the second defendant on a valid purpose trust.

(iii) On trust for those entitled to the residuary estate.

(iv) On any other, and if so what, trusts.

4. That it may be determined whether on the true construction of clause 4 of the will, and in the events which have happened, the sum of £20,000 is held:

(i) On trust for the third defendant absolutely for his own use.

(ii) On trust for the third defendant to be held on valid charitable trust.

(iii) On trust for the third defendant to be held on such non-charitable trust as the court may determine.

(iv) On trust for those entitled to the residuary estate.

(v) On any other, and if so what, trusts.

5. If the answer to paragraph 2 is in the sense (ii), that the court may approve a scheme for the application of the said £20,000.

6. That the first defendant may be appointed to represent all persons claiming to be inhabitants of Roma Parva at the date of the death of the deceased.

7. If, and so far as may be necessary, administration of the estate of the deceased.

8. That provision may be made for the costs of this application.

9. Further or other relief.

Settled by Cyril Cicero

Affidavit in support of the originating summons in 1

IN THE HIGH COURT OF JUSTICE Ch. 1985.C.No

CHANCERY DIVISION

In the matter of the trusts of the will dated 15 March 1981 of J. Caesar, deceased.

BETWEEN(1) MARK ANTHONY
(2) CALPURNIA CAESAR Plaintiffs
and
(1) SOOTH SAYER
(2) ROMA PARVA DISTRICT COUNCIL

(3) MARCUS BRUTUS
(4) HER MAJESTY'S ATTORNEY-GENERAL

Defendants

I, Mark Anthony, of 3, Bury Court, Roma Parva, Gloucestershire, the first plaintiff in this action, make oath and say as follows:

1. I have been a close friend and business associate of the deceased for some 15 years. The matters that I depose to herein are all within my knowledge, or have come to my knowledge in the course of the administration of the estate of the deceased in my capacity as executor and trustee.

2. By his will, dated 15 March 1981, the deceased appointed myself and the second plaintiff to be the executors and trustees thereof, and after directing the payment of his debts and all funeral and testamentary expenses, and giving certain specific legacies which he directed to be paid free of all capital transfer tax, dealt with his estate as follows:

'Clause 2. I hereby give the sum of £50,000 to my executors and trustees to be divided equally among such people as they decide were the inhabitants of Roma Parva at the date of my death.

Clause 3. I give the house, lands, orchards and estate known as Tiber Manor, Roma Parva to the Roma Parva District Council to be used as a public park where all the poor people of Roma Parva can get fit and healthy.

Clause 4. I give £20,000 to my honourable old friend, Marcus Brutus'.

3. The testator died on 15 March 1985 without having altered or revoked the said will, which was proved by the first plaintiff and the second plaintiff, the executors named therein, at the Roma Parva District Registry on 31 March 1985.

4. There is now produced and shown to me marked "M.A.1" a letter which the deceased wrote to the third defendant on 1 January 1985, in which the testator purported to direct the third defendant to give any money he received under the deceased's will to the Order of the Vestal Virgins. The said Order had in fact been closed down on 1 June 1984 due to the lack of suitable candidates to enter it.

5. The gross value of the estate of the testator was sworn for probate at the sum of £900,000, and I estimate that after the payment of his funeral and testamentary expenses and debts, the specific legacies bequeathed by his will and the capital transfer tax thereon, his remaining real and personal estate will amount to approximately £700,000.

6. The testator was married once only, namely to the second defendant, who is entitled to so much of the testator's estate as passes on intestacy. The testator had no children.

Sworn etc.

EXAMPLE 2 ORIGINATING SUMMONS—LIFETIME SETTLEMENT—CONSTRUCTION

IN THE HIGH COURT OF JUSTICE Ch. 1985.A.No .

CHANCERY DIVISION

IN THE MATTER of a settlement dated 1 April 1984 made between Andrew Aguecheek and Malvolio Steward.

BETWEEN

MALVOLIO STEWARD Plaintiff

and

(1) TOBIAS BELCH
(2) OLIVIA ILLYRIA
(3) MARIA MARLENE
(4) FESTE CLOWNE Defendants

TO (1) Tobias Belch of The Manor, Upper Wallop, Somerset, (2) Olivia Illyria of The Manor, Upper Wallop, Somerset, and (3) Maria Marlene of The Manor, Upper Wallop, Somerset, all of whom claim to be beneficially entitled under the terms of the said settlement, and

(4) Feste Clowne of The Manor, Upper Wallop, Somerset, who appears to represent the friends of the said Andrew Aguecheek who may be beneficially entitled under the terms of the said settlement.

LET the defendants. . . (directions as to acknowledgement of service)

BY this summons, which is issued on the application of the plaintiff, Malvolio Steward of Porter's Lodge, The Manor, Upper Wallop, Somerset, the trustee of the above-mentioned settlement, the plaintiff seeks the determination of the court on the following questions and the following relief namely:

1. That it may be determined whether on the true construction of clause 2 of the said settlement, the trust to provide the first defendant with an annuity for the rest of his life sufficient to keep him constantly supplied with alcohol is valid or void for uncertainty or otherwise.

2. That it may be determined whether on the true construction of clause 3 of the said settlement the sum of £50,000 is held;

(i) On trust for the third defendant absolutely.

(ii) On trust for the third defendant as to £10,000 for herself absolutely and as to £40,000 on trust.

(iii) On trust for the second defendant as the person entitled to any property not otherwise disposed of by the said settlement.

(iv) On some other, and if so what, trusts.

3. If the answer to paragraph 2 is in the sense (ii), that it may be

determined whether on the true construction of paragraph 3 of the said settlement, the sum of £40,000 is held:

(i) On a valid trust to be divided equally between the friends of the settlor whom the third defendant considers deserve it for their wit.

(ii) On a valid discretionary trust for the friends of the settlor whom the third defendant considers deserve it for their wit.

(iii) On trust for the second defendant as the person entitled to any property not otherwise disposed of by the said settlement.

4. That the fourth defendant may be appointed to represent the friends of the settlor who may be entitled under clause 3 of the said settlement.

5. That provision may be made for the costs of this application.

6. Further or other relief.

Settled by Iva D. Nuff.

Affidavit in support of the originating summons in 2

IN THE HIGH COURT OF JUSTICE Ch. 1985.A.No

CHANCERY DIVISION

IN THE MATTER of a settlement dated 1 April 1984 between Andrew Aguecheek and Malvolio Steward.

BETWEEN Plaintiff

MALVOLIO STEWARD

and

TOBIAS BELCH and others Defendants

I, Malvolio Steward of Porter's Lodge, The Manor, Upper Wallop, Somerset, the plaintiff in this action, make oath and say as follows:

1. The above mentioned settlement dated 1 April 1984 was made between Andrew Aguecheek (hereinafter called the settlor) on the one part, and myself on the other part. By the settlement, the settlor put £100,000 in trust, and appointed myself as sole trustee of the trust. The £100,000 was paid to me on the same day.

2. The terms of the settlement provided as follows:

'Clause 2. As to one-half of the trust fund, this is to be used to provide my old friend Toby Belch with an annuity for the rest of his life which is sufficient to keep him constantly supplied with alcohol.
Clause 3. As to the other half of the trust fund, this is to be given to Maria Marlene, to keep £10,000 for herself, and to divide the rest among those friends I have whom she thinks most deserve it for their wit.
Clause 4. Any part of the trust fund which is not disposed of by the above gifts is to go to Olivia Illyria, the most beautiful girl in the world.'

3. I know from my own experience as an employee at The Manor, Upper Wallop, Somerset where the said Tobias Belch presently resides that the sum of £50,000 is barely sufficient to provide an annuity large enough to keep the said Toby Belch constantly in alcohol.

4. I have recently been advised by Maria Marlene and verily believe that the settlor had said that he had no friends in the world save the people he knew at The Manor, Upper Wallop.

5. Following an argument at The Manor, Upper Wallop on 25 December 1984 the settlor left The Manor, and despite all efforts I have been unable to contact him. I therefore seek the assistance of this Honourable Court in dealing with the trust fund.

Sworn etc.

EXAMPLE 3 ORIGINATING SUMMONS—SEEKING THE ASSISTANCE OF THE COURT IN MANAGING THE TRUST

IN THE HIGH COURT OF JUSTICE Ch. 1985.S.No .

CHANCERY DIVISION

In the matter of the trusts of the will dated 1 November 1981 of S. Shylock, deceased.

BETWEEN TOPOL TURBAL Plaintiff

and

(1) JESSICA VENETIAN
(2) LORENZO VENETIAN
(3) LAUNCELOT VENETIAN (a minor) Defendants

TO (1) Jessica Venetian of 15, Merchant Terrace, Little Venice, London, the tenant for life under the said will,
(2) Lorenzo Venetian of 15, Merchant Terrace, Little Venice, London, who appears to represent the unborn children of the first defendant,
(3) Launcelot Venetian of 15, Merchant Terrace, Little Venice, London, a remainderman under the said will.

LET the defendants. . .

BY this summons, which is issued on the application of the plaintiff, Topol Turbal of 10, David Court, London E1, executor and trustee of the above-mentioned will, the plaintiff seeks the following relief, namely:

1. That, notwithstanding the absence of any power conferred on the trustee for the purpose under the above-mentioned will, the court may approve the application of the sum of £40,000 from the funds of the trusts of the will as a personal loan to the first defendant to enable her to commence a business.
2. That the court may approve the purchase by the plaintiff of the property known as Shalom House, Little Venice, London, currently property subject to the trusts of the above-mentioned will for a price of £100,000, notwithstanding his position as a trustee of the will.
3. That the second defendant may be appointed to represent the unborn children of the first defendant.
4. That provision may be made for the costs of this application.
5. Further or other relief.

This application is made under section 57 of the Trustee Act 1925.

Settled by I. Costa-Lott

EXAMPLE 4 STATEMENT OF CLAIM—FACTS IN DISPUTE—POSSIBLE CONSTRUCTIVE TRUST

IN THE HIGH COURT OF JUSTICE Ch. 1985.A.No .

CHANCERY DIVISION

BETWEEN MARK ANTHONY Plaintiff

and

CLEOPATRA PTOLEMY Defendant

STATEMENT OF CLAIM

1. The defendant is and was at all material times the legal owner of the property known as Palace House, Alexandria Road, London S.W.33, (hereinafter called 'Palace House'). Palace House is currently valued at approximately £95,000.

2. On 13 September 1977 the plaintiff first met the defendant, and on 14 February 1977 it was orally agreed between them that:

(i) The plaintiff should occupy Palace House jointly with the defendant
(ii) That the plaintiff should carry out repairs and improvements on Palace House, which was then in a dilapidated condition, to the value of £15,000
(iii) That from 1 March 1977 the plaintiff and the defendant should contribute equally to the mortgage repayments on Palace House.

3. On 14 February, pursuant to the said agreement, the plaintiff entered into occupation of Palace House, and lived there with the defendant as husband and wife until 14 February 1981.

4. Pursuant to the said agreement, from 1 March 1977 to 1 March 1981 the plaintiff made payments to the defendant each month of a sum equal to one half of the mortgage repayments, the said mortgage repayments being £300 per month in total.

5. Further, pursuant to the said agreement, the plaintiff began to carry out the repair and improvement work on Palace House agreed by the parties.

6. On 14 February 1981 the plaintiff ceased to occupy Palace House and ceased to contribute to the mortgage repayments. However, he continued to visit the defendant from time to time, and completed the agreed repair and improvement work.

7. On 14 February 1985 the defendant orally informed the plaintiff that she intended to sell Palace House as soon as possible, and to use the entire proceeds of sale for her own purposes.

AND the plaintiff claims:

1. A declaration that the plaintiff is entitled to a beneficial interest in Palace House, Alexandria Road, London SW33 of one third, or such other share as the court may determine.
2. A declaration that the defendant holds Palace House, Alexandria Road, London SW33 on trust for herself and the plaintiff in such proportions as the court may determine.
3. An injunction restraining the defendant from selling the property of Palace House, Alexandria Road, London SW33 before judgment in this action or further order.
4. Further or other relief.
5. Costs.

I. Isis.

EXAMPLE 5 STATEMENT OF CLAIM—BREACH OF TRUSTEE'S DUTIES

IN THE HIGH COURT OF JUSTICE Ch. 1985.B.No .

CHANCERY DIVISION

In the matter of the trusts of the will dated 1 May 1980 of R. de Boys, deceased.

BETWEEN ORLANDO DE BOYS Plaintiff

and

OLIVER DE BOYS Defendant

STATEMENT OF CLAIM

1. The defendant is the sole executor and trustee of the will dated 1 May 1980 of Roland de Boys deceased, who died on 1 June 1980. Probate of the said will was granted to the defendant on 1 July 1980 at the Arden District Registry.
2. Under clause 2 of the will, the deceased directed that his entire estate was to be held on trust in equal shares for his three sons, namely the plaintiff, the defendant and one Jaques de Boys.
3. There was no power in the said will for the trust funds to be invested otherwise than as authorised by law, and there was no power for the trustee to appoint an agent to manage the trust otherwise than as authorised by law.
4. During April 1983, in breach of trust, the defendant invested £200,000 of the trust funds in the purchase of ordinary shares in As You Like It Lingerie Ltd. The said shares were not an investment authorised by law for the investment of the trust funds in that the total issued and paid up share capital of the said company was less than £1,000,000, and in that the said company had not in the five years immediately preceding the purchase, or in each or any of the said five years paid a dividend on all or any of its issued shares.
5. Further or in the alternative, the defendant invested the said £200,000 in breach of trust in that he failed to obtain and/or consider proper advice as to whether the said investment was satisfactory before making it, and/or in that he made the investment without regard to the suitability for the trust of that description of investment, and/or the suitability of the investment as an investment of that description.
6. Further, in breach of his duty as trustee, on or about 3 May 1984, the defendant improperly appointed one Frederick Duke to act as his agent in the management of the trust.

PARTICULARS OF BREACH

(i) The defendant failed to make any or any proper inquiries as to the competence of the said Frederick Duke.
(ii) The defendant failed to make any or any proper inquiries as to the qualifications of the said Frederick Duke.
(iii) The defendant failed to keep any or any adequate check on the activities of the said Frederick Duke in the management of the trust.

7. In fact the said Frederick Duke had no qualifications at all, and was not competent to act, being at the time of his appointment the defendant to proceedings for breach of trust by the beneficiaries of the Duke of Arden's estate. The defendant knew or ought to have known of these matters by reason of his business association with the said Frederick Duke over a number of years. As a result of the incompetence and neglect of the said Frederick Duke the value of the trust funds has been substantially reduced.

8. By reason of the matters aforesaid, the trust funds have been substantially reduced, and have suffered loss and damage.

PARTICULARS

Loss suffered on shares in As You Like It Lingerie Ltd	£150,000
Reduction in capital of trust since 3rd May 1984	£200,000
	£350,000

9. Further the plaintiff claims interest pursuant to section 35A of the Supreme Court Act 1981 on the amount found to be due to the plaintiff at such rate and for such period as the court thinks fit.

AND the plaintiff claims:

1. An account of the monies due to the estate in respect of the losses from the matters complained of.
2. An order for the payment to the trust of the money found due on the taking of the said account.
3. Further or in the alternative, damages for breach of trust.
4. The aforesaid interest pursuant to section 35A of the Supreme Court Act 1981.
5. Further or other relief.
6. Costs.

Wat U. Will.

EXAMPLE 6 STATEMENT OF CLAIM—BREACH OF TRUST—TRACING

IN THE HIGH COURT OF JUSTICE Ch. 1985.L.No .

CHANCERY DIVISION

IN THE MATTER of the trusts of a settlement dated 25 December 1981 made by Rex Lear.

BETWEEN REX LEAR Plaintiff

and

(1) GONERIL ALBANY
(2) REGAN CORNWALL
(3) EDMUND GLOUCESTER Defendants

STATEMENT OF CLAIM

1. By a written instrument dated 25 December 1981, the plaintiff transferred to the first defendant and the second defendant the property known as Brittania Farm, Heath, Wessex ('the farm') and the sum of £1,000,000 to be held on trust for the plaintiff as tenant for life, remainder to the first defendant and the second defendant in equal shares.

2. On or about 1 March 1983, in breach of the said trust, the first defendant and the second defendant transferred the farm into the sole name of the first trustee as sole legal and beneficial owner.

3. In further breach of trust, on or about 3 March 1983 the first defendant sold the farm for a sum of £1,500,000, which sum she then invested in 500,000 shares in Thatcher Armaments plc.

4. In the course of July 1983, in breach of the said trust, the second defendant gave capital from the trust fund to the third defendant to be used for the benefit of herself and the third defendant.

5. By reason of the matters alleged in paragraph 4, the plaintiff has suffered loss and damage.

PARTICULARS

Money spent on a holiday for the second and third defendant	£20,000
Money spent on a car for the third defendant	£30,000
	£50,000

6. Further or in the alternative, the third defendant is accountable to the trust for the said £50,000 as a constructive trustee on the ground that he knowingly participated in the misapplication of the said sum in breach of

trust. His knowledge came from his having been fully informed of the full circumstances of the case by the second defendant.

7. Further, the plaintiff claims interest pursuant to section 35A of the Supreme Court Act 1981 on the amount found to be due to the plaintiff at such rate and for such period as the court thinks fit.

AND the plaintiff claims:

As against the first defendant and the second defendant:

1. An order that the said 500,000 shares in Thatcher Armaments plc be transferred to be held on the terms of the said trust.
2. Further or in the alternative, damages for breach of trust.
3. The aforesaid interest pursuant to section 35A of the Supreme Court Act 1981.
4. An order that Cordelia France and Tom Edgar or some other fit and proper persons may be appointed as trustees of the settlement in the place of the first and second defendants.
5. All other necessary accounts, directions and enquiries.
6. Further or other relief.
7. Costs.

As against the third defendant:

1. A declaration that the third defendant is liable as constructive trustee to restore the amount of £50,000 to the trusts fund.
2. An order that the said £50,000 be paid to the trust fund forthwith.
3. Costs.

Thayer Knuts.

EXAMPLE 7 DEFENCE TO 5—COUNTERCLAIM AGAINST BENEFICIARY

IN THE HIGH COURT OF JUSTICE Ch. 1985.B.No 5678.

CHANCERY DIVISION

In the matter of the trusts of the will dated 1 May 1980 of R. de Boys, deceased.

BETWEEN ORLANDO DE BOYS Plaintiff

and

OLIVER DE BOYS Defendant

DEFENCE

1. Paragraphs 1, 2 and 3 of the Statement of Claim are admitted.

2. It is admitted that the defendant invested £200,000 in shares in As You Like It Lingerie Ltd as alleged in paragraph 4 of the Statement of Claim, but it is denied that the said shares were not an investment authorised by law for the investment of the trust funds at the date of their purchase.

3. Each and every allegation in paragraph 5 of the Statement of Claim is denied. In purchasing the said shares the defendant acted on the advice of one Jester Touchstone, carrying on business at Forest House, Arden, whom the defendant honestly and reasonably believed to be a qualified chartered accountant and experienced financial adviser.

4. It is admitted that the defendant appointed the said Frederick Duke to act as his agent in the management of the trust, but save for this, each and every allegation in paragraphs 6 and 7 of the Statement of Claim is denied. In appointing the said Frederick Duke, the defendant again acted on the advice of the said Jester Touchstone, and acted in good faith in making the appointment.

5. In the circumstances, the defendant acted honestly and reasonably, and if, which is denied, the purchase of the said shares and the appointment of the said Frederick Duke as agent were in breach of trust, the defendant ought fairly to be excused and relieved from personal liability.

6. No admission is made as to the alleged or any loss or damage.

7. Save as is herein admitted, the defendant denies each and every allegation in the Statement of Claim as if the same were individually set out herein and specifically denied.

COUNTERCLAIM

8. Paragraphs 1, 2 and 3 of the defence are repeated.

9. The said investment of £200,000 in shares in As You Like It Lingerie

Ltd was made at the instigation of the plaintiff. On divers dates in March 1983 the plaintiff orally requested the defendant to purchase the said shares on the ground that it was a good investment where an immediate profit could be made, and that the beneficiaries of the trust would benefit from a discount on the price of the items manufactured by the company.

AND the defendant counterclaims:

1. Such order as may be just for the impounding of all or any part of the interest of the plaintiff under the trusts of the will, by way of indemnity against any liability which the defendant may incur for breach of trust.
2. Further or other relief.
3. Costs.

Idon Nuttin.

Advising and drafting in a criminal case

Most of the points on advising and drafting in a criminal case were discussed in Chapter 14. This section adds examples of counts for the most common and most important offences, and also some examples of complete indictments. In a criminal case, drafting is of course solely a matter for the prosecution in drawing up the indictment, though the defence may wish to point out defects in the drafting as part of their case.

Most of the sample counts given here are for complete offences, but the lawyer should always fully consider the possibilities of attempt, aiding and abetting and conspiracy rather than a complete offence if appropriate.

Sample counts for offences against people

Murder

STATEMENT OF OFFENCE

Murder

PARTICULARS OF OFFENCE

Maurice Macbeth on the 13th day of April 1985 murdered Donald Duncan.

Manslaughter

STATEMENT OF OFFENCE

Manslaughter

PARTICULARS OF OFFENCE

Horace Hamlet on the 13th day of November 1984 unlawfully killed Percy Polonius.

Wounding with intent

STATEMENT OF OFFENCE

Wounding with intent, contrary to section 18 of the Offences against the Person Act 1861.

PARTICULARS OF OFFENCE

Claude Cornwall on the 1st day of December 1984 wounded Gerald Gloucester with intent to do him grievous bodily harm.

Unlawful wounding

STATEMENT OF OFFENCE

Unlawful wounding contrary to section 20 of the Offences against the Person Act 1861.

PARTICULARS OF OFFENCE

Andrew Aguecheek on the 1st day of February 1985 unlawfully wounded Sebastian Smith.

Common assault

STATEMENT OF OFFENCE

Common assault.

PARTICULARS OF OFFENCE

Katherina Kant on the 14th day of February 1985 assaulted Petruchio Pyne.

Rape

STATEMENT OF OFFENCE

Rape, contrary to section 1(1) of the Sexual Offences Act 1956.

PARTICULARS OF OFFENCE

Demetrius Goth on the 30th day of January 1985 raped Lavinia Andronicus

or

Demetrius Goth on the 30th day of January 1985 had unlawful sexual intercourse with Lavinia Andronicus, who at the time of the said intercourse did not consent to it, the said Demetrius Goth either knowing that the said Lavinia Andronicus did not so consent, or being reckless as to whether she so consented.

Indecent assault

STATEMENT OF OFFENCE

Indecent assault, contrary to section 14(1) of the Sexual Offences Act 1956.

PARTICULARS OF OFFENCE

Harold Hamlet on the 14th day of February 1985 indecently assaulted Ophelia Osbert.

Sample counts for offences against property

Theft

STATEMENT OF OFFENCE

Theft, contrary to section 1 of the Theft Act 1968.

PARTICULARS OF OFFENCE

Henry Bolingbroke on the 1st day of January 1985 stole a gold crown, the property of Richard Plantagenet.

Burglary

STATEMENT OF OFFENCE

Burglary, contrary to section 9(1)(*a*) of the Theft Act 1968.

PARTICULARS OF OFFENCE

Iago Itch on the 21st day of February 1985 entered a building known as Castle House, Cyprus Place, Brixton, London SE1 as a trespasser with intent to steal a handkerchief therein.

or

STATEMENT OF OFFENCE

Burglary, contrary to section 9(1)(*b*) of the Theft Act 1968.

PARTICULARS OF OFFENCE

Iago Itch on the 21st day of February 1985, having entered a building known as Castle House, Cyprus Place, Brixton, London SE1 as a trespasser, stole therein a handkerchief, the property of Desdemona Moore.

Robbery

STATEMENT OF OFFENCE

Robbery, contrary to section 8(1) of the Theft Act 1968.

PARTICULARS OF OFFENCE

John Falstaff on the 9th day of March 1985 robbed John Merchant of £3,000 in money.

or

STATEMENT OF OFFENCE

Assault with intent to rob, contrary to section 8 of the Theft Act 1968.

PARTICULARS OF OFFENCE

John Falstaff on the 9th day of March 1985 assaulted John Merchant with intent to rob him.

Obtaining property by deception

STATEMENT OF OFFENCE

Obtaining property by deception, contrary to section 15 of the Theft Act 1968.

PARTICULARS OF OFFENCE

John Falstaff on the 1st day of April 1985 dishonestly obtained from Dorothy Tearsheet a pig with intention of permanently depriving Dorothy Tearsheet of the said pig, by deception, namely by falsely representing that he was an Army Officer entitled to requisition the said pig.

Handling

STATEMENT OF OFFENCE

Handling stolen goods, contrary to section 22 of the Theft Act 1968.

PARTICULARS OF OFFENCE

Richard Gloucester on the 3rd day of February 1985 dishonestly received stolen goods, namely a gold crown, the property of Edward Plantagenet, knowing or believing the same to have been stolen.

or

PARTICULARS OF OFFENCE

Richard Gloucester on the 3rd day of February 1985 dishonestly undertook or assisted in the retention, removal, disposal or realisation of stolen goods, namely a gold crown, the property of Edward Plantagenet, by or for the benefit of Henry Tudor, or dishonestly arranged so to do, knowing or believing the same to have been stolen.

Obtaining services by deception

STATEMENT OF OFFENCE

Obtaining services by deception, contrary to section 1 of the Theft Act 1978.

PARTICULARS OF OFFENCE

John Falstaff on the 3rd day of March 1985 dishonestly obtained from the Boar's Head Brewing Company Limited services, namely the laundering of clothing, by deception, namely by falsely representing that it was his intention to pay for the said service.

Evasion of liability by deception

STATEMENT OF OFFENCE

Evasion of liability by deception contrary to section 2 of the Theft Act 1978.

PARTICULARS OF OFFENCE

John Falstaff on the 3rd day of March 1985 dishonestly secured the remission of an existing liability to make payment, namely to pay Ursula Quickly for accommodation provided to him, by a deception, namely by falsely representing to Ursula Quickly that Hal Plantagenet was ready and willing to make the said payment on his behalf.

(Note the alternatives under this section of intending to make permanent default on an existing liability, or of intending to obtain abatement of an existing liability. The correct alternative should be pleaded.)

Making off without payment

STATEMENT OF OFFENCE

Making off without payment, contrary to section 3 of the Theft Act 1978.

PARTICULARS OF OFFENCE

John Falstaff, on the 3rd day of March 1985, knowing that payment on the spot for a meal that he had consumed at the Boars Head Tavern was required of him, and with intent to avoid payment of the amount due, dishonestly made off without having paid.

Criminal damage

STATEMENT OF OFFENCE

Damaging property contrary to section 1(1) of the Criminal Damage Act 1971.

PARTICULARS OF OFFENCE

Henry Plantagenet on the 5th day of April 1985, without lawful excuse, damaged a   belonging to   intending to damage such property, or being reckless as to whether such property would be damaged.

Arson

STATEMENT OF OFFENCE

Arson, contrary to section 1(1) and (3) of the Criminal Damage Act 1971.

PARTICULARS OF OFFENCE

Octavius Caesar on the 9th day of March 1985, without lawful excuse, destroyed by fire a boat belonging to Cleopatra Ptolemy, intending to destroy such property or being reckless as to whether such property would be destroyed.

Sample counts for different types of involvement in an offence

Aiding and abetting

STATEMENT OF OFFENCE

Theft contrary to section 1 of the Theft Act 1968.

PARTICULARS OF OFFENCE

Thomas Percy on the 10th day of January 1985 aided and abetted, counselled and procured Henry Hotspur to steal a crown, the property of Henry Plantagenet. (Note that aiding and abetting can be charged separately from counselling and procuring if appropriate.)

Attempt

STATEMENT OF OFFENCE

Attempted theft contrary to section 1 of the Criminal Attempts Act 1981.

PARTICULARS OF OFFENCE

Henry Hotspur on the 13th day of January 1985 attempted to steal a crown belonging to Henry Plantagenet.

Conspiracy

STATEMENT OF OFFENCE

Conspiracy to murder.

PARTICULARS OF OFFENCE

Marcus Brutus, on a day or days unknown between the 1st day of January 1985 and the 15th day of March 1985 conspired together with Gaius Cassius and Metellus Cimber to murder Julius Caesar.

INDICTMENT AGAINST A SINGLE DEFENDANT

IN THE CROWN COURT AT BOSWORTH

THE QUEEN v RICHARD GLOUCESTER

RICHARD GLOUCESTER is charged as follows:

Count 1.

STATEMENT OF OFFENCE

Murder

PARTICULARS OF OFFENCE

Richard Gloucester on the 1st day of January 1985 aided and abetted Edward Fourth to murder George Clarence.

Count 2.

STATEMENT OF OFFENCE

Murder

PARTICULARS OF OFFENCE

Richard Gloucester on the 25th day of June 1985 counselled and procured Richard Ratcliff to murder Earl Rivers.

Count 3.

STATEMENT OF OFFENCE

Murder

PARTICULARS OF OFFENCE

Richard Gloucester on a day or days unknown between the 26th day of June 1985 and the 1st day of October 1985 counselled and procured James Tyrrell to murder Edward Plantagenet and Richard Plantagenet.

Count 4.

STATEMENT OF OFFENCE

Manslaughter

PARTICULARS OF OFFENCE

Richard Gloucester on the 30th day of June 1985 unlawfully killed Anne Neville Gloucester.

Count 5.

STATEMENT OF OFFENCE

Conspiracy to commit robbery, contrary to section 8 of the Theft Act 1968.

PARTICULARS OF OFFENCE

Richard Gloucester, on a day or days unknown between the 1st day of July 1985 and the 22nd day of August 1985 conspired together with John Norfolk to assault Henry Tudor with intent to rob him.

Date.

Signed Thomas More
Officer of the Court.

INDICTMENT AGAINST CO-DEFENDANTS

IN THE CROWN COURT AT GADSHILL

THE QUEEN v RUDOLPH BARDOLPH, PERCIVAL PISTOL and PERCY PETO.

RUDOLPH BARDOLPH, PERCIVAL PISTOL AND PERCY PETO are charged as follows:

Count 1. STATEMENT OF OFFENCE

Robbery, contrary to section 8(1) of the Theft Act 1968.

PARTICULARS OF OFFENCE

Rudolph Bardolph, Percival Pistol and Percy Peto on the 9th day of March 1985 robbed Franklin Merchant of £3,000.

Count 2. STATEMENT OF OFFENCE

Burglary contrary to section 9(1)(*b*) of the Theft Act 1968.

PARTICULARS OF OFFENCE

Percival Pistol and Percy Peto on the 17th day of March 1985, having entered a building known as Tailor House, Gloucester, stole therein 12 suits, the property of Francis Feeble.

Count 3. STATEMENT OF OFFENCE

Handling stolen goods, contrary to section 22 of the Theft Act 1968.

PARTICULARS OF OFFENCE

Rudolph Bardolph on a day unknown between the 17th day of March 1985 and the 21st day of March 1985 dishonestly received stolen goods, namely 12 suits, the property of Francis Feeble, knowing or believing the same to have been stolen.

Count 4. STATEMENT OF OFFENCE

Theft, contrary to section 1 of the Theft Act 1968.

PARTICULARS OF OFFENCE

Rudolph Bardolph on the 19th day of March 1985 stole £100, the property of Peter Bullcalf.

Date

Signed Robert Shallow
Officer of the Court.

Advising and drafting in a family case

This is an area that many lawyers will come across in practice, and there are a number of special points to be taken into account when advising and drafting. In a family case it is especially important for the lawyer to be very practical, as the problems that arise will often involve the major elements of a person's day-to-day life—such as where they live, how much money they have to live on, and what happens to their children. The lawyer will always have to give detailed consideration to the facts of the case and what may be achieved for the client, and show real sensitivity to the needs of the client. In family cases the courts often have wide discretionary powers as to the orders that can be made, but this does not mean that the lawyer can be vague—it gives him all the more scope to develop strong arguments as to what would be best for the client.

Divorce

With the introduction of the special procedure the lawyer, especially the barrister, is less involved with the mechanics of the divorce itself, and more concerned with ancillary relief relating to property and children. Most divorces will proceed undefended in the county court with the small proportion of defended cases going to the High Court. The petition and any answer will often be drafted by the solicitor, or possibly by the client, but they may be dealt with by a barrister in an important case, and a barrister will often be briefed to draft affidavits or a consent order.

There is now a complete bar on divorce within one year of marriage, but thereafter no bar, Matrimonial and Family Proceedings Act 1984, s.1. When advising on the ground on which to petition for divorce every possibility will need to be considered, with tactful questions to the client, but to save time and costs only one ground should normally be put in the petition, which will probably be that which is most easily proved. Adultery and behaviour are the only immediate grounds for divorce, the others requiring at least two years desertion or separation. It will be necessary to investigate what evidence is available, though detailed evidence will only be needed if the divorce is contested. Adultery is generally proved by circumstantial evidence or a confession, and evidence of behaviour will often be one spouse's word against the other, though independent evidence should be sought if possible. For the fact of two years' separation and consent, the consent of the other party must be specifically given in writing and can in no way be presumed.

There is no set form for a petition that must be used, but the Matrimonial

Causes Rules specify the contents of a petition, and in practice a common form is used, and an example of this is given (see Example 1). There is a brief heading then numbered paragraphs setting out the facts. The first eight paragraphs set out the details of the marriage, any children, and any proceedings relating to the marriage, and no great pleading skills are needed beyond accuracy. The rest of the petition goes on in numbered paragraphs to set out the fact on which the petition is based with appropriate particulars, and here skills may be needed, especially for allegations of behaviour to make clear and concise allegations with sufficient detail. Any period for which the parties have cohabited since the events on which the divorce is based should be pleaded, even if it will not prevent the divorce being granted. If there is an allegation of adultery with a named person, that person must be made a co-respondent in the suit. The prayer at the end of the petition must contain an application for all types of ancillary relief sought.

If the solicitor or barrister has not drafted the petition in the case himself, he should always check it if the case later comes to him to see that it is in order. If there is any defect or omission the petition can be amended. A supplemental petition may be used to allege a further ground for divorce, and this may be done to seek a divorce on the basis of two years separation and consent where a divorce was sought on another fact, but later negotiations have lead to agreement between the spouses.

Many divorces are not defended and stay in the county court, but the respondent should file an answer not only if he does not want a divorce but also if he wants a divorce on a different fact, or if there is good reason for disputing the allegations made against him. The basis for the divorce can be disputed if the respondent says that the ground alleged is not true, or if there is a positive defence such as the fact that the spouses have lived together for more than six months since the alleged ground, or that the respondent will suffer grave financial or other hardship. One or more of these lines should be taken if the respondent does not want a divorce at all, but if he does want a divorce he should either not defend the fact alleged, or cross-petition for divorce.

The respondent should also file an answer if there is good reason to dispute allegations made against him in the petition, though not just because he feels they are not entirely true. Even if he wants a divorce he may wish to deny allegations or raise new facts so that allegations made by the petitioner do not prejudice him when it comes to consideration of ancillary applications for financial relief or custody. This may be more important now that conduct will be taken into account if it would be inequitable to disregard it.

In pleading an answer, there is again no set form, just some rules as to what should be included. There is a form of answer in common use (see Example 2). The respondent does not need to plead to the first eight paragraphs of the petition unless he disputes anything, though he should plead whether he agrees with what the petition says as to children of the family, and it is common to plead whether there is any agreement between the parties for provision. As to the fact and particulars that the petitioner alleges, it is possible just to deny these, but it is preferable to plead in more detail either admitting, confessing and avoiding or adding further information as in a defence, especially where there are allegations of behaviour. The lawyer should go through the petition in detail with the respondent to do this properly. If the respondent wants a divorce on some other fact he should cross-petition pleading another fact fully, and anyone named as committing adultery with the spouse should be made a party-cited.

It is possible, though rare, to have a reply in a divorce suit, but there will be no further pleadings. However the lawyers on both sides should make full use of all possible procedural steps. It is possible to amend the petition or answer, or to get particulars of anything in them, or interrogatories. Discovery may be used, especially to get financial details, and interlocutory injunctions, Mareva injunctions or Anton Piller orders can be sought.

Ancillary relief

The seeking and negotiating of ancillary relief will be the major part of most divorce actions, and here the skills needed by the lawyer will be in drafting affidavits to support applications, negotiating strongly and practically, and in drawing up carefully any agreement or consent order. The basic facts and some of the arguments for ancillary relief will be contained in the affidavits, and it is vital to get full information from the client before drafting, and to file the affidavits properly for the use of the court, see *Practice Note* [1984] 1 All ER 323.

Where there is an application for financial provision, the respondent will have to file an affidavit of means giving full details of all his income and capital. There is a Registry form for this purpose, but it may not be appropriate in all circumstances, though it does give a guide to what information should be given. The spouse seeking financial provision will also have to file an affidavit in support of their application giving details of their own financial position. Examples of financial affidavits are given (see Examples 3 and 4).

The financial affidavit must specify fully and clearly the capital assets and income of the deponent, which will necessitate looking at bank statements, pay slips and so on as well as interviewing the client. If real property is in issue, the Land Registry title number and details of any mortgage should be given. However, the financial affidavit is not merely an objective statement, but a document presenting the client's case that will be signed by him, and it should therefore be expressed in a way that most favours him and raises major arguments in his favour. Such arguments should be put in numbered paragraphs at the end of the affidavit, if for example he needs money to buy a home, or feels that the other spouse should be expected to work. The arguments that most favour the client should be isolated and clearly expressed to get them across to the judge.

When an affidavit has been filed by the other side, the lawyer should go through it with his client in detail to see if it is accurate or anything has been left out. Further particulars of the affidavit can be sought if necessary. The affidavit will also reveal the nature of the case of the other side, so the lawyer can prepare his arguments against it.

In advising on financial matters it is crucial that the lawyer look at the practical details of how much money his client will have and what his expenses will be. This may require complex calculations on income, tax allowances and tax rates. Possible social security benefits should be ignored if there is any alternative, but in fact many divorced women do have to live on supplementary benefit, and if this will be unavoidable the lawyer should be able to advise on the benefits available. Details such as who will pay the mortgage, where the money will come from to run a car and so on must be considered, and the advice of an accountant may be needed, especially if one of the spouses is running a business.

The form of the order must be considered in making calculations. It is generally better for maintenance to be paid direct to a child rather than to a spouse for him to make full use of the child's tax allowance, and if school fees are paid they should probably be part of the order. It will normally be better to have mortgage payments, rates payments etc. as part of a maintenance order rather than payable direct so that they will be tax deductible for the husband.

The lawyer will need to consider all the possible orders that can be made—for lump sums, secured provision, transfer of property or a settlement—and in consultation with the client decide what should be sought in the case. It is not just a question of getting as much as possible for the client, but of getting it in the right form. Alternative bases for provision should also be considered; the one-third rule still survives to some extent, but the alternative of the clean break is preferred if possible, or it may be necessary to have the home settled. If the home is to be settled the lawyer must consider the details of what shares in the property each spouse should have and when it should be sold. The other factor to take into account is of course the possibility of a legal aid charge. Costs should not be allowed to build up in the first place, but if they do the charge must be taken into account in assessing provision.

Arguments on entitlement to provision will centre on the relevant factors listed in the Matrimonial Causes Act 1973, s.25, replaced by the Matrimonial and Family Proceedings Act 1984. Many factors, such as the length of the marriage, remain the same under the new section, but some have changed and remain to be developed in case law. The new section does not aim to put the parties where they would have been if the marriage had not broken down, but puts the interests of children first. It also makes conduct relevant where it would be inequitable to disregard it, so this is something that the lawyer will have to investigate with the client, even though mud-slinging is generally not a good idea as it makes people bitter and makes settlement more difficult. The new section also takes into account any earning capacity which it would be reasonable to expect a spouse to acquire, which is again something to be investigated fully with the client.

Because there are so many possible orders, alternatives for settlement and relevant factors, one can only repeat that the lawyer that does best for the client will be the one that develops possible arguments fully, looks at all the possibilities, and comes up with detailed, concrete proposals to negotiate a settlement or to put to the judge, and a cornerstone of this will be the financial affidavit.

The other main element of ancillary relief will be the custody of children. Again, an affidavit in support must be filed, and again it should set out the relevant background facts and the basic arguments in the client's favour, (see Example 5). This may involve quite a detailed discussion with the client. In many cases there will inevitably be an order for the mother to have custody or at least care and control of the children, with access to the father, but the concepts of custody and access should be clearly explained to the parties. If the parties are likely to be able to agree a very general order for access can be made, but if there is likely to be any difficulty the times and place of access should be spelt out in detail in the order to try to avoid difficulty.

If the application is contested it will be very important to collect evidence in support, as to where the child will live, who he will live with, where he will go to school and how he will be cared for on a day-to-day basis. This will be especially important for the father seeking custody, who will need to impress the judge with his case, or where a party is seeking leave to take the child to live abroad, so that the court will be very concerned about the conditions where the child will be living.

Negotiating a settlement

In many cases financial provision and custody are agreed by the parties, and this puts the lawyers in a vital position. Having taken full instructions from the client as to what he hopes to achieve, the lawyer will have to advise on the most that can be expected and the least that should be offered or accepted. When he does have full information he should make detailed proposals for an offer to the other side, that must take everything into account. Negotiations will take place, but they must never be allowed to drag on too long and build up costs unnecessarily.

An agreed order is desirable wherever possible as it will take some of the bitterness out of the situation, give the parties the chance to agree details, and avoid having to leave matters to the wide discretion of the judge. Once agreement has been reached, there are a variety of ways in which it can be made binding, and these were discussed at the end of Chapter 6, but one of the most common is the consent order. A consent order must be drafted with great care to cover everything, as it will generally not be possible to appeal against a consent order unless there is a vitiating element such as fraud or misrepresentation, and it will usually not be possible to seek further provision, so the terms must take all foreseeable possibilities into account.

In drafting a consent order, there is a clear distinction between orders and undertakings. The court can only order those things which it has the power to order, such as transfers of property, maintenance and custody. If there is anything else that the parties wish to agree, that must go into the undertakings section, if for example they wish to agree that a child should attend a particular school, or that one party should permit the other to do something. Each element in the order must be a separate numbered point, and the wording must be very clear to avoid any enforcement problems (see Examples 6 and 7).

Other types of proceedings

There are a variety of possible proceedings apart from divorce, but to the extent that these involve financial provision or custody, the points already made will apply.

Applications for injunctions relating to the occupation of the matrimonial home or domestic violence are quite common. The lawyer will have to advise on whether to go to the magistrates' court or the county court, which will depend on the types of order sought, whether there has been actual violence, whether the client wants other relief from either court, and on cost. If the client has legal aid they should go to the magistrates' court unless there is good reason to the contrary. Arguments and evidence, especially relating to any violence should be properly prepared. There is sometimes a tendency to rush off for an injunction without considering the position fully, but the courts are making it clear that they will not be prepared to exclude someone from their home without good reason, and that a wife will not easily be able to exclude her husband from the home just because she wishes to live there with the children, *Richards* v *Richards* [1984] AC 174. An injunction is sometimes sought as a strategic move before financial provision or custody is sought, but this should only be done with care in a proper case.

In any event, it is essential to make it clear to the client that an injunction will only be a temporary remedy, and to advise them as to what they should do in the long term, such as seeking a divorce, a transfer of property or a tenancy, rehousing from the council, or some other alternative. An application for orders will only need to state briefly the orders sought, with care being needed in preparing affidavits in support.

There may be an application for a share in property where a divorce is not sought, either under the Married Women's Property Act 1882, s.17 or in a trust action. The lawyer will need to get all the relevant information from the client, and will have to develop detailed arguments not only as to the exact legal reason why there should be a share in the property, but what the size of the share should be. The share may be a set sum or a proportion, and may need detailed arithmetic on contributions made. It will also be necessary to advise the client on whether they can and should seek an order for the sale of the property to get their money out, or whether they can resist an order for sale because they wish to live there. Practical steps like registering an interest or getting an injunction to stop sale may be important. The drafting for court is again a straightforward statement of the orders sought, with the affidavit in support being important.

Lastly, in an application for provision from the estate of a deceased person under the Inheritance (Provision for Family and Dependants) Act 1975, the development of arguments as to why there should be a share and what the size of it should be will be crucial, and the collection of evidence of any agreement made or financial support supplied will be important. Again the application will be a simple statement of the orders sought and the concise and clear preparation of the affidavit will require skill.

EXAMPLE 1 DIVORCE PETITION

IN THE VERONASTER COUNTY COURT No of 1985

The petition of JULIET MONTAGUE shows that:

1. On the 14th February 1978 the petitioner was lawfully married to Romeo Montague (hereinafter called the respondent) at Saint Lawrence's Church, Veronaster, Somerset.
2. The petitioner and the respondent last lived together at Nightingale Cottage, Dawn Lane, Veronaster, Somerset.
3. The petitioner is domiciled in England and Wales. The petitioner is a housewife and resides at Nightingale Cottage aforesaid: the respondent is a fashion photographer and resides at Penthouse Flat, Mantua Road, London NW1.
4. There are six children of the marriage now living, namely Tybalt Montague born on 14th November 1978, Lawrence Montague born on 1st October 1979, Escalus Montague born on 1st October 1980, Paris Montague born on 25th October 1981, Balthasar Montague born on 1st November 1982 and Mercutio Montague born on 1st December 1984.
5. No other child now living has been born to the petitioner during the said marriage.
6. There are or have been no other proceedings in any court in England and Wales which relate to the marriage or are capable of affecting its validity or subsistence, except in that on 1st November 1984 the Veronaster County Court made an order under the Domestic Violence and Matrimonial Proceedings Act 1976 restraining the respondent from molesting the petitioner and excluding the respondent from the matrimonial home.
7. There are no proceedings continuing in any country outside England and Wales which relate to the marriage or are capable of affecting its validity or subsistence.
8. No agreement or arrangement has been made or is proposed to be made between the parties for the support of the petitioner and the said children.
9. The said marriage has broken down irretrievably.
10. The respondent has committed adultery and the petitioner finds it intolerable to live with the respondent.

PARTICULARS

The respondent has committed adultery with Rosaline Starkers on days unknown to the petitioner since February 1984 at places unknown to the petitioner including Penthouse Flat, Mantua Road, London NW1.

The petitioner therefore prays:

1. That the said marriage may be dissolved.

2. That she may be granted the custody of the said children, Tybalt Montague, Lawrence Montague, Escalus Montague, Paris Montague, Balthasar Montague and Mercutio Montague.

3. That the court may order such payments by way of maintenance pending suit and may make such orders for financial provision or adjustment of property for the benefit of the petitioner and the said children as may be just.

4. That the respondent may be ordered to transfer to the petitioner his interest in the property known as Nightingale Cottage, Dawn Lane, Veronaster, Somerset.

5. That the respondent may be ordered to pay the costs of this suit.

Lib Eration.

EXAMPLE 2 ANSWER TO PETITION IN 1

IN THE VERONASTER COUNTY COURT No. 1234 of 1985

BETWEEN	JULIET MONTAGUE	Petitioner
	and	
	ROMEO MONTAGUE	Respondent
	and	
	ROSALINE STARKERS	Co-respondent

The respondent, in ANSWER to the petition filed in this suit says that:

1. No other child now living has been born to the petitioner during the said marriage.
2. No agreement or arrangement has been made or is proposed to be made between the parties for the support of the petitioner and the said children.
3. The respondent admits that the said marriage has broken down irretrievably.
4. The respondent denies that he has committed adultery as alleged in the petition or at all.
5. The petitioner has behaved in such a way that the respondent cannot reasonably be expected to live with the petitioner.

PARTICULARS

(1) The petitioner has never fully committed herself to her marriage to the respondent. On 7th April 1978 the petitioner said to the respondent, 'Mother was right, I should never have married you!' and forthwith left the matriomonial home to stay with her mother, Lucrezia Capulet, for seven days. This behaviour has been repeated frequently throughout the marriage.

(b) The petitioner has frequently made offensive remarks about members of the family of the respondent, alleging that they have Mafia connections. On 28th December 1980, following a visit to her mother over Christmas, the petitioner accused the respondent of causing serious injury to her cousin Tybalt Capulet on 1st January 1978. The injuries caused to the said Tybalt Capulet on that day were entirely his own fault, a fact that the petitioner had previously accepted.

(c) The petitioner has frequently voiced suspicions relating to the respondent's profession as a fashion photographer, alleging that he has had affairs with his models, which is totally untrue. During June 1981 the petitioner found a diary belonging to the respondent and made offensive telephone calls to six models whose names and telephone numbers appeared therein, accusing each of them of having affairs with the respondent and informing each of them 'I'm amazed Romeo's sex-life is not in the Guinness Book of Records'. This conduct caused substantial loss to the respondent's business.

(d) In June 1982 the respondent discovered that the petitioner was drinking heavily. Despite advice from the respondent, the petitioner has continued to drink heavily, and refuses to discuss the problem or to seek professional help.

(e) In February 1983 the petitioner informed the respondent that marrying him had deprived her of her youth and the chance of a good education, and that she had therefore enrolled for a degree in Peace Studies with the Open University. The respondent gave the petitioner £500 to purchase books for the said course, but the sole result of the course was that the petitioner took the five children of the family then living to live in a tent on Greenham Common for six months, from May to November 1982. On her return the petitioner sought an order excluding the respondent from the matrimonial home and to stop him molesting her. The respondent did not feel it necessary to expend money on a lawyer, and the order sought was granted by the Veronaster County Court, but in December 1982 the petitioner voluntarily allowed the respondent to return to the matrimonial home.

(f) On 10th June 1984 the petitioner gave to the respondent a copy of the record 'Two Tribes' by the popular musical group Frankie Goes to Hollywood, together with a birthday card with the message 'This is about our bloody families'. In an effort to show affection for the petitioner, the respondent bought her a card with the message 'Frankie says Relax', but on his return to the matrimonial home that evening he found his belongings packed in suitcases on the front lawn, and the petitioner threatened violence if he re-entered the matrimonial home. As the petitioner had clearly been drinking and the children of the family were clearly distressed, the respondent agreed to leave and found alternative accommodation.

The respondent therefore prays:

1. That the prayer of the petition may be rejected and the petition dismissed.
2. That the said marriage may be dissolved.
3. That the petitioner may be ordered to pay the costs of this suit.

M.C. Pigg.

EXAMPLE 3 AFFIDAVIT OF MEANS

IN THE SOUTH LONDON COUNTY COURT No of 1985

BETWEEN	OCTAVIA ANTHONY	Petitioner
	and	
	MARK ANTHONY	Respondent
	and	
	CLEOPATRA PTOLEMY	Co-respondent

I, Mark Anthony, of 3, Actium Villas, London SW35 make oath and say that the information given herein is true to the best of my knowledge, information and belief, and is a full and accurate statement of my means. Save as set out herein I have no capital or income.

1. I am employed as a Professor of War Studies at the University of Clapham. I am also a journalist writing articles on Middle Eastern affairs.
2. My current gross income from my employment is £18,000 per annum, with a further sum of approximately £2,000 from my journalism. In addition, I receive approximately £300 per annum in interest on my account with the Pyramid Building Society, and £900 per annum from my shareholding in Egypt Holidays Ltd. I have no other source of income.
3. My National Insurance contributions are £15 per week.
4. To enable me to earn the income set out above I incur the following necessary expenses: £10 per week to travel to work, and £10 per week for writing materials.
5. My gross taxable income during the last complete tax year from my employment was £18,000, and my gross taxable income from journalism was £2,300. My income tax liability during the last complete tax year was £5,000.
6. I claim the following to be the necessary expenses of providing myself with a place to live in, namely £50 per week in rent.
7. I make maintenance payments to the petitioner of £100 per month, and maintenance payments for our children Caesar Anthony and Diana Anthony at the rate of £50 per month each.
8. The maintenance payments referred to in paragraph 7 are made under an enforceable agreement, namely a deed dated 16th March 1983.
9. The former matrimonial home is owned solely by myself.
10. The former matrimonial home is still occupied by the petitioner and the children of the family. I estimate its present value to be £80,000. It is subject to a mortgage with the Pyramid Building Society with £20,000 outstanding. The repayments are £300 per month and repayment is due to be completed in 1995.
11. I own two cars. The first is a Volvo Estate made in 1981, and I estimate its current value to be £5,000. The second is a Renault 6 made in 1972, and I estimate its current value to be £400. The second car is used solely by the petitioner.

12. My other assets are savings of £3,000 in an account with the Pyramid Building Society, 1,000 shares in Egypt Holidays Ltd worth £5,000 and a collection of antique swords worth £2,000.

13. My other liabilities are a bank overdraft of £1,000, and a debt of £700 on my Access credit card. I have various hire purchase agreements for the furniture in my flat on which the repayments are £40 per month until May 1988. I have a life assurance policy with an annual premium of £200, maturing in March 1995.

14. The decree absolute has been pronounced. I do not intend to remarry. I do not provide for any other person.

15. I am a member of a pension scheme run by my employer. I contribute £50 per month to it, and my employer contributes an equal amount. My former wife would have been entitled to a monthly pension under this scheme at my death in the absence of a decree absolute. To my knowledge the petitioner is not a member of any such scheme.

16. I would like to urge against the paying of maintenance to the petitioner for more than a brief interim period the fact that the petitioner is well-educated and worked as a research assistant prior to our marriage, and should therefore be able to find remunerative employment easily.

17. I would also ask this Honourable Court to take into account the fact that the petitoner comes from a rich family and can expect to benefit from various family trusts, whereas I have earned all my own money. My resources are under severe strain at present, the flat where I live is very small, and I would ask that the present matrimonial home be sold to release money for me to pay the deposit on a better flat.

18. I would further ask this Honourable Court to take into account the fact that my marriage to the petitioner was relatively short, and that even during the time that we were married we spent little time together as I needed to travel to research my articles.

Sworn etc.

EXAMPLE 4 AFFIDAVIT IN SUPPORT OF AN APPLICATION FOR FINANCIAL PROVISION

IN THE SOUTH LONDON COUNTY COURT No of 1985

BETWEEN	OCTAVIA ANTHONY	Petitioner
	and	
	MARK ANTHONY	Respondent
	and	
	CLEOPATRA PTOLEMY	Co-respondent

In the Matter of section 24 of the Matrimonial Causes Act 1973

And in the Matter of an application by the petitioner for a property adjustment order.

I, Octavia Anthony, of Roman Court, Appia Way, London SW35, a housewife, make oath and say as follows:

1. I am the above-mentioned petitioner, and I make this affidavit in answer to the respondent's affidavit of means dated 1st April 1985, and in support of my application for a property adjustment order.
2. I was married to the respondent on 14th February 1981. We lived together at Roman Court, Appia Way, London SW35 until 1st March 1985, when the respondent left me. We have two children, Caesar Anthony born on 13th October 1981 and Diana Anthony born on 1st October 1983.
3. On 30th March 1985 this Honourable Court pronounced a decree nisi of divorce in my favour on the ground that the marriage had broken down irretrievably because the respondent had committed adultery with the Co-respondent and I found it intolerable to live with the respondent. I was granted custody of Caesar and Diana.
4. I accept the accuracy of the respondent's statements with regard to his financial position as set out in his affidavit of means dated 1st April 1985 save for the following matters.
5. I believe from various things that the respondent has told me that he does intend to marry the co-respondent, as soon as the matters relating to this divorce have been settled. He admitted to me that the co-respondent was his mistress for several years before he married me, and has admitted to me that since he left me he has spent much of his time with her at her house at Palace House, Alexandria Road, London SW33. I believe that as soon as my application for financial relief is decided he will leave the small flat where he currently lives and move in with her. She is a wealthy woman with substantial assets.
6. I dispute that it is open to me to find remunerative employment. Diana is only two years old and needs constant care. Even when she begins school I will need to be at home to see her off in the morning and to be there when she returns. I have no qualifications for any profession. I had

intended to train as a teacher, but when I married the respondent we agreed that I should give this up. If I had not married him I would have completed my training by now, and I feel that he should compensate me for this. In the present economic climate I doubt if I could get any work.

7. Although my marriage to the respondent has been relatively short, I have borne and am bringing up two children that resulted from the marriage. Throughout the marriage I cared well for the children and for the respondent, who consistently refused to do anything in the home, even help with the washing up. The marriage has damaged my career prospects, and did not last purely because of the respondent's adultery.

8. Although it is correct to say that some members of my family are wealthy, I have no entitlement to any money from any of them. My family believe in self-reliance, and I feel it would be wrong to expect anything from them.

9. In addition to the maintenance paid to me by the respondent I receive £10 per week in child benefit. I also receive £1,000 per annum from my shares in Roman Empire Stores plc. I have no other source of income.

10. My other assets are shares in Roman Empire Stores Ltd worth £10,000. Otherwise I have no property whatsoever.

11. The matrimonial home at Roman Court, Appia Way, London SW33 is owned solely by the respondent under H.M. Land Registry Title No. AD 13579. It was purchased on 13th February 1981 for £70,000 with a mortgage of £30,000. My brother paid £30,000 towards the deposit as a wedding present, only £10,000 being provided by the respondent. The respondent has paid and continues to pay the mortgage repayments.

12. I ask this Honourable Court to make an order transferring the whole of the respondent's interest in the former matrimonial home to me, to provide a secure home for myself and the children. In view of the substantial contribution made by my family to the purchase price I feel this would be fair, especially as I believe that the respondent will go to live with the co-respondent, and may in the future go to live in Egypt with her.

13. In all the circumstances I ask this Honourable Court to make an order transferring the respondent's title to the matrimonial home at Roman Court, Appia Way, London SW35 to me absolutely.

Sworn etc.

EXAMPLE 5 AFFIDAVIT SUPPORTING AN APPLICATION FOR CUSTODY

IN THE HIGH COURT OF JUSTICE 1985.R. No .

FAMILY DIVISION

ENDSWELL DISTRICT REGISTRY

BETWEEN BERTRAM ROUSILLON Petitioner
and
HELENA ROUSILLON Respondent

In the Matter of section 42 of the Matrimonial Causes Act 1973.

And in the Matter of an application by the petitioner for a custody order.

I, Bertram Rousillon, of 1, Allswell Road, Endswell, Lancashire, the petitioner herein, make oath and say as follows:

1. I was married to the respondent on 1st February 1977. There is one child of the marriage, Parolles Louis Rousillon, who was born on the 3rd January 1978.
2. At the time of the birth of Parolles our marriage was very happy, and the respondent and I agreed that we should jointly share all the housework and all the work of caring for Parolles.
3. On 24th December 1978 I was made redundant from my post as a Senior Executive with an armament manufacturing company, and since that time I have been unable to find work. As a result, from that date I increasingly took over the day to day care of Parolles, feeding him, bathing him and cleaning his clothes.
4. As I was unable to find work, I agreed with the respondent that she should return to work. She had trained and qualified as a doctor prior to our marriage, and she found a position as a doctor with the Endswell District Hospital, where she began work in June 1979. Due to the increasing pressure of her work, I took over the care of Parolles completely.
5. In January 1981, at the insistence of the respondent, Parolles began to attend a nursery school. The experience clearly upset him, and I suggested that it would be better to withdraw him from the school until he was older. The respondent laughed at this, and said that Parolles should be brought up to face the problems of life, even if I could not cope with them. She insisted that Parolles continue to attend the nursery school, which he did for a week. During this time he became hysterical every morning, and at the end of the week I insisted on withdrawing him from the school, and sought medical help for his hysterical fits.
6. In March 1983 the respondent decided that she wished to widen her

work experience, and contacted associates in Florence, Italy where she had worked for a short time while she was training. She was offered a position as a doctor in Florence General Hospital, which she took up in June 1983, leaving Parolles in my care.

7. Since June 1983 the respondent has only returned to the matrimonial home for periods amounting in total to 12 weeks. She has sent cards and presents to Parolles on his birthdays and at Christmas, but when she returns to the home she has stated that she needs a real holiday and takes no part in the care of Parolles.

8. On 1st February 1985 I was granted a decree nisi of divorce by the Endswell County Court on the ground that my marriage had broken down irretrievably because of the unreasonable behaviour of the respondent. This decree was made absolute on 15th March 1985. The same court granted interim custody of Parolles to me, with reasonable access to the respondent.

9. The respondent has told me that she is seeking custody of Parolles so that she can give him a broad and dynamic outlook on life, and that she intends to renew her contract with the Florence General Hospital and take Parolles there to live with her, with the leave of this court. In this she shows a selfish and inconsiderate attitude as a parent. Parolles has only been to Italy once, in January 1984 for two weeks. On his return he told me that Italy was a silly country where they had food like worms that made him sick, and talked a silly language that he could not understand.

10. Since January 1984 I have found that I can successfully write and sell children's adventure stories. I now have a sufficient income to support myself and Parolles, and can work at home and care for him. My mother, Countessa Rousillon, lives nearby, and she is always available to take care of Parolles if I do need to go out. Since September 1983, Parolles has been attending the Endswell Primary School, where he is well-settled and seems happy.

11. I respectfully ask the court to grant me custody, care and control of Parolles, and to grant limited access to the respondent.

12. There is now produced and shown to me marked 'BR1' a copy of the birth certificate of Parolles Louis Rousillon.

Sworn etc.

EXAMPLE 6 CONSENT ORDER—A SUGGESTED SETTLEMENT BASED ON THE AFFIDAVITS IN 3 AND 4

IN THE SOUTH LONDON COUNTY COURT No .

Before His Honour Judge Jupiter

BETWEEN OCTAVIA ANTHONY Petitioner
and
MARK ANTHONY Respondent
and
CLEOPATRA PTOLEMY Co-respondent

Upon hearing Counsel for the Petitioner and for the Respondent

And upon the Respondent undertaking:

1. To keep contact between the children of the family and the Co-respondent to a minimum during periods of access.

By consent it is ordered:

1. Custody of the children of the family, Caesar Anthony and Diana Anthony to be vested in the petitioner, with access to the respondent on every Sunday between 10.00 a.m. and 6.00 p.m., and for one week in August each year, the exact dates for the latter to be agreed between the petitioner and the respondent.
2. The respondent to pay to the petitioner periodical payments during their joint lives or until the petitioner shall remarry or until further order at the rate of £4,500 per annum less tax, payable monthly, the first payment to be made on 1st May 1985.
3. The respondent to pay to the children of the family, Caesar Anthony and Diana Anthony, periodical payments until they shall attain the age of 18 years or until further order at the rate of £18 per week to each child, the first payments to be made on 1st May 1985.
4. The respondent to transfer the property known as Roman Court, Appia Way, London SW35 into the joint names of himself and the petitioner to be held on trust for sale, not to be sold until the petitioner shall die, or remarry, or until the children Caesar Anthony and Diana Anthony shall both have attained the age of 18 years, whichever is the soonest, and thereafter the said property be sold and the net proceeds of sale be divided equally between the peititioner and the respondent.
5. The respondent to pay to the petitioner a lump sum of £3,000 within 28 days of the date of this order.
6. The respondent to pay the costs of this application.

EXAMPLE 7 CONSENT ORDER—AN ALTERNATIVE TO 6

IN THE SOUTH LONDON COUNTY COURT No .

Before His Honour Judge Jupiter

BETWEEN	OCTAVIA ANTHONY	Petitioner
	and	
	MARK ANTHONY	Respondent
	and	
	CLEOPATRA PTOLEMY	Co-respondent

Upon hearing Counsel for the Petitioner and for the Respondent

And upon the Petitioner undertaking:

1. To allow the child of the family Caesar Anthony to attend a public school chosen by the respondent.
2. To invest all or substantially all of her share of the proceeds of sale of the former matrimonial home in the purchase of a freehold property for occupation by herself and the children of the family.

By consent it is ordered:

1. That custody of the children Caesar Anthony and Diana Anthony be vested jointly in the petitioner and the respondent, with care and control of both to the petitioner, and reasonable access to the respondent.
2. That the respondent do pay to the petitioner periodical payments for the child of the family Diana Anthony, until she attains the age of 18, or ceases to undergo full-time education, or until further order, at the rate of £18 per week, the payments to start on the Monday following the date of this order.
3. That the respondent do pay to the child of the family Caesar Anthony periodical payments, until he attains the age of 18, or ceases to undergo full-time education, or until further order an amount equal to (a) such sum as after deduction of income tax at basic rate equals the school fees at the school the said Caesar Anthony attends in each financial year, payable by three equal instalments on the first day of each school term, and (b) the sum of £1,500 per annum less tax, payable monthly for the general maintenance of the said child. That part of the order which relates to the school fees shall be paid to the Headmaster of the school as agent for the said child, and the receipt of that payee shall be sufficient discharge.
4. That the respondent do sell the property known as Roman Court, Appia Way, London SW35, the net proceeds of sale to be divided between the petitioner and the respondent in the proportion 2/3 to the petitioner and 1/3 to the respondent.

5. That on the payment by the respondent to the petitioner of the petitioner's share of the proceeds of sale of the former matrimonial home, all the petitioner's claims for secured provision, lump sum and property adjustment orders, and periodical payments do stand dismissed.

6. That the respondent do pay the costs of this application, incuding the costs of negotiations and of accountants in connection therewith.

EXAMPLE 8 ORIGINATING SUMMONS—DISPUTE AS TO OWNERSHIP OF PROPERTY

IN THE HIGH COURT OF JUSTICE 1985.S. No

FAMILY DIVISION

In the Matter of an application by Katherina Shrue under section 17 of the Married Women's Property Act 1882 and section 37 of the Matrimonial Proceedings and Property Act 1970.

BETWEEN KATHERINA SHRUE Applicant
and
PETRUCHIO SHRUE Respondent

Let Petruchio Shrue of 13, Verona Villas, Milton Keynes, Buckinghamshire attend before Mr Registrar Grumio in Chambers at the Divorce Registry at Somerset House, Strand, London WC2 on Wednesday the 3rd day of May 1985 at 11 o'clock on the hearing of an application by Katherina Shrue for an order in the following terms:

1. A declaration that the property at 13, Verona Villas, Milton Keynes, Buckinghamshire, is beneficially owned by the applicant and the respondent jointly in equal shares, or such other order as to the ownership thereof as may be just.
2. An order that the said property be sold, and the net proceeds of sale be divided equally between the applicant and the respondent, or otherwise as may be just.
3. A declaration that the items listed in the Schedule hereto are the property of the applicant.
4. An order that the respondent do pay the costs of these proceedings.

SCHEDULE

A Peugeot 205 car, registration number B 111 KS
A Sanyo Music Centre System
A mink coat

Dated etc.

EXAMPLE 9 ORIGINATING SUMMONS—APPLICATION FOR OUSTER ORDER

IN THE HIGH COURT OF JUSTICE 1985.S.No

FAMILY DIVISION

In the matter of an application by Katherina Shrue under section 1 of the Matrimonial Homes Act 1983.

BETWEEN KATHERINA SHRUE Applicant
and
PETRUCHIO SHRUE Respondent

Let Petruchio Shrue of 13, Verona Villas, Milton Keynes, Buckinghamshire attend before the Judge in Chambers, Royal Courts of Justice, Strand, London WC1 on Monday the 9th day of March 1985 at 11 o'clock on the hearing of an application by the applicant for an order in the following terms:

1. A declaration that the applicant is entitled to occupy the premises known as 13, Verona Villas, Milton Keynes, Buckinghamshire.
2. An order that the respondent be prohibited from exercising any right to occupy the said premises from 9th March 1985 until further order.
3. An order that the respondent pay the costs of this application.

Dated etc.

Bibliography

Books on practice and procedure

The Supreme Court Practice (The White Book) (2 volumes with supplements) Sweet and Maxwell
The County Court Practice (The Green Book) Butterworths
Archbold's Criminal Pleading, Evidence and Practice (41st edition with supplements) Sweet and Maxwell
Odger's Principles on Pleading and Practice in Civil Actions in the High Court. (22nd edition) Stevens

Books for reference when advising a client

Kemp and Kemp *The Quantum of Damages.* (2 volumes loose-leaf) Sweet and Maxwell
Kemp *Damages for Personal Injury and Death.* Oyez
Ogus *The Law of Damages.* Butterworths
H. MacGregor *MacGregor on Damages.* (14th edition) Sweet and Maxwell
D.A. Thomas *Current Sentencing Practice.* (Loose-leaf) Sweet and Maxwell

Books for reference for drafting examples and precedents

The Supreme Court Practice (The White Book) Sweet and Maxwell
The County Court Practice (The Green Book) Butterworths
Archbold's Criminal Pleading, Evidence and Practice Sweet and Maxwell
Atkin's Court Forms (2nd edition, 42 volumes with supplements) Butterworths
Bullen and Leake's Precedents and Pleadings (12th edition) Sweet and Maxwell
Chitty and Jacob's Queen's Bench Forms (20th edition) Sweet and Maxwell
Butterworth's County Court Precedents and Pleadings (2 volumes loose-leaf)

Books on the technique of the lawyer

Keith Evans *Advocacy at the Bar.* Financial Training Publications
Richard Du Cann *The Art of the Advocate.* Penguin Books
Francis L. Wellman *The Art of Cross-Examination.* Collier MacMillan
David Napley *The Technique of Persuasion.* Sweet and Maxwell
Robert Hazell *The Bar on Trial.* Quartet Books
Sir William Boulton *Conduct and Etiquette at the Bar.* Butterworths
Senate of the Inns of Court *Code of Conduct for the Bar of England and Wales*
Lawrence Shurman *The Practical Skills of the Solicitor.* Oyez Longman
Colin Shuttleworth *Check-Lists for Solicitors.* Oyez Longman

Index